States and Women's Rights

States and Women's Rights

The Making of Postcolonial Tunisia, Algeria, and Morocco

MOUNIRA M. CHARRAD

University of California Press

BERKELEY   LOS ANGELES   LONDON

This book is a print-on-demand volume. It is manufactured using toner in place of ink. Type and images may be less sharp than the same material seen in traditionally printed University of California Press editions.

University of California Press
Berkeley and Los Angeles, California

University of California Press, Ltd.
London, England

Library of Congress Cataloging-in-Publication Data

Charrad, M. (Mounira)
    States and women's rights : the making of postcolonial Tunisia,
Algeria, and Morocco / Mounira M. Charrad.
        p.   cm.
    Includes bibliographical references and index.
    ISBN 0-520-07323-1 (cloth : alk. paper) — ISBN 0-520-22576-7 (pbk. :
alk. paper)
    1. Women's rights—Africa, North—History.   2. Muslim
women—Government policy—Africa, North—History.   3. Domestic
relations (Islamic law)—Africa, North—History.   4. Tribes—Africa,
North—History.   5. Africa, North—Politics and government.
I. Title.

    HQ1236 .5 .A355 C43   2001
    323 .3'4'0961—dc21   00-051172

Manufactured in the United States of America

To M., A., A., E., and M.

Contents

List of Maps and Tables

Maps

Tables

Preface

This is a book about the making of states. It is also about women's rights in the context of Islamic Middle Eastern societies. The intersection of the two themes provides the focus for the book. The analysis centers on the structural forces that led to different state policies on family law and women's rights in Tunisia, Algeria, and Morocco in the era following independence. The question posed is: why did the national state reform Islamic family law in radical ways and promulgate laws expanding women's rights in Tunisia, quickly adopt a conservative policy in Morocco, and become stalled between alternatives for a long period before enacting a conservative legal code in Algeria?

In order to understand differences in state policy in the three countries, I develop a framework focusing on the process of state formation and especially on how the integration of tribes into each nation-state affected the political foundations of the state and thereby the fate of family law. The framework is meant to sharpen our sense of pivotal state/society relations in countries where kinship has served as a major mechanism of social organization. It is also intended to offer an approach for analyzing the political origins of state policies on family law and women's rights in those nation-states and time periods in which kin-based tribal groups, or kin groupings, historically have been significant political actors.

This book developed from a blend of personal experience and scholarly interests. Growing up in Tunisia in a bicultural French and Tunisian family and then living in the United States, I was forced to navigate among cultures. My primarily French-speaking upbringing in a predominantly Arabic-speaking society gave me the vantage point of a partial outsider to the general culture. As a woman living in several cultural worlds at once, I became attuned to similarities and differences with respect to the rights that women had or did not have. I thought that women's rights as defined in family law raised issues at the heart of social organization, such as the place of individuals or collectivities in the social order. I saw how critical laws regulating marriage, divorce, polygamy, and inheritance could be in defining women's life options in the Islamic world. Often referred to in brief as "women's rights," issues of family law have become the stuff of high drama in the Middle East at large in recent times. Yet, much remains to be known about long-term historical and structural forces behind family law policies in different countries. It has been a pressing intellectual question for me to understand why the Tunisian state reformed the law while the other two Maghribi states did not.

As a comparative-historical sociologist trained in French and American universities, I have been interested in the structural analysis of political outcomes, whether they be Weber's bureaucracy, Barrington Moore's dictatorship or democracy, Skocpol's revolutions, Wallerstein's core-periphery relations of domination, or Tilly's collective protest. A focus of my training and teaching has been the study of the class origins of politics in the history of Western Europe and the United States. When I considered political developments in Tunisian and Maghribi history, however, the models used for predominantly class-based and capitalist societies did not seem to apply. Although classes certainly developed in the Maghrib, tribal kin groupings appeared to be a key variable differentiating the process of state formation and political outcomes in Maghribi countries. I became convinced that, even after capitalist economic arrangements had developed, kin-based social formations made an enduring imprint on Maghribi history. State-tribe relations and kinship as a key principle of social organization thus had to be brought to center stage in the analysis of state formation and state policy on family law and women's rights in the Maghrib.

Acknowledgments

The intellectual journey represented by this book has taken me to places on three continents where many people have generously given inspiration, time, money, comments, and moral support. It is a pleasure to acknowledge their contribution. My first debts are to those who introduced me to the intricacies of political sociology and to the scope of comparative history. I had the good fortune to learn essential conceptual tools from Raymond Aron, Georges Balandier, Daniel Bell, Seymour Martin Lipset, and Barrington Moore. They were formidable teachers, and I am grateful to them.

An early formulation of my comparative research on the Maghrib centered on the precolonial, colonial, and nationalist periods. I am deeply indebted to Ann Swidler, whose influence was fundamental to the maturing of my thoughts about this project and to the development of my theoretical framework. Seymour Martin Lipset, Daniel Bell, and Nathan Glazer gave encouragement and invaluable suggestions. Crucial, too, was Theda Skocpol, who provided support and provocative comments. A second phase of my comparative research focused on the newly formed national state in the period of independence in the Maghrib. Julia Clancy-Smith, Randall Collins, Suad Joseph, and John Markoff gave much appreciated advice that helped sharpen the analysis. Mary Freifeld gave valuable comments on manuscript organization, theoretical themes, and documentation that improved the clarity of the entire text. Betty Farrell read the manuscript more times than she may care to remember and made astute suggestions. I had the privilege to rely on the expertise of Lynne Withey as my editor at the University of California Press. Her guidance and encouragement helped bring the book to completion.

Several colleagues and friends commented on the book manuscript or parts of it. Others read related papers and provided feedback that influenced the development of the book. Still others provided encouragement at critical moments along the way. I was fortunate to receive input from Julia Adams, Lisa Anderson, Belkacem Baccouche, Rainer Baum, Lilia Ben Salem, Bennett Berger, Rae Blumberg, Herbert L. Bodman, Rahma Bourqia, Abdelhy Chouikha, Esther Chow, Cynthia Deitch, John Esposito, Elizabeth W. Fernea, Nancy Gallagher, Akiko Hashimoto, Naima Karoui, Zeinouba Khomsi, Kristin Luker, Richard Madsen, Susan Miller, Jeanne Mrad, Chandra Mukerji, Jelal Rhaiem, Magali Sarfatti-Larson, Mark Tessler, Judith Tucker, Lucette Valensi, Christine Williams, I. William Zartman, and Abdelkader Zghal. While I cannot name them all here, I also have benefited greatly, both personally and intellectually, from stimulating discussions with other colleagues at the University of Tunis, Harvard University, the University of California, San Diego, the University of Pittsburgh, and the University of Texas at Austin.

A series of papers based on parts of this work were presented at conferences. Those organized jointly by the Social Science Research Council and the American Council of Learned Societies offered an exceptionally propitious forum for scholarly exchange. I am most appreciative of the opportunity these and other conferences gave me to present the structural framework that is at the core of this book and to receive comments that stimulated my thinking. I was privileged in the course of this project to receive kind hospitality and intellectual support from the Research Center of the Law School, University of Tunis, the Center for Middle Eastern Studies at Harvard, and the Center for Maghribi Studies in Tunis (CEMAT).

The resourcefulness of professionals in fine libraries made my research forays more productive than I could have made them on my own. I profited from the skill of reference librarians at Widener Library at Harvard, the libraries of the University of California in Berkeley and San Diego, the Library of the Law School at the University of Tunis, the Centre de Documentation Nationale in Tunis, and Hillman Library at the University of Pittsburgh.

Several institutions generously funded parts of this work. I am grateful for grants from the American Association of University Women, the Andrew Mellon Postdoctoral Program at the University of Pittsburgh, the American Institute for Maghrib Studies, and the National Endowment for the Humanities Travel to Collections Program. The Regents of the University of California awarded me a Faculty Fellowship and the University of California, San Diego, aided my research with grants from the Committee on Research.

I owe a special debt to Linda Frankel who has been a long-standing source of intellectual nurturance, good ideas, and sound advice. My gratitude goes to Susan McCoin and Bobbie Kalmanson for their stalwart support over many years. I thank Carolyn Spicer Russ whose editorial skills and personal generosity find no equal. Sara Scalenghe kindly checked the transliteration and I am grateful to her. I received the research assistance of Ramdas Menon and Pam Pears who brought to the task more energy and ingenuity than one could wish. Kathy Rud ushered the manuscript to its final printing with her usual competence and poise. Needless to say, the opinions expressed and the conclusions reached in this book are my own, and none other than myself is to be held accountable for its shortcomings.

I have enjoyed the love and unfailing encouragement of my parents, A. and A., whom I thank for fostering in me the life of the mind and the belief in an international intellectual community, even though they never suspected any of it to take me this far from Tunisia. I wish that my father could have lived to see this book completed. M. B., my husband, has read drafts of the book with good humor and patience, suffered with me the periods of high stress, and joined me in the excitement of ideas. I thank him for all this and for listening as I talked out this book.

—Mounira M. Charrad

Note on Foreign Terms and Transliteration

The transliteration of Maghribi names into English poses particular problems and requires choices on the part of everyone studying the Maghrib. Names of people and places have multiple origins including classical Arabic, spoken Arabic, Berber regional or local dialects, Ottoman Turkish, and French. They have been transliterated by the French in a form that renders the Arabic sounds satisfactorily to a French ear. That form often fails to render the proper sound in English, however. For example, the French transliteration "Maghreb" becomes "Maghrib" in English. In another example, what is transcribed as *ou* in French is more accurately transcribed as *u* or *w* in English. The system adopted by the *International Journal of Middle East Studies* (IJMES) is increasingly used for the transliteration of Arabic into English. It has the advantage of offering a basis for standardization in what has been a world of disparateness.

The transcription of proper names remains a difficult issue, however. Proper names in the Maghrib have historically been written in the French transliteration that has predominated in some cases for more than a century. They have become known in that form, and readers are likely to find them as such in bibliographies, indexes, and scholarly writing, especially with respect to the colonial and nationalist periods. For example, the name of a political party in Tunisia is Destour in its French transliteration. In the IJMES system, the word becomes al-Dustur. In another example, the city of Fez in Morocco becomes Fas. In still another example, the name of a tribal group is changed from Beni Mtir to Banu Mtir.

I have given priority to the objective of clarity in making choices about transliteration. When writing proper names, I have respected common usage in the Maghrib as much as possible and kept the form that readers are likely to find in other sources on the historical periods considered in this book. Thus, I use Destour, Fez, and Beni Mtir. When a proper name frequently appears in the literature in an English transliteration, however, I have used it and indicated in parentheses the French form. For example, I use Abd al-Qadir rather than Abdelkader and include the latter in parentheses the first time the name appears in the text. When appropriate, I use the English *u* or *w* instead of the French *ou*.

Since common words do not pose the same problem of identification, the glossary at the end of the book includes them transliterated in accordance with the IJMES system. In the text itself, I basically use that system for common words but I have omitted diacritics in order to make the text less burdensome for readers interested in comparative history outside of the Maghrib and the Middle East. Readers will find diacritics in the glossary, where I indicate the transliteration that I have used in the text and immediately next to it the IJMES system with diacritical marks. As this note suggests, issues of transliteration in the Maghrib are complex and likely to remain so for some time to come. They reflect the rich history of the region and in part are a legacy of its colonial past.

All translations from the French are my own unless otherwise specified.

Table 1 Landmark Dates

	Tunisia	Morocco	Algeria
Instances of major tribal resistance to central power	1860s (against the bey)	1890s–1900s (against the sultan)	1830–1840s (against the French)
Beginning of colonization	1881	1912	1830
Height of nationalist struggle	Mid-1950s	Mid-1950s	1950s–1962
Proclamation of national independence	20 March 1956	2 March 1956	3 July 1962
Promulgation of a national family law	13 August 1956 Code of Personal Status	November 1957– March 1958 Code of Personal Status	9 July 1984 Family Code
Interval between independence and family law promulgation	5 months	1 year and 8 months	22 years

Introduction

In the summer of 1956, when the winds of independence from French colonial rule were sweeping through Tunisia, the newly formed national state made a bold move. It reformed family law in radical ways by promulgating the Code of Personal Status, a legal code that constituted a sharp break from preexisting Islamic law. Among other changes, the Tunisian Code outlawed polygamy or the right of a man to have as many as four wives. It abolished repudiation, the unilateral right of the husband to terminate the marriage at will without court proceedings. Divorce now could take place only in court. The code also entitled women to file for divorce on the same grounds as men. It increased mothers' custody rights and expanded inheritance rights for daughters and granddaughters. The Tunisian reforms became a yardstick against which to judge changes in family law in other Middle Eastern countries. Commenting on family law, an international report stated four decades later: "One of Tunisia's greatest achievements since independence is the body of laws which [gave] women rights not enjoyed anywhere else in the Arab world."[1]

In contrast, Morocco promptly adopted a conservative family law after achieving national sovereignty in 1956. Its Code of Personal Status, promulgated in 1957–58, remained faithful to the prevailing Islamic legislation. For example, it maintained polygamy and repudiation and kept inheritance laws unchanged. In Algeria, family law became caught in a paralyzing gridlock between reformist and conservative tendencies for more than two decades after independence in 1962. During that time, reform plans aborted repeatedly until a conservative family code faithful to Islamic law was promulgated in 1984.

These differences occurred despite the fact that Tunisia, Algeria, and Morocco share several historical and cultural characteristics. All are located on the western tip of the Arab world. They are collectively referred to as the "Maghrib" or "West" in Arabic.[2] They are geographically contiguous; they are Arab-Islamic societies; they experienced a period of French colonization; and they became independent nation-states in the same historical period, in the mid-1950s and early 1960s. And, in Tunisia, Algeria, and Morocco alike, actions on family law came "from the top." Nowhere in the Maghrib was there a broad-based, grassroots women's movement demanding the expansion of women's rights in the 1950s. Despite these similarities, upon gaining independence from French colonial rule, the newly formed national states in the three countries followed markedly different paths with respect to family law.

The core question posed in the book is: what are the structural and historical forces that led the three newly formed national states to follow different paths with respect to family law and women's rights in the aftermath of independence? The central argument is that the process of state formation, especially the pattern of integration of tribes or tribal kin groupings in each nation-state, has been critical in shaping the state and its family law policy. In societies where social organization has historically been based on kinship, as in the Maghrib, state formation has generated contests for political power between the state and tribal kin groupings. Tunisia, Algeria, and Morocco differ on a key dimension: the extent to which the newly formed national state built its authority in alliance with kin groupings or, on the contrary, on bases independent of them. The study shows how states treated issues of family law differently, depending on the structure of the polity that emerged with national independence, and especially the relationship between state and tribe.

The theory developed in the book identifies three distinct paths to state formation and family law. In the first path, the newly formed national state emerges from colonization in close alliance with tribal kin groupings and promptly adopts a conservative family law policy, as in Morocco. In the second path, the state develops in partial alliance with tribal kin groupings and stalls between alternatives before finally enacting a conservative family law policy, as in Algeria. In the third path, the national state evolves in relative autonomy from tribal kin groupings and immediately promulgates a liberal family law, expanding the legal rights of women, as in Tunisia.

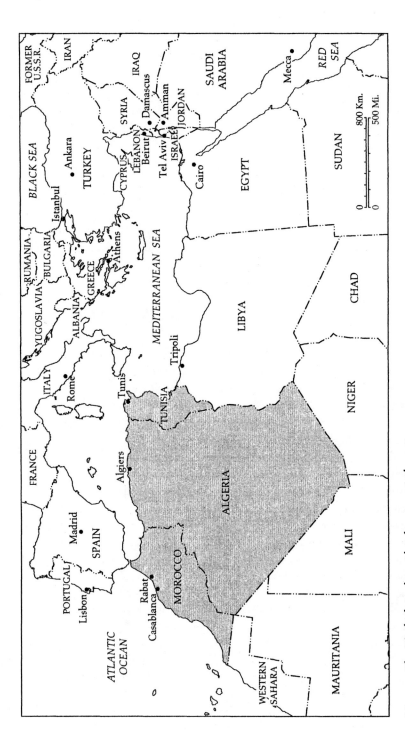

Map 1. The Maghrib in the mid to late twentieth century

THE STATE AND WOMEN'S RIGHTS

Why the relationship of the state to tribe or kin grouping is key to reforms of family law and women's rights can be understood only in the context of the historical development of the Maghrib. The formation of a national state with administrative control over fixed territorial boundaries is a relatively recent phenomenon in Tunisia, Algeria, and Morocco alike. In the absence of strong centralized states, kin groupings organized as tribes were a major locus of social organization, political authority, and economic activity. The political significance of kinship was manifested in the relative autonomy of tribes or kin groupings from central authority—in whatever form central authority existed at a given time—and in the continuing tension between these two poles of power. To varying degrees in the history of the Maghrib, political conflicts were played out between kin-based local communities and semibureaucratic states whose effective authority had ambiguous boundaries. The kin-based communities jealously safeguarded their autonomy while the states attempted to expand their control over wider segments of the society.

The importance of the central-local dialectic in the process of state formation is not specific to the three countries under investigation. It applies to the formation of many nation-states, but with different parameters. What is specific to the Maghrib, and to a number of other Middle Eastern countries, is the extent to which local solidarities have been defined by kinship ties. In the Maghribi context, the issue of state formation must be cast in terms of the confrontation between central authority and local kin-based collectivities. Important variations among the three countries notwithstanding, tribal kin groupings everywhere had retained enough strength through the colonial period to matter in the web of political alliances and conflicts that affected the emergence of the national state at the time of independence.

To call Maghribi societies "kin based" in the precolonial and colonial periods is to indicate that local ties understood in broadly defined kinship terms (tribe, kin group, clan, or lineage) served as a basis for political association and action. In a kin-based society, when people unite for political action, they do so primarily as members of a kin-based community rather than as members of a class, occupational group, or ideological movement. Despite economic changes in the broader social structure, kin groupings remain agents of social control, enforcing behavioral norms and ordering political life in their local areas.

Family law raises questions that are at the intersection of kinship and state. Law in general is best thought of as a boundary-setting device. It does not determine what people do, but it restricts their choices. Family law is promulgated by the state to regulate relations in the kinship unit. Any body of legislation regulating family relations contains a concept, an image, a normative model of the individual, the family, the society, and the relationships among them. Family law by definition embodies an ideal of the family and social relationships. Whether the legislation of a country conforms to the ideal of the family embodied in Islamic family law is central to the analysis presented in this study. As interpreted here, Islamic family law legitimizes the extended male-centered patrilineage that has served as the building block of kin-based solidarities within tribal groups in the Maghrib. It supports the patriarchal power not only of husbands, but also of kin, over women. Islamic family law is treated in this book as a "precision instrument" for the stability of patrilineages and tribal kin groupings.[3]

By remaining faithful to Islamic law, the Moroccan postindependence legislation retained the model of the family as an extended patrilineage. After being caught in political gridlock, the long-delayed Algerian Family Code was grounded on a similar concept. In contrast, by moving away from traditional Islamic law, the Tunisian legislation focused instead on individual rights and obligations within a nuclear family system. In promulgating the family law of the newly sovereign country, each Maghribi state presented its vision of kinship and the family. Each vision included different norms on kinship relations and at the same time a different set of rights for women.

Referring to the Islamic world in general, Asma Khadar, a lawyer and human rights activist, declared: "Family law is the key to the gate of freedom and human rights for women."[4] In the Maghrib, as in other parts of the Islamic world, women's rights as defined in family law are the crux of the matter. They are experienced as fundamental, as is reflected in the use of the expression "women's rights" in the Maghrib to refer to family law. At stake is the set of legal rights and responsibilities that men and women have in the family and, by extension, in the society at large. Involving matters of legal personhood, the central questions concern procedures for marriage, rights and obligations of each spouse, polygamy, conditions for divorce, custody of children, and inheritance. At issue is whether traditional Islamic family law prevails unchallenged or whether legal reforms alter the balance of power that the law gives to men and women in their roles not only as spouses but also as members of larger kin groups. At the heart of the issue is the fundamental organization of society and the place of individuals and kin-based collectivities within it.

When family law reforms were made, as in Tunisia, they challenged identities that historically had been based on extended patrilineal kinship ties and that had served as a major anchor for social solidarity, social control, and collective political action. When Islamic family law was promptly reaffirmed as in Morocco, or tacitly maintained due to political paralysis and eventually ratified as in Algeria, the state preserved the form of kinship organization that had kept tribal kin groupings together. Since it defines the place of individuals and kin-based collectivities in society, family law in the Islamic world in effect contains within itself a blueprint for the social order. Policy choices with respect to national family legislation unavoidably brought to the fore the divisions and alliances of national politics. The choices embodied in each new Code of Personal Status or Family Code were an outcome of the structure of political power in each society. More specifically, they were shaped by the extent to which the newly formed state derived its support from political forces tied to tribes or kin groupings and by the place that the leadership intended to give to kin-based solidarities in the future society.

The achievement of national sovereignty represents an exceptional moment in the history of a society. This is a time when the national state is in the making and when contests over state power generate conflicts and alliances among potential contenders. Politics in that era reflect the social forces that previously united to overturn the colonial regime, but now tend to become rivals in the pursuit of power in the newly independent state. Focusing on the crucial period of independence, the book shows how family law policies resulted from the strategies pursued by the newly sovereign states to establish authority over the society as a whole. The strategies varied depending on the extent to which the political leadership found a basis for power in coalitions centered on tribal kin groupings in the period of independence.

Understanding the conflicts and alliances that entered into the state-building strategies pursued by the national leadership requires, however, that attention be paid not only to the period of independence itself, but also to the legacy of long-term structural forces inherited from previous eras. Historical trajectories over the long run created the context in which the state-building strategies of the political elites later unfolded. Developments before and during colonization combined with the characteristics of nationalist movements to leave Tunisia, Algeria, and Morocco with different political configurations on the eve of independence. This gave the nationalist movement and then the state leadership unequal chances for achieving autonomy from tribal kin groupings.

The degree of reliance on—or autonomy from—tribal kin groupings in turn offered the political leadership of the newly formed national state different possibilities and incentives for the reform of family law. Since leaders of the newly formed states derived their power from different sets of alliances, they were unevenly inclined to make reforms that risked disrupting kinship arrangements and undermining alliances with political coalitions anchored in tribal areas. Political leaders had high stakes in preserving Islamic family law when their support came primarily from social groups tied to kin-based solidarities. Further, it is precisely where local areas had remained heavily marked by divisions among separate tribal kin groupings and patrilineages, as in Morocco especially and to some extent in Algeria, that Islamic family law provided the most meaningful symbol of national unity readily available to the newly formed state.

In contrast, where tribal kin groupings had been largely subsumed within a national entity, as in Tunisia, the political leadership had more leeway for reform, for it operated in a context where bases other than Islamic family law existed to set national goals. This was also a context in which it was possible and realistic for the leadership to envision a future society where tribal kin groupings would become even more marginalized. Besides, the leadership in this case had incentives for reform, as family law reform was likely to further weaken what was left of already attenuated kin-based tribal solidarities. Tribal kin groupings that remained not only offered no support to the state leadership but constituted a potential basis for mobilization by other contenders for power, an additional reason for the leadership to undermine kin-based solidarities. As variations in the Maghrib suggest, newly formed states all have to address the restructuring of society after colonization, but they do not all march down the same road. Indeed, states in culturally similar societies may follow markedly different paths.

A FOCUS ON THE POLITY

In developing a structural model, I draw on a body of theoretical and comparative writings on the state. A common thrust of the writings is to emphasize the impact of state structures and political organization on social change. Some scholars show how the conditions surrounding the formation of central states influence their policies or analyze the role of the state in social transformation.[5] Others propose an approach focusing on the potential autonomy of the state, reminding us that state policies are sometimes best explained by reference to state structures, interests, or capacities.[6] These theories have called attention to the interaction between state and social class in shaping politics and policies. Taken together, the writings offer a perspective centering on the polity. That perspective has proven useful to analyze a wide range of political outcomes, particularly in societies where social class divisions have provided the main basis for collective political action. There is still much to be done, however, to apply the insights of state theories to political outcomes in times and places such as the precolonial, colonial, and postcolonial Maghrib where tribal kin groupings, rather than social classes, historically have played a major political role.

A key question to consider for such cases concerns the extent to which the state has been autonomous from, or, on the contrary, dependent upon, kin-based tribal groupings in the process of historical development. When dealing with the development of the state in the Maghrib and in other parts of the Middle East, we must confront the central importance of kin-based tribal groupings in the structure of the polity.[7] Many policies of Maghribi (as well as other Middle Eastern) states in the last half century become more intelligible if one keeps in mind that they occurred in societies that were in part kin based and where tribal kin groupings represented a political force when sovereign nation-states were emerging from colonization.

With its focus on the relationship between state and tribe, the framework of this book departs from the prevailing model of the forces shaping state policies on gender. Influential studies have shown how state policies that either expand or limit women's opportunities and rights are responses (positive or negative) to pressures from below by social and political movements (including women's groups or women's rights advocates).[8] Developments in the Maghrib do not conform to that model, however. The effect of feminist activism from below does not account for state policies on family law and women's rights as they evolved in the Maghrib in the aftermath of independence. Strikingly, the government of the country where the most radical reforms occurred (Tunisia) was not the object of pressures from below by an organized women's movement. In the Maghrib, the strategy of state building as shaped by the relationship between state and tribe has been key.

In considering the region of the Middle East, scholars have emphasized the gendered and patriarchal practices of Middle Eastern states.[9] These important contributions have deepened our understanding of gender policies in that part of the world. All Middle Eastern states are not alike, however. They vary in their gender policies with some being more patriarchal than others. Why this is so remains to be fully explained and provides the starting point for my inquiry into the political origins of women's rights. I focus on variations among states and, in considering such variations in the Maghrib in the postcolonial period, I take state-tribe relations as a critical variable shaping state policies on women's rights in family law.

In brief, the relationship between state and tribe made reforms of family law possible in Tunisia, uncertain in Algeria, and unlikely in Morocco. As this book shows, the structure of the polity made it more or less possible and advantageous for the political leadership to reform family law. Reforms were made in the Maghrib when they were in conformity with the interests of those political forces controlling the newly formed national state. They were rejected or avoided when they would have threatened alliances deemed critical to the existing political and social balance of power.

TRIBE AND AUTONOMY

Because the concepts of tribe, kin grouping, state autonomy, and tribal autonomy are pivotal to this study, definitions are in order at the outset. The meaning of "tribe" in particular varies greatly depending on the context. A Maghribi tribe is best conceptualized as primarily a political entity, bound by shared conceptions of patrilineal kinship serving as a basis for solidarity, and oriented toward the collective defense of itself as a group. I use the term "larger kin groupings" to refer to segments of a tribe, thus to a group that tends to be smaller than a tribe but shares the same logic of organization. I also use "tribal kin groupings" to emphasize the overlap between the political and kinship dimensions. Other terms used in the literature on the Maghrib include lineages, patrilineages, clans, kin groups, kin networks, kin-based forms of association, and sometimes large family groups.

The definition of a Maghribi tribe rests on a consideration of the links between tribes and the wider society. The tribes have combined a quest for autonomy with a degree of participation in a social whole larger than themselves.[10] Elbaki Hermassi remarks: "If by tribe, we mean a self-sufficient social unit constituting a world unto itself—perceiving itself as the whole of mankind and recognizing no right or obligation beyond its limits—then tribes [did] not exist in North Africa."[11] The quest for tribal autonomy in the history of the Maghrib refers to the struggles in which tribes engaged in order to escape interference in their affairs by central authority. Most often, tribes defended their autonomy in order to avoid taxation.

At the same time, however, tribal organization historically has coexisted with markets, states, and the religious universalism of Islam. Maghribi tribes have experienced a process of partial inclusion in the broader society at least since the early nineteenth century. Most tribes came into contact with the larger environment because they could not avoid altogether exchanging goods with other groups. Most tribes also encountered the agents of central authority at one time or another, despite their efforts to resist all forms of intrusion. In addition, Islam enveloped the cultural particularisms of nearly all tribal areas. It permeated the particularisms even where it did not eradicate them. Maghribi tribes thus existed in the context of universalizing forces that they sometimes resisted but could rarely escape altogether. Cultural unity and political fragmentation have gone hand in hand in Maghribi history.

By state autonomy from tribes, I mean that state actors did not seek political support from social groups that found their base among tribal kin groupings. This further suggests that state actors found political support in other sectors of society and had little incentive to make a place for tribes in the social order. The relationship between state and tribe is a complex one with several dimensions. In the period of nationalism and national independence, that relationship was shaped by: a) the extent to which kin-based tribal groupings remained as a potential basis for political mobilization in the fight against the colonizer; b) how much the nationalist leadership actually mobilized them; c) how kin-based tribal solidarities entered the politics of the newly formed national state; and d) the potential for bureaucratic centralization inherited from the precolonial and colonial periods.

COMPARATIVE HISTORY AND TIME PERIODS

The book uses a comparative-historical method. I draw on the tradition of examining how long-term trajectories combine with short-term developments at critical historical moments to lead to different political outcomes.[12] More specifically, I use what John Stuart Mill called the "Method of Difference."[13] It consists of selecting cases (Tunisia, Algeria, Morocco) that exhibit different outcomes (family law policy) and that can be matched on as many dimensions as possible (Arab culture, Islam, French colonization), except the dimension hypothesized to have made the difference (state formation as shaped by the relationship between state and tribe from precolonial times to independence). The method thus involves an effort "to control" for similarities. Differences in state policies on women's rights are then ascribed to the divergent patterns of state formation exhibited in each country. Departing from a narrative chronological history, the analysis highlights instead variations among cases in the relationship between central power and kin-based solidarities over time. As Max Weber has taught us, systematic comparisons among cases give us an opportunity to perceive or highlight relationships that may otherwise be less visible.[14]

The time periods examined vary depending on the specific issue at hand. There are basically three. First, because the relationship between the state and tribal kin groupings evolved over the long term, I trace its development in each Maghribi country from the precolonial period in the nineteenth century, through colonization, to the time of independence in the mid-twentieth century. Historical trajectories over the long run must be considered because they provide the structural context for the emergence of the sovereign national state. Second, when I examine the conflicts and alliances of the nationalist and then national political leadership, I take the time period immediately before and after national independence. This represents the critical time for state building. It is then that each state made basic choices and equipped the country with a national body of legislation, as in Tunisia (1956) or Morocco (1957–58), or was stalled between alternatives and experienced paralysis, as in Algeria (1962–84). The choices made—or avoided—after independence set the foundation for the future of family law in each country. Third, when I analyze cultural similarities among the three cases, I concentrate mostly on the two decades that surrounded the strategic policy choices in the aftermath of independence, and thus on the period from the 1940s to the 1960s.

This book combines the use of several forms of evidence. Primary sources have provided information on the position of the political leadership on family law and women's rights in the period of independence. When considering the law of each country, I have analyzed studies by legal scholars in addition to primary sources. I have found it necessary to examine closely the text of the law to reach my own judgment about its sociological implications, even though legal commentaries offered a useful perspective. In examining state formation over time and cultural similarities in the Maghrib, I draw much of the evidence from the work of area studies specialists who have concentrated on particular periods in the history of the Maghrib.

Comparative-historical sociologists such as myself are indebted to scholars who have conducted primary research on single countries and periods. We are fortunate to have an expanding reservoir of research on the Maghrib by Maghribi scholars, most of whom are trained and publish in French. In drawing on their and other scholars' research, I have applied the comparativist's strategy of balancing several sources on the same issue when such sources were available. I have followed the practice of citing and quoting sources as much as possible to share with the reader the origins of the information I use in formulating my interpretation on specific points. I have also tried to make the evidence intelligible to scholars other than specialists on the Maghrib.

LOOKING AHEAD

In keeping with my methodology, the book considers similarities and differences. It unfolds in three parts. Part 1, Similarities, presents the shared heritage of the Maghrib. Theoretical issues involved in the analysis of common features of state formation in kin-based societies such as those of the Maghrib are discussed in chapter 1. Islamic family law as it existed in the three countries before the emergence of sovereign nation-states is the subject of chapter 2. The status of women as key resources for the patrilineages that served as building blocks for tribal kin groupings is covered in chapter 3. Tribal solidarity and tribal politics as they pervaded the history of the Maghrib at least until the time of national independence are examined in chapter 4.

Part 2, Historical Differences, opens the discussion of variations among the three countries and is devoted to the precolonial and colonial periods. The capacity of kin groupings to resist the control of central authority in precolonial times and the reflection of that capacity in family law are considered in chapter 5. The different forms that colonization took in the three countries and its differential effect on state-tribe relations as well as family law is examined in chapter 6. Together, chapters 5 and 6 lead to an appreciation of the differences in structural conditions in Tunisia, Algeria, and Morocco at the end of the colonial period. These conditions formed the context in which national states would later emerge.

Part 3, Three Paths to Nation-State and Family Law, compares the different paths followed by Tunisia, Algeria, and Morocco during the nationalist struggle and the period of independence. It focuses on the type of relationship that each political leadership had to tribal solidarities. It shows how this affected the state-building strategy in each country and the outcome with respect to family law and women's rights. The coalition between palace and tribe in Morocco and the preservation of Islamic family law are the subject of chapter 7. The partial reliance of the state on tribal kin groupings in Algeria and the political conflicts that held family law hostage are examined in chapter 8. State autonomy from tribes in Tunisia and the major family law reforms enacted after independence are discussed in chapter 9. A conclusion compares the paths followed by the three countries and briefly discusses implications of the framework developed in the book.

Part 1

SIMILARITIES
Common Heritage of the Maghrib

If your subject is law, the roads are plain to anthropology.
Justice Holmes

To appreciate the common cultural and socio-political heritage of the Maghrib, it is helpful to turn to politics, law, and anthropology. A process of state formation in a kin-based context, the predominance of Islamic family law, the place of women and men in the patrilineage, and the power of tribes in politics are major aspects of the common heritage.

1 State Formation in Kin-Based Societies

Tunisia, Algeria, and Morocco share a common denominator with many postcolonial nation-states in that they are "old societies" at the same time that they are "new states," to use Clifford Geertz's classic formulation.[1] What makes them new is the novelty of their political independence. Until fairly recently on the world historical scene, these countries were colonies or enjoyed only limited sovereignty.[2] Their populations, however, are not new. They have had a cultural identity for centuries. Upon gaining sovereignty, a major imperative confronting postcolonial nations such as those of the Maghrib was to develop a national state and nation-wide institutions in the context left by colonial rule.[3] The task often was to be done in a society characterized by a segmented social organization, as colonization had left many new nations with separate collectivities that were not integrated into a national whole. The separate collectivities varied in nature. They could be ethnic, caste or kinship-based, tribal, religious, or linguistic. In the case of the Maghrib, they were largely tribal and kin based.

The important similarity among many old societies and new states is that loyalties and foci of solidarity rested with the collectivities themselves rather than with nation-wide institutions. Postcolonial newly independent nations had to become nation-states in which the territoriality of the nation was coterminous with that of the state. Following a worldwide wave of decolonization in the mid-twentieth century, the development of nation-states generated tensions with local solidarities in many parts of the world. The problem of state formation, nation building, or national integration has been widespread in the postcolonial world, as is demonstrated by references "to 'dual' and 'plural' or 'multiple' societies, to 'mosaic' or 'composite' social structures, to 'states' that are not 'nations' and 'nations' that are not 'states,' to 'tribalism,' 'parochialism,' and 'communalism.' "[4]

This chapter discusses the conceptualization of state and state formation in societies characterized by politically significant local solidarities. The essential starting point is an appreciation of the tensions inherent to nation building and state formation in postcolonial nation-states in general and in the kin-based societies of the Maghrib in particular.

STATES, NATIONS, AND LOCAL SOLIDARITIES

When analyzing state formation, it is more appropriate to consider the *extent* to which a given collectivity meets criteria that are part of statehood in given periods than to ask whether a collectivity does or does not constitute a state. The same applies to nationhood. Max Weber offers a definition useful for the conceptualization of the state used in this book. He writes: "A compulsory political association with continuous organization will be called 'a state' if and in so far as its administrative staff successfully upholds a claim to the monopoly of the legitimate use of physical force in the enforcement of its order."[5] A state thus is an institution that places a claim on the authority to make binding decisions for all, on the monopoly of force, and on a territory. In the modern world, a state is usually associated with an administrative apparatus in the form of a bureaucracy.

By implication, state formation involves the expansion of administrative reach over a territory combined with authority within national boundaries.[6] Nation building refers to the development of a collective identity and the integration of separate collectivities into a national whole. The connections between state formation and nation building are intricate and vary from case to case. Some countries face nation building and state formation all at once. Others already have a collective identity when they develop a central state. Still others become national entities only after the development of a central state.[7]

As an overall concept for the social ties binding communities in old societies with separate collectivities, Geertz speaks of "primordial attachments." He sees the attachments as stemming from the "givens of social existence," mainly "immediate contiguity and kin connection," including kinship, ethnicity, language, region, religion, or custom.[8] The concept of primordial ties taps a crucial reality in the new nations because it highlights the segmentation of social organization. Primordial ties often serve as a source of solidarity and cohesion for communities in local areas. They serve as a basis for members of communities to claim their separateness both from other communities and central power. If primordial ties remain strong and separate collectivities persist, it is generally not because people refuse to relinquish centuries-old, deep-rooted beliefs that no longer make sense in a modern era. The ties remain, not as meaningless vestiges of the past, but as social forms that serve a useful function in the here and now. In some cases, ties previously forgotten are reinvented. In the Maghrib, as elsewhere, traditions are invented, abandoned, reinvented, and transformed for reasons rooted in the present.

There is a direct conflict between local solidarities based on primordial ties (which I refer to in brief as local solidarities) and a nation-state. Each institution requires loyalties of its members. Each involves mutually exclusive definitions of what the maximal political unit ought to be. Insofar as primordial solidarities sometimes become candidates for nationhood, they compete with the state or challenge its very existence. Precisely because they represent alternative institutions of power and social control, primordial communities and national institutions find themselves in a relationship of ongoing tension. The tension may be open or latent. Considering other nations may help to place the Maghrib in perspective. In India, for example, the tension has crystallized into violent conflict. Many of the problems of Indian society involve managing the complexities of a society that includes several languages, castes, religions, and ethnic groups. Similar conflicts based in part on similar kinds of solidarities have arisen in places as diverse as Morocco, Nigeria, Rwanda, China, the former Soviet Union, and the former Yugoslavia, to name only a few. One may think of Lebanon and Afghanistan as countries where in recent history, for a variety of national and transnational reasons, loyalties grounded in kinship, ethnicity, or religion challenged the state and one another.

The tension between communal solidarities and society-wide institutions is not unique to new nation-states. It was also experienced, but in a different way, by the West. Reinhard Bendix reminds us that Max Weber's lifework was an effort to analyze the tension. Bendix writes about Weber's work: "[It was an effort] to document the proposition that Christian doctrine and the revival of Roman law militated against familial and communal ties as foci of loyalty which compete effectively with the universal claims of legal procedure . . ."[9] Such familial and communal ties as foci of loyalty competed also with *national* political, social, and economic entities. Some communal ties, particularly ethnic, linguistic, and religious, remain to this day social and political issues in advanced industrial nations. Witness, for example, French-speaking Canada, Basque nationalism in Spain or, on a more limited scale, the Corsican movement in France. In general in Western Europe, however, communal solidarities were broken, or at least weakened, in a gradual fashion, over several centuries by industrial capitalism and political struggles in absolutist regimes. Jack Goody traces the weakening of solidarities grounded in extended kinship ties to an even earlier period and associates it with the expansion of the Christian Church in Western Europe.[10]

In the Maghrib as in other new nations, there are two essential differences. First, the timing of state formation is different. Whereas England and France, for example, were already nation-states when industrialization took place, the new nations sometimes had to face state formation, nation building, industrialization, and a host of other imperatives all at once. Second, some of the primordial communities have remained basic social institutions up to the present in many new nation-states. This is not to say that there was no change in those societies until recently. In many cases, however, the dynamic of change was such that primordial communities were able to maintain themselves, either by making necessary but minimal adjustments or by openly struggling for their autonomy.

The development of a national state requires the redirection of resources previously embedded in local networks of obligation toward national goals.[11] As new states attempt to channel resources away from local communities, they challenge primordial ties. Members of separate collectivities find their autonomy jeopardized and their life affected in all respects, sometimes even the most private. To establish the hegemony of the state, the groups in power must transfer social control at least in part from its prior basis in local, ethnic, or kin-based communities to national institutions. Only then is the state in a position to make binding decisions for all. Although new nation-states share the primordial-national dialectic, the particular way in which this dialectic is played out varies greatly, as is evinced by the diversity of institutional configurations in the postcolonial world.

There are multiple kinds of national unity, multiple kinds of nation-wide institutions, and multiple forms of state hegemony. In theoretical terms, central power may a) confront kin-based solidarities and try to subordinate them; b) tolerate them and timidly chip away at their political leverage; or c) manipulate them in a divide-and-rule approach to politics.[12] Conversely, kin-based corporate structures may exist in a variety of relationships to the state. Such structures may a) compete with the state by representing a focus of loyalties for those groups trying to escape state control; b) support the state in both direct and indirect ways; or c) compete among themselves in an attempt to gain the favors of the state. Groups in power can establish state hegemony in a variety of ways, thus giving different forms to the relationship between central power and local solidarities. There also can be shifts in the strategy of any given state, resulting in variations from one historical period to another in the same country. And the process may reverse itself. As Lisa Anderson reminds us, "the march of bureaucratic domination," to use Weber's phrase, is reversible and states may lose power they once had over the periphery.[13]

CENTRAL/LOCAL TENSION
IN THE HISTORY OF THE MAGHRIB

The nation-state had an ambiguous identity in the political history of the Maghrib. Only with the achievement of independence from colonial rule has the modern state emerged to challenge or undermine the authority of traditional structures of solidarity and social control. Historically, authoritative institutions were of two types in the Maghrib: the immediate kin-based community or tribe on the one hand and the world Islamic community on the other. Neither unit of reference overlapped with the boundaries of a nation-state. One unit of identification, the tribe, did not reach the level of the nation-state. The other unit, the world Islamic community, bypassed the nation-state altogether. It transcended it geographically, and it subsumed the political within an all-encompassing religious frame of reference.

In terms of social organization, the tribe or kin grouping is critical because it historically has constituted the basic community in the Maghrib. A feature shared by Maghribi and other Middle Eastern societies is their origin in a tribal structure. Nikki Keddie states that, when analyzing the history of the Middle East, it is necessary to consider how a large-scale tribal presence has affected the society as a whole.[14] Tribal origins do not belong to a forgotten past. There are entire regions where individuals continue to identify themselves as members of a tribe. Scholars have documented the existence of a tribal structure to varying degrees in Tunisia, Algeria, and Morocco well into the twentieth century. Elbaki Hermassi, for example, indicates that most rural areas in the Maghrib "remained predominantly tribal, preserving their social structures intact until the beginning of the twentieth century."[15] Tribal solidarities may overlap with linguistic, ethnic, or other identities. In the Maghrib as a whole, however, significant local solidarities have rested primarily upon tribal roots.[16]

The Maghribi experience derives in large part from a history of tension between a social group holding power in the political center and autonomous local collectivities resisting its control. Precolonial states, with varying degrees of administrative capacities, expanded and contracted depending on how much control they could master over tribal areas in the periphery. Tribes coexisted with partially bureaucratic centers that had shifting boundaries and often lacked stable systems of administration at the regional and local levels.[17] Keddie has suggested that Middle Eastern history could be reconstructed by looking at the "various permutations and combinations of a nomadic-agricultural-urban synthesis."[18] This applies well to the Maghrib. The nomads were usually at the periphery, resisting control by the center. Settled agricultural populations occupied a middle position; they reluctantly submitted to partial control by central authority when it was ascendant. Urban groups, those at the center, constituted the core of the state's domain. They submitted to taxation and provided a pool for the armed force of the ruler.

A phrase attributed to the Prophet Muhammad reads as follows: "The plow will not enter a family's dwelling without also bringing debasement."[19] Whoever uses a plow is attached to a piece of land. The notion expressed in the phrase is that with the tie to land comes the obligation to submit to the demands of central authority and, in particular, to pay taxes. The nomad, who has neither plow nor land, has freedom to move and thus to escape obligations. The nomadic way of life is often glorified in Maghribi culture. Even today, it is not uncommon to hear that whoever has Bedouin blood (i.e., nomadic ancestors) belongs to the authentic core of Maghribi society. Until the nineteenth century in most of the Maghrib, power was the basis of wealth, which was under constant threat if it did not go hand in hand with control over tribes. Ruling elites usually had little or no stable landed patrimony and therefore lacked an enduring basis for support. Wealth in the form of land for the settled population and cattle for nomads could disappear suddenly in case of war among tribes—and these wars occurred frequently. It would also vanish if the social group in the center were displaced by another group—and this too happened quite often. The best way, then, to retain wealth was to be in a position of political power, that is to say, to be in control of other tribal groups.

The clash between tribes and central authority in precolonial times characteristically was less acute where central authority infringed little on the life of the population. In areas where central authority restricted its demands to the payment of a tribute and to respect for peace, settled agricultural communities could tolerate these demands. They did not feel overly threatened as long as the institutions of social control, the organization of production, and the general orchestration of communal life were still in their own hands. Furthermore, numerous communities were altogether out of the reach of central authority. The relative autonomy left to separate social groups—even to those from which the political center succeeded in extracting tributes—contributed to the preservation of different social norms and to the ongoing cohesiveness of each group.

THE "REPUBLICS OF COUSINS" IN POLITICS

Reflecting the importance of kin-based solidarities in the Maghrib, there has been a revival of the work of Ibn Khaldun, the great Maghribi historian of the fourteenth century (1332–1406).[20] There are obvious differences between Ibn Khaldun's time and modern times. In particular there are now territorial nation-states with fixed boundaries. Yet, there is good reason for turning to Ibn Khaldun. His analysis provides insights for the understanding of the Maghrib in the nineteenth century and the first half of the twentieth. The main question preoccupying Ibn Khaldun was that of "solidarity" or "group cohesion." He was concerned with what held a collectivity together, gave it strength and power, and prevented its atomization.

The concept of *asabiyya*, central to Ibn Khaldun's work, has proven particularly useful for the analysis of Maghribi history. Asabiyya is often translated as "solidarity" or *"esprit de clan."* A more accurate translation proposed by David Hart is "unifying structural cohesion" or "agnation in action."[21] What mattered greatly for the history of any group was the strength of its asabiyya, its "unifying structural cohesion" based on ties among agnates, or male kin in the paternal line. The groups with the greatest asabiyya were those best capable of resisting control by other groups, including central authority, and sometimes to displace central authority altogether. Hence, a strong asabiyya was politically advantageous and instrumental for the survival of the tribal group. The French anthropologist Germaine Tillion effectively captures this linkage between kinship and politics by referring to the many "republics of cousins" in the traditional political order of the Maghrib.[22] The patrilineage historically has been the building block of tribal communities or larger kin groupings with political functions. Members of a tribe typically perceived themselves as related to one another through kinship ties, however broad the definition of a meaningful link might be.

Colonization did not fundamentally alter extended kinship systems in the Maghrib. Its effect on kinship was far from a simple restructuring. The era of colonization in the Maghrib as a whole covered part of the nineteenth century and the beginning of the twentieth. At that time, the world-historical setting was such that colonizers primarily were interested in the economic advantages provided by colonies. They were concerned with matters of social organization such as kinship or the family only insofar as these matters facilitated or hindered colonial rule and economic domination. Often, the objective of the colonizer was to make tribal kin groupings serve as conservative, stabilizing elements of the social order, as political power at the center was monopolized by colonial authority. Among the colonized, the extended kinship unit acquired further value as a refuge from those dimensions of society being transformed by the colonizer. Kin-based solidarities thereby were reinforced in response to the experience of colonial domination.

Kin groupings historically acted as corporate structures striving for autonomy from the centers of political power. In the precolonial and colonial periods and in some instances after independence, the republics of cousins engaged in intermittent conflict, latent or overt, with the political center. Because local collectivities found their source of cohesion in the nexus of kinship ties, the process of state formation demanded everywhere in the Maghrib a social transformation involving the integration of republics of cousins. Throughout the Maghrib, a transformation from a locally based society to a centrally integrated nation-state confronted the political leadership after independence, even where the process had started before colonization. The transformation was not smooth; on the contrary, it was accompanied by conflicts serious enough to threaten the stability of the polity.

During the nationalist period, kin-based local solidarities entered the political equation in all three countries in the Maghrib. Although it had developed a semibureaucratic state earlier than its neighbors because of developments starting in the precolonial period, Tunisia nevertheless experienced the turmoil of tribal politics during the anticolonial struggle. Algerian and Moroccan societies exhibited an even more segmented social organization in which ties of lineage and tribe remained stronger. About Algeria at the end of colonization, Jeanne Favret remarks that "social discontinuity [was] more marked than in any other country freed from colonial rule."[23] About the formative history of Morocco, Clifford Geertz notes: "The critical feature of Morocco is that its cultural center of gravity lay . . . in the mobile, aggressive, now federated, now fragmented tribes who not only harassed and exploited [the cities] but also shaped their growth."[24] Commenting on the later phase of the colonial period in Morocco, Ernest Gellner writes: "For the tribesmen, political life was the conflict of local groups, alignments, lineages, families, for local power, and the game was played out within the region."[25]

Solidarities based on kinship may respond to change in numerous and complex ways: they may resist it; they may tighten up protectively in the face of external threats; they may change in limited ways so as to adapt to new situations; or they may change in substantial ways. Instead of treating kinship as an institution that is immediately altered in response to changes in the society at large, it is thus helpful to use a broader conceptualization of how kinship systems respond to social transformations. Furthermore, interesting questions can be raised if one considers the relationship between changes in kinship and in other institutional spheres. Kin groups or families have been primarily defined as economically relevant units, whether these units are seen in their productive function in preindustrial societies or in terms of their socio-economic status in advanced industrial countries.[26] Once the economic aspect of kinship units is emphasized, the main question that arises concerns the reciprocal effect between kinship and the economy. This is an important question, but not the only one worth considering.

Kinship systems also can be seen in their political and integrative functions, and therefore in relation to the polity. This is especially the case in parts of the world where clans, lineages, and other kin-based forms of association remained meaningful social entities in the modern era. For example, Judith Stacey shows how kinship systems in China not only persisted but played a crucial role in shaping the course of social and political change.[27] In the Maghrib, throughout the nineteenth century and in many regions in the first half of the twentieth, kin-based solidarities remained strong in local areas, although profound changes were affecting the region. Even when they had not maintained enough separate identity to be properly called a tribe, many republics of cousins had retained a sense of themselves as corporate entities and remained operative in the political order. In several regions of the Maghrib, the coming of national independence heightened the tension between local collectivities and central authority. The intervention of nationalists and then of the national government in rural politics reactivated kin-based local solidarities in all three countries but it did so within different scenarios.

In Morocco in the aftermath of independence, the monarchy was the key arbitrator in an intricate web of loyalty and dependence within a system of segmented politics. I. William Zartman indicates that the royal strategy was to form alliances with tribal notables in rural areas. John Waterbury calls attention to the king's ability to manipulate, encourage, and balance off factions.[28] Given that many factions were anchored in rural coalitions that included a tribal base, it would not have been advantageous for the monarchy to challenge kin-based solidarities. It was more sensible to maintain them and to leave unthreatened the kinship structure that served as the basis of social organization in rural areas.

In Algeria, the strategy of the political leadership was double-sided. A major postindependence insurrection showed a republic of cousins coming together. According to Favret, it was an example of the manipulation of kin-based groups in rural areas by what she calls their "elite city cousins" in national politics. She remarks that the primordial groups in newly independent Algeria survived "not as unconscious anachronisms but as a result of deliberate reaction."[29] This was only part of the story, however. There was a tension in independent Algeria between the manipulation of local kin-based solidarities and an attempt to create a polity independent from such solidarities.

In Tunisia, conflicts involving kin-based solidarities flared up in violent outbreaks during the nationalist struggle and immediately following independence, but the conflicts ended with the defeat of tribally based coalitions. In the aftermath of independence, the balance of forces was favorable to those elements of the national leadership that were most interested in reducing the political weight of social groups attached to kin-based solidarities. As a result, the national state in Tunisia had a better chance to achieve autonomy from tribal kin groupings than either its Algerian or Moroccan counterpart.[30]

To emphasize the importance of kin-based solidarities is not to say that the Maghrib was classless until the mid-twentieth century. Once capitalism developed as a world system, no world region escaped its influence.[31] Furthermore, there was some form of semibureacratic state with uneven control over territory and frequently changing boundaries in each Maghribi country already in the precolonial period. "State" by definition implies appropriation of surplus and therefore class inequality. The important point is that kin-based political organization and noncapitalist social formations coexisted with capitalist interests. Where kin-based political solidarities existed during the colonial period, they continued to make their mark on politics after independence, this time within a national context.

When nationalist leaders mobilized tribal areas in the nationalist struggle or after independence, most did so to increase their power in national politics, not to create a separate nation. It would be an anachronism to treat the politics of the mid-twentieth century as nothing other than a sheer reenactment of tribal dissidence in the precolonial period. Coalitions based on tribal kin groupings played a role in nationalism and then in the independent nation-state, and they did so by entering the modern politics of the mid-twentieth century.

· · ·

In the context of the Maghrib, the solidarity of tribal kin groupings as political communities claiming the loyalty of their members thus must be given central place in the investigation of issues of political authority at least until the period of national independence. Whatever institution or policy at the national level is studied in the period of independence, it is necessary to ask how it was affected by the interaction between the local areas where tribal organization prevailed and the newly formed central state. The integration of tribes into a nation-state was a long process, often accompanied by bloodshed and violence. The timing and particular mechanisms of that process have shaped the development of the national state, its relationship to social groups, and the policies it adopted in the aftermath of national sovereignty. I turn next to another major similarity in the Maghrib, the centrality of Islam and family law.

2   Islam and Family Law
An Unorthodox View

Islam constitutes the idiom of unity throughout the Maghrib. It has historically linked otherwise diverse populations into the world Islamic community. And, within that world community, family law occupies a special place. It is at the core of the Islamic tradition. Several legal principles that apply to family life appear in the text of the Qur'an itself and therefore represent the word of God directly transmitted to the believer through the Prophet Muhammad. As such, the legal principles must be revered by all Muslims. Islamic family law regulated family life in Tunisia, Algeria, and Morocco until each country made reforms of varying significance after independence. Local codes of customary law coexisted with Islamic family law, resembling it in many respects, differing from it in others, borrowing from it and modifying it. They applied to minorities in local areas or regions. Enclaves of customary law notwithstanding, Islamic law provided a common umbrella for the majority of the population in the history of the Maghrib.

Any family law contains within itself a conception of gender and a conception of kinship. The most explicit aspect of Islamic family law concerns gender relations. Islamic family law places women in a subordinate status by giving power over women to men as husbands and as male kin. Islamic law in effect sanctions the control of women by their own kin group. Any family law also offers an image of kinship in that it defines some relations in the kinship unit as privileged and other relations as less significant. Conceptions of solidarity in the kinship unit pervade family legislation, even though they may be implicit. In the West, for example, family legislation on the whole has defined relations between parent and child and between spouses as privileged, since the emergence of the modern nuclear child-centered family.[1] Quite different in this regard, Islamic law presents an image of the conjugal bond as fragile and easily breakable. It identifies instead the patrilineage as a web of enduring ties. Islamic family law sanctions the cohesiveness of the extended patrilineal kin group. It presents a vision of the family as an extended kin group built on strong ties uniting a community of male relatives.

In analyzing Islamic family law and codes of customary law, I concentrate on the vision of society behind the law. This chapter discusses the law as it appears in texts that guided the work of religious judges and shaped people's conceptions of proper behavior.[2] I present normative images of gender, which is the aspect of Islamic family law that has received much attention in the literature on it.[3] My analysis also offers a somewhat unorthodox approach to Islamic law. It emphasizes how the law defines power relations, lines of division, and bonds of solidarity in the kin group. I suggest that the way in which these dimensions combine with gender is key to an understanding of Islamic family law in the broader social structure of the Maghrib. The discussion proceeds by examining the place of law in Islam, the substance of Islamic family law, and, briefly, codes of customary law.

THE LAW IN ISLAM

There is no differentiation in Islam between the secular and the sacred, between theology and the principles guiding life in society. The sacred and the civil are one and the same thing. Laws regulating social life represent an integral part of the religion itself. No distinction is made between the role of the theologian and that of the lawyer because, in Islam, one cannot be a theologian without knowing the law or be a judge without being well versed in theology. Being a Muslim entails accepting a system of jurisprudence. The set of regulations that comprise Islamic law plays a central role in defining the Islamic way of life.

Islamic law is called the *Shari'a*. At the core of Islam, the Shari'a has shaped the social and moral order of Muslim populations from one end of the Muslim world to the other. The Shari'a covers many aspects of private and social life, but it is in the field of kinship and the family that it includes the most explicit recommendations. Dealing with a wide range of issues, it specifies principles to be followed in matters of personal status, family life, relations among kin, and property rights.

A set of ethical imperatives presented in several religious texts constitutes the Shari'a. There is no single manual. The law stems from four sources in decreasing order of authority. The two most authoritative sources are first, the word of God as embodied in the Qur'an, and second, the *Sunna* or model behavior of the Prophet Muhammad, as recorded in compendia called the *Hadīth*. The third and fourth sources, *qiyas* and *ijma*, involve interpretation and legal reasoning on the basis of the first two. Qiyas means reasoning by analogy and ijma is community consensus. When a new issue arose, which the two primary sources did not address, jurists and scholars devised a solution through a process of consensus among themselves and by analogy with the principles contained in the primary sources. This has generated a number of texts.[4]

Reasoning by analogy and community consensus provided Muslims with a method for legal innovation within a framework of faithfulness to the two primary religious texts. The period from the first century of Islam (seventh century) to about the fourth witnessed much creativity in legal thinking. Jurists and scholars adapted and expanded the law beyond the primary sources, while respecting their basic orientation. A number of political reasons stifled innovation in the fourth century of Islam, opening the way to conservatism. The substance of the primary sources, adapted to suit the social reality of the first to fourth centuries of Islam, became the fundamental jurisprudence of Islam.

In the two most authoritative sources of Islamic law—the Qur'an and the Hadīth, or pronouncements of the Prophet—the wording of the statements that pertain to the family and women leaves room for more than one interpretation. The relative ambiguity has caused controversy among Islamic scholars over the exact meaning of the statements. It has also led to several major accepted interpretations. The plasticity of Islam is in part attributable to the absence of an organized clergy in the dominant Islamic tradition, the Sunni tradition.[5] Sunni Islam has no church, no institutionalized hierarchy or central organization that could serve as the guardian of religious doctrine everywhere in the Islamic world. Abdelwahab Bouhdiba aptly notes that there is no "rampart of orthodoxy" in the Sunni tradition.[6]

Islam consequently has taken a somewhat different character depending on the specific setting in which it took root, even though Islamic thought in general, and Islamic law in particular, contain a core of principles shared throughout the Islamic world. Most aspects of Islamic family law originate in the religious texts themselves. Others find their source in the customs and ways of life of particular populations. Clifford Geertz demonstrates how Islam has taken different faces in different parts of the world.[7] In a theoretical analysis of culture, Ann Swidler shows how world cultures offer a range of strategies for meaning and action.[8] As is the case with other world religions, Islamic principles and local culture have intermingled in the course of history. This has combined with various interpretations of the original texts by religious scholars to give rise to different schools of thought within Islam.

Four major legal schools have developed within the dominant Islamic Sunni tradition. They present slight, yet noteworthy, variations in legal regulations pertaining to women, family, and kinship. The four schools are also called the four "rites" of Islam.[9] Religious authorities within each school consider different scholastic interpretations of the doctrine acceptable and trustworthy. The school called *Maliki* has historically predominated in the Maghrib. It is named after the religious scholar Malik, who founded the school in the eighth century. Members of the *Hanafi* school are also found in some areas, but as a distinct minority. Of the four legal schools in Islam, the Maliki school historically has been the best adapted to the social structure of Maghribi societies. It allowed the people of the Maghrib to adopt Islam with minimal adjustments in kinship structure in that it conforms to the extended patrilineage. E. F. Gautier comments about the Maliki school: "It is not the Maghrib that 'islamized itself . . . it is Islam that 'maghribized' itself."[10] With a few exceptions, the common heritage of the Maghrib centers on the Maliki school of Islamic law.

ISLAMIC FAMILY LAW

Given the overwhelming presence of Malikism in the Maghrib, the discussion of Islamic family law focuses on the Maliki school of law, whenever that school differs from the others.[11] The thrust of Islamic law in general is to permit the control of women by their male relatives and to preserve the cohesiveness of patrilineages. The subordinate status of women constitutes one of the most apparent and distinctive themes in the legal texts that show how the law places women in an inferior position and gives men power over them.[12]

Other aspects of the law are less visible, yet equally important for an understanding of the vision of society inherent to Islamic family law. First, the law leaves room for marriages to be arranged and controlled by kin. Second, it tolerates a fragile marital bond, with the attendant instability of the conjugal unit. Third, it identifies ties among agnates (male kin in the paternal line) as the critical bonds for individuals even after marriage. The fragility of the marital bond appears, for example, in the laws on divorce and polygamy and in the separation of property of marriage, since each spouse retains control over his or her own property, which never becomes part of a common conjugal patrimony. The fragility also appears in the laws of inheritance, which favor agnatic relatives to the detriment of the spouse. In the model of kinship inherent in the law, there is little competition, if any, between loyalties to the conjugal unit and loyalties to extended kin. Seen in this perspective, Islamic family law shows a concept of kinship in which the patrilineage occupies a privileged position. The concept of kinship corresponds in large measure to the kin-based, tribally organized social structure in which Islam took root.

Marriage as a Contract between Families

Islamic law defines marriage as a contractual rather than a sacred institution. Marriage is a contract through which a man gives a bride price to a woman and commits himself to support her as long as they are married. In counterpart, the man receives the right to have sexual intercourse with her. The religious texts hardly mention the formation of a new family unit as a new social cell. Instead, they emphasize marriage as legitimation of sexual relations.

The law does not require any ceremony, either religious or civil, for the marriage contract to be valid. The "offer" and the "acceptance," which have to be made in the presence of witnesses, constitute the marriage contract. Once verbal consent has been expressed, the marriage is concluded.[13] Marriage is an important community event in the Maghrib, however, in that it unites two kin groups and, as such, takes on a highly public character. The social celebration can be quite elaborate. In Tunisia, for example, I had occasion to attend festivities that lasted for several days or, in some cases, a whole week. In towns and villages, I saw long processions accompany the move of the woman and her belongings from her father's house to her husband's. The procession was done on foot, lasted several hours, and was frequently headed by a group of musicians. This turned the wedding into an event of significance for the entire community.

Islamic law makes marriage essentially a private agreement between two families. The presence of two witnesses suffices to insure the validity of the marriage. The original texts do not require the registration of marriage either with civil or religious authorities who would then have the responsibility to record it with the civil registry. Marriage is therefore not sanctioned by the state. It is a social and familial matter in which the state has no jurisdiction. It could not have been otherwise, since there was no state administrative apparatus when Islamic law was formulated. Even at the time when a state—or some form of it—did exist, however, as in the nineteenth century in the Maghrib, marriage remained in most areas a private agreement between families, with no required intervention on the part of civil authorities.

Legal Subordination of Women

Although several aspects of Islamic family law legitimate the control of women's lives by male members of their kin group, the stipulations on marriage do so with particular clarity.

Age at Marriage. The law gives no minimum legal age for marriage. A marriage can be legally contracted at any age, but with a condition. Although the contract itself may be entered into before puberty, the actual consummation should not occur until after puberty. Since no exact age can be given for puberty, the time when a marriage may be consummated is left to the determination of each family.[14] The contract and the consummation of marriage may thus take place at different times. In actuality, they may be as far apart as one or two years and, in some cases, they may be many years apart. The stipulation in effect empowers families to contract their daughters and sons in marriage when the bride and groom are still children. By requiring no minimum age for the marriage contract, the law leaves open the possibility of child marriages. Islamic law thus places the power of decision directly in the hands of families and makes it possible for them to control marriage alliances.[15]

Consent for Marriage and Matrimonial Guardian. The Maliki rite gives prerogatives to the woman's father or legal guardian in regard to the marriage contract. A bride need not express her consent to marriage when the contract is established. The law actually does not require the bride's presence at the marriage contract for the marriage to be valid. The bride has a "matrimonial guardian," usually her father or, in his absence, another male relative whom family members designate as her legal guardian. The matrimonial guardian speaks in the name of the bride. He transmits her agreement to two witnesses who attend the marriage contract. Only the guardian's verbal expression of consent, and not the bride's, makes the marriage legally valid. In case of disagreement between the woman and her father over the choice of a spouse, the right of decision is legally granted to the father or legal guardian.[16] It is thus to a man that Maliki law gives the last word over a woman's marriage.[17]

A specific legal concept—*jabr*—expresses the father's or guardian's constraining power over a woman's marriage. The term refers to a man's legal prerogative to constrain a woman under his guardianship to marry the husband of his choice, if he considers the marriage beneficial to the woman. Maurice Borrmans notes that over the centuries, law combined with customs and practices to strengthen paternal power over daughters in the history of the Maghrib.[18] The Maliki legal rite in effect grants the father the right to contract his daughter in compulsory marriage. Combining this paternal right with the possibility of child marriages, Maliki law legitimizes the control over marriage alliances by male members of the kinship network. In practice, daughters may resist parental decisions. In case of conflict, however, the law validates the power of the kin group rather than individual choices.

Rights and Responsibilities of Each Spouse. The Shariʿa specifies responsibilities and obligates the husband to support his wife and children. Defined as the head of the family group, the husband has rights over his wife. He may choose the place of residence, dispose of the physical person of his wife, control her whereabouts, forbid her to have visitors, and chastise her whenever is necessary. As to the woman, she is entitled to financial support, but owes unconditional faithfulness and obedience to her husband.[19]

At marriage, the legal control over women is transferred from the father or guardian to the husband. A daughter is under paternal guardianship until she gets married or, if the marriage contract and consummation occur at different times, until the consummation of the marriage.[20] A son is under the father's guardianship until puberty. Whereas a man becomes legally emancipated at puberty, a woman never does. Before marriage, the law grants a woman's father or legal male guardian the prerogative to make major decisions for her. After marriage, a woman is under the control of her husband. She has a subordinate legal status throughout her life.

The absence of a minimum legal age for marriage, the fact that the law requires neither the woman's verbal expression of consent nor her presence at the marriage contract for the marriage to be valid, the right of the father to contract his daughter in marriage, and the prerogatives given by law to the husband, all reflect gender inequality and women's subordination in Islamic family law.

Fragility of the Marital Bond

Islamic family law portrays the marital bond as fragile. Far from fostering the development of long-lasting, strong emotional ties between husband and wife, the law underplays the formation and continuity of independent and stable conjugal units. This shows in particular in the procedure to terminate marriage, the legality of polygamy, and the absence of community of property between husband and wife.

Divorce and Repudiation. Maliki law facilitates the termination of marriage. It offers three procedures to end marriage: a unilateral repudiation of the wife by the husband, a repudiation "negotiated" between the spouses, or a judicial dissolution of the marriage through an appeal to a religious judge (*qadi*). The most striking forms of divorce are the first two. In the unilateral repudiation, the husband has the legal right to end the marriage simply by pronouncing the formula "I repudiate thee" three times. This suffices for the divorce to become effective. The law does not require the intervention of judicial or religious authority. The husband in effect has the privilege to terminate the marriage at will, without going to court.[21]

Several characteristics of the divorce by unilateral repudiation must be underscored. First, the law makes repudiation the exclusive prerogative of the husband and gives no equivalent right to the wife. Second, a woman has no legal recourse. Once her husband has made the decision to repudiate her, a woman can only accept it. She finds herself divorced. Third, repudiation is a domestic act in which courts do not intervene. It is a private matter. If a man wishes to terminate his marriage, the law places few obstacles in his way.

According to the original texts, a repudiation could not be an instantaneous decision. The formula of repudiation had in principle to be enunciated at three different times, with an interval of three to four months between the first and second times, and again between the second and third times. The intervals were meant to give the husband a chance to ponder his decision and perhaps to recall his wife. They also provided the time necessary to establish paternity, if need be. Originally then, a repudiation could become effective only after a period of six to eight months. Over time, however, a single enunciation of the triple formula of repudiation became widely accepted. Borrmans indicates that one utterance, instead of three, came to be the predominant form of repudiation in Maghribi law, which evolved in the direction of gradually greater permissiveness with respect to repudiation.[22]

The Maliki rite obligates the man to pay a bride price to the woman at the time of the wedding. The bride price is necessary for the marriage to be valid. The bride's and groom's families negotiate the amount. According to the Shari'a, the bride price becomes the property of the bride, who may dispose of it as she pleases. As to the woman and her family, the law does not obligate them to provide a dowry or to pay anything in money or in kind. Since it does not require the bride's family to provide a trousseau, the law defines any contribution the family makes as an optional donation and not as a condition for the marriage to be valid. Socially, however, the bride's family is expected to provide a trousseau commensurate with its financial status.

The bride price serves several functions. It represents a form of security for women. In a legal system that provides little protection for women, the bride price is a sum of money that, according to the law, belongs to the woman and that, therefore, gives her a minimum of financial security. The bride price may also serve as a deterrent to divorce. In negotiating the amount before the marriage, the bride's and groom's families have the option of deciding that only part of the bride price be paid at marriage and that the remainder be paid later. The law stipulates that, in case of repudiation, the husband must remit to his wife the remainder of the bride price held back at the time of marriage. If a man does not repudiate his wife, he may never have to pay the full amount of the bride price agreed upon by the two families prior to the wedding. Furthermore, in case a man wants to marry again, he has to produce another bride price to obtain a new wife. The clause of the deferred bride price introduces a pressure toward stability in a system that otherwise facilitates the dissolution of marriages.[23]

The significance of the deferred bride price as a deterrent to repudiation should not be exaggerated, however. Another legal provision allows the husband to repudiate his wife, yet escape payment of the deferred bride price. The husband may end the marriage through what is called a "negotiated repudiation." This is a termination of marriage resulting from an agreement between the spouses or their representatives.[24] Maliki law considers a negotiated repudiation equivalent to a regular repudiation in that, once it is done, the spouses may not resume conjugal life. The difference is that, in the former, the husband does not have to pay any compensation to the woman, not even the portion of the bride price that he did not deliver at marriage. If the woman's family, in effect her father or male guardian, does not require the full payment of the bride price or can be persuaded to accept the repudiation without it, the husband is then freed from any obligation. The negotiated repudiation resembles closely the unilateral repudiation, except in its financial implications. In both cases, the husband holds legal power that allows him to break the marital bond at will.

If a husband may divorce his wife simply by declaring his intention to do so, a wife cannot do the same. She must go through a legal procedure if she wants a divorce. She must appeal to a qadi who may, if he considers that the woman has a case, order the end of the marriage. Maliki law advises the judge to grant the woman a divorce if any of the following occurred. First, the husband did not reveal a problem already there at the time of marriage, such as a serious physical or mental illness or sexual impotence. Second, the husband had a prolonged absence for unknown or illegitimate reasons. Depending on the particular circumstances, the absence has to last one to four years to be considered cause for divorce. Third, the husband fails to support his wife and children while he has the financial means to do so. Fourth, the husband abuses his wife physically. The religious judge decides whether the wife has been able to provide enough convincing evidence. If she has, the law urges him to grant her a divorce.

Maliki law makes the dissolution of marriage easier than other schools of Islamic law. Compared to the Hanafi school for example, Maliki law offers a greater number of conditions under which a woman may ask the judge to grant her a divorce. The Hanafi minority in the Maghrib admits only two such conditions: the husband's impotence and his refusal to follow his wife in Islam, if the woman converts after marriage. For the Hanafis of the Maghrib, unrevealed illness, unjustified long absence, and unwillingness of the husband to support his family do not constitute legitimate grounds for the judge to grant a woman a divorce. A plausible interpretation of the Maliki relative leniency toward women's right to divorce centers on the fragility of the marital bond in Maliki law. Men may repudiate their wives as they wish. Women may obtain a divorce more easily than in other schools of Islamic law. Both unilateral repudiation and the variety of conditions under which a woman may obtain a divorce attest to the lack of legal mechanisms among the Malikis to keep the conjugal unit together.

Polygamy. Polygamy combines with unilateral repudiation to threaten the marital union. Islamic law allows a man to marry as many as four wives, with a mild restriction. The text of the Shari'a indicates that a man who has several wives should treat them equally and avoid injustice. If he feels incapable of treating several wives equally, he is advised to remain monogamous. A famous verse of the Qur'an states: "[M]arry other women who seem good to you: two, three, or four of them. But if you fear that you cannot maintain equality among them, marry one only...."[25] No further specification appears in the Shari'a as to what would constitute unequal treatment. The husband's subjective appraisal of his ability for fairness constitutes the only restriction.

Commanding much attention in discussions of Islamic family law, polygamy has been appropriately considered a major factor of gender inequality.[26] The very fact that a woman may have to share her husband and home with co-wives says much about the gender inequality built into the law. A woman lives with the constant possibility that her husband will take another wife. If she fails to behave in accordance with her husband's wishes, she runs the risk of having to live in a polygamous household. This creates an incentive for women to comply with their husband's decisions and preferences. Coupled with the threat of unilateral repudiation, polygamy is a major source of inequality in the relationship between husband and wife. To understand the full significance of polygamy, it is important also to take into account some of its complex implications for women's lives and for the kinship structure.

Polygamy is often an heir-producing device in the Middle East, but it is a device available only to some. If his first wife is barren, the legality of polygamy allows a man to marry a second wife in the hope of having heirs, particularly male heirs.[27] This matters because the presence of sons has historically contributed to a man's social status, his power in the kin group and his security in old age. Not everyone can afford a polygamous marriage, however. A man has to be rather well-off to pay two or more bride prices and to support several wives. If several of his wives have children, he must support the children as well.

Although images of harems have captured the imagination of Western observers, it must be noted that polygamy can only be practiced by a few. William Goode makes the point that, "as is obvious on sober thought, only a tiny minority of Arabs ever lived in the classical harem of Western fantasy."[28] The numbers of polygamous marriages vary from one social group to another. Some studies give an indication of the proportion of polygamous marriages in the Maghrib in the mid-twentieth century, one of the periods covered in this book. In way of brief illustration, an analysis of census data in Algeria indicates that out of a thousand married men, thirty were in a polygamous marriage in 1948, twenty in 1954, and eighteen in 1966.[29] In a study published in 1953 and considering one thousand households in the city of Casablanca, A. M. Baron indicates that 2 percent of the marriages were polygamous.[30]

While not numerically widespread in the Maghrib, polygamy has important implications for women's lives. Paradoxically, polygamy provides a form of economic security for women who have no independent means.

A man may take a second wife and, at the same time, keep his barren first wife instead of divorcing her. Polygamy allows the first wife to remain legally married. Since, according to Islamic law, marriage obligates a man to support his wife, the first wife remains entitled to economic support. Polygamy also makes levirate marriages possible. A man who is already married may nevertheless marry his brother's widow and support her and her children. Since in the Middle Eastern patrilineal kinship system children belong to their father's kin group, a levirate marriage allows the woman to go on living with her children in the family of her deceased husband. Without the levirate marriage, she might be separated from her children for the rest of her life.

The legality of polygamy also has another, very different set of implications. It is likely to affect the emotional life of the spouses and the nature of the tie between husband and wife. The legality of polygamy by definition implies a conception of the marital bond as nonexclusive. Since a man may either repudiate his wife or take a second, third, and fourth wife, there is little incentive for him to invest much of himself in the relationship with any one wife. The same pressures apply to the woman, but for different reasons. She may be repudiated on her husband's whim, or she may have to share her husband with one, two, or three other women. The law discourages attachment to the spouse and emotional investment in the marital union. Although she analyzes the Islamic tradition in a perspective different from the one developed here, Fatima Mernissi notes, "Polygamy is . . . a direct attempt to prevent emotional growth in the conjugal unit and results in the impoverishment of the husband's and wife's investment in each other . . ."[31]

Separation of Ownership in Marriage. Islamic law prescribes separation of ownership in marriage. It does not offer joint ownership as an option for a married couple. The husband's patrimony and the wife's remain separate throughout the duration of the marriage. The wife has no legal responsibility to provide for the household. Her property is hers, and the law entitles her to manage it as she pleases, except for a small restriction included in the Maliki rite. She may freely give her property away to a member of her family, in which case the husband has no right to intervene. If, however, she tries to give more than one-third of her assets to someone other than a family member, the husband has the right to stop her and a donation already made will be declared void. Otherwise, the woman has authority over the management and use of her wealth.[32]

The husband has complete control over his own assets with no restriction whatsoever. His wife has no legal right to intervene in the management of his property under any circumstances. The law entitles her to food, housing, clothing, and furnishings from her husband. Once she has received this, she has no say as to what her husband does with the rest of his assets or income. The separation of ownership is total between husband and wife, making property matters more manageable in case of repudiation or death. Under Islamic law, marriage may result in few, if any, financial ties between spouses.

The facilitation of divorce, especially in the form of unilateral repudiation, the legality of polygamy, and the absence of common property between husband and wife, all combine to define the marital bond as fragile. The regulations on marriage and divorce in Islamic law do not promote strong marriages. On the contrary, they discourage the formation of stable, independent conjugal units.

Privileged Status of the Patrilineage

Islamic law identifies the extended patrilineage (called *ayla* in the Maghrib), rather than the married couple, as the nexus of enduring solidarities. This is especially apparent in the system of filiation, the provisions for the custody of children, and inheritance laws.

Filiation and Custody of Children. Filiation has historically served in the Maghrib as the basis of an individual's social identity. Prior to changes brought about by national independence in Tunisia for example, the majority of the population had no patronymic name.[33] Throughout the Maghrib, one expressed one's identity by reference to his or her paternal lineage, by stating the first name of one's male ascendants. For example, a man whose first name was Ali would be called Ali ibn Salah ibn Muhammad ibn Tijani.[34] Salah would be his father, Muhammad his paternal grandfather and Tijani his paternal great grandfather. A woman, Ali's sister, would be called Aisha bint Salah bint Muhammad bint Tijani.[35] Both men and women expressed their identity by citing their male relatives in the male line. Social identity was thus primarily rooted in the paternal lineage.

In Islamic law, filiation can be established only through blood ties. The law does not recognize adoption. Even if practiced, adoption has no validity before the law, in that it does not allow the adopted child the rights of blood children. It does not, for example, carry any rights to inheritance. A married couple cannot choose to introduce a stranger into the kinship network. The actual blood connection to the lineage has to exist for an individual to have a full identity and be part of the kin group.

In case of divorce, the rules regulating custody of children differ for sons and daughters. Sons are in the custody of their mother until they reach puberty, whereas a daughter remains in the custody of her mother until she gets married.[36] Once a son reaches puberty, custody passes automatically from the mother to the father. If the father cannot take care of his son, one of the father's relatives will then have custody. In a patrilineal descent system such as has historically predominated in the Middle East, sons matter more than daughters for the perpetuation of the lineage. Accordingly, Islamic law prescribes that males be recovered by the paternal lineage as soon as they reach early adulthood. Daughters, who will be lost to their father's lineage anyway if they marry outside of it, are allowed to remain with the mother and her kin group.

Succession and Inheritance. No other area of Islamic law sanctions the rights of paternal male kin as much as does the law of inheritance and succession. Whatever the specific regulations in particular cases, the basic thrust of the law is twofold. First, the law favors men over women. A woman always receives half as much inheritance as would a man in a similar situation. Second, the law grants inheritance privileges to agnatic relatives (or male relatives on the paternal side). For example, given the appropriate kinship configuration, a distant male cousin in the paternal line may inherit as much as the wife or the daughter of the deceased, and more than his grand-daughter. Prescriptions on inheritance lie at the heart of Islamic family law. Many Muslims consider them the most sacred and untouchable part of the Shari'a. Strict and precise, inheritance laws include detailed prescriptions and allow few personal choices in matter of succession. Rights of inheritance rest upon family ties. An individual may dispose of only one-third of his or her property, which he or she may include in a will. The law distributes the other two thirds to specific relatives on the basis of kinship relations.

The religious texts carefully identify the recipients of the two-thirds and the shares that each heir should receive. One may not deprive an heir of his or her inheritance right, change the size of an heir's share, or modify the order of the various individuals called by law to inherit. There is a set hierarchy in the order of heirs and shares. And the prescriptions are imperative.[37] For example, the Qur'an includes inheritance rules with the following degree of detail. Note that the rules constitute a divine commandment:

> If there be more than two girls, they shall have two-thirds of the inheritance; but if there be one only, she shall inherit the half. Parents

shall inherit a sixth each, if the deceased have a child; but if he leave
no child and his parents be his heirs, his mother shall have a third. If he
have brothers, his mother shall have a sixth after payment of any
legacy he may have bequeathed or any debt he may have owed. . . . You
shall inherit the half of your wives' estate if they die childless. If they
leave children, a quarter of their estate shall be yours after payment
of any legacy they may have bequeathed or any debt they may have
owed. Your wives shall inherit one quarter of your estate if you die
childless. If you leave children, they shall inherit one-eighth. . . . If a
man or a woman leave neither children nor parents and have a brother
or a sister, they shall each inherit one-sixth. If there be more, they
shall equally share the third of the estate. . . . This is a commandment
from God. God is all knowing and gracious.[38]

Agnatism pervades Islamic law, in that the law grants significant inheritance rights to male relatives on the paternal side (or agnates).[39] At
the same time, the law deviates from pure agnatism. It gives a share to
relatives whom a rule of pure agnatism would altogether exclude from
inheritance. Islamic law identifies two basic categories of heirs, the "quota
sharers" and the closest agnates. The quota sharers are those relatives
whom the text of the Shariʿa specifically identifies as heirs and whose share
(or quota) it defines. The Shariʿa identifies the following quota sharers:
father, mother, spouse, daughters, son's daughters, sisters, uterine brother,
grandfather, and grandmother.[40] A rule of pure agnatism would have excluded most of them from succession, whereas Islamic law defines them
as heirs. Given their number, however, the quota sharers usually each
receive a small fraction of the inheritance.

The second category is made up of the closest agnates. Inheritance by
agnatism dictates that the nearest agnate exclude the most remote. For
example, a son excludes a brother who, in turn, excludes a cousin. Sons,
brothers, and paternal cousins inherit as agnates.[41] As to the father, he
inherits as nearest agnate, if the deceased had no son. If the deceased had
a son, however, Islamic law defines the son as nearer to the deceased in
the agnatic line than the father. Following the principle that the nearest
agnate is the one who inherits, the law makes the son an heir as closest
agnate and excludes the father. In that case, the law reintroduces the father
among the quota-sharers. One of the basic principles is that certain relatives, such as the father, must be taken care of in the transmission of
property. The first task in applying inheritance rules to a particular case
consists in figuring out who inherits as quota sharer and who inherits as
closest agnate. Once the members of each category of heirs have been
identified, the law then distributes the inheritance between the two cate-

gories of heirs. The quota sharers first receive their prescribed (and usually small) share. The rest goes to the nearest agnate.

It has been suggested that agnates had even greater inheritance privileges before the advent of Islam and that Islamic law in effect reduced agnatism.[42] Even though Islamic law modified agnatism, it nevertheless did not eradicate it. Islam took root in tribal federations built around patrilineages. In adapting to its environment while transforming it, Islam retained definite forms of agnatism in its law. Ever since its inception, Islamic law has granted considerable rights of inheritance to the closest male relatives on the paternal side.

The rule according to which a woman inherits half as much as a man applies to all cases. Regardless of her position in the hierarchy of heirs and her kinship relation to the person whose property is being inherited, she receives only half of what a man in the same position would receive.[43] If, for example, a brother of the deceased gets the equivalent of ten thousand dollars, a sister would get only five thousand. Another example may show more dramatically the consequences that gender inequality in inheritance rights, coupled as it is with the rule of agnatism, has for women. Let us take the case of a man who leaves an estate and whose only living relatives are a son and a distant paternal male cousin. Since the nearest agnate excludes the most remote, the whole estate goes to the son. Suppose now a man whose only relatives are a daughter and a distant paternal male cousin. As a female quota sharer, the daughter will receive half of the estate, while the other half goes to the distant cousin who inherits as nearest agnate. Both cases present the same kinship configuration. Gender alone makes the difference in outcome. The son gets twice as much as the daughter. In the second example, a distant male cousin inherits as much as does a daughter.

A religiously sanctioned institution has provided a way to escape some of the strict regulations on inheritance. The institution, called *habus* in the Maghrib, or sometimes *waqf*, is a pious donation of a piece of land or other property usually to a religious organization.[44] The term refers at once to the act of donation and the piece of land donated. The habus institution introduces a loophole by separating ownership and right of usage. The act of donation makes the religious organization receiving the land the final heir holding ownership. The donor may, however, give and restrict the right of usage to one or more family members of his or her choice. This constitutes the loophole. The arrangement enables the donor to exclude the other heirs who are, by law, entitled to inherit and who would have received part of the inheritance, had the land *not* been given in habus. The institution of the habus thus allows the owner to transfer property to relatives of his or her own choosing. In that it provides a way to select one's actual heir or heirs, a procedure contrary to the principles of Islamic law when it applies to more than one-third of one's property, the institution is in effect a curtailment of the law.

Habus also served to avoid the fragmentation of property and to deprive women of their inheritance rights. Sophie Ferchiou shows how the habus system was used to keep property within the agnatic kinship network by excluding women or making them temporary beneficiaries.[45] Lucette Valensi indicates that, in the case of a habus she studied, the testator's evident objective was to exclude his daughters' husband and children from the succession.[46] In a study of 101 Maliki judicial opinions, David Powers comments that a habus often (although not always) was set up by men in favor of other men. He writes that "fathers were three times as likely to create an endowment for sons as for daughters."[47] Germaine Tillion reports that, in areas where she did field work, the beneficiaries of the exclusive right to use the land were male and that the women were consistently among the excluded heirs.[48] Given the Maghribi kinship system and the position of women within it, it should come as no surprise that the institution of the habus would be used to strip women of their property rights. If women married outside the patrilineal kinship network, the property given to them would be lost by that network. A habus conveniently allowed the patrilineal kin group to retain its holdings. In providing a way to exclude women and other relatives entitled to inherit as quota sharers, it could only help keep the property of the ayla together and further strengthen agnatic ties.

In another practice used to escape the rigidity of inheritance laws, female heirs would receive an indemnity in cash instead of inheritance in the form of land.[49] The piece of property that should legally have become theirs would be withdrawn. Instead, women would be compensated with a sum of money or with movable property equivalent, in principle, to the value of the land they did not receive. This is another mechanism, in effect another deviation from the law, that could help an ayla prevent the fragmentation of its property, in case women married outside the patrilineage. The two practices, donation in habus and compensation in cash for women, have historically reinforced Islamic inheritance law to keep property within the extended patrilineal kin group.

With gender inequality and inheritance by agnates as two of its central features, the Islamic law of succession fits a society in which tribal organization and extended kin groupings predominate. In favoring distant male kin over women, the law sanctions the solidarity of the ayla and its extension, the larger kin group. The law in effect favors tribal heirs. Inheritance by agnatic relatives is adapted to a social structure in which one relies on agnates for help and where the main source of solidarity lies with the kin or tribal group.

CUSTOMARY LAW

Customary law, also called customary codes, coexisted with Islamic family law in the history of the Maghrib. In embracing Islam over the centuries, most of the Maghrib adopted Islamic family law. Some Berber areas, however, retained their distinctive, particularistic codes of law. Berber-speaking tribes generally partook in the umbrella identity of Islam, but they adopted Islam selectively. While most Berber-speaking tribes considered themselves Muslim, outsiders often refused them the label, precisely because the tribes subscribed only in part to Islamic family law or because they took much liberty in interpreting it. Customary codes were based on local custom, which was permeated by Islamic law to different degrees depending on the region. The extent of the resemblance between customary law and Islamic family law therefore varied from one region to another.

Using the same lens as in the case of Islamic law, I consider customary codes by focusing on the vision of kinship and gender embedded in them. The key question concerns the extent to which the codes sanctioned the extended patrilineage and kin-based solidarities. Instead of describing every code, I highlight the connections between some of the major codes and Islamic family law. Compared to Islamic law, a few codes gave greater freedom to women. Most codes, however, tended to legitimate even more an extended agnatic kinship structure and to grant women a more subordinate status.

Enclaves of customary law existed in Algeria and Morocco during the precolonial and colonial periods. Customary codes applied to a substantial minority of the population in both countries, mostly to Berber-speaking areas.[50] The codes were officially abolished in Morocco and Algeria after each country achieved national sovereignty. The issue did not apply to Tunisia, which had practically no customary law to speak of in those historical periods. It is important to consider customary codes, even though they have been officially abolished, because the codes are indicative of the kinship structure that has historically existed in the Maghrib at the same time as they have contributed to shaping it. Customary codes also became politically charged in the colonial period, when they served as a weapon in a divide-and-rule strategy of colonial domination.

The Berber world has blended with the Arab-Islamic culture of the Maghrib, yet has retained its originality by mixing the particularism of local communities or regions with the religious universalism of Islam. For example, Jacques Berque indicates how Berber-speaking tribes related to the original texts of Islam. He writes, "Glossaries in the Berber tongue were appended to the sacred texts, together with particularistic legal comments."[51] How much originality any particular group retained depended largely on how independent the group had been from the centers of political control and cultural influence throughout its history. Those groups that submitted most completely to central authority tended to be influenced by—or forced to adopt—Islamic law, predominantly in its Maliki version. Others, which remained more independent, kept their own customary laws with fewer Islamic influences.

The Berber groups that retained their own customary codes fell outside the jurisdiction of Islamic judges. For many tribes, the retention of an autonomous judicial system mattered even more than the substance of customary law. A communal or tribal council called a *jamaa* applied the customary law of the area. The jamaa was responsible for the collective matters of the tribal group, including matters of personal status, family life, and inheritance. Each tribe had its jamaa whose decisions were binding for all members of the tribe. Negotiations for resolutions of conflicts thus took place entirely within the social world of the tribe.

Customary law is sometimes referred to as "Berber law" in the singular. The label is misleading, however, because there was no single body of Berber customary law. There were many codes of customary law and the codes differed among themselves, some considerably so. They were transmitted essentially through practice and oral tradition. Some codes were recorded at various times for administrative purposes, while others have become known through anthropological or sociological studies of particular Berber areas. As a result, information on customary law is often fragmented.[52]

In Algeria, there were at least three clearly identifiable codes of customary law, which were found among the Berbers of Kabylia and those of the Aures, and the Touaregs. Since the Kabyles represented one of the most politically and culturally distinct Berber groups in Algeria, their code is the best known. When reference is made to customary law in Algeria, the reference often is to its Kabyle expression. Strongly agnatic, the Kabyle code contained a model of kinship that emphasized the primacy of relations among the men of the patrilineage. Several Kabyle regulations were identical to those of Islamic law, but others differed in giving men even greater power over women. Like Islamic law, the Kabyle code required the presence of a male guardian at the marriage ceremony for the marriage to be valid. The male guardian consented to the marriage on behalf of the bride, who did not express consent directly, and a bride price was mandatory. The husband had the same privilege of unilateral repudiation as in Islamic law.

Other regulations of Kabyle law were quite different from Islamic law, however.[53] Whereas under Islamic law a woman inherits half as much as a man, but inherits nevertheless, Kabyle customary law deprived women of inheritance altogether. Not only did a Kabyle woman inherit neither from her parents, siblings, husband, nor anyone else, but she was legally part of a man's inheritance.[54] The man who inherited her could dispose of her hand and thus, according to the Kabyle code, give her in marriage to a man of his choice.[55] Whereas under Maliki law the bride price belongs to the woman, it became the father's or guardian's property under Kabyle law. If the woman had been inherited by a man, this man was her guardian and the bride price therefore belonged to him. Coupling the lack of inheritance for women with the appropriation of the bride price by a male member of the family, Kabyle customary law deprived women of some of the few sources of security granted to them by Islamic law. At the same time, it included strict obligations for men to help female kin. If Islamic law places pressure on men to take care of their female relatives in case of need, Kabyle customary law did so even more. When, for example, a Kabyle woman found herself repudiated or widowed and with no means, men of her kin group had little choice but to provide for her.

Under Kabyle law, a woman could practically never have custody rights. At best, she had the custody of her children for the period of nursing, after which the father's kin group had custody. Sometimes, a mother was refused even this much and infants were taken care of by female relatives of their father's. In case of repudiation by her husband, the woman received no compensation of any kind. Moreover, in what was called a repudiation *à la Kabyle*, the woman, or rather her male guardian, had to return the totality of the bride price to the husband after she was repudiated. In addition, the woman could not remarry without her family or her new husband paying an indemnity to the first husband as a way of buying her back.

As this brief presentation indicates, the subordination of women and the control of their lives by male members of the kin group were more pronounced in Kabyle customary law than in Islamic family law. The woman owned nothing of her own, she might be part of a man's inheritance, and her children could be separated from her at an early age. Stringent rules also historically applied to women's behavior in Kabylia. G. H. Bousquet, for example, found that Kabyle custom subjected women to the "strictest surveillance."[56] He noted that the position of women in Kabylia was inferior to that of women in other Berber areas.[57] Several aspects of the Kabyle customary code offered an image of kinship of the purest agnatic type. Ties within the male line defined the kinship structure. The rights of male relatives in the paternal line were even more extensive in Kabyle than in Maliki law. If Maliki law sanctions the extended patrilineal kinship network, and facilitates its cohesiveness, Kabyle law went still further in that direction.

The people of the Aures, one of the other Berber groups of Algeria, and the Touaregs, who constitute a minority living in a remote region in the southern part of the country, also had their distinctive customary law. In both areas, customary law placed women in a less subordinate status than did Kabyle law. The customary code of the Touaregs provided women with greater rights than did codes in other predominantly tribal areas. The customary law of the Aures was also more favorable to women than Kabyle law. It let women retain the bride price for themselves, for example. Under the law of the Aures, however, as in Kabyle law, women did not inherit, the patrimony was kept undivided in the hands of the males of the kin network, and marriages often took place within the tribal faction. The customary code of the Aures has historically been infiltrated by Islamic law and more influenced by it than was its Kabyle counterpart.[58]

In Morocco before independence, a mosaic of codes of customary law was juxtaposed to Islamic law.[59] As in Algeria, the codes varied from one tribal area to another. Similarly, variations concerned mostly the rights of women and the degree to which the customary code sanctioned the extended patrilineage. The codes varied as to whether the woman had a right to inheritance, kept the bride price, and was entitled to own property. Other variations concerned whether the amount of the bride price was left to the choice of individual families or fixed by the tribal council for the whole tribe, whether only the man could divorce his wife through unilateral repudiation or whether the woman (or her family) could appeal to the tribal council for divorce, and whether the woman received compensation after repudiation or nothing at all. These elements combined in various ways to constitute the customary codes of the Moroccan tribal groups. Basically, the codes ranged from extreme agnatism and legal subordination of women—as in Kabyle customary law—to modified agnatism—as in Maliki law.

• • •

Islamic family law is usually analyzed in reference to gender relations and male dominance. Analytically speaking, I have proceeded in an unorthodox way. The approach I have used to analyze the law highlights not only relations of gender, in which women are legally subordinate to men, but also relations of power and solidarity. When one takes such a perspective, it becomes clear that Islamic law legitimates patrilineages and kin-based tribal cohesion. The same is true of most codes of customary law that applied to minorities. Since it requires no minimum age for marriage, and because only the expression of consent by the father or guardian (but not that by the bride) makes the marriage valid, Islamic law leaves the door open to compulsory and child marriages. It gives legal prerogatives to male kin over marriage alliances and the choice of marriage partners. Under these conditions, marriages may be used to reinforce the ayla, either through marriages within the extended patrilineage itself or through controlled exogamous alliances that benefit the kin group.

An aspect of Maliki family law emphasized in this chapter is the fragility of the conjugal unit. The legality of polygamy, the unilateral right of repudiation, and the absence of common property between husband and wife, all tend to facilitate the dissolution of the marital bond. The message of the law is that the nuclear family does not constitute the significant locus of solidarity. Islamic law in effect defines the conjugal bond as potentially short lived. By contrast, it identifies the blood ties uniting the extended patrilineage as those likely to endure. It implies that support and ongoing ties of loyalty are to be sought in the extended patrilineal kin group.

The analysis has shown that Islamic laws of inheritance directly sustain the ayla. By giving to men a share twice as large as to women and by explicitly identifying agnatic relatives as recipients of property, Islamic inheritance laws contribute in a major way to the consolidation of patrilineal kinship ties. Codes of customary law, such as in Kabylia and the Aures, reinforce this tendency by excluding women from inheritance altogether. Inheritance laws are crucial for the understanding of a society, particularly in an economy not entirely dominated by market relations, because they reveal the favored patterns in the distribution of resources in that society. Islamic law makes agnatic relatives the privileged target in the distributive process. The codification of agnatic inheritance rights in the Islamic law of succession can only have facilitated the persistence of patrilineages as cohesive entities. Robert Descloitres and Laid Debzi appropriately see the law of succession as a "precision instrument" for the maintenance of relations among agnates.[60]

This chapter has suggested that Islamic family law in general should be conceptualized as such an instrument. Islamic law does more than define relations internal to the family such as relations between husband and wife or between parents and children. It also has implications for the broader social structure. By placing the control of marriage alliances in the hands of the kin group, by favoring agnatic heirs, and by defining the ayla as the stable family unit, Islamic family law favors the continuation of kin-based solidarities in the society at large. Historically, there has been a parallel in the Maghrib between the concept of kinship inherent in Islamic—especially Maliki—law and features of kinship organization. This is not to say that religion or law shapes social structure, but only that there is a measure of fit between the two. The strongly agnatic Maghribi kinship structure is likely to have influenced the agnatism pervasive in the Maliki version of Islamic law that came to prevail in the Maghrib. Once a law develops, however, it then offers general norms for social action. It is useful, therefore, to think of Islamic and customary law as having provided a basic framework for relations within the larger kin group and the smaller family unit. I next examine the organizing principles of kinship and gender relations in the social structure of the Maghrib.

3 Women Ally with the Devil
Gender, Unity, and Division

A Maghribi saying goes as follows: "Angels and men work towards unity. The devil and women work towards division." The saying captures the structure of kinship in the Maghrib. Two contradictory principles historically have operated at once: a principle of unity, based on ties among men in the agnatic lineage, and a principle of division, introduced by the necessity to accept in the kin group a number of women from other lineages. The particularism of conjugal units represents a potential threat to the solidarity of the agnatic kin group, since conjugal units may break away from the group and thus bring division. Many of the social norms governing kin and gender relations have functioned to strengthen the unity among the men of a lineage and to keep at bay the threat of division symbolized by women.

Indicating the focal position of the kinship unit in the history of Maghribi societies, Jacques Berque has called it the "structure of structures."[1] Writing in the 1920s and 1930s, René Maunier stated that one could not understand Algerian society without a prior knowledge of kinship organization.[2] Half a century later, Nikki Keddie and Lois Beck noted the continuing importance of lineage ties in the Middle East in general.[3] In a study of kinship structure in Algeria, Robert Descloitres and Laid Debzi pointed out that kinship figured in most of the major issues facing the Algerian leadership after independence in the 1960s, such as the development of a socialist economy, the management of agricultural units, and the quest for cultural authenticity.[4] With variations in degree, the statements on Algeria apply to the rest of the Maghrib where kinship has historically been the main axis of social organization. An understanding of the common heritage of the Maghrib requires the analysis of "the structure of structures," its composition, its internal dynamics, and its articulation with other institutions.

A discussion of the characteristics and dynamics of the kinship structure raises issues of time and space. Can one speak of the Maghribi kinship structure in a general sense, without taking into account changes over time? If one takes a temporal perspective, the task is then to trace changes in the organization of kinship over a specified time period. In the same way, can one validly speak of the kinship structure in global terms without considering variations across the countries of the Maghrib or even across regions and social groups within the same country? As soon as the attempt is made to delineate the features of the kinship structure, the necessity arises to consider, in the same stroke of the pen, specificities of time and place.

Treating the Middle East as a global region, a number of scholars point to the backdrop of homogeneity in Middle Eastern kinship, whatever particular national or regional variations might exist. For example, emphasizing fundamental similarities in kinship organization throughout the area, Carroll Pastner locates them in the predominance of the patrilineal extended family and the ideology that applies to the female role.[5] In the same vein, Suad Joseph underscores the centrality of the family and kinship throughout the Arab world.[6] Keddie and Beck call attention to the existence of remarkably similar patterns in different parts of the Middle East.[7] Descloitres and Debzi point to an identical profile in the organization of kinship throughout the Maghrib. While recognizing that the profile is embodied in a variety of regional, urban, or rural concrete realizations, they consider its basic structure to be pervasive in the Maghrib in general.[8]

With respect to the issue of changes over time in kinship structure, much of the literature suggests that certain organizing principles continue to give Middle Eastern kinship its distinctive character, differentiating it from kinship in other world regions. Researchers whose work is sensitive to historical specificities emphasize continuity in kinship structure. Presenting a nuanced analysis, Halim Barakat notes that Middle Eastern kinship retains some essential features, despite modifications undergone under the pressure of large-scale structural changes.[9] Lilia Ben Salem and Carmel Camilleri indicate that traditional kinship forms serve as a basis from which individuals respond to the demands created by a changing environment.[10] Maurice Borrmans remarks that kinship patterns in North Africa seem to have shown a "promise of eternity."[11]

Holding aside for the moment questions of change and variations, I identify here key relationships and organizing principles in the kinship system in the Maghrib.[12] In this chapter I offer an ideal-typical model, rather than an exact description of any particular kinship unit, by distilling several studies that reveal similar patterns. With respect to time, the general period that is of greatest concern in this chapter extends approximately from the 1920s to the 1970s, when all countries of the Maghrib completed the process of national liberation and developed the context in which family law policies were formulated.[13] Issues that I consider central to kinship organization in the common heritage of the Maghrib include: the bases for unity and division in the kin group; a normative preference for cousin marriage; and the walls, veils, and other social norms that have served to reinforce the unity of the kin group by keeping women in their socially assigned place.

MEN AS UNITY

The principle of community—or basis for solidarity—traditionally has been anchored in the bonds connecting male members of the same paternal lineage. In the Maghribi kinship structure, agnates (male relatives on the paternal side) form the social unit whose members expect reciprocal obligations and mutual assistance. The socially meaningful ties unifying the network thus bind men together and bypass women. It is one's place in the patrilineage that matters for one's position in the kinship network and in the larger social world. This contrasts with a kinship system where both sides of the family enter into the definition of kinship affiliation. With very few exceptions,[14] the principle of kinship in the Maghrib has historically been unilineal descent in the agnatic line, even though different communities have adapted and modified the basic principle in a variety of ways.[15]

Maghribi kinship units have tended to be patrilocal. Upon marriage, if the newly wed couple does not move to a separate dwelling, they take up residence in the house of the husband's family. In rural areas, in cases where the husband and wife come from different villages, the wife moves to her husband's village. With only a few rare instances of matrilocality, patrilocality has been the general tendency among urban, rural, and nomadic groups alike.

In everyday social interaction, relations with extended kin on the wife's side are often devalued. A number of anthropologists report on this pattern in the Maghrib. In their study of Algerian kinship, Descloitres and Debzi note that interaction with kin on the wife's or mother's side generally involves only visits with the closest kin such as parents, sisters, and brothers. In her research in Morocco, Vanessa Maher finds that strong ties link women to their close female relatives such as mothers, daughters, and sisters.[16] Relations with kin on the wife's side are usually restricted to the closest connections, however, whereas relations on the father's side often extend to distant relatives. Descloitres and Debzi note that, when relatives on the woman's side come to visit, they are received with considerable formality instead of being treated as "family."[17] I noticed a similar phenomenon during visits to Tunisian towns and villages. Cousins on the husband's side would go in and out of the house freely, whereas those on the wife's side would be greeted at the door and escorted to a room reserved for visitors. In her work on Morocco, Germaine Tillion reports that it is the paternal cousins in particular, and relatives on the male side in general, that make up networks of regular interaction and mutual support.[18]

Linguistic distinctions often reflect significant social categories. In Arabic as spoken in the Maghrib, different linguistic terms exist to refer to relatives on the paternal and maternal sides, thus highlighting the distinction between the two kinship lines. A son's son and a daughter's son are not both simply called grandson. Two separate terms refer to each of them. The son's son has a special status. He will remain in the lineage of his paternal grandfather, whereas the daughter's son, given the rule of patrilineality, belongs to a different lineage.[19] In the same way, distinct terms refer to the paternal and maternal uncle and to paternal and maternal cousins. Arabic gives as many as eight different terms to translate the single English word "cousin," depending on the nature of the kinship link.

Table 2 shows a major distinction between the two kinship lines. Each one of the terms includes information on whether the relation is on the paternal or maternal side, thereby emphasizing the kinship line in which the relation is located. As the table indicates, all the terms that apply to

Table 2 Terminology of Familial Relationships (cousins)

Father's Side	Mother's Side
ibn ʿamm	*ibn khal*
father's brother's son	mother's brother's son
bint ʿamm	*bint khal*
father's brother's daughter	mother's brother's daughter
ibn ʿammt	*ibn khalt*
father's sister's son	mother's sister's son
bint ʿammt	*bint khalt*
father's sister's daughter	mother's sister's daughter

paternal relatives are variations (masculine and feminine) on a basic root-word, *amm* or father's sibling. Similarly, all the terms that apply to maternal relatives are variations on another rootword, *khal* or mother's sibling. Next to the father, the role that commands most respect in the kinship structure is that of the father's brother. Deferential behavior toward one's paternal uncle is socially prescribed and calling someone who is not a blood relative "amm" (paternal uncle) is a sign of respectful affection. The father's brother occupies a pivotal structural position in the system of unilineal descent that characterizes the Maghribi kinship structure. He commands respect because he symbolizes the unity of the branches that constitute the patrilineage.

Styles of interaction with relatives, linguistic expressions, and norms of respect all converge to emphasize the distinction, as well as opposition, between the two sides of kinship relations. They also reflect the predominance of the agnatic line.

WOMEN AS DIVISION

Women represent a potential source of rupture in the web uniting the men of the patrilineage. Division may come from the particularism of conjugal units, which is in a state of tension with the unity of the agnatic community formed by the *ayla*. Division may also result from the necessity to conclude alliances with outside groups and exchange women with them. Since the ties unifying the network are agnatic and run among the men on the paternal side, the significant links exclude women. For the solidarity of the kin group to remain effective, agnatic ties must continue to predominate in the kinship structure, unbroken by the threat of conjugal particularisms.

Two types of relations exist within the ayla: those among agnatic relatives in the extended patrilineal kin group and those among members of conjugal units. For the extended patrilineage to operate as a community, a balance has to be found between the two types of relations, but a balance that protects agnatic solidarity. A preference for marriage within the kin group, or kin endogamy, has long prevailed in the Middle East. It has served to further agnatic solidarity in that the retention of women for the men of the lineage or the tribe helps strengthen the ties among the men. In practice, however, kin endogamy is not always possible or desirable. Most kin groups have had to tolerate a degree of wife taking and wife giving. Conjugal particularism and inevitable exogamy thus both constitute sources of possible division in the lineage. Women who are not part of the lineage are particularly threatening to agnatic solidarity. In exogamous marriages, the woman belongs to a lineage other than her husband's. Her allegiances are divided between her own kin group, to which she retains connections, and her husband's, of which she never fully becomes a part.

For reasons of economic security, a woman has incentives to keep strong ties with her own lineage, since such ties remain important especially in case of divorce and sometimes in matters of inheritance. In a social system in which the law facilitates divorce, and where most women have no independent source of support, reliance on one's kin group represents the main and most stable basis for security.[20] Typically, divorced women go back to their father's house, or they go to live in the household of a male relative such as a son, brother, or uncle. The woman is also tied to her husband's lineage, however, if only by the fact that her children belong to it. She is thus in an ambiguous status.

A wife remains, in L. Massignon's phrase, "l'hôtesse étrangère de la maison" (a hostess who is a stranger in her own home), if she is not related to her husband's lineage through blood ties.[21] Only in cases of marriage with kin does a wife have as much interest as the husband in furthering the solidarity of the common extended kin group. In exogamous marriages, the woman entering her husband's extended patrilineage has no particular incentive to work toward the solidarity of that lineage. Her attention is likely to go to her husband and children. Women who are not related by blood to their husband's lineage are often perceived and treated as outsiders. For example, in the Algerian countryside, people worry that such women may favor their own children in the presence of other children of the ayla, when the prescribed behavior is to treat all children equally in public situations.[22] In the same vein, if a man tries to break off from the ayla, the blame is usually put on his wife.

Images of female sexuality reflect the position of women as a potential source of division among the men of the kin group. The Islamic tradition represents female sexuality as overpowering, destructive, and divisive. Fatna Sabbah has deciphered the cultural symbols and the representations of the female body and mind that pervade several male Middle Eastern writings on sexuality.[23] The writings portray the woman as a formidable force, animated by animal energy, and in constant search of pleasure. Endowed with an all-triumphant sexuality and relating only to nature, the woman is depicted as blind to social barriers. When left to her own instincts, she lacks all sense of social propriety. In the texts analyzed by

Sabbah, female sexuality is described as irresistible. The man has no choice but to give in to the temptation.

Yet, when he gives in, he must avoid emotional investment in the woman, since the Islamic ideal requires a man's affectivity to be channeled entirely to the worship of God, at the exclusion of all other possible attachments. A man's affective investment in a woman would undermine his total submission to the divine and therefore must be neutralized. Pursuing gratification with impunity, the woman is described in the texts as threatening the moral and social order. She embodies danger and is associated with the forces of evil. An Islamic religious authority comments: "She resembles Satan in his irresistible power over the individual."[24] The Prophet Muhammad is quoted as having said: "When the woman comes towards you, it is Satan who is approaching you. . . . after my disappearance, there will be no greater source of chaos and disorder for my nation than women."[25]

What is feared in the Islamic tradition, and what must be controlled, is not sexuality in general. It is female sexuality, since female nature is the symbol of destruction. Left unbridled, a woman's very nature is likely to lead to chaos. Her subversive tendencies must therefore be restrained, and her behavior regulated, if social disruption is to be avoided. Conceptions of the moral order require that, from a formidable force, the woman be tamed to become all obedience and passivity. There is a parallel between a woman's place in the kin group and her image in the moral order. As an outsider to her husband's lineage in case of exogamous marriage, or if she steers her husband away from his patrilineage, the woman is a threat to the solidarity of the agnatic kin group. As a sexual being, she is described as a threat to morality and the social order.

MARRIAGE ALLIANCES: IDEOLOGY AND REALITY

At the same time that she symbolizes division, the woman is also a potential resource for power in her capacity to become a wife. She may contribute to the welfare of the kin group by marrying a cousin or another male relative in the patrilineage. Patrilineages in the Maghrib and the Middle East historically have enhanced their solidarity through cousin marriage or other forms of kin endogamy. The rule of kin endogamy involves in particular the preference for marriage with the first parallel paternal cousin. According to the rule, the preferred marriage for a man is, first, with his father's brother's daughter (referred to as FBD) and, if not, with another female kin. In general, a patrilineage will show a preference for keeping its women for its own men when possible. Middle Eastern endogamy contrasts with the rest of the world, where exogamy usually prevails, with kinship groups exchanging women. Anthropologists have pointed out the special place of the Middle Eastern FBD marriage in the ethnographic literature. Robert Fernea and James Malarkey write that "[the Middle Eastern FBD marriage is] the only example in the ethnographic literature where those in the lineage have rights of access as well as rights of disposition over women."[26] Middle Eastern endogamy implies that, instead of wife giving and wife taking occurring between lineages as in most of the world, the processes occur within the same lineage. A man's claim over his female kin has shown diverse patterns in the Maghrib and the Middle East more generally. What is common is a value placed on kin endogamy. How compelling a right a man has over his cousin's hand has varied across areas, however.[27]

FBD marriage has the advantage of militating against the fragmentation of property by keeping the estate of a kin group intact. Since Islamic inheritance laws allow women to inherit, marriages between first parallel paternal cousins resolve the risk of agnatic property being divided. The preference for kin endogamy has served as a major device against partition of property in the Middle East. Other societies have developed other devices such as primogeniture or ultimogeniture to the same end.[28] In a society where size and strength of the lineage matter for economic and political power, giving a woman in marriage to her paternal cousin also has another advantage for a kin group. Given the principle of patrilineality, the lineage of the woman's father will retain the woman's children and thus increase its size.

The prescription to marry within the lineage and the preference for marriage between first parallel paternal cousins are grounded in social norms found throughout the Middle East and the Maghrib. Expressing the norms, a woman interviewed in the early 1980s said about marriages between first cousins: "Relatives, in our part of the world, always seek each other out as marriage partners. Theirs [is] an expected union."[29] Another woman relates how she became engaged to her paternal uncle's son who approached her father and received from him the following reply: "My son, she is your first cousin and, come what may, you have priority above anyone else."[30] Among some groups, a man has an exclusive right to his father's brother's daughter (FBD), who cannot marry anyone else without his prior consent. He may even be paid a sum of money as compensation for renouncing his privilege over her hand. A man is usually free to use or not to use his right.

The preferential right of a man to his FBD actually entails a relation between two men, the groom's and the bride's fathers. Hildred Geertz indicates that, in the Moroccan town of Sefrou where she studied family ties, the person holding the right over the woman is not the groom-to-be, but his father. A man in effect has a claim to marry off his son to his brother's daughter.[31] The significant relation is between two brothers, for whom their children's marriage is an occasion to strengthen the agnatic bond. H. Geertz reports that the people with whom she spoke rarely expressed the preference unsolicited, but, when asked about it, some people stated a proverb according to which "a girl's father's brother's son has priority."[32] The priority is not absolute, nor is it a moral right. It implies, however, that if a man wants to marry his father's brother's daughter, he can make a stronger claim than would another man.

Because of the preference for FBD marriages, the relationship between paternal cousins of opposite sex often takes on a special character. The cousins sometimes are matched and promised to each other from an early age. In reporting on the behavior of cousins in their study in Algeria, Descloitres and Debzi write: "From the age of ten or twelve, they start acting like fiancés."[33] In Tunisia, I often saw little girls giggle and act embarrassed when they were in the presence of their father's brother's son. If a woman has no first parallel paternal cousin, she falls in principle to the next male in the patrilineage, with the rule of kin endogamy extending to other men in the agnatic line. Other male relatives do not, however, hold as compelling a preferential right as does the first paternal cousin.

FBD marriages often involve a lower bride price than do marriages between strangers. Sometimes, the bride price is made negligible. The lower bride price that applies to FBD marriage reflects the preference for this type of union. Essentially a transaction from the groom's family to the bride's, and required by Islamic law for the legitimation of a marriage, the bride price becomes a transaction between brothers in the case of FBD marriage.[34] Instead of seeing the bride price as lower in endogamous marriages, it may be more accurate to view it as higher in exogamous marriages because such unions are less valued.[35] Considered less honorable, marriages between strangers would require a higher price to be paid by the groom's family to the bride's. This suggests further evidence that marriages among kin are considered more advantageous to the group.

The ideology of kin endogamy has been enacted in social practice to varying degrees. FBD marriages and kin endogamy have been found to occur throughout the Arab-Islamic world. On this point, scholars agree. However, controversies have arisen over the actual frequency of endogamous marriages. In the 1950s, when social science writings in the West tended to emphasize the uniqueness of Middle Eastern culture, scholars highlighted the norm and practice of endogamy, which were seen as a distinctive feature of the Middle East. Then the emphasis shifted to those aspects of culture that the Arab-Islamic Middle East shared with other cultural areas of the world. Hence, kin endogamy was underplayed. A fuller and potentially more accurate understanding of Middle Eastern kinship and marriage strategies has since developed.

Stating that the custom of cousin marriage has been practiced everywhere in the Islamic Middle East, Raphael Patai gives unreasonably high figures for the occurrence of FBD marriages. Using a 1952 source on Egypt, which he evidently judges reliable, he contends that 80 percent of all the marriages among peasants took place between first cousins.[36] Taking a more balanced view, Goode sees some of the reports used by Patai as possibly untrustworthy and generally presents lower figures for FBD marriages, ranging from 12 to 50 percent.[37] In a 1973 summary of a number of studies, Barth shows that FBD marriages vary from 10 percent to 20 percent and in some communities up to 30 percent of all marriages.[38] Considering more than twenty studies published between 1931 and 1988, Bonte indicates that the frequency of FBD marriage in the Islamic Middle East ranges from 3.3 percent for some populations to 38 percent for others.[39] In the same vein, Ben Salem notes that FBD marriages typically represent from 10 to 30 percent of marriages in most of the Middle East.[40]

Research on the Maghrib confirms this range. In her anthropological work in a Moroccan village between 1970 and 1972, Susan Davis found that 12 percent of the marriages involved spouses related by blood.[41] Hildred Geertz reports that 12 percent of the marriages took place between first parallel paternal cousins in the group that she studied in the Moroccan town of Sefrou.[42] In a field study conducted between 1968 and 1970 in the town of Boujad in Morocco, Dale Eickelman found that FBD marriages varied from 14 to 30 percent depending on the particular social group.[43] In his research in Tunisia, Kilani finds a stated preference for FBD marriages, even when exogamy is practiced. He interprets the stated preference as a reflection of the high value placed on kinship ties and lineage solidarity.[44]

In considering the practice of kin endogamy, we must take into account other forms of marriage within the kin group, in addition to marriages between first cousins. Marriages between members of the same lineage also constitute kin endogamy. Like FBD marriages, they serve to consolidate the lineage and its property. Figures on the frequency of endogamy must therefore include them. Fredrik Barth estimates that the combined frequency of FBD and intra-lineage marriages varies between 40 and 80 percent, thus indicating that approximately half of the marriages take place among kin. Camilleri reports kin endogamy rates varying from 15 percent in the capital city of Tunis to 20 percent in other cities and 24.5 percent in Tunisian villages.[45]

Jean Cuisenier finds that, in a rural area of Tunisia, more than half of the marriages occurred between members of the same tribal group from the late nineteenth century to the middle of the twentieth. In a 1953 study of Casablanca, Anne-Marie Baron reports that 30 percent of the married men took a wife in their tribal group of origin. Maher indicates that, in a Moroccan hamlet in the Middle Atlas, 22 percent of the marriages were between relatives. H. Geertz finds that nearly one-third of the marriages entered by the men of a given lineage over three generations are with women of that same lineage, in an area of Morocco.[46] Taken together, the studies report an average of 30 percent of all marriages taking place within the same lineage or tribe. The figure is within the range of 28 to 62 percent for intra-lineage marriages indicated by Bonte in his review of eleven studies on various communities of the Middle East, published between 1931 and 1988.[47] The evidence therefore suggests that the preference for kin endogamy is put into practice in approximately a third of the marriages.

Kin endogamy has been a key mechanism of social integration in Middle Eastern societies, where it has served to strengthen the solidarity of the extended patrilineal kinship network. This has been the case even though kin endogamy has been practiced to various degrees and in different ways in different communities. The retention of women within the lineage and its extension has historically been a major process by which Middle Eastern kin groups have maximized their cohesiveness.

VEILS AND WALLS

For endogamy and collectively useful exogamy to be possible, marriages cannot be left to personal preferences. The interests of the kin group must instead be allowed to shape individual destinies. In shielding women from the outside world, several institutional arrangements help maximize the likelihood that the collective interests of the kin group will prevail. The walls and veils that surround women are among such arrangements.

Men and women share a responsibility for preserving the cohesiveness of the ayla in that everyone is expected to behave in a way that enhances the prestige and unity of the collectivity. Nothing in individual behavior should break the united front of the males in the patrilineage. Although both men and women are expected to comply with what is best for the ayla, the organization of the Maghribi kinship system rests upon a stricter control of women than men. If left free, the woman may "ally with the devil" and foment division. The retention of women for the men of the kin group and the preservation of male solidarity within the patrilineage require control over women's lives. They require a defense against women's divisive potential and symbolic destructive power, a defense that is grounded in social and moral norms. Even though individual women find ways to escape the norms in everyday life, the norms are important in themselves in that they define the female role in the social order.[48]

Several institutional mechanisms and codes of behavior facilitate the control of women. One such mechanism is the institution of guardianship for women, required by Islamic law.[49] Legal guardianship often overlaps with a more broadly defined responsibility for female kin. Some kin groups explicitly designate a man to be legally, economically, and morally responsible for a female relative in the patrilineage. Men sometimes remain responsible for a kinswoman even after her marriage. In some areas, for example, if a woman commits adultery, the obligation to avenge the shame falls upon her father or brother. Socially unacceptable behavior on the part of a woman creates more shame and embarrassment for the males of her kin group than for her husband. Conversely, men sometimes claim a greater sense of economic and moral responsibility for their female relatives than for their wives.

The men's commitment to the women of their kin group goes together with control over their behavior. On the one hand, the kin group is responsible for its women and, in particular, for the provision of economic support if the woman is no longer supported by a husband. On the other hand, since the reputation of the tribe, kin grouping, or ayla is of utmost concern, men will make sure that their kinswomen behave in such a way as to preserve the collective reputation. This concern on the part of men does not apply only to their closest family members such as daughters or sisters. Men will also watch over the behavior of other, more distant, female relatives. Men are expected to provide assistance to their female kin. In return, they demand proper behavior.

Preoccupation with female purity and modesty is at the center of the social norms governing gender relations in the Middle East. The preoccupation appears in the value of *ird* and the general code of honor.[50] The term "ird" includes several notions that have to be expressed in different ways in English. It refers inclusively to the honor or moral purity of a group, its prestige in the community, and its strength. It is a collective characteristic. An individual man has ird, but his is essentially a reflection of the ird of his family and lineage. The ird of a lineage depends on the behavior of its women and can be lost in case of female misconduct. Women thus carry a large share of the burden for safeguarding the family, lineage, and tribal honor. Gained or lost through the conduct of women, ird is mostly an attribute of men who either possess it or are left without it. The men of a patrilineage, father, brothers, paternal uncles, and cousins, are the ones who must enforce the norms upon which their honor depends. The male is enjoined to protect the female. He has to guard her against herself because her actions are unpredictable. Since her very being as a woman may create temptations in other men, he also has to guard her from men who are liable to hurt the ird of his kin group.[51]

Family reputation depends on the virginity of daughters and sisters, the fidelity of wives, and the continence of widowed and divorced daughters or sisters. Accordingly, norms of chastity and modesty apply to women's behavior in public. Sometimes, much less than sexual transgression may entail a loss of ird. A challenge may be enough. Even though the woman may have done nothing to encourage the advances of a man, such advances in themselves affect the honor of the kin group, particularly if made in public or known to others. By simply casting doubt on the modesty of the women of the lineage, such action on the part of men may be sufficient to bring about a loss of ird.

The value of ird thus has two central characteristics. First, a man's ird is not nearly as affected by his wife's behavior as it is by his kinswomen's. Blood ties matter more than marriage in this respect. The males of the patrilineage, rather than husbands, primarily hold the right and carry the responsibility to watch over women's behavior. Second, the men of a lineage all share in each other's honor, since each man should concern himself not only with the conduct of the women most closely related to him, such as daughter or sister, but with the conduct of other women in the lineage as well. A collective characteristic, ird is also a collective responsibility. With the entire lineage made responsible for the reputation and proper conduct of its women, powerful mechanisms operate to control women's behavior. In such a social system, clear lines must delineate the realm of the socially acceptable and the socially proscribed. Women have to be kept away from circumstances that may bring a loss of ird and the boundaries of women's lives must be strictly circumscribed.

Several institutional arrangements, such as sex segregation and the veil, help prevent the exposure of women to men other than kin. There is a divide between the world of women and that of men, a symbolic wall that isolates women and restricts their contacts with men to the domestic circle. Descloitres and Debzi remark that the relations between men and women are limited "to the indispensable."[52] Segregation is grounded in the organization of daily life. Examples of sex-segregated activities include the eating of meals separately and separate leisure activities for men and women. Weddings and the celebration of other life events often involve separate ceremonies for women and men.

The veil is the most "visible" instance of the symbolic divide—it is the one that makes women "invisible." Specific features of the veil vary depending on the country, region, or even community.[53] A veil may cover the whole body, including the hair and the face while leaving the eyes uncovered, or it may leave only one eye uncovered, or it may be worn in conjunction with a mask covering the eyebrows, nose, and mouth. Regardless of the specific features, the general principle is the same. The veil is meant to cover and hide the female body, and women are expected to wear it when they are in public spaces.

One useful way to think about the veil is as a device defining the boundaries of kin endogamy. Delineating the world in which marriages are preferred, veiling rules indicate the outer limits of the groups that form alliances. They make explicit the units within which the exchange of women is allowed or at least preferred. Veiling rules in the Middle East require that women wear a veil only when they can be seen by non-kin and that they remain uncovered when they are in the presence of kin. The group within which the veil is dropped, the kin group, is precisely the social unit within which marriage alliances are preferred. More women traditionally have worn a veil in urban areas, towns, and villages than in the countryside. In tribal areas, women often do not wear a veil except when they take a trip to a town or village. Since most people in a tribal area tend to be members of the same kin grouping, women are unlikely to encounter strangers. A veil thus is not required. It is only in settings where they may be seen by non-kin, as in villages, towns, or cities, that women must hide under the protective shield that the veil represents.

In hiding women from male strangers, the veil minimizes the risk that a woman's family will lose ird. Since female sexuality is thought of as having no bounds, one way to guard against it is to keep it hidden.[54] Veiling protects the family from the humiliation that women might cause in transgressing norms of proper conduct. Tillion aptly interprets the phenomenon of the veil as a defense mechanism of tribal communities when their cohesiveness and autonomy are threatened.[55] It is when these communities face the danger of disintegration that it becomes most important for them to hide their women in order to retain them for the males of the lineage. The veil is one way of ensuring the continuation of endogamy in a world in which endogamous alliances risk being superseded by other forms of marriage. The veiling of women serves two basic functions with respect to the maintenance of the kinship structure. It protects the family against the loss of ird and it facilitates the retention of women for the males of the descent group.

If we treat architecture as culture visible on the ground, we see that traditional architecture in the Maghrib has contributed to shielding the family or kin group from the outside. Tillion's metaphor of an "iron curtain" applies well to the isolation of the kin group, especially of its women, from the street and visitors. Joëlle Bahloul speaks of the "logic of enclosure."[56] With an orientation inward and turning its back to the outside, the traditional Maghribi architecture serves to "veil off" women from strangers and to keep them away from contact with non-kin males. The spatial organization of dwellings is such that all the rooms are built around a central courtyard. Each room has only one door, which opens to the courtyard. Windows are so high that no one can look in. Only a small opening connects the house to the outside. Since the opening is located at the end of an elbow-shaped passage, visitors coming to the entry door cannot see inside the courtyard or any of the rooms.

During visits to Tunisia and Morocco, I often heard the voices of women safely hidden in the courtyard, while a man or a child greeted me at the door. Women should not be seen before a male relative or a child has screened visitors. Non-kin males, falling in the category of unacceptable visitors, are not let into the main part of the house. They are taken to a special room called a *hanut*.[57] Unconnected to the female space, the hanut is reserved for male strangers. It is located next to the entry door, is clearly separate from the rest of the house, and opens only to the street. Since there is no access to the hanut from the house, women cannot reach it from inside or be seen by visitors received in that room.

The layout of old Maghribi cities also facilitates the separation of the female and male worlds. A woman moves in urban spaces surrounded with a "triple shield": her veil, a cluster of children generally accompanying her on errands, and the tiny winding streets of old Maghribi cities where no one can be seen for long.[58] Already protected by their veil and the circle of children surrounding them, women also escape quickly from the sight of passers-by. Furthermore, streets are for men. They are not the place for women. In urban areas, there is a quasi-public female space where much informal socializing takes place. Women get together on rooftops. Elizabeth Fernea reports that, after a few months in the city of Marrakesh, she still had not made her way into the world of Moroccan women until, one day, she went to her roof. It is on the neighboring rooftops that she found the women of Marrakesh, talking, relaxing, or working.[59] Similarly, in attending a wedding on the Tunisian island of Kerkennah, I saw women sit on rooftops to watch a wedding procession pass through the town. Men rarely spend time on rooftops. Streets are primarily for men, rooftops are for women.

• • •

The principles of unity and division historically have operated at once in the Maghribi kinship structure. To ensure the welfare of the kin group, unity must be maximized against the danger of division. The logic of organization of the kinship structure requires that women be prevented from "allying with the devil," or introducing ruptures in the web of bonds connecting the men. The unity of the males, all from the same lineage, represents "a firm rampart" protecting the agnatic kin group against the conjugal particularisms symbolized by the women.[60] Accordingly, the consolidation of the agnatic ties that constitute that rampart takes precedence over the conjugal bond in the social organization of kin groups.

While they bring a risk of division within the agnatic kin group, women also represent potential power for the kin group in their capacity to become wives. The preference for marriage within the lineage, or ideology of kin endogamy, has been accompanied by substantial practice in the Middle East in general and the Maghrib in particular, relative to other world regions. Kin endogamy has served as a major mechanism of integration for Middle Eastern kin groups, even though it has combined with exogamy. Without the retention of at least some of its women for its own men, it is difficult for the Maghribi kin group to preserve its cohesion. Whether they are kept for the men of the lineage or given to outsiders in collectively useful marriage alliances, women represent a critical resource for the kin group.

Several institutional arrangements such as veils, walls, and segregated activities have facilitated control over women on the part of the kin group. Veils and walls protect women from encounters with non-kin males. Superfluous in tribal areas where women are likely to be seen only by kin, veiling has been more prevalent in towns and urban spaces where there is a higher risk of contact between women and non-kin. Part of a complex system of social control, veils and walls ensure a separation of the sexes. They also serve to keep women within the kinship network. The continued responsibility of men toward their kinswomen, the value of ird, the importance of women's behavior for family honor, and the veiling of women constitute social norms that have converged toward facilitating the control of women by male members of the kin group.

In the Maghrib as in other parts of the world, gender and kinship have been linked to each other and to the broader social structure. The control of women, as discussed in this chapter, has implications for the broader politics involving kin groupings. The organizing principles of kinship and gender that apply to the ayla by extension have been operative in the formation of larger kin groupings with political functions. The political leverage that the larger kin groupings have been able to acquire and retain has been, to a considerable degree, dependent on their internal solidarity. Women thus have represented power not only for the ayla, but also for its extension, the larger kin groupings or tribes. The internal organization and political roles of larger kin groupings are the subject of the next chapter.

4 Men Work with Angels
Power of the Tribe

Kinship historically has provided a vehicle for political organization in the Maghrib as a whole. It has delineated conditions for individuals to come together and cooperate. In particular, kinship ties have served as a basis for political action and collective defense. The same structural patterns have prevailed in the organization of kinship and politics, insofar as the male-dominated agnatic kin group has operated as a building block for larger groupings with political functions. The control of women, critical for the cohesiveness of the *ayla* (extended patrilineage), also enhanced the power of tribes vis a vis other tribes and central authority. As the Tunisian sociologist Abdelkader Zghal remarks, "It is at the level of the patrilineage that we find the basic political unit in all rural communities in the Maghrib; this unit is at the same time the structural model for larger political groupings."[1] Throughout the Maghrib, rural areas remained predominantly tribal, and kin-based solidarities continued to operate to varying degrees at least until the mid-twentieth century and later in some cases.[2] The nexus of significant solidarities was made up of patrilineal kinship ties that extended from the lineage to larger kin groupings.[3] Within this nexus, Islamic family law and customary law sanctioned the subordination of women to male kin. Expectations of loyalty and mutual support overlapped with patrilineal kinship ties linking the men. As the proverb goes, "Men and angels work towards unity."[4]

The relationship between unilineal descent and segmentary political organization has often been noted.[5] The existence of the relationship has been widely acknowledged, even though the issue of the direction of causality has generated controversy among anthropologists. Meyer Fortes sees segmentary political structure as stemming from the nature of kinship relations. He thus derives the characteristics of political systems in the

Middle East from the unilineal descent system.[6] For Fredrik Barth, the terms of the relationship are reversed. In contrast to Fortes, he sees the Middle Eastern descent system resulting from political and economic structures.[7]

Another theoretical debate revolves around the use of the segmentary lineage model in the social anthropology of the Maghrib, especially Morocco.[8] Whereas some conceive of political relations primarily in terms of descent and lineage, others emphasize the fluidity of social interaction and the role of institutional arrangements other than tribe and kin in shaping the cultural order of Morocco.[9] The debate concerns the *extent* to which kin and tribe are the key to understanding political and social relations, not whether they are important—a point on which scholars tend to agree. Furthermore, while they disagree about causality, most scholars agree that, once a patrilineal descent system and tribal political organization coexist, kinship ties provide a vehicle for politics, regardless of which came first historically.

What matters for the argument of this book is that such a relationship between kinship and political organization has existed at all. My concern is twofold. It is to examine the nature of the larger kin groupings, and it is also to emphasize that agnatic solidarity, which is legitimated by Islamic law, has been a basis of internal cohesiveness and political leverage for tribal groups in Maghribi history. Because the concept of tribe has been used in the literature with many different meanings, it is important to call attention to some of the identifying characteristics of Maghribi tribes and to their partial inclusion in the wider society. This chapter analyzes the structure of tribal groups, the processes by which they are brought together when collective action is needed, and the dynamics of tribal politics. The focus is on common elements of kin groupings in the shared heritage of the Maghrib.

For some areas of the Maghrib, the analysis applies best to the nineteenth century. In others, the analysis remains valid for the early twentieth century, while in others still it continues to apply to the mid-twentieth century at the time of decolonization and even later. Larger kin groupings, or tribes, historically have exhibited similar basic principles of organization throughout the Maghrib, despite variations on specific traits. The same holds true for the relationship between tribe and central authority, which has played itself out in similar terms. Differences among countries notwithstanding (to be considered in part 2), the state in each Maghribi country faced the issues discussed in this chapter in one form or another, at one time or another in its history.

TIES THAT BIND: TRIBAL SOLIDARITY

The concepts of tribe and tribal organization are useful for the analysis of the Maghrib if one treats them as flexible. As an ideal type, a tribe represents a grouping brought together by shared understandings of bonds and obligations resulting from blood or marriage ties. The kinship ties may be real or they may be mythic, in that only some tribes may be able to identify an actual common ancestor while others rely on fictive ancestry. Also as an ideal type, a society in which tribal organization predominates is one in which blood and marriage ties represent the major mechanism defining who has access to economic and political resources and who does not. Like other ideal types, the concepts of tribe and tribal organization constitute heuristic devices for the analysis of several instances, not faithful descriptions of any single instance.

It is best to think of kinship ties in the history of the Maghrib as a resource, rather than a fixed frame for action. Members of tribal communities could activate the ties when they were faced with a collective threat or crisis. Saying that lineage ties served as bases for political action in the Maghrib implies that the ties provided a readily understood medium for solidarity. They delineated conditions for cooperation, even though the cooperation and solidarity could occur to various degrees according to circumstances. This is not to mean that the ties set rigid rules for social interaction between two individuals under all conditions. In the Maghrib, members of "republics of cousins" to use Tillion's metaphor, historically have placed a value on *asabiyya*, or "agnation in action," or in David Hart's words "unifying structural cohesion."[10] The republics of cousins took common descent as one good reason for collective political action.

Maghribi tribes claimed common kinship.[11] Each tribe would claim a male ancestor common to all members of the tribe. Every one of the tribal segments would, in addition, claim another male ancestor common to members of the segment. Kinship could be real in that some tribes could trace their genealogy back to a person who had existed. Kinship also could be fictive. As Wendy Griswold and Benedict Anderson remind us in discussing ethnic groups and nations, many communities are imagined.[12] They are products of human minds in response to specific historical circumstances. Maghribi tribes are no exception.

A tribe required a clear definition of membership in order to operate as a unit. All the members had to know who was in and who was out at any particular time, since membership defined by descent served as the basis for cooperation. In some cases, occupants of a given territory attributed descent to individuals who had acquired rights in the territory by whatever means. They invented common ancestry by constructing genealogies that artfully linked all the various groups into a tribe. Whether a tribe could identify actual links in its genealogy, or whether it developed primarily as a political entity for the defense of its territory, the agnatic principle remained the same. In both cases, members of kin groupings identified themselves as related through patrilineal kinship relations. The very act of constructing a common kinship root strengthened solidarity within the tribal unit.

Common ancestry generated the sense of collective kinship necessary for a group to act as a corporate unit in defending its territory and in other political conflicts. In that it elicited loyalty and a sense of reciprocal obligations, a myth of common ancestry united members of a tribe as effectively as did actual ancestry. Once the kinship relation was established through fictive ancestry, it served as a basis for law and order, cooperation, and defense. And, it was a basis readily understood and accepted by all. The tribe then reinforced the imagined links within itself through actual intermarriage, or tribal endogamy. In this process, kin control of marriage alliances, facilitated as it was by Islamic family law and customary law, helped cement patrilineal and tribal solidarity.

Group Formation and Loyalties

Aylas typically have come together in larger kin groups that united to form a tribe. Although names and classification varied across areas, a fairly common hierarchy in size included the conjugal (rarely) or extended (usually) household as the smallest unit, followed by the ayla, then a group of lineages or subclan, a larger circle of lineages or clan, sometimes also referred to as the tribal faction, and the tribe as the largest configuration. The size of a tribe would vary greatly, ranging from a few hamlets to an entire province. Hart notes, "[A tribe] may range in size from a tiny cluster of hamlets dotting one or two mountain slopes to a huge (though not necessarily amorphous) unit, covering most of a whole province or even spilling over into neighboring provinces."[13] Among nomads, a tribe might vary from twenty to several hundred or even a thousand tents. The group actually engaged at a given moment might include all the descendants of a common (real or fictive) ancestor for several generations or only the members of two or three extended households.

Maghribi tribes have used two major processes of group formation, one driven by the issue at hand and the other by the kinship position of the individual in need of help. In the first process, members of a tribe, or members of one of its segments, would join together for collective action. Which segments of the tribe united depended on the subject and context of conflict. Different issues required different political alignments and therefore called for the coming together of different parts of a tribe. The operational group might be restricted to a clan within the tribe, or a lineage within the clan, while at other times it might involve several clans or lineages.[14] All the clans that constituted a tribe usually would unite in political matters that concerned the whole tribe. Some tribes might form tribal confederations for specific purposes, usually to enhance their ability to oppose a common enemy.

The other major process of group formation centered on the man (not the woman) in need of help, thus activating a different configuration of kinship ties for each individual. In the first process, the membership of the group, be it a tribe, a clan, or a lineage, was fixed. In the second process a group was constituted on an ad hoc basis to help a specific person. In the latter, group membership fluctuated, as every man was the center of a circle of kinship links that might be activated when necessary. Women entered the web of bonds and obligations indirectly, through their male relatives. If a woman needed help or had been wronged, her close male relatives such as father, brother, or son, carried the first responsibility toward her. Should the issue require the involvement of a larger group, networks of support would form to help the woman's male relative address what then became redefined as an issue facing a man.

The group that came together in the second process of group formation usually involved all the males within five degrees of patrilineal relationship to the individual needing help. Specific to each male, the group constituted to provide help was a function of the location of that particular individual in the kinship structure. Although the individuals who came together in this way did not form a stable group, they were nevertheless among those to be counted on for support when an individual had been wronged and vengeance was required. In addition to the tribe and its segments as units capable of corporate action, the Maghribi kinship system thus involved a nexus of reciprocal obligation that, although fluid in composition, was a crucial component of the network of support provided by the larger kin groups.

The outer limits of loyalties overlapped with the boundaries of agnatic relations in a series of concentric circles. The loyalties usually went first to closer kin, the members of the ayla, and then to members of the same agnatic lineage. They extended to the *beni amm* (or *banu amm*, meaning the "circle of cousins" or, literally, the sons of the father's brother), that is, the tribal faction or the whole tribal group, depending on the region. The circle of loyalties went no further. It stopped with the tribal entity. The overlap between solidarity and agnatic relations in a series of circles has been documented in different regions of the Maghrib. For example, in studying tribal organization in Tunisia in the nineteenth century, Lucette Valensi locates individual identity "at the center of a series of concentric circles of which the last, the largest, is the tribe."[15] In the same vein, and writing about Morocco in the early twentieth century, Hart comments that "[i]n the tribal regions, the widest terminal loyalty was to the widest agnatic group, in [a] series of concentric circles."[16]

Functioning first and foremost as a political entity, a Maghribi tribe could redefine itself in response to compelling changes in political circumstances. A new tribal entity could develop through a process of political amalgamation between two tribes or through splits within a tribe. The growth of tribal units resulted in the shifting of tribal segments from one tribe to another and in the development of new tribal confederations. The boundaries thus were fluid and new units formed, usually because of political pressures. Fragmentation would occur in cases of insoluble conflicts among segments of one tribe or because a tribe had grown to dimensions that made the regulation of collective life impractical. Amalgamation would occur to enhance the capacity of the amalgamating tribes to defend themselves against a common offender.

Community and Power

The principle of unity within the patrilineage and within its extension, the tribe, has been embedded in a number of patterns, particularly in patterns of ownership and in several cases in patterns of residence. Studies of household size show that the extended kin group remained important as a residential unit as late as the 1950s in several regions of the Maghrib. A study done in 1959 in a Berber village in Morocco indicates that the entire population of the village, about two hundred people, lived in twenty houses, which made an average of ten individuals per household.[17] In her study of kinship structure and agricultural work in Algeria, Claudine Chaulet reports that households included as many as seventeen individuals.[18] Writing in 1963, Descloitres and Debzi report that in eastern Algeria three and sometimes four generations lived in a household, with a total of thirty to forty members and in some cases up to fifty.[19]

Community and kinship solidarity also have appeared in patterns of ownership. Women as legally defined recipients of inheritance shares under Islamic law, despite the gender inequality in inheritance, have been a significant part of these patterns and, through endogamy, have contributed to the stability of the land holdings owned by the patrilineal kin group. Property might be held in common by the ayla. In some cases, communal ownership might extend beyond the lineage to the circle of lineages that constituted a tribal faction, the beni amm, or even to an entire tribal unit. Issues of property and territory were of central concern to lineages and tribes. Barth notes: "Descent group affairs focus on property and the control of territory. They relate to a particular tangible estate."[20] In addition, some lineages engaged collectively in production. Among ninety kinship units that she studied in Algeria, Chaulet found that sixty-six were collectively engaged in production as well as consumption. Thirty-four units worked the land collectively but left consumption to the various conjugal units that formed the kinship network. Underlining the importance of the kin group in matters of ownership and production, Chaulet concludes that kinship relations functioned as relations of production.[21]

Attempting a general characterization of the mode of ownership in large parts of the Middle East, Robert Fernea and James Malarkey suggest that it has historically consisted of a combination of private access and collective ownership.[22] This applies to the Maghrib where small, individually owned plots coexisted with collectively owned pasture land. The system of tribal land ownership often reflected the social organization of the tribe. Hart comments that "[t]he overall system of tribal land ownership [was] in effect nothing but the segmentary system . . . flopped down spatially onto the ground."[23] For most nomadic populations, land ownership was usually of minor relevance, as wealth was held primarily in the form of cattle. Depending on the particular group, cattle were owned either entirely in common or part of the cattle might be individually owned by conjugal families, while another part belonged to the ayla, the larger circle of lineages, or the tribe as a whole. Brands borne by cattle in some rural areas manifested the combination of communal and private ownership. The animals in the cattle herd of the ayla all bore the same mark of the ayla. Each son or brother might also acquire one or several animals for himself besides the collectively owned herd. These animals would then bear his individual brand, in addition to that of the ayla. The individual brand existed only for internal purposes. It had no relevance for the delineation of grazing territories in the larger context of a village or a region where the mark of the ayla was the only one that mattered.[24]

The allocation of power within the tribe involved a tension between diffusion and concentration of authority.[25] The internal distribution of power rested in principle on a system of opposition and balances between lineages and tribal sections, bringing about alternatively unification and fragmentation within the tribe. The same segments might cooperate at one time and oppose each other at another time. Two lineages might, for example, be in conflict over the sharing of irrigation waters in their adjacent territories.[26] At another time, they might unite and form a corporate entity, when faced with a common threat to their land by another tribe, or even by a third segment of their own tribe. Lines of alliance and opposition thus would shift and positions of authority could change accordingly. Since the composition and boundaries of the group uniting varied, this favored a diffusion of authority and could function to restrain the concentration of power within a single group.

Kin groupings of various size, tribes, clans, or lineages, generally vested a council with decision-making power. Some kin groupings, acting through the male members of the lineage—the agnates—chose members of their council by holding elections once a year or, more precisely stated, by making a designation based on agreements reached after negotiations or sometimes after bloodshed. In periods when conflicts with the outside world occurred only occasionally, top chiefs with emergency or special powers were chosen in times of war or for action requiring that the whole tribe unite. Meant to be only a *primus inter pares*, the top chief was expected to relinquish his authority once the tribe had resolved the issue that caused him to gain power. In considering power within the tribe, it is useful to borrow from Edward Evans-Pritchard's classic formulation in his work on the Sanusi tribes of Cyrenaica. He writes:

> Authority is distributed at every point of the tribal structure and political
> leadership limited to situations in which a tribe or segment of it acts
> corporately. With a tribe, this only happens in war or in dealings with
> an outside authority . . . The status of a *shaikh* can only be defined
> in terms of a complicated network of kinship ties and structural relations.
> It is only necessary here to emphasize that his social position is
> unformalized and that he must in no sense be regarded as a ruler or
> administrator.[27]

Relations with the outside world often precipitated a concentration of power in the hands of either an entire lineage or an individual chief, however. Armed conflicts with other tribes or with central authority required effective and sustained leadership. Since very few tribes operated in total isolation, most faced conflicts with the outside. Rare were those that could dispense with some form of leadership for any appreciable length of time. Lineages or individuals within them sometimes succeeded to acquire and retain power for longer than expected. In the competition for internal leadership, the lineages or individuals most likely to succeed were those that managed at once to convince the tribe that they would protect it against central authority and persuade central authority that they would maintain peace in the tribe.

The sphere of action of Maghribi kin groupings as corporate entities has included the social, the economic, and the political. In the absence of centralized state institutions, kin groupings served as the functional equivalent of regulating and supporting agencies. Arranged marriages between tribal lineages supported the development of cooperative bonds in such large-scale endeavors. In this process, kin control over marriage alliances served as a critical political resource in building tribal cohesion and group solidarity. The larger kin groupings functioned as economic agencies for endeavors beyond the capacity of the ayla, such as the working out of an irrigation plan for a large area or a project of agricultural improvement. Larger kin groupings also played an important role with respect to the maintenance of law and order. Sensitive to criticism and facing strong social controls, members of Maghribi tribes were attached to their own customs, which they guarded jealously. Infractions to tribal norms were severely punished. In some cases, they even required blood vengeance. Generally, when the offense was between close relatives, such as between first cousins, some attempt was made to avoid bloodshed and settle the matter with a payment in money or in goods, even in cases of serious infractions.[28]

The most important function of larger kin groupings was political. The defense of its territory constituted the major objective of a tribe coming together as a corporate group and calling all its segments to cooperate.[29] Each tribe had a name and a territory. Each clan within a tribe also had its own name and subterritory. Since nomadic tribes did not move randomly but within a well-defined area, the defense of a territory in some cases mattered to them as much as it did to settled populations. Many Maghribi nomadic tribes were actually transhumant, a word borrowed from French and adopted into English, meaning that the groups in question made two moves a year. In the spring, they moved to the mountains to find pasture for their cattle (generally sheep) and, in the fall, they went back to their dwellings in the lower valleys, where they spent most of the year. Transhumant tribes treated the defense of their territory in the lower valleys as a matter critical to survival.

Whether settled or transhumant, larger kin groupings typically entered into collective action when they had to defend themselves against outsiders. Potential threats that triggered internal solidarity and cooperation included a broad range of strangers. Barth comments: "The prototypical opponent to which the whole 'we' descent group is counterposed is characteristically composed of strangers: armies, caravans, city-ruled police, nomads for the villagers, villagers for the nomads, other ethnic groups, other religious communities, unrelated neighbors."[30] Whatever their particular characteristics, settled or transhumant, based on real or mythical ancestry, tribes had in common the fact that they were primarily *political entities* oriented toward the defense of their autonomy. As E. Braunlich comments about a tribe in this context, it is "a political, not a somatic entity."[31]

TRIBES, ISLAMIC UNITY, AND MARKETS

Two broad historical processes have contributed to the partial inclusion of Maghribi tribal groups in the wider society: the development of religious unity throughout the Maghrib and the necessity for exchange in the market. Far from being isolated, self-sufficient units, most Maghribi tribes in the nineteenth century interacted with other tribes or central authority. Although only partial, the relative inclusion of tribes in the wider society is the reason that threats to tribal autonomy existed at all. Had they been cut off from the larger environment, tribes would have had fewer reasons to defend themselves against the outside world.

The Maghrib developed as a homogenous religious area in the course of time, since the Arab conquest in the eighth century. As discussed in chapter 2, Islam has provided an umbrella identity. It has, among others, sanctioned the persistence of a common cohesive kinship structure in which women are subordinate to male kin. The overwhelming majority of the Maghribi population shares in the creed of Islam and perceives itself as part of the world Islamic community, despite the existence of several interpretations. Even some of the areas that at one time had their own code of customary law historically have seen themselves as belonging under the umbrella of Islam. By contrast to other parts of the world, where segmentation and tribal fragmentation often went hand in hand with religious separatism, in the Maghrib, tribal units strove for autonomy and remained segmentary at the same time that they participated in a universalistic system of values.

Scholars from different perspectives converge in emphasizing the significance of religious unity in the Maghrib. Carl Brown writes that "Islam is the most important common denominator in the Maghrib . . . [it is] a symbol of unity and identity."[32] Jean Dejeux notes that Islam has served as a politico-religious bond among different Maghribi groups under common religious symbols.[33] Ernest Gellner notes that within the Muslim community in the Maghrib, "religious homogeneity is almost complete."[34] He further points out that "differences stop short, considerably short, of an avowed separation or schism."[35] There was, and there still is, diversity in religious practice among regions and local areas, as is evinced in the existence of numerous cults and brotherhoods. The diversity has failed, however, to give rise to religious separatism. Maghribi tribes have shared an Islamic identity despite the existence of local particularisms.

A degree of exchange in the market place has provided another mechanism for the partial inclusion of tribal groups into the larger social environment. During the nineteenth century and even earlier, Maghribi tribes did not live in economic autarky, despite a widely shared ideal of economic self-sufficiency. Many tribes managed to come close to the ideal by producing most of the goods needed for food consumption, since production of essential food items guaranteed independence from other tribes in times of tribal warfare. It also helped a tribe reduce its vulnerability to agents of central authority, by allowing it to retreat into isolation when necessary. In his study of markets in Morocco, Marvin Mikesell indicates that, although differences in soil and climate required some specialization, tribes avoided specializing so much that they would be forced to depend on others for basic food staples.[36]

While striving toward self sufficiency, most tribes nevertheless exchanged goods in times of relative peace. Interregional and intertribal exchanges have been documented throughout the Maghrib. Habib Attia's study of tribal groups in the Hautes Steppes, one of the most remote areas of Tunisia, shows that in the nineteenth century, members of tribal groups went to the northern part of the country to sell their labor during grain harvest. They received in payment one tenth of the crop and brought back home their reserve of grain for the year. They also went to markets in the east where they would sell wool, dried meat, and honey, and buy items that their land did not allow them to produce, such as oil and sugar.[37]

Julia Clancy-Smith writes that ". . . despite apparent isolation, the pre-Sahara's oasis and tribal communities shared in a number of local, regional and transregional networks."[38] In Algeria, even the groups most resistant to the control of central authority had to go, at least occasionally, to market places. Some Kabyle groups, notorious for their fierce sense of independence, needed to exchange their oil and figs for wheat. This forced them to come out of their northern mountains and enter into trade relations with other groups. The same applied to the Algerian south where tribes that produced wool, livestock, and dates, exchanged these products for grain.[39] It applied as well to tribal groups in Morocco.[40] The "route of salt" was particularly important in this respect. Tribes living in mountainous areas had to go to places where they could obtain salt, which was unavailable in their own regions.

Tribal solidarities were preserved in the Maghrib despite partial economic and trading dependency. Even though it gathered several tribal groups in a given location, exchange in the market failed to erode tribal organization. One of the reasons is that Maghribi tribal markets were periodic assemblies and not stable settlements. After a visit to the market place, each group returned to its own territory where it could live in temporary withdrawal and in isolation from other groups. Thus, markets did not in themselves undermine mechanisms of internal cohesion, such as the preference for endogamy in the extended patrilineage or the tribe. In some cases, markets could provide an opportunity for arranged marriages that would cement trading relations between different tribes. In this instance, exogamy was pursued to further the collective interests of the kin group, as tribes would use marriage alliances as part of a broad economic tribal strategy.

Market places historically also have had a political function. There were two types of markets, local and regional. Each tribe held its own local market once a week for its own members. Attracting larger numbers of people, regional markets were often located on the lines that marked the frontier between the territories of different tribes. Held in the open at predetermined sites, markets took place on a given day of the week. Local and regional markets served as informal, yet regular, political assemblies in tribal areas. Marvin Mikesell notes that "[b]y night fall tribal authorities [had] resolved most of the problems of the week."[41] Market day was the time not only for the trading of goods, but also for the exchange of political information, announcements of news, transactions among tribes, and various kinds of negotiations.

Because they allowed for commercial exchange without requiring the settlement of populations in trading centers, weekly periodic markets helped perpetuate the separation of local collectivities in rural areas from the representatives of central authority located in cities. At the same time, however, market sites offered a strategic place for episodic attempts on the part of central authority to exert control on recalcitrant tribes. In Morocco in the early twentieth century, for example, representatives of colonial powers, French and Spanish officers, established headquarters at the larger regional markets, where they tried to collect taxes.[42] Although they managed to escape paying other kinds of taxes, tribes in principle still had to pay for their rights to the market place.[43] Yet, since markets were held in open-air areas with no gates or walls, it was sometimes possible for tribal groups to avoid paying even their market dues. Market places provided but another stage for the ongoing conflict between central authority and tribal groups.

TRIBES AND CENTRAL AUTHORITY

A state of unstable truce between the center and the periphery constituted the most common denominator of Maghribi political structures in the nineteenth century. A monarchy occupied the center, and tribal groups the periphery. There was an ever changing balance between the power of the monarchy and the autonomy of tribal groups. The stronger the monarchy, the more the tribes had to relinquish their independence and recognize central authority, even if only grudgingly. As soon as the monarchy faltered, tribal groups quickly regained their autonomy. Then, they either ignored central authority or sometimes attempted to overthrow it. Although with significant differences among Tunisia, Algeria, and Morocco, the Maghrib in the early nineteenth century on the whole had not developed stable centralized states. None of the countries in that period had a state able to control effectively a clearly defined territory and to extract taxes regularly. Instead, in the early part of the nineteenth century, the Maghribi state was "perched precariously on top of a mass of tribal communities," in Gellner's apt phrase.[44] The state was made up of a monarch, his court, and a generally feeble army based in a city.[45] Some dynasties were able to retain power for several generations. Others were quickly brought down by more powerful tribal collectivities, capable of taking over and establishing a new dynasty that would then find itself in a similar relationship of conflicts and alliances with other tribes. Strategic marriages between competing patrilineages played a role in reinforcing this pattern of alliance and consolidation.

Because it lacked both a bureaucratic apparatus and an efficient army, the state only partially controlled rural areas. Tribal groups would be its allies or enemies, depending on circumstances and on the relative strength of the particular state and tribe in question.[46] Some form of order prevailed, but it was fragile and interrupted by tribal rebellions. In the areas that it controlled, central authority was sometimes able to place representatives who were either its direct agents or, more frequently, tribal leaders whose position of local leadership it had ratified. In areas beyond the reach of central authority, order was maintained by a complex system of agreements, negotiations, and alliances among tribal groups.[47]

The fundamental issue at stake in the conflict between central authority and tribal groups was taxation.[48] Tribes constantly struggled to escape taxes. They defended their autonomy from other tribes as well, but the state was the greatest threat because it was potentially the most powerful challenger. Some tribes succeeded better than others at escaping taxation and only a few succumbed entirely to central administrative authority. Tribal dissidence, or opposition to the state, was endemic in Maghribi history. Consequently, in the nineteenth century and in some areas well into the twentieth century, states had no choice but to tolerate the refusal of numerous tribes to pay taxes. The degree of bureaucratic and military state centralization was directly related to the capacity of the state to extract taxes. States that lacked the means to coerce local collectivities into submitting to taxation found themselves in a difficult position to develop a bureaucratic and military apparatus. A basic issue for central authority in the nineteenth century was how to levy taxes to support a bureaucracy and an army, despite the predominance of a near-subsistence economy in many areas.

Political organization in the nineteenth-century Maghrib can be described as three concentric zones.[49] The first and smallest zone represents central power. Based in cities, ruling dynasties combined military, commercial, and religious functions. They surrounded themselves with tax-exempt tribes whose members assumed military responsibilities. The second circle represents an intermediary zone composed of subject tribes, which were under the control of central authority and submitted to heavy taxation. Third, tribes that were in a state of quasi-constant dissidence made up the largest and peripheral zone. Most tribes in this zone generally escaped taxation and some of them intermittently tried to displace established dynasties through warfare.

The history of the nineteenth-century Maghrib was characterized by an ongoing tension between the first and third zones. Watching faltering dynasties at the center and sometimes preparing to invade them, dissident tribes in the third zone were those that posed a permanent danger to central authority. Subject tribes, those in the second zone, did not play a direct role in the struggle for power. Weakened by taxation, they had no capacity to resist the raids of dissident tribes and had to rely on central authority for protection.

The zone of dissidence and the zone of subject tribes should be understood as fluid and fluctuating sociological categories, not as neatly delimited geographic areas. What remained constant was the organization of society in three basic categories: one raising taxes, another submitting to them, and a third evading them. Rapid shifts occurred, however, in the size of the zone under dissidence. Any particular group could switch from one category to another over a short period of time. A given tribe might be in dissidence for several years and then fall under the grip of central authority. Or the reverse might occur in that a tribe could be forced to pay taxes for a while and later regain its autonomy. Some tribes, usually situated in mountainous areas of difficult access, succeeded in maintaining a fairly constant state of dissidence. Powerful dynasties managed to reduce considerably the zone of dissidence and bring more tribes than their predecessor into their tax-paying orbit. By contrast, a crisis, such as when one dynasty displaced another, could reduce the subject zone to cities and surrounding plains. In periods of generalized dissidence, tribal violence extended all the way to city walls.

Dissidence is best conceptualized as a range covering a continuum from total submission to total independence; that is, there were degrees of dissidence. Furthermore, rulers did not submit all the tribes within their orbit to the same amount or kind of taxation. They took whatever they could get. Sometimes rulers obtained a certain amount of taxes through a local chief, but less than they would have liked. At other times, they obtained only an agreement of nonhostility, levied no taxes at all, had no representatives of their own in the area, and left the political institutions of the tribe intact. Shrewd enough to avoid open confrontation with tribes in the zone of dissidence, rulers often exerted only as much control as any given area would take.

The existence of two linguistic groups in the Maghrib, Arabs and Berbers, has been used, especially in colonial writings, to suggest an overlap between Berbers and dissidents on the one hand, and Arabs and subjects of the monarchy on the other.[50] Arabs and Berbers have also been treated as two antagonistic corporate entities. These interpretations are misleading in that they seriously misread Maghribi political history.[51] The distinction between Arabs and Berbers is primarily linguistic. To be precise, one should say Berberophones and Arabophones. Maghribi Arabs are in fact Berbers who were "arabized" after the Arab conquest in the eighth century and have since adopted the Arabic language.

More importantly, there was no single Berber identity or language that could have served as a vehicle for a unified movement of dissidence against central authority. "Berber" is in effect a cluster of dialects among which mutual intelligibility is not always possible. In Morocco, for example, there are at least three important Berber dialects: the Tachelhit, or language of the Shleuhs Berbers of the south, the Tamazirht, or language of the Berbers of the Middle Atlas, and the language of the Berbers of the Rif in the northern part of the country. In Algeria as well, different Berber dialects are spoken among the Kabyles, the Shawiyas and the Mzabites.[52] In Maghribi history, neither Arabs nor Berbers acted as a single group. If a Berber was a menace to an Arab, he was a menace because he belonged to a different tribe. Gellner comments: "The Berber is a menace *qua* tribesman, not *qua* speaker of gibberish-sounding language. As tribesman, he might also be ally . . . So, the difference which exists in linguistic fact and history is not underscored, for it lacks a connection with any of those ideas in terms of which men do see their world."[53] In the nineteenth century, Berbers saw themselves as members of this or that tribe and not as members of a Berber entity. Regardless of linguistic differences between Arabs and Berbers and among Berbers themselves, all shared in kin-based tribal politics and in the conflict between tribe and central authority.

• • •

Tribes and their segments, the larger kin groupings, historically have shared the same basic principles of organization throughout the Maghrib, despite variations on specific traits. An emphasis on patrilineal kinship ties, defined as either real or fictive common ancestry, went together with the political strength of a tribal group. The ties served as a basis for solidarity and cooperation. As the proverb says, "Men and angels work towards unity." Until at least the early twentieth century, tribes constituted meaningful social entities and retained political functions with respect to the maintenance of internal order and dealings with the larger environment.

The tribes participated in a world larger than themselves. Religion and market exchange acted as forces of unification in bringing tribal groups into contact with one another and sometimes with central authority. At the same time, however, political fragmentation prevailed as a result of the ongoing quest for political autonomy on the part of tribal collectivities. Maghribi tribes engaged in continuous efforts to ward off intrusion from other tribes and central authority. Politics involved a tension between central authority attempting to expand its control over larger territories and tribal groups struggling to escape it. Who won in this contest—state or tribe—depended on the particular period, area, and set of circumstances. Often, there was no definite winner for any length of time, making success a short-lived state of affairs.

Part 2

HISTORICAL DIFFERENCES

The central task is to discover, or invent, the appropriate terms of
comparison, the appropriate frameworks within which to view
material phenomenally disparate in such a way that its very
disparateness leads us into a deeper understanding of it.

Clifford Geertz

Using the lens developed in the analysis of similarities in part 1, part 2
opens the discussion of differences among the three Maghribi countries
by focusing on the precolonial and colonial periods. Unity and fragmentation coexisted in an ever changing balance throughout Maghribi history.
How unity and fragmentation played themselves out over time shaped the
long-term trajectory of each country, and more specifically, the balance of
power between center and periphery, or state and tribe.

Part 2 shows how the structure of the precolonial polity combined with
the differential effect of colonization to influence the development of the
state. The political origins of much that was to be distinctive about the
polity of each country can be traced back to these early periods. The greater
centralization and weaker tribal structures that characterized Tunisia
throughout its history had their early origins here, as did the greater power
of tribes in Morocco and Algeria.

5 The Precolonial Polity
National Variations

Tunisia, Algeria, and Morocco exhibited similarities and significant differences in the basic framework of politics in the precolonial period. Throughout the Maghrib in that period, the polity was neither a stateless society nor a modern nation-state, but one in which issues of control were negotiated and renegotiated between central power and local areas. The model of power outlined in the previous chapter applied to some extent to all three countries, which displayed the two key elements of tribal politics: a tension between state and tribe, and the advantage provided by the support of a cohesive kin grouping to build a power base at the local and regional level.[1] Although they shared these characteristics, Tunisia, Algeria, and Morocco differed with respect to the political leverage of kin groupings and the form of central authority in the precolonial era. This chapter examines differences in the polity of the three Maghribi countries in the precolonial period with an emphasis on political unification versus fragmentation. The implications of these differences for family law are then considered at the end of the chapter.

Tunisia experienced early state centralization, coupled with a weakening of the tribes as political actors. Algeria had powerful tribes and a weak state that often ignored each other. In Morocco, a division between a shaky *bilad al-makhzan* (land of government) and a feisty *bilad al-siba* (land of dissidence) caused frequent and bloody confrontations. Family law mirrored political organization in each country. The judicial system and the number of codes of family law in each territory reflected the degree of political unification, or on the contrary, the degree of fragmentation. Tunisia had a more unified system of family law and even attempted a few reforms of that system. Algeria and Morocco had a more diverse and fragmented system of law, with a substantial number of particularistic codes of customary law in regions and local areas.

I use two categories of indicators to analyze national differences in the capacity for control on the part of central authority versus the degree of autonomy of tribal groups. The categories of indicators are the incidence and character of tribal rebellions and the centralizing reforms attempted or actually implemented by central power. The first category, tribal rebellions, taps the degree of segmentation of the society. Within that category, the frequency of tribal rebellions refers to the actual occurrence of acts of dissidence and resistance to central power. It indicates the frequency with which local areas activated kin-based solidarities to oppose controlling efforts on the part of the state. The features of tribal rebellions, whether tribal groups revolted each in isolation or could generate a measure of coordination among themselves, reflect social organization in the region considered. The nature of the grievances made by rebelling tribes tells us something about the nature of the relationship between kin-based groups and the state. Whether tribal groups revolted to preserve their autonomy or on the contrary to demand assistance from central power reflects a different kind of relationship.

The second category of indicators—centralizing reforms—taps the characteristics of the state. It shows the ability of the state to extract taxation from the population and channel resources toward developing its bureaucratic and military apparatus. In the absence of systematic information on the overall amount of taxation that each state extracted at different times, I made a judgment. If a state were able to strengthen its bureaucracy and army and to extend its administration over a larger territory, I took the evidence as a reason to assume that the state had the resources to do so and thus levied taxes with some degree of success and that tribal groups had surrendered some of their autonomy.

At the outset, the time periods and the geographic areas considered in this chapter must be clear. The precolonial era covered different chronological periods for the three countries. Colonial rule started in 1830 in Algeria, in 1881 in Tunisia, and in 1912 in Morocco. In considering the polity in the decades before colonization, this chapter thus examines different time periods for each country. With respect to geographic area, precolonial Tunisia, Algeria, and Morocco did not constitute nation-states as we usually understand the concept today, with (more or less) fixed borders and a territory under the (more or less) accepted authority of a state. Julia Clancy-Smith shows how the borders represented "zones of exchange, compromise and contest."[2] It was not until Tunisia and Morocco became sovereign states in the mid-1950s that borders became more or less fixed, although conflicts over territorial boundaries also have occurred since then. Map 2 indicates the changing borders over time. To be precise, one should say "in the territory that later became Algeria or Tunisia or Morocco," when considering Maghribi politics in the precolonial period. For the sake of simplicity, however, I refer to the countries by their current names in all historical periods.

TUNISIA: EARLY DEVELOPMENT
OF CENTRALIZED INSTITUTIONS

Historians agree that the precolonial Tunisian state was the most centralized of the three Maghribi states. Pointing to differences among the three Maghribi societies prior to colonization, Abdelkader Zghal notes that Tunisia was the country with the weakest zone of dissidence (bilad al-siba) and where the contacts between cities and rural areas were most frequent.[3] Lucette Valensi indicates that the Tunisian precolonial state successfully levied taxes.[4] Referring to the precolonial period, Henri de Montety speaks of "a feeling of national cohesion."[5] Nazih Ayubi writes that ". . . Tunisia was perhaps the most integrated and centralized of the Maghrib countries."[6] Jean Lacouture comments that nineteenth-century Tunisia was characterized by a relatively stable community and recognized boundaries.[7] Carl Brown also remarks that people in many parts of Tunisia shared "a greater sentiment of belonging to a geographically-defined *watan* [nation] than did peoples in other parts of the Arab-Muslim world."[8] This is in contrast to general descriptions of precolonial Algeria and Morocco. Brown describes Algeria as separate villages and tribes and Morocco as a territory two-thirds of which stood outside the orbit of the sultan's power.[9]

Tunisia was a geographically more accessible country than either Algeria or Morocco, where mountainous areas allowed for the prolonged isolation of independent tribal units. A sequence of foreign conquests, culminating in Ottoman domination in the eighteenth century, had opened Tunisia to trade and manufacture, which in turn facilitated contacts among collectivities and intercourse between central power and local groups. The stability of the Husaynid dynasty, functioning nominally under the umbrella of the Ottoman empire, but ruling in effect as a national monarchy, had further differentiated Tunisia from the other two Maghribi societies.[10]

Precolonial

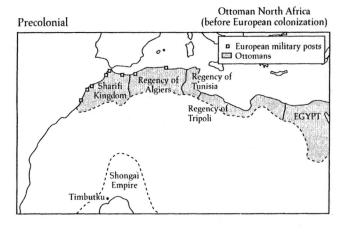

Colonial   The Maghrib in 1939

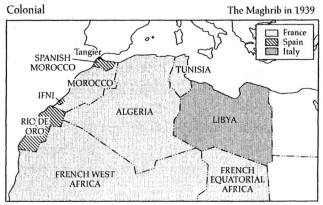

Independent Nation-States   Decolonization

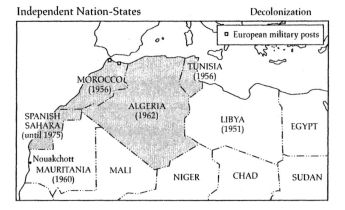

Map 2. The Maghrib in different historical periods (adapted
from Camille Lacoste and Yves Lacoste, eds., *L'Etat Du Maghreb*.
Tunis: Cérès Productions, 1991, 41).

Unresolved Tension between State and Tribe

If one had compared tribal fragmentation in the precolonial Maghrib, one would have found that it increased as one went from Tunisia to Morocco and then to Algeria. Referring to tribal organization in the three countries, Augustin Bernard wrote in 1906: "There is something of a gradation across North Africa: in Morocco, there are enormous confederations like the Beraber in Algeria, powerful tribes like the Larba and the Ouled-Nayl; and in Tunisia, only weak and minuscule tribes. . . . the tribes had already dissolved before our arrival, and some of them, like those of the Sahel, have even lost their names."[11] One would be mistaken, however, to conclude that tribal groups and kin-based solidarities had entirely disappeared from Tunisia in the nineteenth century. While less prominent than in Morocco or Algeria and existing in more muted forms, they were nevertheless present. The tension between state and tribe was far from resolved in that period. In a clear assessment of precolonial Tunisia, Valensi states that a centralized political authority coexisted with "undeniable tribal autonomy."[12] In his study of the Hautes Steppes of Tunisia in the nineteenth century, Habib Attia comments that tribal solidarity and internal cohesion were essential to the survival of social groups in that area.[13] As with other tribal groups, ties of solidarity were not always activated, but they became manifest as soon as an external threat arose.

The region of the Hautes Steppes was the territory of tribal groups such as the Hamamma, the Frechich, the Zlass, and the Majeurs. In 1911, the region had a population of about 176,000, approximately one tenth of the overall Tunisian population, which was estimated at 1,740,000.[14] Each tribe in the Hautes Steppes had its own pasture land and land ownership was collective. A tribal council regulated tribal life, made collective decisions concerning production, irrigation, and transhumance (or periodic nomadic moves). Grains were stored in the collective granary and the form of dwellings reflected the social structure of the tribe. The council orchestrated the life of the tribal group, made all important decisions about moves on tribal pasture lands, regulated internal conflicts and, in case of crime, decided on punishment and compensation.

As a general comment on social organization in the Hautes Steppes of Tunisia in the nineteenth and early twentieth century, Attia remarks that group solidarity was maintained "by a tribal social structure, with the patriarchal (or agnatic) kinship unit as the basic social cell."[15] The Hautes Steppes represented the area of Tunisia where tribal organization persisted in its purest form. There is also evidence of the activation of kin-based solidarities in other areas, particularly at times of conflict with central authority, when the state impinged upon the autonomy of local groups. Throughout the nineteenth century, tribal ties became more evident when rural groups rose in opposition to taxation.

The most striking and generalized instance of the reactivation of tribal solidarities was the rebellion of 1864. An examination of the rebellion provides insight into the tension between state and tribe in Tunisia in that period. It shows at the same time the extent to which the rebellion was tribally rooted and the capacity of the state to contain it. The immediate cause of the rebellion was a decision of the bey (monarch) to increase the poll tax. In November 1863, the bey decided to double the tax from thirty-six to seventy-two piasters.[16] The rebellion started among the most tribally organized communities, those with a long history of dissidence, in the region of the Hautes Steppes and in the extreme south of Tunisia. The principal leader of the rebellion, Ali Ibn Ghadhahim, was a member of the tribe of the Majeurs in the Hautes Steppes. The rebellion spread quickly to other rural communities, where tribal groups replaced the representative of central authority *(qaid)* with elected tribal members. One of the first acts of the tribes was to oust the agents of central power and to reassert their autonomy by reinstituting tribal institutions.

Along with a general increase in taxation, the bey also had decided in 1863 to levy the poll tax on the inhabitants of towns and cities previously exempted from it. The decision applied especially to the villages of the eastern coast in the Sahel, Sousse, and Sfax.[17] From tribal groups and rural communities, the rebellion extended to villages and towns, where common people supported the rebellion. Only notables, such as those in the religious and military establishments, gave continued allegiance to central power. Notables were against new taxation from which they had previously been exempt, but they were frightened by the magnitude of the rebellion and particularly by the active role of tribal groups. They therefore considered it safer to remain loyal to central authority. They did not want taxation, but they were even more afraid of the tribes than they were of the state.

In April 1864, the bey skillfully retreated. He announced that the taxes would be kept at their previous amount of thirty-six piasters and that the urban population would continue to be exempt from the poll tax.[18] Tribal demands were not restricted to taxation, however. The demands also included "an administrative system more accessible to the tribes," which meant a replacement of the qaid by elected members of the tribes.[19] Local groups were not only refusing an increase in taxation, they also wanted to maintain or restore their own independent system of administration.

The rebellion of 1864 does not lend itself to any simple interpretation. It shows at once the reactivation of kin-based solidarities and the extent of state control over the country. The evidence in support of an explanation emphasizing primordial ties and kin-based solidarities includes the fact that the rebellion was initiated by those tribal groups with the longest history of autonomy and resistance to central authority. The first victories against the bey's army in the early phase of the revolt were achieved by local communities and kin groupings through the reactivation of their tribal institutions. Furthermore, the coordination of the various local uprisings was the most difficult task for the leader of the rebellion and the least successfully accomplished. Leaders of different tribes met a few times and made an attempt to discuss the possibility of unified strategy against the bey.

The tribes revealed themselves as incapable of common action, however. For example, during a meeting on 5 May 1864, tribal leaders failed to unite their resources against the bey's army. Instead, they resolved that each group would return to its own territory and concentrate on defending it. The loyalty to the kin grouping predominated over the capacity for co-ordinated action. The retreat of each local group to its own territory greatly facilitated the action of the bey's army, which could then attack only one group at a time rather than face a collective, coordinated resistance. John Waterbury comments that "the alliance [among tribes] was not to survive the harvest, during which the bey was able to cut deals with various tribal alliances. . . ."[20] Valensi captures the overall nature of the rebellion in stating that it was "vigorous in its local solidarity," and "weak in its overall coordination."[21]

These three elements—the tribal nature of the groups that took the initiative of the rebellion, the difficulties of coordination faced by its leaders, and the demands for greater administrative autonomy on the part of local collectivities—all attest to the ongoing strength and autonomy of kin groupings in Tunisia in the nineteenth century. Hermassi writes that what he calls "ethnic" in the broad sense, and what I have called kin-based solidarities, "rarely took a primordial turn capable of undermining national unity."[22] He further suggests that the demands formulated during revolts in nineteenth-century Tunisia show "how deeply central authority had penetrated the fabric of society."[23] True, national cohesion and the capacity of the state to control the country were greater than in Algeria and Morocco. The tension between the state and kin-based local collectivities was still somewhat unresolved, however. As is evinced by the rebellion of 1864, the tension at times could flare into open conflict and lead to violence.

Yet, the rebellion of 1864 also reveals other features of Tunisian society in the precolonial period. Although sustained coordinated action failed to occur, there nevertheless was communication among various tribal groups that were in contact enough to call meetings. The remarkable point is that tribal groups in revolt in different areas communicated at all about strategy, even though in the end they could not agree on a collective course of action. The other significant feature of Tunisian society was revealed by the response of central authority to the rebellion. The bey gave in to the rebelling tribes by reducing the taxes to their previous amount and replacing his administrative representatives with local chiefs. At the same time, however, he sent his army to crush the rebellion, and it was strong enough to force tribal groups to surrender their arms.

In summary, the rebellion of 1864 shows that kin-based local groups were still struggling for their autonomy in several areas in Tunisia. The main motivation for the rebellion was to reduce the intervention of the state in local affairs and to resist taxation. Nonetheless, the rebellion shows that Tunisian society was becoming less segmented. Local groups were capable of communicating with one another for political purposes. The rebellion was a test for central power. In the end, the bey could not increase taxation as he had wished, but his army proved strong enough to suppress the local groups that refused to surrender.

Preliminary Steps toward a State Bureaucracy

During the nineteenth century, the Tunisian administrative apparatus was more developed than its Algerian and Moroccan counterparts.[24] The apparatus covered most of the Tunisian territory, whereas large segments of the Algerian and Moroccan population escaped the control of central authority during the same period. The political structure was strongly centered on Tunis, where the bey surrounded himself with an administration, an army, and a corps of *ulama* (religious scholars). De Montety remarks that "even though the ties between the beylical administration and its subjects had always been loose, the entire territory acknowledged its authority."[25] Elbaki Hermassi also remarks that, in comparison with Algeria and Morocco, "for the same period, Tunisia's administration was far more comprehensive and centralized."[26]

Administration of local areas was in the hands of about sixty qaids, or governors. According to Hermassi, all the qaids were appointed by the bey, whereas De Montety describes some of them as tribal notables whose position was ratified by the center.[27] What seems clear is that, regardless of the basis on which a qaid was selected, a measure of administrative uniformity prevailed over the whole country. The evidence suggests that the corps of qaids included both direct appointees of central power and tribal notables. The bey used both strategies depending on the acceptance of particular groups. The issue of whether the qaid was principally a tribal leader or an outsider appointed by the government was a contentious one. It should be remembered that this was one of the points of conflict between the bey and local collectivities during the rebellion of 1864.

In the nineteenth century, central administration penetrated even those areas where tribal organization was most clearly prevalent. Henia shows how central power affected the region of the Jerid in southern Tunisia where lineages and tribes were operative social units. In the same vein, Attia indicates that tribal areas in the Hautes Steppes of central Tunisia were far from being "under-administered."[28] His careful investigation of archives showed that central administration had a presence even in that region. Fiscal registers were well and regularly maintained. A reading of the correspondence of the qaids showed that many of the letters sent to them came from members of tribal groups in the area and particularly from tribal councils. The letters expressed complaints about an increasingly heavy bureaucratic apparatus attempting to control the economic and political affairs of the tribes. For example, people of the Hautes Steppes complained in the following terms in one of the letters: "We used to be administered by six shaykhs and only one qaid; now we have four qaids and eighteen shaykhs."[29]

Another indicator of the relative strength of the Tunisian precolonial state was its capacity to launch reforms aimed at centralization and at developing nation-wide institutions. A series of reformers whose efforts met with varying degrees of success ruled Tunisia in the nineteenth century.[30] One of the most daring reformers for the time was Ahmad Bey (1837–55) and another was Khayr al-Din, who served as prime minister from 1873 to 1877. Clancy-Smith remarks about the former that "Ahmad Bey's reign represents a sea change in modern Tunisia's history mainly, but not exclusively, because of the reforms imposed upon his largely unwilling subjects."[31] Ahmad Bey started with an effort to modernize the army and to launch military conscription of the general population.[32]

The impetus for reform was foreign challenge. The Tunisian dynasty realized that it had to strengthen its army, its administrative apparatus, and the economy of the country if it were to resist foreign domination. In a chain reaction, the implementation of military reforms then required changes in other areas, such as transportation, industry, administration, and education. Brown indicates that further reforms included a program aimed at abolishing slavery, a telegraph system, the creation of small industries, and measures to develop the administration of the country.[33] A military school, the Ecole du Bardo, was founded in 1840 in the vicinity of Tunis to train army officers. The school included foreign instructors, and cadets received instruction in French and Italian in addition to Arabic. The army was expanded to about twenty-six thousand men in the 1840s, a sizable force for Tunisia at the time. Revenue to finance the military reforms came from two sources, foreign loans and additional taxes on the Tunisian population. For example, new taxes applied to olive and palm trees and to the sale of all agricultural products, sheep, and cattle.[34]

Prime Minister Khayr al-Din launched administrative and tax reforms between 1873 and 1877. He proceeded to strengthen the authority of government by increasing the surveillance of the qaids and their expenditure. He let the qaids retain as salary one-tenth of the taxes they gathered but required them to submit regular accounts of their tax collection to the government. This allowed for greater supervision of the state over the procedure to collect taxes and over the amount collected. The collection of taxes was no longer a matter of personal agreement between central power and each qaid. The process became more formalized and therefore standardized while it was placed directly under state control.

Another major area of reform, the great significance of which was to be felt during the nationalist period and at independence, was education. It was exemplified by the creation of the Collège Sadiqi. Founded by Khayr al-Din in 1875, the Collège Sadiqi was the first nonmilitary Tunisian school to have a modern curriculum that included instruction in Arabic, French, Italian, mathematics, and the sciences. The principal mission of the Collège Sadiqi was to train civil servants. The college did in fact fulfill this mission. It trained the Tunisian leadership from its creation in the late nineteenth century to the period of independence.[35] The Collège Sadiqi was reserved for Tunisian Muslims, a competitive examination determined entrance and enrollment was kept small (a student population of about seven hundred), thus creating a sense of solidarity among graduates. Far from being a simple copy of foreign schools, whether French or Italian, the college was designed to adapt Western knowledge to the Arab-Islamic identity of Tunisia. It formed civil servants who were well versed in foreign culture but also retained a knowledge of their own society.

Khayr al-Din introduced other educational reforms. Arnold Green indicates that Khayr al-Din revamped instruction at the Zaytuna Mosque, the center of Islamic scholarship and higher learning. The reforms introduced modern subjects into the curriculum and placed the Zaytuna under the control of the prime minister's office.[36] The Zaytuna thus remained a center of Islamic learning after the reform, but it was "modernized" through the introduction of subjects of study other than theology. The prime minister also set standards for Islamic primary schools by requiring that teachers be certified by the government.[37] In an effort to coordinate the expansion of education, he established a new bureau to supervise all educational institutions in Tunisia.

As could be expected, several of the reforms met with serious opposition. The ulama, who had been the educators of Tunisian society, did not look favorably upon the introduction of modern subjects into the educational system. Nor did they approve of the reformers' efforts toward coordination, centralization, or supervision by the state. Tribal groups in local areas often only grudgingly accepted administrative reforms and shaky compromises had to be made between the state and tribal communities. Taxes could not be expanded sufficiently to finance all the reforms started by Ahmad Bey and Prime Minister Khayr al-Din.

The Tunisian state had little choice but to turn repeatedly to loans from foreign banks to sustain its reformist policy. Centralization, modernization of the army, and bureaucratic expansion had been possible only at great financial cost. Mohamed Hédi Cherif comments that "the fiscal burden increased regularly to become paralyzing, intolerable, absurd."[38] Plunging into further and further borrowing from abroad, the state finally reached financial collapse and gave in to French domination. In 1881, the bey signed the Treaty of the Bardo, which established a French protectorate in Tunisia.

Tunisian society presented the following features at the end of the precolonial period: a centralizing state; a college training potential civil servants—in small numbers but effectively—in the art of administration and leadership; an administrative apparatus able to reach most of the territory, even though it was unable to implement the decisions of central power in many regions or local areas; and an overall degree of homogeneity that neither Algeria nor Morocco had experienced. Remote villages did not always accept the decisions made at the center and on occasion actively opposed them, but most of their inhabitants knew about the decisions. Central power in Tunisia at the eve of colonization was able to communicate with kin-based local collectivities and affect their lives far more than was the case in either Algeria or Morocco. Although the age of the early reformers ended with the humiliation of colonial occupation, it was nevertheless a critical period in the history of the country, one that laid the foundation for the future development of modern Tunisia.

ALGERIA: TRIBAL ISOLATION AND WEAK STATE

The periodization of Algerian history differs from that of Tunisia because of the particular pattern of colonization. The French conquest of Algeria was a long, drawn-out process. Although France officially colonized Algeria in 1830, the date of the treaty that established colonial rule, substantial sections of the country still escaped French control several decades later. Precolonial conditions continued much after 1830 for the largest portion of the territory that later became Algeria. The analysis in this section therefore considers some of the events that took place in the mid and late 1800s as revealing the outlook of Algerian society before the penetration of the French.[39]

During the precolonial era, Algeria exhibited a weakly centralized political system and a highly segmented form of social organization. Like Tunisia, Algeria experienced Ottoman rule, but the Turks never established in Algeria the kind of centralizing state that they implanted in Tunisia. Turkish authority actually covered only the eastern part of Algeria, in contrast to Tunisia where the bey ruled over most of the country in the name of the Turks. Furthermore, Turkish government in Algeria was incapacitated by its organization into four separate divisions with little, if any, coordination among the divisions. The rugged terrain and the size of the territory, which was much larger than Tunisia, contributed to making coordination difficult. The control that the Turks exerted over the Algerian territory was so restricted that, when they signed the Treaty of 1830 establishing French colonization, they turned over only the city of Algiers and its surroundings.[40]

This was all the Turks could give because of their limited control over the territory known today as Algeria. The major portion of the population, organized in tribes and tribal confederations, remained in a state of tribal autonomy. In 1853, Carette estimated that, out of a population of about 3 million, 2,670,410 were organized in identifiable tribal groups.[41] Louis Rinn's survey of French reports, published between 1897 and 1899, gives a good indication of the numerical importance of politically independent tribal groups in the Algerian territory.[42] The survey includes information on the portion of the territory occupied by different social groups. A summary of the results, table 3, shows the number of tribes by region in each of four major political categories in Algeria.

The table suggests that over half of the population was made up of tribal groups that maintained their autonomy from central power and usually escaped taxation. The groups that constituted the *makhzan* (central power) and the subject tribes, which had submitted to taxation but not necessarily to any other form of control, represented together 230 units. These two categories combined occupied only 16 percent of the territory. The semi-independent tribes, which had entered into some form of agreement with central authority but frequently oscillated between acquiescence and hostility, occupied about 15 percent of the territory. The independent tribes, numbering about 200 units of the 516 studied, occupied the largest part of the territory, or 69 percent. More than two-thirds of the Algerian territory thus belonged to tribal groups that had successfully maintained their autonomy from central power, escaped taxation, and sustained dissidence. Adding the 86 semi-independent to the 200 independent tribes, Hermassi notes that in the nineteenth century more than half the population was never brought under the orbit of central power in Algeria.[43] Reaching a similar conclusion on the basis of research on the same period in French archives, André Nouschi considers that two-thirds of the Algerian population escaped paying taxes to central authority.[44]

Further evidence of the segmentation of Algerian society is suggested

Table 3 Distribution of Tribes in Precolonial Algeria

Political Categories	Tribal Units by Region				Total Number of Tribal Units	Percentage of Territory Occupied
	Algiers	Titteri	Oran	Constantine		
Makhzan	19	14	46	47	128	16%
Subject tribes	11	23	56	14	104	
Semi-independent chiefs	20	12	29	25	86	15%
Independent tribes	23	13	26	138	200 / 516	69%

SOURCE: Adapted from Hermassi, *Leadership and National Development in North Africa*, p. 47.

by the frequency and magnitude of tribal revolts. One of the most important instances of tribally rooted resistance to the French conquest was the movement led by Amir Abd al-Qadir (also often transliterated Abdelkader).[45] Building on the tribal structure, Abd al-Qadir forged a confederation of several tribal groups prepared to act together in defense of a common interest: to defend their autonomy by opposing the French military conquest. He led the tribal warriors and became the chief of the confederation. His principal instrument of control over the tribes was a central council responsible for directing military activities. He was able to levy his own taxes, form a small army (about ten thousand men) under his personal direction, and also recruit local tribal auxiliaries in the regions that were the sites of the battles.[46] Abd al-Qadir's "army" fought in the traditional tribal style with surprise attacks and skirmishing rather than sustained fighting. With all the limitations of an organization based primarily on tribal strength, Abd al-Qadir's resistance nevertheless lasted for more than a decade, from 1832 to 1843 and, on a smaller scale, even longer.

In the absence of a central state representing the Algerians and negotiating with the French, the movement formed by Abd al-Qadir and tribal confederations filled the vacuum of power. The relations between the French and Abd al-Qadir were complex. At first, the French treated him and his warriors as tribal rebels to be overpowered by military means. But then, several times during the 1830s, the French entered into negotiations and signed agreements with him recognizing his authority over the districts that he controlled. This was the case, for example, in the district of Oran in western Algeria where Abd al-Qadir controlled the whole district except the towns, which were occupied by the French. The French even signed a treaty, the Treaty of Tafna in 1837, defining the limits of the localities under Abd al-Qadir's authority. Map 3 shows how his sphere of influence expanded in the 1830s.

Abd al-Qadir's authority, based as it was on the alliance of several tribes, met with tribal resistance in several parts of Algeria. The segmentation of Algerian society made national unification under Abd al-Qadir highly unlikely. He was in fact maneuvering between two opponents at once: the French occupants and numerous tribes that fought to escape his control, as was the case, for example, in the west and the south of the country.[47] These tribes wanted to retain their autonomy from Abd al-Qadir just as much as they wanted autonomy from the French colonial state. With his limited resources and his tribally rooted organization, Abd al-Qadir could not succeed against French military power in the long run. His movement continued to gain strength for a while by bringing together several tribes

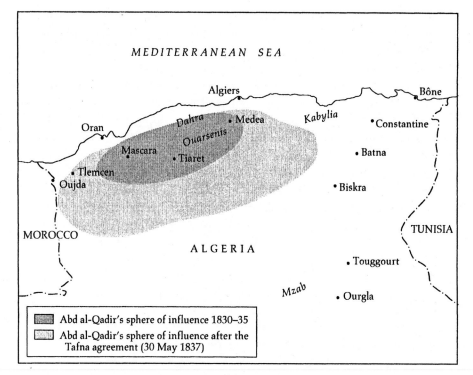

Map 3. Algeria in the 1830s (adapted from Magali Morsey, *North Africa 1800–1900: A Survey from the Nile to the Atlantic*. London, Longman, 1984, 137).

that rebelled against French occupation. For example, Abd al-Qadir formed alliances with rebelling tribes in the region of the Dahra in 1845 and with tribes in the Rif in northern Morocco in 1847.[48] Ultimately, however, the French gained control and forced Abd al-Qadir to surrender in 1847.[49]

Because of the segmentation of Algerian society and the absence of a centralized state, opposition to the French could only be initiated by tribally based movements. The movement of Abd al-Qadir came closest to the embryo of an indigenous state. Commenting on Algeria, Alexis de Tocqueville wrote: "Abdelkader [Abd al-Qadir], who probably never heard of what took place in fifteenth-century France, is acting vis-à-vis the tribes precisely in the same way that our kings, and in particular Charles VII, have acted against feudality . . . he scatters or destroys everyday the old and powerful families. . . . [he] is in the process of building a form of power more centralized, more agile, stronger, more experienced, and more ordered than any of its predecessors for centuries in this part of the world."[50]

Other tribal revolts against the French attest to the continued strength of kin groupings in Algeria throughout the nineteenth century. Clancy-Smith shows how tribes participated in major uprisings that spanned part of the pre-Saharan region.[51] In 1864, a rebellion broke out in a branch of the Awlad Sidi al-Shaykh tribe in the southwest, which refused the taxes that the French wanted to levy. The tribal rebels defeated the French troops sent to face them and the rebellion spread to other tribes. This led the French to increase their military intervention to bring the tribes under control.[52] One of the most important revolts after the signing of the 1830 convention establishing French colonization was the tribal rebellion led by Moqrani (also transliterated as al-Muqrani) in Kabylia in 1871.[53] The French recognized Moqrani as the chief of his tribe, a tribe that belonged to an area of long-standing dissidence. Even after the agreement between Moqrani and the French, Moqrani's tribe maintained considerable autonomy over its own affairs. As in other cases, the rebellion was triggered by the French imposition of taxes on the tribe—a decision that, coming at a time when agricultural production in that area was declining, threatened to bring about financial ruin. Taking advantage of the crisis started by Moqrani's, several other tribes joined in the uprising.

At no point did the rebellion become a unified movement. Although it involved practically a whole region, the rebellion never had a single leadership for any length of time. It remained instead the action of separate kin groupings, each participating in an independent fashion.[54] The tribal rebellion had the same outcome as previous ones. It was crushed by French military power and French settlers occupied the best tribal lands. From then on, the French engaged in a systematic and extensive policy of occupation of tribal lands, provoking tribal revolts, but facing no single enemy strong enough to oppose French settlement on Algerian lands.

On the eve of colonization, Algeria thus was quite different from Tunisia. Whereas Tunisia had a tradition of centralized institutions, a state capable of extracting taxes—albeit not consistently and systematically—Algeria had no central state to speak of when the French conquered it and made it a French territory. The majority of the population was organized into tribal groups and primary loyalties remained embedded in kin groupings. Tribal groups retained considerable autonomy, with the majority living in a condition of close to total independence from the political center. The initiative of resistance to colonial encroachment on Algerian lands was taken by tribal groups in a coordinated fashion, as in the case of Abd al-Qadir's movement, and in a separate, autonomous way in the case of other tribal revolts. The relative lack of centralized institutions coupled with the strength of kin groupings shaped conditions for the development of the polity in Algeria in the next historical periods.

MOROCCO: LAND OF GOVERNMENT
VERSUS LAND OF DISSIDENCE

The dichotomy between land of government and land of dissidence (bilad al-makhzan/bilad al-siba) applies most directly to Morocco.[55] In contrast to Tunisia and Algeria, Morocco never experienced Ottoman rule. A long-standing but weak dynasty ruled the country throughout the nineteenth century.[56] Morocco essentially remained closed to the outside world until the 1830s, when it then opened to trade with Europe and to the penetration of European commercial interests.[57]

Whereas Tunisia developed centralizing institutions relatively early and Algeria remained extremely segmented with most tribal groups having little or no contact with a weak political center, Morocco was characterized by an ongoing opposition between central power and autonomous tribes. Some of the tribes were powerful enough to challenge the ruling dynasty directly. Two features differentiated Morocco from its neighbors. In contrast to Tunisia, Morocco did not develop a central state capable of implementing reforms and extracting resources from the population. In contrast to Algeria where the majority of tribes were left to themselves, Moroccan tribes were in a constant state of tension with the center.

Volatile Alliances

Boundaries between the areas that accepted the sultan's authority and those that opposed it shifted off and on. Waterbury appropriately refers to "islands of submissiveness in seas of defiance" with respect to Moroccan history.[58] There were also pockets of defiance in areas of submissiveness. On the whole, the land of government often included the plains, the towns, and villages, even though dissidence could spread to those areas. The land of dissidence covered mountainous areas, such as the Rif and the Middle and High Atlas, which provided a niche to tribal groups fighting for their autonomy. Ernest Gellner indicates that the land of dissidence correlated with mountainous areas where it was possible to physically evade the reach of central authority.[59] Clifford Geertz notes that the land of government, where the authority of the sultan was recognized, had appointed governors, market inspectors, religious judges, and other representatives of the sultan.[60] As to the land of dissidence, it contained none of the above. It was the land of tribal organization.

Geography combined with history to heighten the opposition between makhzan and siba in the history of Morocco. Geertz explains the situation in Morocco in part by reference to the terrain, which is more mountainous than in Tunisia and thus better suited to tribal dissidence.[61] Another factor suggested by Geertz is the existence of a relatively large Berber population that tended to live precisely in the mountainous areas, in the Rif and the Atlas. It is estimated that Berbers represent approximately 40 percent of the total population in modern Morocco.[62] Although there was no simple correlation between Berber and dissident, the gradual penetration of Arab culture and the Arabic language in Morocco left several Berber tribes little affected by them. Berber tribes had a ready-made basis in their linguistic distinctiveness to oppose the sultan and refuse his authority. In summary, Gellner suggests that "most mountainous and desert terrain and most but not all Berber areas, were siba."[63]

In the eighteenth and early nineteenth century, Morocco had no stable bureaucracy that could have ensured continuity of governmental authority. Nor did it have a standing army. The exercise of power depended on each sultan's capacity to develop the armed forces necessary for controlling tribal groups or for forming alliances with some of them. Crises of succession were frequent. It was precisely during those crises that tribal solidarities were most likely to come actively to the fore. The dominant political concern of each sultan was how many tribal groups he would win over either by granting them privileges or subduing them by force. A critical and recurrent question in Moroccan history was how much authority each reigning sultan would have over the country, especially over tribal areas.

In conformity with the model of politics outlined in chapter 4, central power surrounded itself with tax-exempt tribes that rendered various services, such as fulfilling military and administrative functions. The rest of the country was divided into areas that paid taxes and others that evaded them. Although which tribes were in active opposition to the sultan fluctuated over time, about half of the territory constituting Morocco was in a near permanent state of dissidence in the precolonial period. Dissident tribes were an ever present threat to central authority, a source of potential dynastic rivals. Conversely, central power posed a constant threat to tribal independence since the sultan would attempt to bring dissident tribes into his taxpaying orbit whenever he had the military means to do so.

Political organization in Morocco showed remarkable continuity from about the seventeenth century to the nineteenth and, some authors claim, even until 1912, the date of colonization. For example, Jamil Abun-Nasr writes that "Morocco entered the nineteenth century with the political system it developed in the sixteenth century little altered."[64] Making a similar statement about the early twentieth century, Waterbury notes: "In 1912, the organization of the Alawite dynasty bore a close resemblance to that established in the seventeenth century by the first great Alawite sultan, Moulay Isma'il."[65] Continuity is emphasized in the literature on Morocco because the problems facing central authority remained similar. In the precolonial period, every sultan faced the problems of raising taxes, sustaining an army, and subduing dissident tribes. Waterbury describes Morocco in the period as "[a] stable system of continuous violence . . . collect taxes to pay the army to crush the tribes to collect still more taxes."[66]

Rarely could a new sultan simply build upon the situation left by his predecessor. He usually had to reconquer parts of the territory where tribes took advantage of the period of political transition to assert their independence. The military ventures in which a sultan engaged upon coming to power frequently occupied a major portion of his reign. The tumultuous nine-year period following the accession of the sultan Moulay Hassan to the throne in 1873 illustrates the task facing a new sultan. Moulay Hassan first set out to fight and subdue the Sussi tribes, then the tribe of the Beni Hassan, then the Beni Mtir. During those years, he went to war twice against the Ghiyyata, once more against the Beni Mtir, fought the Beni Moussa and the Ait Attab and faced several other tribal revolts. Once a tribe was subdued, there was no guarantee that it would grant allegiance to the sultan for longer than the period of direct military occupation. When the sultan's forces were called elsewhere, a tribe could revolt again as soon as it had gathered its own forces. In some cases, as it happened with the Beni Mtir and the Ghiyyata tribes, this could occur within as little as one year.[67]

The military and administrative apparatus of the makhzan was rudimentary, giving central authority only limited means of control.[68] The sultan's army was poorly organized. The troops, drawn from the tax-exempt tribes, lacked discipline and training. Auxiliary forces, furnished by a number of tribes, were sometimes called upon in time of crisis, but they received no regular payment and failed to provide a reliable force for the sultan. The administrative apparatus was hardly more developed. The sultan's ministers had vaguely defined responsibilities. With positions that tended to become hereditary, the ministers had no fixed salaries and relied heavily on commissions for their livelihood. The administration of the regions was in principle in the hands of qaids responsible to the sultan. Most Moroccan qaids were not direct representatives of central authority, however, but local notables whose influence in the tribe the sultan had ratified. Even this ineffective method of administration held true only for the subject tribes in the land of government since dissident tribes did not have any representative of the makhzan, however nominal. The power of the sultan thus was not institutionalized. Instead, as Waterbury notes, "It consisted of the sum total of the power of his momentary allies at any one time."[69]

A system of fragile alliances and counter alliances connected the sultan and local leaders. In Tunisia the state was able to appoint its own representatives in several regions. By contrast, in those parts of Morocco where the sultan was able to exert control, his power depended on volatile tribal allies. Often the sultan exploited existing tribal hostilities by using one tribe or one tribal faction against another. For example, in 1907, the sultan's brother rebelled by forming an alliance with the Rahmana and the Glawis, two powerful tribal groups that had a long tradition of dissidence toward the sultan. The sultan responded by making an alliance with the Mtugis, another powerful tribal group that had a long-standing hostility with the Glawis.[70]

In some cases, the alliances and counter alliances between the sultan and tribal areas involved favoring a particular tribal leader. Once the leader of a lineage or a tribe had established a cohesive following at the local level, he would try to be recognized by the sultan as the leader of that tribe or of several tribes. He would try to be named qaid and become the representative of central authority in the area. Local leaders thereby became clients of the makhzan, but they were under the conflicting pressures of their tribe and the makhzan. Their obedience to the sultan was limited and they might quickly withdraw support under the pressure of their tribe rebelling against the sultan.

Potentially short lived, alliances between the sultan and local leaders were nevertheless mutually beneficial. For a local leader, there were advantages in becoming qaid, even if only temporarily. A qaid received no salary, but retained for himself part of the taxes that he collected for the sultan. If he were successful in levying the tribal tribute (*hadiya*), a qaid could end up keeping considerable sums for his personal use.[71] Although it was a politically difficult position, it was therefore profitable for a local leader to serve as an intermediary between a tribal group and the makhzan. The arrangement also suited central authority. In areas where he was unable to establish a more direct control, the sultan was satisfied—since he had no other choice—with establishing a simple zone of influence. If the local leader-become-qaid could enforce taxation, that was all the better for the sultan. If the qaid levied only minimal taxes or even no taxes at all, but could maintain order and prevent tribal rebellions, that was still better for the sultan than facing armed conflict with the tribe.

The use of local chiefs as intermediaries thus was essential to a policy of shifting alliances and counter alliances with tribal groups in Morocco in the nineteenth century. Waterbury remarks: "Historically the political process was one of constant and confusing flux . . . To survive and certainly to prosper, one had to assess all the possibilities for alliance with others as well as all the possibilities of counter-alliances."[72] David Seddon also notes: "[The makhzan used] subtle manipulation and intrigue, calming with promises, withholding favors, blocking economic exchange and soothing with tactful mediation."[73] Local leaders strove for recognition from above and the sultan looked for alliances with critically placed local groups. The sultan's political strength in large part was a function of his skill at maneuvering in the tribal maze of Moroccan society.

Regional Pockets of Power

A central feature of Moroccan society prior to colonization was the development of regional centers of power ruled by minor potentates with their own armies. Known as the "Lords of the Atlas" and commanding most power between 1897 and 1916, the chiefs were able to exert control over entire regions with little or no interference from the central government.[74] In addition to owning their own armed force, the regional chiefs also controlled fortified grain storehouses. This placed them in a position to withstand sustained attacks from the makhzan.[75] The sultan had to acknowledge his inability to bring the chieftaincies under control. He had no alternative but to recognize their power.

The chieftaincies headed by the Lords of the Atlas were formed by the domination of a kin grouping over several others. They retained a tribal form of organization, as the chief relied on the support and cohesiveness of his own kin grouping to gain a following and then to subdue other tribes. Waterbury identifies the main chieftaincies as those of the Glawi, the Gundafi, and the Mtugi.[76] The sultan granted the chiefs the title of qaid and often exempted the chieftaincies from paying taxes. At times, violent clashes opposed the armed forces of the makhzan and those of a powerful chief.

The revolt of Bu Hmara illustrates the clashes with the makhzan and the power that the Lords of the Atlas were able to gather on the basis of tribal support. For several years after the death of the sultan Moulay Hassan in 1894, the country was in a restive state. The makhzan was increasingly losing control over sizable segments of the population and beset by a series of tribal rebellions. Bu Hmara raised a revolt among tribes in the area of Fez and, with the help of tribes in other areas, successfully defeated the troops of the sultan. He was then able to exert what Seddon refers to as an "effectively makhzen-like" control over the population in northeast Morocco.[77] Given the extent of Bu Hmara's power, it became important for other local chiefs to establish good relations with him. The rules of the political game were the same. Local chiefs still needed the following of their tribesmen to gain credence but, in this case, they did not seek recognition from the sultan. Bu Hmara had become so powerful that it is from him that local chiefs sought recognition.

In the same way that a sultan depended on alliances with tribal groups and on the allegiance of these groups for the exercise of power, Bu Hmara depended on the same type of support. He needed the support of local leaders for recruitment into his "army," and he entered into the same type of alliances with tribal groups and their leaders as a sultan would have. Just as they would have done if the sultan were the dominant power, tribal groups that had previously supported Bu Hmara rebelled against him. After a defeat by the Ait Warryaghel tribe of the central Rif, Bu Hmara ultimately lost his power in 1908. His makhzan-like organization and his rivalry with the sultan had nevertheless lasted five years.

The Moroccan sultanate attempted mild reforms in the late nineteenth century, during the reign of Moulay Hassan (1873–94), but the reforms could not be enacted. The sultan made plans to create a modern army, recruited military instructors from European countries, and purchased weapons from abroad. He also tried to reorganize the administration of the country by creating 330 administrative units each headed by a qaid. He contemplated a reform of the tax system that would include new taxes and stipulate that the qaids should not only collect taxes, but also pay some themselves.[78] The reforms met with such opposition that they had to be abandoned. The next sultan (Moulay Abdul-Aziz, 1894–1908) did not even make an effort to pursue his predecessor's reformist policy. The qaids refused to pay taxes. The new taxes were never collected and, as usual in Morocco, tribal insurrections challenged the authority of the sultan. Tribes of the Middle Atlas (the Sanhaja) and other tribes (the Jbala) rose in rebellion.[79] It is also during the same period that Bu Hmara organized his sustained opposition to the makhzan, in the northeast of Morocco.

The northeast is the area of Morocco closest to Algeria where the French were already established. Claiming that the tribal rebellions could harm the interests of the French who had settled in Morocco and "cause serious problems to the authorities in Algeria,"[80] the French used this pretext to intervene in Morocco. They established frontier posts between Algeria and Morocco and declared their intention to use military force to subdue any tribe that would oppose the sultan on the Moroccan side. As the activities of the French expanded in Morocco, so did tribal resistance. Tribesmen attacked the French, providing an excuse for France to intervene militarily in 1907. In 1910, several tribes rose in rebellion and marched on Fez, the capital city.[81] The French intervened again on the pretext of defending the sultan as well as the Europeans. French forces defeated the rebelling tribesmen and a French protectorate was established in Morocco in 1912.[82]

By the end of the nineteenth century in Morocco the state had become stable enough, and the Alawi dynasty strong enough, to discourage or to defeat attempts by tribal groups or chieftaincies to take over altogether. But it was a weak state and a weak dynasty. The existence of the Lords of the Atlas with their own armies, no matter how poorly equipped and how rudimentary, meant that central authority did not have the monopoly of military force in the country. Instead, the makhzan in effect shared its control over Moroccan society with regional pockets of power, in addition to facing smaller units of tribal dissidence. Tribal revolts occurred throughout the second half of the nineteenth century and well into the twentieth. Writing in 1961 and referring to his field work experience in the rugged mountains of the High Atlas, Gellner notes: "*Lokt n'siba* (in the time of dissidence) was a frequent opening of a sentence. It was a concept with a contrast and, indeed, the very contrast that the historians and sociologists attributed it with: *makhzen*, government."[83] As Gellner's statement suggests, images of tribal dissidence survived in Morocco until quite recently. Tribes would continue to play a political role beyond precolonial times and would have an effect on the polity of Morocco in the next historical periods.

FAMILY LAW AS MIRROR OF THE POLITY

Family law mirrored similarities and differences in political organization in the three countries. Everywhere, family law defined the lineage as the basic social unit. Everywhere too, the law permitted kin groupings to control marriage alliances as a strategy to gain influence and build a power base. In all three countries, support of the patrilineage and broader kin group was essential to success. A local leader was someone able to acquire, and retain for a while, wealth and influence within his own tribal group. Underscoring the importance of agnatic and other kin support for the purpose of building power at the local level, Seddon writes that a leader relied "on the support of a following drawn from among his agnates and other kinsmen, but also including a number of unrelated dependents, friends and allies."[84]

In all three countries, family law made endogamy within the lineage or the tribe possible. Marriage alliances and tribal politics of the type discussed in chapters 3 and 4 entered into strategies to gain power in local areas, as the practice of kin endogamy and collectively useful exogamy helped tribal groups build political influence. Although exogamy aimed at forming an alliance with another tribe or lineage was politically useful, endogamy was an even more successful strategy in tribal politics. Seddon points to a higher proportion of endogamous marriages in powerful lineages than in politically weak lineages. He notes: "[T]hose lineages forming the core of an important leader's following tended to have a higher proportion of endogamous marriages than those without leaders or split by internal quarrels and dissension."[85] This generally held true for the Maghrib as a whole, where family law made it possible everywhere to maximize power by using kinship appropriately.

The three countries of the Maghrib differed with respect to the extent of legal unification versus internal diversity in family law in the precolonial period. National differences in social and political segmentation were reflected in the legal sphere. Precolonial Tunisia had a relatively more homogeneous legal system, one that was based on Islamic law, than the other two countries. In contrast, several local, particularistic codes of customary law coexisted with Islamic family law in Algeria and Morocco in the precolonial period. Although Islamic law of the Maliki school predominated in the Maghrib as a whole, it did so in a variety of relationships to other schools of Islamic law (especially the Hanafi school) and to local, particularistic codes of customary law. This created different kinds of situations with different political implications. Two schools of law (Maliki and Hanafi) existed in Tunisia, a distinction that was politically less divisive than the enclaves of customary codes in Algeria and Morocco, which represented a more significant form of division. As discussed in chapter 2, in regard to substance, customary codes bore various degrees of resemblance to Islamic family law in that they blended local particularism and general Islamic principles. Some of the areas under customary law even considered their law to be Islamic and the minor differences to be of no consequence.[86]

Politically more significant than the substance of the law itself, judicial institutions differentiated areas under Islamic family law from areas under customary law. Judicial functions were exercised by a religious judge (qadi), sometimes by a qaid, or by a standing local assembly in the form of a tribal council (jamaa), or sometimes on an ad hoc basis by elders considered wise and fair by members of their communities. Usually, the land of government had religious judges and Islamic law, whereas enclaves of customary law and tribal councils tended to fall in the land of dissidence. There was no clear-cut overlap between law and politics, however, in that the land of dissidence also included areas under Islamic law.

Family law as such was not the primary cause of conflicts between state and tribe in the precolonial period. The conflicts occurred over issues of overall autonomy—not over family law alone—as the retention of customary law and tribal councils was part of the general quest for autonomy on the part of the tribes. If a tribe historically had enjoyed an autonomous judicial system, keeping it was a pressing concern. Tribes strove to retain their jamaa, which applied customary law, free from the participation of religious judges. Since the tribal council remained responsible for the collective matters of the tribal group in areas under customary law, rejection of Islamic judges meant less interference by central authority in the affairs of the tribe. Preservation of customary law and the safeguard of local autonomy thus mutually reinforced each other, as the groups that retained their own code could by the same token keep the judicial arm of central authority at bay.

Even though it had no particularistic family codes of any significance, Tunisia nevertheless faced the problems caused by the existence of two schools of Islamic family law in the country. Most of the religious judges relied on the Maliki school of law. The fact that some judges based their decisions on the Hanafi school caused confusion, however, and made the work of religious judges cumbersome. Alone in the Maghrib in that period, the dynasty ruling Tunisia and its ministers raised the issue of legal unification. They tried to abolish the distinctions between the two schools of Islamic law. As part of the broader set of centralizing reforms that he launched in the 1870s, Prime Minister Khayr al-Din formed the project to standardize Tunisian law. In 1876, he appointed a commission formed of three ulama and a secular member to unify Islamic family law in the country.[87]

The commission had the mandate to draft a comprehensive legislation faithful to Islamic law and to abolish all distinctions between the Hanafi and Maliki schools of law. The commission had a short life. Lack of financial resources resulting from the rulers' inability to increase taxes made it difficult to finance reforms in general, including reforms of family law. Members of the beylical administration had already increased taxes as much as they thought the Tunisian population would bear before rising in revolt. The memories of the bloody and widespread rebellion of 1864 were still fresh. In addition, the project met with the opposition of the religious establishment, which tended to oppose modernizing reforms whether the reforms concerned law, education, or any other area in which religious scholars perceived change as a threat to their authority.[88] Impoverished finances and the ulama's opposition caused the commission on family law to stop its work in the same way as they jeopardized other attempted reforms.

Although it failed, the plan of the Tunisian rulers nevertheless constitutes a meaningful indicator of the Tunisian polity at the time. The attempt to abolish the distinctions between the two schools of Islamic family law in itself shows that unification was posed as a salient issue early on in Tunisia at a time when no comparable attempt took place in the other two Maghribi countries. The predominance of Islamic family law throughout Tunisia, despite the distinction between the Maliki and Hanafi schools, and the attempt at unification are signs of the relative integration of Tunisian society at the eve of colonization.

In contrast, the existence of several local, particularistic codes of customary law along with Islamic law in Algeria and Morocco reflects the social segmentation of the two countries in the precolonial period. Algeria had major enclaves of particularistic law in Kabylia, the Aures, the Mzab, and among the Touaregs. Morocco had even more diversity.[89] The dynasties that ruled Morocco and Algeria in the precolonial period had been unable to install their judges in dissident tribal areas, just as they could not extract taxes from them. All they could do was acknowledge the tribal customary codes and let the tribes continue to apply them. For example, the Kabyles of Algeria, one of the groups that had been most recalcitrant to the control of central authority and that led a rebellion in 1871, had most jealously guarded their code of customary law. In Morocco as well, the groups that had most successfully escaped the control of central authority were precisely those that kept their own local customary codes.

• • •

To sum up the characteristics of the polity toward the end of the precolonial period, it is fair to say that Tunisia, Algeria, and Morocco all shared in the turmoil of tribal politics. A tribal form of social organization existed throughout the Maghrib, where primary loyalties were oriented toward the tribe or kin grouping. At the same time, the polity also differed in critical respects in the three countries. Differences concerned the degree of tribal isolation, the capacity of tribes to evade taxation, and the extent of emerging bureaucratization.

Tunisia had developed stronger centralizing institutions. It had reformed its incipient military and bureaucratic apparatus. It was also more politically integrated than its neighbors insofar as there was greater communication between central authority and local areas. Algeria was the most segmented society. The majority of tribal groups lived in relative independence and the state interfered only minimally with their autonomy. Moroccan society was segmented as well. There, central authority and tribal groups faced each other in an ongoing antagonism. Central authority struggled to extend its control, either by using force against—or forming tactical alliances with—tribal groups ready to revolt as soon as central authority ventured to demand more taxes or sometimes any taxes at all.

Family law reflected differences in the polity. Tunisia had a more unified legal system than the other two countries, and its rulers made attempts to bring even more unification, although their effort ultimately aborted. In contrast, Algeria and Morocco had local and regional pockets of particularistic customary law. The diversity that prevailed in the two countries was indicative of the greater importance of local autonomy and tribal social organization. The relative autonomy of tribal groups in Morocco and Algeria, compared to the greater centralization of Tunisia, created different conditions for politics in the next historical periods.

6 Colonial Rule
French Strategies

The French used different strategies to rule over each of their Maghribi colonies. This had implications for the degree of political centralization, the strength of tribal solidarities, and the legal system of each country. The particular form of colonial rule depended in part on the characteristics of the colonized country and those of the colonizer in the historical period when colonization began. Covering part of the nineteenth and twentieth centuries, colonization occurred in a different context in each country. Each context, shaped by the local-central dialectic in precolonial politics, generated opportunities for, and obstacles to, different forms of domination. This intersected with reasons related to historical timing, colonial economic interests, and availability of French military resources to produce different modes of administration. These different modes of administration in turn resulted in a differential impact of colonization on the polity of the colonized society. Key differences concerned the extent to which colonial domination preserved or weakened tribal organization and the effect of colonial rule on bureaucratic centralization.

Throughout the Maghrib, the issue of family law became intertwined with the politics of colonial rule. Often believing in a *mission civilisatrice* (civilizing mission) while imposing colonial domination, the French had a vision of turning everyone into a French man or woman, in the Maghrib as in their other colonies in the world. As a practical matter, however, they knew when not to try, because of the anticipated cost that the attempt would bring. French colonial authorities knew that moves on family law quickly inflamed anticolonial feelings and could lead to widespread violence. Nowhere in the Maghrib did the French simply try to impose French civil law on all. Instead, they pursued differentiated policies depending on the characteristics of each one of their Maghribi colonies. In each country, the colonial state handled family law in ways that protected or enhanced its power.

In Tunisia, colonial rule furthered bureaucratic centralization, weakened the tribes, and generated a laissez-faire policy on family law. By contrast, colonization had the effect of maintaining kin-based segmentation in the other two countries. In Algeria, the colonial state failed to dissolve kin-based solidarities, even though it fragmented the tribes into smaller units. It maintained particularistic codes of customary law. It also took steps toward codification of Islamic family law and made partial reforms that facilitated colonial control over the Algerian population. In Morocco, the French colonial state actively preserved tribal organization by using a divide-and-rule strategy. It overtly politicized family law by emphasizing existing divisions among regions, local areas, and tribal groups. Of the three societies, Algeria was the most segmented before colonization in that the greatest number of tribal groups had the greatest autonomy from central authority. By the end of the colonial period, mainly as the result of different forms of colonial rule, Algeria switched positions with Morocco where tribes retained the greatest political leverage.

This chapter examines the different strategies of domination pursued by the French colonial state in Tunisia, Algeria, and Morocco. Focusing on the French policy toward tribal groups, the chapter first shows how colonial rule affected the degree of segmentation and the potential for state bureaucratization in each country. It then considers how the colonial state manipulated the legal system and family law as part of its overall strategy of domination in each colony.

FORM OF COLONIAL DOMINATION

The French colonial state exerted a tighter grip on Algeria than on Tunisia or Morocco, in part because it had higher stakes in that country. Colonization lasted over a century in Algeria, from 1830 to 1962, about three quarters of a century in Tunisia, from 1881 to 1956, and less than half a century in Morocco, from 1912 to 1956. Declaring its Algerian colony a French province and thus part of the French national territory, the French looked upon it as France in the making. Tunisia and Morocco were only French protectorates, a status that, in principle at least, placed some limitation on French domination, since Tunisians and Moroccans were to be associated, if only nominally, to the running of their country. Algeria also had a greater proportion of French settlers. At its height, in 1955, the European population, which was overwhelmingly French, constituted 13 percent of the total population in Algeria and between 6 and 8 percent in Morocco and Tunisia.[1] Finally, experience with colonial administration that the French accumulated in Algeria played a role when they devised strategies in the other two countries. In part because they knew the costs and benefits of different administrative methods by the time they arrived in Tunisia and Morocco, French officials developed a broader panoply of strategies to exert colonial rule.

Tunisia: Further Bureaucratic Centralization

In ruling over Tunisia, the French essentially maintained the Tunisian administrative structure that they found when they occupied the country. They used it to govern the country and superimposed their own apparatus.[2] They relied less heavily on military occupation in Tunisia than in Algeria or Morocco. Instead of sending military personnel to conquer and then administer the conquered territory as they did in the other two countries, the French co-opted the Tunisian officials who represented the ruling dynasty in the regions. Two basic reasons help explain why the French could do this in Tunisia and not in the other two countries. They encountered a relatively weak tribal organization and therefore did not face the same tribal violence as they did in Algeria and Morocco. Tunisia also had already developed an administration that colonial state officials could use, even though they modified it for their own purposes.

French colonial officials introduced changes aimed at centralizing local and regional administration in order to consolidate administrative authority. Elbaki Hermassi aptly remarks: "It is ironic that France's major contribution was to re-enforce the pre-existing . . . centralized bureaucracy."[3] In the same vein, Nazih Ayubi comments in referring to Tunisia that "[i]n general French policies under the protectorate . . . worked to strengthen the state."[4] The French grafted onto the existing Tunisian administration features of the French bureaucracy. Their major objective was to introduce what they saw as necessary to increase efficiency and enhance their control over the Tunisian population. For example, finding too much dispersion of authority in the administration of regions, they reduced the number of *qaids* from eighty to thirty-seven for the whole country as a measure toward bureaucratic centralization.[5]

The French kept in place the Tunisian monarch, the bey of Tunis, who had been ruling as a member of an independent dynasty under a nominal and distant Turkish suzerainty. They took effective power away from the bey, however, and placed it in the hands of a French *résident général*, the supreme representative of France in Tunisia. As the *de jure* ruler, the bey issued decrees in his own name, but a decree took effect only if the résident général, the de facto power holder, gave his approval. While the French kept the existing administration at the regional and local levels, they placed it under French supervision. For example, Tunisian qaids continued to head the provinces, but French governors supervised their activities, especially the collection of taxes. In some cases, the French governor took over the qaid's activities altogether, making the qaid no more than a figurehead.[6]

The principle of colonial administration in Tunisia was cosovereignty. While it never entailed an equal sharing of power between the French and the Tunisians, the arrangement involved in cosovereignty had the advantage of not totally excluding Tunisians from the political and administrative institutions of their country. For example, a decree issued in 1922 reorganized regional administration by creating provincial councils throughout the country. In those councils, eighty-six seats were reserved for the French and sixty-nine for Tunisian representatives.[7] As was typical of French rule in Tunisia, Tunisians were included in the councils, but the French made sure to outnumber them. In addition, the French governor of the province, the highest colonial authority in the administration of regions, automatically presided over the council.

While French occupation provoked fewer and less extensive tribal rebellions in Tunisia than in Algeria or Morocco, there were nevertheless some violent uprisings, mostly in the tribal regions of the south and the central part of the country. The French had to use military force to suppress the uprisings. Several tribes united in opposition to the French in the Hautes Steppes of central Tunisia, one of the predominantly tribal areas that had revolted against Tunisian rulers several times in the past. The Frechichs, the Zlass, the Hammamas, and the Majeurs formed a tribal coalition against French troops. After resisting successfully for a while, they were defeated by the French and pulled back to remote areas in the southern region. Some of the tribal groups retreated across the southern border to Libya.[8] In addition, tribal resistance to French occupation also occurred in the northwest region of Khroumirie.[9]

Colonial rule in Tunisia had the effect of further weakening tribal organization, thus continuing a trend already markedly present in the precolonial period. Bureaucratic expansion during colonization, coupled with the intensification of a market economy, continued to erode the raison d'être of tribes, which was first and foremost political. In the face of an increasingly intrusive colonial administration, it became more and more meaningless for most tribes to engage in the collective defense of a territory, free of interference by a central state or other tribes. Lisa Anderson writes that "[a]dministrative territorialization undermined the position of tribal leaders, as they became office-bound functionaries and lost contact with the daily preoccupations of their less favored kin."[10] Anderson also gives a useful indicator of the change affecting the tribes by considering official correspondence. Until the end of the nineteenth century, tribal councils signed official letters to the central administration, thus serving as the collective voice of a tribe or a tribal faction. By the end of the First World War, individuals signed the letters, speaking in their own name or that of their families and no longer in the name of a tribe or a tribal faction. This does not mean that kin-based solidarities dissolved. Tribes continued to hold land collectively and identify themselves as tribes, especially in the south of the country and in other arid regions. The change in official correspondence does suggest, however, that some tribes increasingly were losing their role as political actors.[11]

In some cases, kin-based solidarities came to serve as a basis for political organization in a new way. No longer flaring up in rebellions, they expressed themselves in more organized collective action, such as in the first Tunisian workers' movement. M. Dellagi's study on the origins of trade unions in Tunisia shows that it was on the basis of kin-based connections that striking dockers built a movement in 1924–25.[12] The dockers derived organizational strength and mutual trust from the fact that tribal affiliations created a web of connections among them. The difference with earlier times, however, was that the groups that engaged in collective protest identified themselves as dockers and no longer as members of tribal groups. Instead of serving as a basis for breaking away from the political system and maintaining local autonomy from the state, kin-based solidarities now were mobilized within a broader framework to make demands on the state. In a major change, social groups thus used kinship ties to organize collective action aimed at putting pressures on the state rather than as a mechanism to evade its authority.

The dominant economic interests of the French helped mold the form of colonial rule and shape the development of social forces within Tunisian society. Especially in the early phase of colonization, powerful landowners and large companies dominated colonial agriculture. This differed markedly from the pattern of land settlement that was still occurring in Algeria by the time France colonized Tunisia. In Algeria, the French military acquired tribal lands by physically displacing tribal groups. Algerian land was distributed free of charge to individual French settlers, many of whom ran small family farms. In part because the reliance on sheer force in the colonization of Algeria had cost France a high price in human lives and military resources, the French were not about to repeat the same policy in Tunisia. Aware of the cost involved in gaining land through violent means, a French official, State-Councilor Pascal, stated in 1886: "If our government is not capable of restraining itself, if it transforms Tunisia into (another) Algerian department, it would be *only* a source of expense . . ."[13] French officials learned an important lesson from their experience in Algeria and used a different land policy in Tunisia. Instead of receiving land free of charge from the French government, French settlers in Tunisia had to purchase it, even if at unfairly low prices, from Tunisian tribal or individual owners.

As a result, capitalistic enterprise coupled with concentration of property characterized colonial economic domination in Tunisia. French land ownership was concentrated in a few hands, not as scattered among a multitude of small farmers as it was in Algeria. For example, in 1892, eleven years after the treaty that established colonial rule in 1881, the French owned 443,000 hectares of land. Indicative of the concentration of ownership was the fact that sixteen French owners held 416,000 hectares out of the 443,000. In addition to individual owners, large companies also invested in land and owned a sizeable portion of it. By the late 1930s, four companies owned as much as 23 percent of the lands that belonged to the French. Many of the same French companies were involved in other economic activities such as mining, transportation, and various industries.[14]

The pattern of economic exploitation in Tunisia resulted in the formation of an agricultural and industrial Tunisian proletariat, made up mostly of the agricultural laborers and industrial workers employed by French landowners with extensive property and by companies. When a labor movement emerged in the 1940s, labor grievances merged with nationalist issues, as the grievances directed against French owners often took an anticolonial turn. Joining labor demands with those of the nationalist movement, the Tunisian proletariat later became an important political force in the struggle for national independence, when the alliance of the labor union and the nationalist party proved a powerful tool against colonial domination.

The French colonial policy, ruling Tunisia through the Tunisian bureaucracy while expanding it, had significant implications on the polity. First, since the existing institutions constituted the major vehicle of colonization, the French tried to make them as efficient as possible. The trend toward bureaucratization begun before colonization consequently continued during the colonial period. Second, most tribes lost the ability to preserve their autonomy from central authority, even though kin-based sol-idarities could still serve as a basis for political action in some cases. Third, the beylical dynasty, which the colonial state had kept in place as a figure-head, lost its credibility. So did the Tunisian administrators who were in office during the colonial period. Discredited in the eyes of the Tunisian people, the bey and his administrators came to be perceived as the instru-ments of colonial rule and were later dismissed by the nationalist move-ment. Finally, capitalistic enterprise and concentration of ownership helped generate the development of a labor union that would form a powerful alliance with nationalist forces later on. Summarizing the characteristics of the polity in Tunisia in the later phase of the colonial period, Jean Lacouture comments that Tunisia was "a markedly unified country. . . . the elements of both a nation and a state were already present."[15]

Algeria: Fragmentation of the Tribes

Because France had higher economic and political stakes in Algeria than in its two other Maghribi colonies—and did not hesitate to do what it took to protect its interests—colonial rule had a greater impact in destabilizing Algerian society. Covering 132 years (1830 to 1962), colonization lasted considerably longer in Algeria than in Tunisia or Morocco. Securing land for settlement at any cost and breaking the power of the tribes represented twin objectives for the French in Algeria. The methods that they used to attain their objectives resulted in the fragmentation of tribes into smaller units, without, however, dissolving kin-based solidarities.

The French knew that, if they were to rule over Algeria, they had to do away with powerful tribal groups and destroy them as centers of po-litical loyalty. This goal conformed to their own interests as rulers of the country. Expressing the French awareness that tribal groups had to be broken to enhance colonial power in Algeria, the Comte de Raousset-Boulbon, a wealthy settler, remarked in 1847: "If one wanted to prepare the tribes for assimilation with France instead of reconstituting the government of Arabs by Arabs, would it not be wise to disorganize them . . . ?"[16] The French faced a dilemma, however. They had to destroy the tribes in such a way that the colonial state could function and control the population, yet without fostering a sense of nationhood that would transcend tribal identities.

In their combined attempt to secure land for settlement and break the tribes, the French pursued a systematic policy of acquiring productive lands usually to give, or occasionally to sell, to French settlers in Algeria. They overwhelmingly used military means for the colonization of the Algerian territory, crushing any resistance with armed force.[17] Map 4 shows the stages of the colonial conquest. Hermassi comments that "the military was the foremost agent of total colonialism in Algeria."[18] Julia Clancy-Smith notes that "by the mid-1840s, France had committed tens of thousands of troops to the conquest of Algeria."[19] Prochaska indicates that, in addition to using force, the military paved the way for the settlers by building bridges and roads.[20] The administration of Algeria was under the responsibility of the French Ministry of War for a long time, and French colonial officials held military powers. Using force whenever they judged it necessary,[21] they waged a war against Algerian tribes to obtain land.[22]

The French secured tribal lands for settlers by expropriating Algerians and using the methods of "confinement," "transplantation," and "segregation" in tribal areas.[23] Confinement consisted of occupying the most fertile lands of a tribe, then confining the tribe to a restricted area. This measure left the tribes with a fraction of the land on which they had previously lived. Transplantation meant that the French physically transplanted entire tribal groups to another part of the country, usually to the south or to areas of poor arid land and then occupied the tribal territory. The third measure, segregation, consisted of fragmenting tribes and segregating the different parts in different geographic areas. In addition, French authorities restricted the mobility of members of Algerian tribes, thus hindering communication among their segments. In rural areas, Algerians had to obtain the authorization of the French military or administrative official in charge of the area, before they could leave their village or district.

Among the three measures, segregation had the most devastating effect on the social fabric of Algeria because it shattered local communities and scattered their pieces throughout the Algerian territory. Looking at it from a sociological angle and writing in 1949, René Maunier described the effect of this measure on tribal groups: "Their societies [are] broken up, their unity destroyed, their traditions swamped, their customary law obliterated ... [This] means the destruction of the tribal order, the dissolution of the ancestral group, which often forfeits even its name, even the memory of its past exploits."[24]

Direct colonial rule, or administration of local areas by French officials, usually followed successful military intervention. Once they had subdued an area, the French placed their own officials in strategic sites and endowed them with military powers. Although they succeeded in exerting direct rule in several parts of Algeria, the French could not generalize it through-

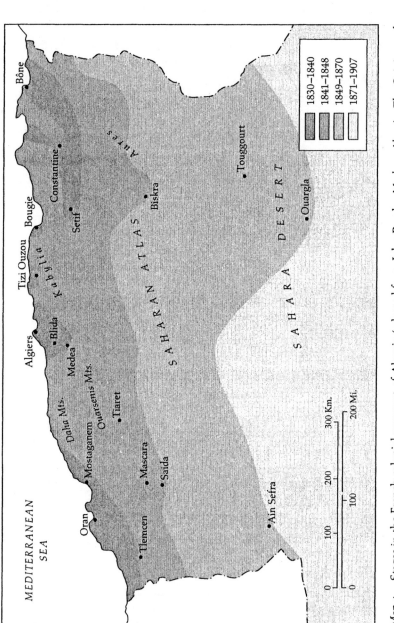

Map 4. Stages in the French colonial conquest of Algeria (adapted from John Ruedy, *Modern Algeria: The Origins and Development of a Nation*. Bloomington and Indianapolis: Indiana University Press, 1992, 57).

out the territory because of a shortage of resources. Such generalization simply proved unfeasible over the long run. Extending direct rule everywhere in Algeria would have required more settlers, more military input, and more administrative expenditures than the French had at their disposal. The problem posed by limited resources and insufficient numbers of French colonial officials persisted well beyond the early stages of colonization. Indeed, it was still being felt in the 1930s, a century after the beginning of French occupation.[25] Unable to exert generalized direct rule, the French had to find another alternative to administrate local areas. They turned to indirect rule under tight French supervision, accompanied by increased administrative partitioning of Algeria.

Colonial officials set up indirect rule by enlisting the help of tribal leaders in an effort to create a group of petty functionaries faithful to the French.[26] The French endowed tribal notables with administrative titles and gave them administrative responsibilities. They asked the notables to collect taxes, maintain order in the area, control markets, and, in some cases, organize a small armed force subsidized by the colonial state. In selecting tribal leaders, the French knew how to manipulate the local power structure and use criteria designed for a segmented, tribally organized society such as Algeria. They chose leaders who had the allegiance of their kin group and whose tribe was involved in a sizeable network of tribal alliances, as was appropriate in that setting. For example, in eastern Algeria, the French gave administrative responsibilities to notables in three of the most important and powerful kin groupings, those that had a network of influence in the region: the Beni (often transliterated as Banu) Gana, the Bu Akkaz and the Beni Shanuf. The French expected the kin groupings whose help they enlisted to maintain order in their entire regions, something that happened only occasionally.

In setting up indirect rule, the French were trying to inject elements of a centralized administration into the decentralized power structure of tribal politics. The policy brought two very different political systems to clash with each other. Neither the ideal of local autonomy nor the ever shifting pattern of alliances among tribes were compatible with the French objective of a bureaucratic and centralized rule. The French-sponsored tribal leadership, artificially created for the purpose of colonial administration and often motivated by sheer self-interest, proved incapable of accomplishing the tasks assigned to it. The French were seeking the long-range domination of the Algerian population through the progressive development of bureaucratic administration. As for the indigenous leaders, they were engaging in the politics to which they were accustomed. They were more interested in building alliances useful to their tribe and to themselves than in establishing bureaucratic rule over neighboring tribes, much less over their own tribe. As a result, and despite repeated attempts at organization and reorganization on the part of colonial officials in local areas, indirect rule in Algeria never produced the kind of bureaucratic order that the French were seeking.

The divergent interests between the French colonial state and those to whom they had delegated administrative powers were only one reason for the difficulties that the French encountered in establishing indirect rule. The constant outbursts of hostility among the tribes that indigenous leaders were expected to control also made the maintenance of law and order tenuous, if not altogether impossible. Rivalries flared up among the French-appointed leaders themselves and among their kin groupings. In case of demotion of a leader, his whole kin grouping rose in revolt. Tribal uprisings threatened, and often made null, the shaky arrangements constructed by the French. For example, Peter von Sivers indicates that in 1849 a revolt occurred against the Beni Gana, one of the kin groupings selected by the French for leadership positions in eastern Algeria. A tax increase on palm trees precipitated the revolt, which spread in the area, involving thousands of people and taking on proportions that the Beni Gana could not handle. French troops had to be dispatched and it took them seven weeks of serious fighting to break the revolt.[27]

In their quest for autonomy, Algerian tribes had not yet lost the battle, however. During the 1870s, thirty years after the beginning of the experiment with indirect rule, violent and lengthy revolts took place.[28] Insurrections broke out intermittently in the areas officially placed under the control of the Bu Akkaz, the Beni Shanuf, and the Beni Gana, to whom French power had been delegated. In 1870, many tribes refused to pay taxes. Von Sivers notes that in 1870 only 12 percent of the expected taxes had been collected.[29] A concomitant rebellion in the south made the crisis worse and disturbances went on through the 1870s, culminating in uprising in the Aures in 1879. In the early 1870s, French military forces in Algeria were considerably reduced in numbers because most of the troops had been called back to France to fight in the Prussian war of 1870–71. Without them, French authorities and their tribal auxiliaries found themselves incapable of mastering the tribal revolts until the late 1870s, when French regiments returned to Algeria and proceeded with the work of subjugation. The incidents of the 1870s revealed the limitations of French control over the population and the weakness of the tribal leaders appointed to serve French domination. They also demonstrated an ongoing capacity for resistance on the part of Algerian tribes.

After the experience of the 1870s, French colonial officials refined their strategy to administrate local areas. They partitioned administrative units by reducing the size of the area over which the appointed tribal leaders were to exert control. In refining methods of colonial administration, the French kept in check the ambitions of the largest and most powerful tribes that historically had been their fiercest enemies. Colonial officials sometimes divided into four or more separate districts a territory that previously had been under one tribal leader. They then placed the four districts under the jurisdiction of four different leaders. Von Sivers indicates that the Beni Gana, the Bu Akkaz, and the Beni Shanuf controlled only a few districts after the administrative changes of 1879, whereas they had held administrative responsibilities over entire regions at the beginning in the 1840s.[30] The three kin groupings thus saw their power reduced from the regional to the local level.

The French combined administrative partitioning with an increased supervision of indigenous leaders by French officials. Colette Establet indicates that the autonomy of Algerian qaids was increasingly limited at the same time that bureaucratization and formal rules increased.[31] In 1850, ninety-three French officers supervised indigenous tribal leaders. By 1884, the French colonial state put in place what von Sivers refers to as "a veritable army of two hundred eighty nine mayors who watched over the Algerian population."[32]

Greater and greater administrative partitioning resulted in the long run in a loss of power on the part of the tribes that had been among the most powerful in Algerian history. These could no longer hope to control a region, but they retained power in their immediate local areas. By taking the best tribal lands and refining methods of colonial administration, the French weakened those tribal groups that had been best able to form regional tribal confederations aimed at resisting French domination. They did not, however, eliminate tribal solidarity.

Morocco: Tribes Tamed but Preserved

A major effect of colonization on Moroccan society was to tame but preserve the tribes. Shorter than in Tunisia and Algeria, the colonial period in Morocco lasted forty-four years, from 1912 to 1956. The French found powerful tribes in Morocco, as they had in Algeria.[33] In a consciously devised divide-and-rule strategy, they used and exacerbated the existing divisions among tribes in the Moroccan polity. In sharp contrast to what they did in Algeria, where they tried to break the tribes, the French maintained the tribal structure of Morocco as much as possible. John Waterbury writes: "Morocco is unique in that so much of the traditional government and political system survived the half century of . . . French rule relatively intact."[34] In the same vein, Abdeslam Baita speaks of the "retraditionalization" of political institutions in Morocco under colonization.[35] As they did in Tunisia, the French ruled in the name of the sultan, whom they kept as a nominal ruler, while the résident général held the real decision-making power. France shared colonial power over Morocco with Spain, to which a Franco-Spanish treaty signed in 1912 gave authority over a relatively small area in the northern part of the country.[36]

What the French called "pacification," in reality the conquest of the country, took more than twenty years (1912–34) and required extensive military involvement in rural areas. Map 5 indicates the stages in the French occupation of Morocco. At the time of the colonial conquest, Mo-

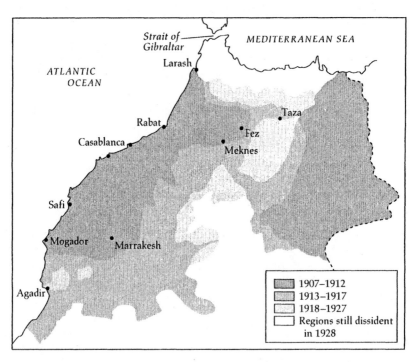

Map 5.   Stages in the French colonial conquest of Morocco (adapted from Robert Montagne, *The Berbers: Their Social and Political Organization*. London: Frank Cass, 1973, 18).

rocco included areas under the sultan's control and areas that escaped his control almost entirely, or *bilad al-makhzan* and *bilad al-siba*. The primary interest of the French was in the bilad al-makhzan. Some form of administration already existed in that part of the country, which also had the advantage of including most of the fertile lands and mineral resources. Less interested in the land of dissidence, at least initially, the colonizers moved only gradually to bring it under colonial administration.

Tribal rebellions broke out as soon as the colonial powers tried to establish control over the land of dissidence. The most violent uprising and the most serious opposition to the Spaniards erupted when Abdulkrim led a tribal revolt that brought together a powerful group of Berber tribes in the Rif region.[37] Aware that they could not escape Spanish rule altogether, the Berber tribes under Abdulkrim's leadership were hoping to maintain as much tribal autonomy as possible within the context of Spanish colonization. They wanted a compromise, one that would involve indirect rule by their own tribal leaders and thus would preserve tribal institutions and customs.

In 1922, Abdulkrim declared the formation of an "Independent Republic," which consisted of a confederation of Rifian tribes. Declaring himself president of the "Republic," Abdulkrim gathered an impressive force of about 120,000 troops. He was able to recruit European instructors, force the Spaniards to withdraw from some of the territory that they had occupied, and attack French forces at the same time. He won several victories against the Spaniards and maintained his republic for four years, from 1922 to 1926. Facing the combined military force of France and Spain, Abdulkrim was defeated in 1926, when his tribally based republic was brought to an end.[38]

The French military ultimately got the upper hand over Moroccan tribes in the 1930s, two decades after the signing of the treaty establishing colonization. Map 6 indicates that many tribal areas were still resisting the French in 1940 and had to be placed under direct military intervention. Long and difficult, the process of occupation shows the extent of tribal autonomy in Morocco in that period. It also shows the capacity of Moroccan tribes to engage in sustained resistance until then. Writing in 1946, a French general, Général Guillaume, remarked, "No tribe ever came to us spontaneously. None ever surrendered without a fight, and some only after having exhausted all means of resistance."[39] Several tribal regions, such as the Middle Atlas, the Tafilalt, the Jabal Saghro, and the Anti-Atlas, repeatedly resisted colonial forces. Indicating the difficulties that the French encountered in subduing Moroccan tribes, Waterbury calculates

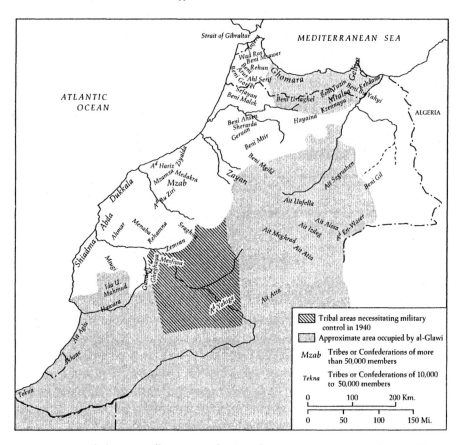

Map 6.   Tribal areas still resisting the French in Morocco in 1940 (U.S. GPO, Geography Division, Map no. 908, August 2, 1942).

that the French casualties were high for the period from 1907 to 1935, coming as they did to twenty-seven thousand dead and fifteen thousand wounded.[40]

Once they subdued the tribes, the French (and the Spaniards in the small zone under their jurisdiction) then faced the task of administering tribal areas. They opted for indirect rule, or administration through tribal leaders, similar to one of the methods used in Algeria. Having learned the high cost of direct and sustained military occupation from their experience in Algeria and realizing that administration by French civil officials required more human and financial resources than they had at their disposal, colonial authorities found it more economical to rule through the existing tribal institutions. Lyautey was the first résident général in Morocco

(1912–25), and he was instrumental in devising the colonial administrative policy in that country. He was surrounded by administrators who had served in other colonies, especially in Algeria and Tunisia. The administrators brought from personal experience a belief in the value of indirect rule, which they saw as the only feasible form of administration in tribal territory. Lyautey's style of ruling though traditional institutions, developed in the early phase of the colonial period, continued to dominate colonial administration in Morocco.[41] In addition to using tribal leaders for administrative purposes, France also developed a limited regional administrative network of its own by putting in place French personnel headed by a French governor in each region.

Wherever they found tribal chiefs powerful enough to exert influence at the regional level, the French tried to gain their allegiance instead of confronting them. Appointing them qaids, the French mandated the tribal chiefs to rule over their areas in the name of the French colonial state.[42] An arrangement between the French and the Glawi of the Atlas is one of the best known examples of the relationship between the French colonial state and some tribal chiefs. French colonial officials lavished deference and privileges on Madani al-Glawi, the head of a large chieftaincy, who was "treated as the supreme chief," Abun-Nasr notes.[43] Map 6 shows the area under al-Glawi's control in the 1940s. The French treated other leaders of tribal chieftaincies in similar ways, also making them qaids (as, for example, the Mtugi, the Gundafi, and al-Ayyadi). Some of the chiefs even received arms to conquer areas still in a state of dissidence and to rule them in the name of the French.

In contrast to the colonial policy in Algeria, the French did not attempt to fragment, uproot, or divide the Moroccan tribes. On the contrary, they left them in place and kept each tribe together. Map 6 shows tribes of ten thousand to fifty thousand and others of more than fifty thousand members in Morocco in 1940, three decades after the beginning of colonization (and sixteen years before the advent of national independence). In Algeria, the French in effect had tried to turn tribal leaders into surrogate French administrators. In Morocco, the French used tribal institutions by taking them much more on their own terms. They refrained from intruding on the internal organization of local areas. As a result, local life remained essentially the same in many areas, where tribes saw little difference from the past. French administrators, or a tribal chief acting in the name of the French, rather than the sultan, now levied taxes, but the change did not transform the internal organization of the tribe. In other areas, the difference from precolonial times was greater, as tribes now had to pay taxes, an imposition that they had successfully avoided before colonization.

For Moroccan tribal groups, political life in the colonial period continued to consist primarily of conflicts among lineages and competition for power in the immediate local area. Although the relationship between central power and tribes had changed insofar as tribes could no longer escape taxes for long periods of time, political life at the local level went on largely as it had before the French occupation. The links that the French established among local areas had little meaning for most people in those areas.[44] Ernest Gellner remarks, "Basically local life was local life, self-enclosed and self-sufficient."[45] In the same vein, Waterbury notes, "The administrative and economic infrastructure introduced by the French remained, throughout the protectorate period, an exogenous and basically exotic creation imposed upon an uncomprehending population."[46] Politics at the national or even the provincial level did not concern the tribesmen.[47] Metaphors suggesting preservation abound in the social history of Morocco under French rule, even after the conquest of the land of dissidence in the 1930s. For example, Gellner notes that "traditional institutions were placed in a kind of sociological icebox," and Waterbury comments that political organization was "put in mothballs."[48]

In ruling rural Morocco, the French repeatedly resorted to a divide-and-rule strategy that further contributed to keeping the tribal structure in place. They politicized differences between Arabs and Berbers and used the division between makhzan and siba in a well-thought-out policy. For example, R. Gaudefroy-Démombynes, a high-ranking official of the French Residency, wrote in 1928: "We must utilize to our advantage the old dictum 'divide and rule.' The presence of a Berber race is a useful instrument for countering the Arab race; we may even use it against the makhzan itself."[49] Differences between Arabs and Berbers existed no more than among all tribes, but they were useful to the French. Berbers in Morocco in that period thought of themselves as members of such and such a tribe, not as part of a Berber movement and even less as members of a "race," a term that is used loosely and inappropriately in the quotation above.[50]

The French response to the resistance of the Berber group of the Beni Mtir shows how colonial authorities used their divide-and-rule strategy to demarcate Berbers from others in Moroccan society. Like other tribes, the Beni Mtir had escaped control by the makhzan prior to colonization. They had led a successful tribal revolt against the makhzan in 1911, before the establishment of the French protectorate. In 1912 and 1913, immediately after the signing of the protectorate, they rose against the French.[51] The internal organization of the Beni Mtir was loose and segmented, with no tribal chief influential enough for the French to use as their representative. In this particular case, colonial authorities found no tribal leader to cajole, thus precluding the usual method of co-opting a tribal leader to establish French rule over a tribe.

Playing upon existing differences, French colonial officials proposed to the Beni Mtir to surrender to the state—meaning the French colonial state—but not to the Moroccan makhzan, still nominally in place with the sultan as a figurehead. Submission to the makhzan would have required the Beni Mtir to accept institutions such as in particular a qadi and Shari'a law. The acceptance of such institutions usually was part of submission agreements. The Beni Mtir rejected these institutions. Edmund Burke III comments, "The Beni Mtir . . . saw submission to the makhzan as representing not only submission to the political authority of the sultan, but also acceptance of the full panoply of makhzan administration, including qaids, qadis, and Shari'a law. It thus represented a direct threat to their custom, institutions and way of life."[52] Like many other dissident tribes, the Beni Mtir had their own code of customary law, which varied to some degree from the Shari'a.[53] More importantly, they were governed by their own autonomous tribal councils (or assembly of elders). The least of their desire was to have qadis start intruding in the affairs of the tribe.

As for the French, the issue was one of political domination, not family law. They wanted to end the Beni Mtir's belligerence. The French and the Beni Mtir agreed that the tribe would surrender to the French, but keep both its customary law and tribal council. The arrangement satisfied the Beni Mtir who stopped their violence against the French. The Beni Mtir had obtained what they wanted most, which was the preservation of their internal institutions and customs.

Later applied to other tribes in several areas, similar arrangements successfully brought many Moroccan tribes to lay down their arms and recognize French authority. Coupled with the method of indirect rule that used tribal leaders to administer local areas, the policy had an important implication. It maintained tribal institutions, kept the internal social organization of tribes essentially intact, and preserved tribal identity in Morocco during the colonial period.

COLONIAL MANIPULATION OF FAMILY LAW

In all three countries, the French policy on family law was shaped by the form of colonial domination at the same time that it contributed to it. In

Tunisia, the French could exert colonial rule without changing family law. Neither the colonial economy, heavily based as it was on large commercial interests, nor the expansion of the preexisting Tunisian bureaucracy, made changes in family law a pressing agenda for the colonial state. The French left family law in place, essentially as it was at the beginning of colonization.

By contrast, the French manipulated family law in Algeria and Morocco. In Algeria they introduced a number of changes that aimed overwhelmingly to tighten the colonial grip over the Algerian population. Maintaining the basic framework of Islamic family law, most of the French initiatives converged toward the objective of facilitating bureaucratic rule. Taking advantage of the existence of customary law in several regions in Algeria, the French also encouraged the divisions among regions and the particularism that prevailed in each. In Morocco, the French overtly politicized family law. Playing on the existing diversity of Moroccan society, they exacerbated the divisions in family law and set one part of Morocco against another. They encouraged the divisions between Islamic and customary law, makhzan and siba, and Arabs and Berbers. Map 7 shows the significance of areas of Berber speech in Algeria and Morocco and their absence in Tunisia. Not all, but many, Berber areas had their own codes of customary law. Among other factors, linguistic diversity offered the colonizer different opportunities for a divide-and-rule strategy.

Algeria: Reforms and Colonial Grip

When they occupied Algeria in 1830, the French pledged to respect the codes of personal status and family law of the various Algerian populations. On the whole, they kept that pledge for reasons of political expediency and self-interest. They preferred to avoid causing more violent resistance than they already faced. They knew Algeria well enough to realize that Algerians overwhelmingly saw Islam as the cornerstone of their identity. When the French introduced reforms, they made only relatively small ones and kept the framework of Islamic law.[54] Allan Christelow shows how in the 1850s the French maintained Islamic law for the majority of the population in Algeria while placing the courts under French control. In tribal areas, colonial authorities often had no choice but to respect customary law when they negotiated with tribal communities to gain their allegiance or minimize their resistance. In addition, the French also found it politically advantageous to keep customary law as a way of exacerbating divisions among Algerians.

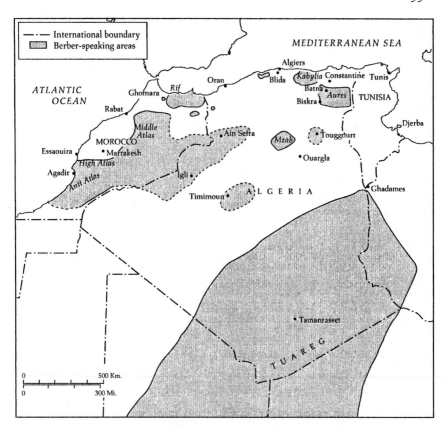

Map 7. Berber-speaking areas in the Maghrib (adapted from Ernest Gellner and Charles Micaud, eds., *Arabs and Berbers: From Tribe to Nation in North Africa*. Lexington, Mass.: D.C. Heath, 1972, 16–17).

The French encouraged regional and local particularisms by granting legal recognition to particularistic codes of family law. For example, in 1889, Kabyle customary law in the Berber region of Kabylia received official recognition.[55] This was not meant to change actual practice but only to give a stamp of approval to an existing situation. In most of Kabylia, tribal councils were applying Kabyle customary law, although in some areas, such as Tizi Ouzou and Bougie, French judges or local officials legislated on the basis of their interpretation of Kabyle law. In 1902 and 1925, French officials in Kabylia made some attempts to codify Kabyle law, but these were sporadic and unsystematic attempts with limited impact.

In another example, the French colonial regime gave official recognition to the family law of the Ibadites of the Mzab region, in the south of

Algeria. The Ibadite code of family law followed the Shari'a, but it consisted of a more austere and intransigent interpretation of Islam than the
Maliki school of law, which predominated in other parts of the Maghrib.
Ibadite interpretation of Islamic law was even more conservative regarding
women. The Mzab region traditionally had been involved in trading with
other regions. This took some of the men to other parts of Algeria while
women, even married, usually stayed in the Mzab as their husbands came
and went.

Following the French conquest of the Mzab, one of the French officers
in charge, Général Randon, and the tribal confederation of the Beni Mzab
came to an understanding in 1853. The French promised to accept the
legitimacy of Ibadite law and local institutions if the Ibadites accepted
French authority.[56] In January 1883 and December 1890, the French issued
formal decrees officially granting the Ibadites the right to have their own
courts, meaning their own local assemblies, not only in the Mzab but in
every geographic area where Ibadite groups were present. This allowed the
Ibadites to have their own law and assemblies in those areas where their
trading activities had taken them. There were twenty-six such courts or
assemblies throughout the Algerian territory, most of which legislated for
the essentially male Ibadite population scattered outside the Mzab.[57]

In 1950, a hundred years after the initial conquest of the Mzab, another
decree reiterated the same policy in maintaining the legitimacy of specifically Ibadite courts. It also added an option that allowed members of the
Ibadite community to refer matters of personal status and inheritance either to their own courts or to Islamic judges, if they so wished.[58] This
additional option changed nothing; it was meant only to expedite judicial
cases when a member of the Ibadite community wanted a quick resolution
to a simple matter. Jules Roussier explains the care taken by the French
colonial regime in asserting and reasserting the privileged status of Ibadite
law and courts in terms of political prudence.[59] The French wanted to keep
areas such as the Mzab and Kabylia quiet. They also wanted to maintain
the particularistic law that distinguished these areas from other parts of
Algeria.

Another major aspect of the colonial policy in Algeria was an attempt
to codify Islamic family law to facilitate the work of French courts. The
French instituted French courts that had the responsibility to apply Islamic
family law as defined by the Shari'a and customary law where it prevailed.
The French gave Algerians who fell under the Shari'a the choice between
going either to Islamic judges or to the French courts that applied Shari'a

law for cases involving Muslims. French law regulated all penal cases and civil matters other than the family for everyone in Algeria.

Colonial officials undertook to codify Islamic law in 1905. The résident général formed a commission under the chairmanship of Marcel Morand who lent his name to the report that became known as the "Code Morand." Morand raised the issue of heterogeneity in Algerian law and underlined the desirability to unify the law. He argued that it would be useful to formulate a code faithful to Islamic precepts and at the same time applicable to all Algerians.[60] Unification of family law would have made practical sense from the point of view of colonial administration in that it would have helped the work of judicial authorities in Algeria.

Thoughts about unifying family law raised a number of complex and conflicting considerations for the colonial state, however. Any effort to develop a unified family law immediately raised the issue of tribal customary codes. After the sustained tribal revolts of the nineteenth century and the high military cost paid to subdue Algerian tribes, the French were not about to confront tribal groups on this sensitive question, thereby running the risk of renewed resistance. Unification of the legal system under French law was out of the question because the French expected it to inflame anticolonial feelings. The imposition of French law by the colonial state might even have brought Algerians to overcome their divisions and unite around the defense of Islam, precisely what colonial officials feared most. Because of the significance of customary codes in several regions, unification under Islamic law was also problematic. Nor would it have been advantageous to the French. Even though the diversity of family law caused difficulties for the judicial system, colonial authorities found it politically useful to maintain differences among Algerians instead of running the risk of fostering unity.

The résident général avoided facing those sensitive political questions by giving the Morand commission a mandate that precluded it from considering issues of a political nature. The role of the commission was limited to systematizing existing Islamic laws and regulations. "Our mission is not to innovate," wrote Morand, "we have no other goal than to formulate clearly, in a methodical order, the true principles of Islamic law."[61] Doing just that, the commission produced the Code Morand, a text that presented in a methodical style legal principles and rules that appear in several Islamic sources.[62] Composed of judicial commentaries, the Code Morand was what it was meant to be, nothing more than a clarification of Islamic regulations. Published in 1916 and never meant to become law, it remained a convenient source of reference on family law and a guide for French judicial authorities.

As of the 1940s, more than a century after colonization, Algeria still had a multiplicity of codes of personal status and family law. The result was inextricable complexity. There were so many judicial authorities applying so many codes that the authorities themselves had difficulty deciding under whose competence and under which code a particular case should fall. Algerians could opt for French citizenship, in which case they had to give up their own code of personal status and come under French law. Two laws, one in 1944 and the other in 1946, reversed the situation by giving Algerians the option to acquire French citizenship without renouncing Islamic law.[63] Similarly, the Kabyles, who had their own customary law, and members of other areas of customary law, could opt for French citizenship while remaining under their own code. They could also decide to fall under French law, however, in which case all they needed to do was to declare their intent to do so. Despite these accommodations, the overwhelming majority of the Algerian population opted neither for French citizenship nor for the French civil code. This would have meant giving in to the colonizer and losing their identity, something that few Algerians were prepared to do.

As a result of the policies in force, the situation looked something like the following in Algeria. The French were under French law, while Algerians who had opted for French citizenship were divided among French law, Islamic law, and customary codes. After a law confirmed the legitimacy of customary codes in 1944, the Kabyles, the Ibadites of the Mzab, the people of the Aures, and other local groups all kept their respective customary law.[64] Members of Arab tribes living in Kabyle areas fell under Islamic law or under the French code if they had opted for the latter. Members of the Kabyle tribes, however, could not opt for Islamic law as long as they resided in Kabylia. They could do so only after they established residence outside of Kabylia, in which case they could choose between the Hanafi or Maliki rites. To complicate matters further, someone falling under Islamic law could go either to Islamic judges (qadis) or to French courts that would then apply Islamic law. Judicial institutions were of three kinds. Tribal councils applied customary laws, Islamic judges applied Islamic law, and French courts applied French law, Islamic law and, in some cases, customary law.

It was a maze, one that created considerable difficulties in the handling of cases. Despite the confusion that the situation caused, the French nevertheless maintained the multiple codes. When reforms were introduced late in the colonial period, in the late 1950s, they concerned the application of the Shari'a. The reforms essentially left intact the diversity of local codes. The very diversity continued to be advantageous to the colonial state and preferable to a policy of unification that might have fostered a sense of unity among Algerians.

The period from 1954 to independence in 1962 was critical for Algeria. The war of national liberation, which intensified in that period, brought turmoil, violence, and misery. The French increased their efforts to maintain their rule in Algeria, while Algerians intensified theirs to strengthen resistance in the hope of national liberation. It is during that period that the French made changes in family law. The first step concerned the registration of marriages in civil records. Already in 1882 and again in 1930, colonial officials had made some attempt in that direction by urging Algerians to register their marriage with the qadis.[65] But there was no sanction in case of noncompliance. Marriages contracted in the Islamic fashion, as a private act unrecorded by civil authorities, had remained valid after the attempts of 1882 and 1930.

In 1957, the colonial state promulgated a law concerning marriage certificates.[66] Containing many exceptions, the 1957 law was meant to facilitate the work of French courts. It was not meant to introduce deep-reaching changes in the practices of the Algerian population. The law required that a proof of marriage in the form of a certificate be delivered at the time the marriage was registered. In actuality, the certificate served mostly to prove marriage to a French court. It was made mandatory only for further legal procedures that might be handled by French courts on the basis of French law at a later time, but it was not mandatory for procedures handled by qadis or by French courts applying Islamic law. Since it concerned only those legal actions that would take place outside the framework of traditional family life as defined by Islamic law, the law of 1957 did not institute a compulsory registration of marriages for everyone. The same law also set the age of legal majority at twenty-one for all Algerians, again with exceptions. It made an exception for the Kabyles, who had their own customary code and for whom majority had been set at eighteen by an earlier law.[67] It also made an exception for the Ibadites of the Mzab, who had already been entitled to keep their own code unaffected by the new law.

In 1959, in the midst of the struggle of national liberation, the French promulgated another law on the registration of marriages.[68] The 1959 law made marriage a public act, made its registration mandatory, and established a system of civil registry records similar to that existing in France.

Requiring the registration of birth, death, marriage, divorce, and other civil matters in records available to every branch of the administrative apparatus throughout the country, a civil registry could only help the proper functioning of the French administrative apparatus. It also facilitated colonial control over the Algerian population. In a politically motivated caveat, the first article of the law of 1959 asserted that Islamic law would continue to regulate all other aspects of marriage. This kind of caution accompanied every legal modification, however slight. Colonial officials meant it as a reassurance to the Algerian population, a way to claim that the change did not call into question the basic principles of Islamic law.

Despite the claim made in the caveat, the move represented by the law of 1959 had implications for the substance of family law in Algeria. In requiring the registration of marriages, the law of 1959 took marriage out of the private realm, where Islamic law located it. It made it a civil matter to be recorded by state authorities. The same law stipulated that marriage was to be contracted in the presence of two witnesses and a civil authority or a qadi. The civil authority or the qadi had to deliver to the couple a document, in effect more than a marriage certificate since it later would include information on the birth of children. The document became the only valid proof of marriage for all further legal procedures.

The same law of 1959 brought a few other changes. It suppressed the principle of matrimonial guardian as it existed in Islamic family law, thus taking away the father's or guardian's power to express the woman's consent to marriage in her stead. This potentially undermined the power of kin in the patrilineage. The law permitted the guardian's consent only when the bride had not yet reached the age of legal majority, twenty-one. The law also set the minimum age for marriage at eighteen for a man and fifteen for a woman. The 1959 law made a minor change with respect to repudiation. It maintained repudiation as a legitimate form of divorce in that the husband kept his unilateral right of dissolving the marriage at will, without any court decision. The only difference from Islamic law was that now all forms of divorce, including repudiation, had to be recorded by a qadi or a judge.

The French took 129 years to introduce reforms of family law in Algeria. The reforms show an attempt on the part of colonial legislators to counteract the practice of child marriages. The abolition of the matrimonial guardian's prerogative made compulsory marriages more difficult. Marriages and divorces now had to be recorded in the civil registry, making the country more amenable to administrative control. Many aspects of Islamic family law remained untouched, however, such as repudiation, polygamy, rights and responsibilities of the spouses, filiation, and inheritance. Although some changes made by the French in 1959 were noteworthy, such as the abolition of matrimonial guardianship, most did not challenge the framework of Islamic family law. Instead, the changes were meant to tighten the colonial grip on Algeria by facilitating bureaucratization.

Morocco: Overt Politicization

In Morocco, the French overtly politicized family law. They manipulated it for political purposes and exacerbated the divisions that they found in place. The dynasties that ruled Morocco before colonization had been unable to apply Islamic family law to tribal areas just as they had been unable to impose taxation. As in Algeria and in contrast to Tunisia, the French found enclaves of tribal customary codes in Morocco, and they used the situation to their advantage.[69] In Morocco as in Algeria, they refrained from creating a homogenous legal system that might have contributed to the development of a sense of national unity in the country. On the contrary, the French accentuated existing differences among tribal groups as a way of strengthening their rule. In so doing, they not only acknowledged the segmentation of Moroccan society; they actively encouraged it. The diversity of codes of personal status existing in Morocco offered the French colonial regime an ideal weapon for its strategy of divide and rule in that country.

In 1914, only two years after the signing of the protectorate, a *dahir* officially recognized the right of tribal areas to apply their customary laws. A dahir was a decree signed by the sultan and having value of law. Issued whenever French colonial officials judged it necessary, a dahir was a device through which French policy in all domains was carried out in colonial Morocco.[70] The dahir of 1914 stated: "The tribes of the so-called Berber custom are and will remain ruled and administered according to their laws and customs under the control of the authorities."[71] Referring to colonial authorities, the last clause, "under the control of the authorities," was in effect gratuitous. In 1914, most of the tribal areas, particularly Berber, violently opposed and successfully escaped colonial control. Map 8 shows the Berber speaking areas of Morocco in that period, the areas targeted by the dahir.

The purpose of the dahir was not to introduce any change in how tribal areas handled their laws and customs, something over which the French had no control in any case. The purpose was instead to let the Berbers know that they could submit to the French without losing their judicial autonomy. In 1924, a committee appointed by the French résident général

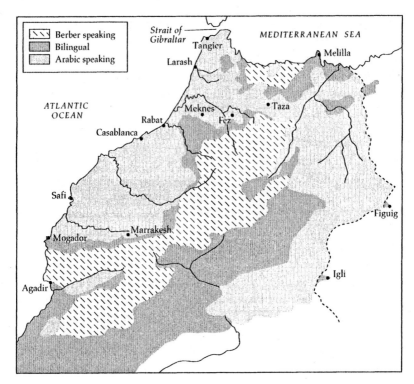

Map 8. Linguistic map of Morocco in the colonial period (adapted from Robert Montagne, *The Berbers: Their Social and Political Organization*. London: Frank Cass, 1973, 18).

to look further into the matter of customary codes presented a report that stated a major objective. The report read: "By destroying the unity of the Moroccan judicial system, the Berbers could be strengthened as a counterpoise to the city Arabs."[72]

A few years later, the French made a policy move in the direction suggested by the report and issued the Berber dahir or Berber decree of 1930.[73] Exacerbating once again political and legal divisions between Berbers and Arabs, the decree reasserted the legitimacy of Berber customary law and tribal councils. This was nothing other than an open and official recognition of the judicial competence of the jamaas, the tribal councils that had hitherto administered tribal areas with no or minimal interference from central authority. The decree formalized the tribal councils by making them "tribunals of customary law." It also created courts of appeal for the application of that law. It gave "customary tribunals" competence over all matters of personal status, family law, and inheritance, as well as over civil and commercial matters. In all cases, the "customary tribunals" were to apply the local customary law of the area and not Islamic family law. The same dahir also introduced changes in the sphere of penal law by establishing French tribunals that were to apply French penal law to all criminal matters in the tribal areas.[74]

The decree of 1930 was a continuation of the colonial policy of setting one part of Morocco against another. The French saw Berbers in the bilad al-siba as potential allies. Catholic circles in Morocco believed that the distinctiveness of Berber customary law implied that Berber allegiance to Islam was shaky, even in Islamicized areas. They entertained the notion that, with some encouragement, the Berbers could be weaned away from Islamic faith.[75] Adoption of Christian values, it was presumed, would make Berbers culturally closer to the French and more amenable to French rule. By openly recognizing the customary codes as legitimate and by bringing French penal law to Berber areas, the dahir of 1930 in effect placed those areas outside of both the jurisdiction of Islamic law and the authority of the sultan. In the same way that he signed other decrees issued by the French colonial state, the sultan signed this one.

The reactions were tremendous. The Berber decree triggered strong protests in Morocco, from both Islamic and Berber groups. Many Moroccans saw the 1930 dahir as an attack on Islam combined with a threat to the country. They saw it as an attempt on the part of the French to divide the country into two blocs. The decree became a powerful symbol of colonial injury to Moroccan identity then and later, for it has remained inscribed in collective memory as a vivid example of colonial domination. Setting Berbers apart from the rest of the Moroccan population, the Berber decree suggested that Berber areas had not fully adopted Islam and that this state of affairs should be encouraged to continue. The irony is that a large segment of the population, mostly Berber, had in fact not been under Islamic law until then. To have this state of affairs officially recognized and politically manipulated, however, shed a disturbing light on the issue. The decree placed in sharp focus the lack of unity of Moroccan society. It provided a rallying cause to the nationalist movement that was developing among intellectuals in Morocco. Family law became an overtly political issue that ignited national consciousness as no other issue had done so far.[76]

Recitations of the *latif*, an invocation to God, were organized in mosques throughout the country to deplore the Berber decree of 1930.[77] Street demonstrations took place. Shops closed and there was a general atmosphere of national mourning. In several cities, the Friday prayer was of the kind called for "in case of grave danger threatening the community."[78] The French arrested those whom they deemed responsible for leading the opposition. This only furthered the determination of many Moroccans to organize more recitations of the latif. After the arrests, the latif increasingly included an invocation of God's help in the national struggle against the French.[79] Throughout the Islamic world, a latif was recited in support of Morocco. Articles on the Berber decree appeared not only in Morocco, but also in the Middle East and in France. Muslims in other countries perceived the decree as a way to isolate the whole Berber population of Morocco and pull it away from the world Islamic community. Voices to save the Berbers and Islam were heard in far away places. Gellner notes that "protests were echoed in Muslim lands as far as Indonesia."[80] Clifford Geertz writes that "committees to save the Berbers for Islam were set up in Egypt, India, and . . . Java."[81]

In 1934, four years after the promulgation of the Berber decree, a political association made up in part of intellectuals, and called "Committee of Moroccan Action," presented a petition to the sultan demanding a unified judicial system for the whole country. The committee requested the creation of Islamic courts responsible for all matters of civil law, including therefore family law. It also requested that all courts be placed under the authority of the sultan. Finally, it asked that a single Moroccan legislation be developed and made applicable to all Moroccans. The petition was only partly satisfied. The French never rescinded the Berber dahir of 1930. A new dahir, promulgated in 1934, reversed the parts of the 1930 dahir in regard to penal cases only, which were now placed everywhere in the country under the jurisdiction of Islamic judges (qadis) and administrative officials (qaids).[82] Nothing was done to reverse the parts of the 1930 dahir that concerned family law, however. Morocco was left with two sets of codes: Islamic law and Islamic judicial organization in parts of the country, multiple customary codes and tribal councils in other parts. This situation remained unchanged throughout the remainder of the colonial period.

•   •   •

Colonization had a major effect on the local-central dialectic throughout the Maghrib, but a different one in each country. The different strategies of colonial rule used by the French had a differential impact on tribal organization and state centralization in Tunisia, Algeria, and Morocco. The policy on family law was part and parcel of the form of colonial domination in each colony. Fearing violent protest if they touched Islamic family law, French colonial authorities handled the issue cautiously, sometimes doing nothing for long periods of time. When they intervened, they manipulated family law in ways dictated primarily by the particular form of colonial rule in each country.

In Tunisia, French rule expanded and strengthened centralization. At the beginning of colonization, the state was already more bureaucratized in Tunisia than in the other two countries, with an administrative apparatus that was more developed and better able to extract taxation. The French ruled by using the existing Tunisian administration on which they grafted a bureaucratic apparatus of their own. The effect of colonization was to weaken tribal organization further and to reinforce the trend toward state bureaucratization. Left with greater centralization than its Maghribi neighbors at the end of the colonial period, Tunisia in effect had the foundation of a modern state. Throughout the colonial period in Tunisia, the French left Islamic family law essentially as they found it when they came. The kind of bureaucratic expansion that they undertook and the absence of significant areas of customary law required no particular action with respect to family law.

In Algeria, the French set out to "break the tribes." Did they succeed in doing this? Measured against the initial objective of destroying the tribe in an Algeria defined as France in the making, success was quite limited. Although colonial rule resulted in the fragmentation of many Algerian tribes, it did not eliminate tribal solidarity, even though it changed tribal politics in a significant way. Large tribes could no longer form powerful confederations, and regional competition among tribal groups was no longer an issue. The cohesiveness of kin groupings remained an asset for political influence, however, in that smaller tribal units continued to be important political actors at the local level. Although French military and administrative domination inevitably fragmented many tribes, colonial rule in Algeria failed to dissolve kin-based solidarities altogether.

Algerian society in effect withdrew into itself when faced with the threat of disintegration. In the absence of any other forms of associative and political life, which colonization precluded, Algerians "adhered to a traditionalism of despair"[83] by tightening the networks of kin-based solidarities in search of a refuge from French domination. The French made some changes in family law in Algeria. Even though any change in family law felt at the time like a painful aggression on Algerian identity, in retrospect, the French initiatives do not appear as a shift in the basic framework of Islamic law. Most of the initiatives reflected instead the French objective of maximizing the bureaucratic efficiency of the colonial state and its control over the Algerian population. In addition, the French encouraged local particularism by maintaining enclaves of customary law in Algeria.

In Morocco, the particular form of colonial rule combined with the precolonial social structure to preserve tribal organization. It took the French twenty-five years longer to conquer the land of dissidence than the land of government. After they had tamed the land of dissidence, the French actively preserved the tribes as part of a conscious strategy of divide and rule. They manipulated tribal rivalries and used tribal leadership to administer local areas. The tribes came under the authority of a state— the colonial state—and lost their ability to effectively resist central authority through armed struggle for sustained periods. At the same time, however, the internal life of Moroccan tribes remained insulated, for much of the French administrative structure was simply superimposed over tribal organization. Rarely did it penetrate or truly transform collective life in tribal areas. Although the subduing of the tribes is a major turning point in the history of Morocco, the fact that the colonial state preserved tribal organization is equally significant. Colonial handling of family law in Morocco reflected the divide-and-rule strategy that was central to French domination in that country. Just as the form of colonial rule contributed to preserve the tribes in Morocco, the colonial policy on family law helped preserve particularistic customary law and divisions among tribal areas.

The different forms of colonial rule and the different family law policies in the three countries created different conditions for nationalist movements and sovereign national states in the next period.

Part 3

THREE PATHS TO NATION-STATE AND FAMILY LAW

The basis of government is jugglery. If it works, and lasts, it
becomes policy.

A ninth-century wazir

Building on the analysis of historical differences in part 2, part 3 considers
the transition from anticolonial struggles in the era of nationalism to the
building of new nation-states. It shows how Morocco, Algeria, and Tunisia
followed different paths with respect to the development of the sovereign
national state and to postindependence family law. A key difference was
the central-local dialectic that took on different forms in each country
depending on the political role of kin groupings in the nationalist struggle
and then in the newly formed nation-state. This dialectic gave the political
leadership uneven incentives to capitalize on kin-based solidarities. It made
it more or less advantageous to pursue a reform of Islamic family law.

In analyzing postindependence family law in Tunisia, Algeria, and Morocco, I focus on the message of the law, on the vision of society embodied
in the law. I consider whether the new laws sanction a nuclear family
system with individual rights and obligations, and therefore with greater
rights for women or, instead, whether they condone the extended patrilineage and larger kin-based solidarities. The objective of the analysis is to
show how family law policies in the Maghrib were shaped by the strategy
of state formation and nation building in each society. The discussion of
family law reform in part 3 is organized theoretically according to outcomes rather than chronologically. It underscores the significance of long-
term structural forces and short-term political strategies that made reform
in the aftermath of independence highly unlikely in Morocco, first uncertain then improbable in Algeria, and possible in Tunisia.

7 Palace, Tribe, and Preservation of Islamic Law

Morocco

The nationalist struggle in Morocco culminated in the revival of the monarchy as a key institution based on a coalition with rural notables against the influence of an urban-based nationalist party. Tribal areas in effect provided the throne with some of its strongest allies. In part because the French colonial state had left tribal structures intact in most of the countryside as part of its administrative strategy, kin-based local solidarities remained a salient feature of Moroccan politics throughout the nationalist period. When Morocco became independent in 1956, the country continued to exhibit a contrast between areas of government influence, mostly the cities, and rural areas where tribal authority and kin-based patronage networks predominated. In contrast to Tunisia (where they quickly receded from the political scene) and more recognizably than in Algeria (where they were laced with many other issues), loyalties and interests rooted in tribal affiliations shaped the nationalist struggle and the newly formed national state in Morocco.[1]

The policy on family law after independence reflected the coalition between monarchy and tribe and the continued importance of kin-based solidarities in Morocco. Once victorious, the monarchy engaged in political actions and policies that protected—or avoided disturbing—the tribal order that provided it with a base for power. The policy on family law was part of this overall strategy. After independence, the law was codified in a concise text that appeared in 1957–58. Following a conservative choice on the part of the monarchy, the text remained faithful to the Islamic family law of the Shari'a. The codification institutionalized the model of the family as an extended patrilineage based on agnatic ties, the kinship model that was the cornerstone of the tribal system. The content of the law and women's legal status thus were left essentially unchanged. With the codification, the monarchy protected the agnatic kinship structure in Morocco and cemented its alliance with the tribal areas of the country. This chapter traces the political struggles and coalitions that led to that outcome. It examines the forces involved in the formation of the national state that kept family law unchanged in the period after independence.

COALITION BETWEEN PALACE AND TRIBE (1940S–50S)

The coalition between palace and tribe developed during the struggle for national liberation. Conflicts and alliances of the nationalist period left the Moroccan monarchy with close ties to tribal areas, as the sultan came to play a critical role in the anticolonial struggle. Maintained as a figurehead by the colonial state, the sultan emerged from the period with his power not only restored but strengthened. Divisions within Moroccan society left him the most likely candidate for the role of unifying antagonistic social forces in the anticolonial struggle, such as urban nationalists and tribal areas.

An urban-based party named the Istiqlal (meaning "independence" in Arabic) initially spearheaded the nationalist struggle. During most of the nationalist period, in the 1940s and early 1950s, the Istiqlal was the main actor in the anticolonial fight (by 1947, it already had fifteen thousand members).[2] Its leader, Allal al-Fasi, who combined nationalist goals with religious revivalism, had great appeal among nationalists in Morocco.[3] He became the apparent spokesman of Moroccan nationalism. His broad appeal, further increased by the fact that the French sent him into exile from 1937 to 1946, contributed to the ability of the Istiqlal to expand its membership.[4] The impression that the Istiqlal would succeed in becoming a mass-based nationalist party did not last long, however.

Tribal Opposition to Urban-Based Nationalism

The Istiqlal party failed to develop nationwide support, mostly because it faced fierce opposition from tribal areas. The segmentation of Moroccan society and the persistence of tribal organization in rural areas made it difficult for the party to reach out to the countryside. Drawing its leadership mostly from families of the urban, commercial, and religious establishment of the cities, the Istiqlal succeeded in mobilizing urban areas such as Fez, Casablanca, and Rabat. Its implantation in tribal areas, by contrast, was virtually nonexistent, thus leaving open the possibility of countermobilization. The French colonial regime seized the opportunity.

The French responded to the predominantly urban-based Moroccan nationalism by manipulating tribal notables in rural areas as a counterweight to the urban nationalists. As in their other colonies, French colonial authorities resorted to direct repression against nationalist leaders, whom they arrested or sent into exile. In addition, when the French decided that it was time to use force against the nationalists, they found allies among some tribes and rural notables. In 1953, al-Glawi, the chief of a powerful tribal confederation, headed a rural coalition against the Istiqlal and sultan. He led warriors who marched on the cities of Fez and Rabat. The coalition circulated a petition signed by more than 75 percent of the rural notables to whom the colonial regime had delegated administrative responsibilities. Benjamin Stora mentions that the petition presented 270 signatures including mostly rural notables, and Elbaki Hermassi indicates that 309 out of 325 rural qaids signed the petition.[5]

Addressed to the chief representative of the colonial state in Morocco, the French résident général, the petition asked him to "deliver the people from the extremists of the Istiqlal party and from whoever [helped] them."[6] By "whoever helped them," the rural notables referred to the sultan. In 1953, al-Glawi toured Morocco, demanding the removal of the sultan whose position he identified with that of the Istiqlal. He also threatened the French government to withdraw his support unless the French showed more firmness against the nationalists. He declared: "If, contrary to our expectation, [the French government] does not show the firmness which the Moroccan people expect of it, France will lose her place in Morocco."[7] The presence of the Berber warriors in Rabat and Fez was meant as a show of force principally against the Istiqlal and at the same time against the sultan, as long as the latter allied himself with the party.[8] After the sultan refused to abdicate, the French deposed him in 1953 and sent him into exile. From then on, the urban-based nationalist movement made the return of the sultan its rallying cry.

With several tribal groups helping the French and forcefully opposing the Istiqlal, it was unlikely that the party would become the uncontested voice of the Moroccan nation. Rural notables in tribal areas feared above all the urban nationalists of the Istiqlal. They expected that, if allowed to take power, the urban elite would transform the countryside in its own interest and to the detriment of rural notables. Unable to galvanize popular resistance in the country at large, Istiqlal leaders came to realize that they lacked the support required to lead the nationalist struggle effectively. They also came to accept that the sultan was in a better position to elicit rural support than they were.[9] Essentially restricted to urban areas and facing opposition in the countryside, the Istiqlal had only one ally to turn to, the sultan.

Even though they had treated the Istiqlal and the sultan as a common enemy in their show of force, rural tribal groups could consider accepting the sultan's authority. Some tribal notables even saw him as a potential ally, if he could dissociate himself from the Istiqlal. The sultan drew legitimacy from the history of the Moroccan sultanate, which combined temporal and spiritual power, even though its power had been rejected by the zone of dissidence. He belonged to the Alawi dynasty, which first established itself in the mid-1600s and traced its descent to the Prophet Muhammad through blood lines.[10] The area of influence of the dynasty had fluctuated considerably in the two hundred years of its rule before colonization, since dissident tribes in mountainous areas usually refused to pay taxes.

Despite long periods of serious weakness in its history, the fact that the Alawi dynasty had occupied a position of authority for more than three hundred years, coupled with its descent from the Prophet, could nevertheless serve as a source of legitimacy, especially when conditions were favorable to such a development. M. Combs-Schilling insightfully remarks: "It is no accident that the sharifi [descendant of the Prophet] model of rule emerged when more mundane undergirdings of central power were destabilized."[11] The long (albeit tortuous) history of the dynasty provided it with a legitimacy that helped it obtain the allegiance of tribal areas, which could see the sultan as a counterweight to the threat of the Istiqlal, when the issue of nationhood came to a head in the mid-1950s.

France finally recognized the independence of Morocco on 2 March 1956, after armed bands bearing the name of Moroccan Liberation Army attacked French posts in several regions. Violence and riots also had shaken Moroccan cities. Poorly organized, the Liberation Army took sporadic and uncoordinated actions. This was a time when the Algerian war already was consuming French resources and energies. Eager to avoid a reenactment of the Algerian war in their other colonies, French officials were neither willing nor ready to become involved in fighting in Morocco as well. Even though the Moroccan Liberation Army in no way compared to the Algerian resistance, France agreed to end the colonization of Morocco. With the Istiqlal party unable to take the reins of the nationalist struggle, Moroccan independence was achieved under the leadership of the monarchy. When the sultan returned to Morocco from exile, the politically volatile tribal areas recognized his authority. The sultan remained in power and, with a change in title at independence, became the king of sovereign Morocco.[12]

The politics of the nationalist struggle in Morocco had some features in common with the Tunisian case. By contrast to Algeria, both Tunisia and Morocco were spared a prolonged anticolonial guerrilla war and the ensuing emergence of multiple, armed decision-making centers at the time of independence. Developments in Morocco nevertheless differed from the situation in Tunisia, where the monarchy lost its prestige in supporting the French regime and where a tightly coordinated party that combined an urban *and* rural base took the leadership of the nationalist struggle. It was in large part because of the segmentation of Moroccan society and the strength of tribal groups that the Istiqlal could not play a leading role in the nationalist victory. The structural context in which organized nationalism emerged in Morocco made it unlikely that the urban elite could mobilize rural areas under its leadership. Upon attaining independence, the strengthened monarchy, the weakened urban-based Istiqlal party, and potentially powerful rural notables in tribal areas represented key actors in the politics of the new national state.

Tribes in the New Nation-State

The political discourse reflected the role of tribes in Morocco in the period of independence. Whereas the leadership dropped the concept of tribe in Tunisia and made more or less veiled references to it in Algeria, Moroccan political leaders made direct references to tribes in their statements. And they made them with pride. In 1956, for example, a Berber chief, who was Minister of Interior and had decided to resign his position, returned to his mountains in the Middle Atlas, where he encouraged the tribes of the area to revolt. In justifying his move, the former Minister of Interior declared: "It is the tribes who made the glory of Morocco."[13] He further suggested that political parties be dissolved and that more power be given to representatives of the tribes. He also made the following comment: "It is contrary to the interests of the country to confer responsibility on men who totally ignore the tribes."[14]

The place of tribal areas in the overall population of Morocco shows the significance of tribes in the new state. The first national census of independent Morocco indicated a total population of 11,626,000 in 1960.[15] Rémy Leveau estimates that Morocco in the aftermath of independence counted approximately six hundred tribes, each with an average of ten thousand to fifteen thousand members.[16] This suggests that 6 million to 9 million people out of 11,626,000, or 51 to 77 percent of the total population in Morocco were members of tribes. Similarly, Douglas Ashford indicates that 80 percent of the population lived in rural areas at the time of independence, and scholars agree that tribal organization prevailed in most of the countryside.[17]

Despite the support given to the monarchy by the tribes, independence carried with it the challenge to integrate tribal areas and their kin-based solidarities into national politics. After Morocco became a sovereign state, some tribes mounted opposition to the central government.[18] Tribes in mountainous areas once again challenged the authority of the state as they revived old patterns of tribal dissidence by refusing to pay taxes and retreating to their mountains. Tribal uprisings went on during 1957 and 1959, particularly in the region of the Rif, but also in other areas throughout the country.[19] A combination of military action and negotiations between the king's government and the leaders of the revolts contained the uprisings. The resolution of the conflicts often included words of benevolence and forgiveness on the part of the king, in a symbolic assertion of a direct and personal link between king and tribe. For example, in 1958, the king addressed a tribal delegation in the following terms: "All the injustices that have been reported will be repaired. All legitimate rights will be satisfied. Return to your tribes in tranquility and without fear. Transmit to your brothers our paternal solicitude. Transmit to them equally our order: that each return to his village since we have given our instructions that no one should be troubled."[20]

By their unrest, Moroccan tribes now expressed their fear of being relegated to second-class citizenship within a modern civil order. Tribal unrest was no simple repetition of the precolonial *siba* rising against the *makhzan*.[21] Although tribal dissidence in Morocco took the same form after independence as in earlier periods, its meaning had shifted. Whereas during the precolonial and colonial periods, tribes revolted to escape the control of central authority, postindependence tribal unrest occurred when tribes "found themselves neither left alone nor helped by the new Moroccan government," as I. William Zartman remarks.[22] Clifford Geertz writes that the restlessness of the tribes expressed their concern "to find a secure and accepted place in [the] nation."[23] In the same vein, David Seddon explains the general dissidence in tribal areas after independence by their fear of being left out.[24]

By revolting, tribes were trying to attract the attention of the state, which they expected to dispense benefits. They sought to obtain more government investments in their areas, more jobs, more schools, more roads, more clinics. At the same time, some of the tribes rose up in arms to protest interference by the central government in the administration of their affairs. They complained that the interference brought no improvement in their lots.[25] Tribes could accept the authority of the central government if this brought them benefits, but they were unwilling to give up control over their own affairs for no return.

Tribal areas entered the political system of the new Moroccan nation-state as active partners, not as useless relics from the past. Moroccan politics at independence can be understood only if one considers the strategic position of notables in tribal areas and their place within the national political system. The notables could mobilize support in rural areas because they had a following based on a combination of kin-based ties and patronage networks. They could use the support to back or refuse policies of the central government in their own areas. They could also use the support to help a political figure, as strength in rural areas brought influence in national politics. In Moroccan politics at independence, power often was determined by the number and influence of one's followers, represented by the people who would provide backing in a show of force.[26] The best followers in this context, those who could be counted upon most surely and most consistently, were members of one's tribal area, and by extension, members of one's region.

Because they offered a way of securing a following that could serve as a basis for power at the national level, tribal areas played a key role in the political life of the country. They connected to systems of patronage for which Ernest Gellner uses the metaphor of "central nervous systems" with nerve ends reaching into the villages.[27] The systems of patronage overlapped with long-standing networks of tribal loyalties and rivalries. When one tribe supported a given politician or faction, the neighboring tribe, its traditional rival, often supported an opposing politician. Such systems of patronage based on tribal solidarities could be activated quickly. Comparing them to equipment with detonators, Gellner writes: "They [were], so to speak, with detonators in place and barely a safety catch on. From time to time, they [were] triggered off . . ."[28] The threat of reactivation of tribal ties was ever present in the Moroccan countryside in the aftermath of independence. Although the manipulation of tribal alliances was played with more restraint than in the precolonial and colonial periods, it remained nevertheless central to the functioning of the Moroccan political system in the period when a sovereign national state took shape.

Tribal Areas as Allies of the Monarchy

One of the ways the monarchy responded to the challenge of integrating tribal areas in the new nation-state was by making them its allies. The Moroccan monarchy in effect capitalized on the strength of kin-based solidarities. As long as the system of patronage in tribal areas continued to provide power at the center, it was not to the advantage of the Moroccan monarchy to engage in any policy that might hasten the disintegration of tribal solidarities. On the contrary, it made good political sense to keep them in place. Leveau sees the monarchy as holding a wealth of political credit in tribal areas, where it was perceived in part as protection against the urban elite of the Istiqlal party. Referring to the countryside as the "defender of the throne," Leveau further suggests that the monarchy restored the power of tribal notables, who in return brought the support of their world against the urban political parties.[29] Jean-François Clement shares this view in arguing that the stability of the Moroccan regime resulted from a privileged alliance between the monarchy and rural notables.[30] In the same vein, Abdellah Hammoudi writes that rural notables "are the ones who, so far, have been responsible for the stability of the regime."[31]

Rural support allowed the monarchy to restrict the influence of urban elites and thus to protect itself, since the urban elites of the Istiqlal would have been likely to reduce the monarchy to a symbolic role, had they succeeded in taking power at independence. Abdelali Doumou indicates that the monarchy gave advantages to rural notables, such as easy credit, subsidies, and tax relief.[32] It should be noted that the alliance between rural notables and the monarchy was far from being a case of determinism by attributes. By training, culture, and style, King Muhammad V (1956–61) and his successor Hassan II (1961–99) resembled members of the educated and cosmopolitan elite from the city of Fez, an elite that constituted the major segment of the nationalist leadership in the Istiqlal party, more than they resembled rural notables.[33]

The allegiance of tribal areas to the monarchy and their opposition to the Istiqlal were understandable. In contrast to the monarchy's support for tribal areas, several leaders of the urban-based Istiqlal were hoping to undermine the tribal framework of Moroccan society. They wished to replace ties of solidarity based on kinship with new forms of association based on social and economic interests such as markets, schools, hospitals, and networks of agricultural production.[34] Leveau writes, "The [Istiqlal] reformers' guiding idea was to destroy the tribal framework, that is the ties of solidarity and obligation generated by actual or fictive kinship that maintained the cohesiveness of social groups in the traditional rural order."[35] Referring to the "unifying zeal" of the Istiqlal reformers, Leveau indicates that the touchstone of nationalism as they saw it included the suppression of particularism, the abolition of customary tribal law, the end of the power of local notables, and their replacement with officials appointed by the central government.[36] Leaders of the Istiqlal wanted a single party organized in local branches throughout the country and working hand in hand with the government administration. In part because of continued rural opposition, they failed to develop it.

Although nationalist cadres of the Istiqlal succeeded in taking office as administrators in many regions and local areas in 1956 immediately following independence, they did not last long. Rural areas rejected their authority and the king accepted the rejection, with the result that rural notables gradually were integrated as new *qaids* into the administration of the Ministry of Interior to replace the nationalist cadres in the late 1950s and early 1960s.[37] The revolt of Addi ou Bihi in 1957 illustrates the process. As governor of one of the regions, the Tafilalt, Addi ou Bihi refused to apply the decisions of the Ministry of Interior, who wanted to appoint "modern qaids," most of whom had graduated from the College of Azrou. Perceiving the qaids about to administer his area as "strangers with allegiance to the Istiqlal,"[38] Addi ou Bihi refused to have them appointed. Leveau explains that "[Addi ou Bihi] considered himself as the king's deputy in his province and therefore entitled to be the one choosing his qaids."[39] King Muhammad V understood Addi ou Bihi, whose notion of what made a qaid had little to do with a college education. Addi ou Bihi's notion was much closer to the description that John Waterbury gives of a qaid. Waterbury indicates that a qaid's "alliance group and not his administrative position confer[red] elite status upon him. Moreover, it [was] his alliance group that won him the administrative post in the first place."[40]

The incident caused by Addi ou Bihi represented a common occurrence, for most tribal areas rejected administrators associated with the Istiqlal. Power returned to tribal areas, where Istiqlal administrators lost their positions to local notables. As a result of the shift in administrative personnel in tribal areas, local notables came to participate in the national administrative apparatus, thanks to their ability to mobilize interpersonal ties of kinship and patronage. This further strengthened the alliance between tribal areas and the political center organized around the monarchy.

Agricultural land policy illustrates the alliance between palace and tribe, and the determination of the monarchy to safeguard tribal organization.

The monarchy in effect defined social relations of production on the basis of kinship ties rather than social class. After it appropriated some of the land that had previously belonged to French settlers (an appropriation that was part of the decolonization process), the Moroccan government distributed land to Moroccans. A decree regulating agricultural production accompanied the distribution. It required land recipients to hire relatives for help and to refrain from wage labor. Land recipients had to "work the land themselves with the help of their relatives living under the same roof and without wage labor. . . . Such individuals [had to] refrain from engaging in paid labor themselves."[41] Offering a convincing interpretation of the policy, Doumou describes it as an instrument to maintain kin-based forms of association in agricultural production and to slow down the development of capitalist relations of production in the rural world.[42] Striving to safeguard the family or kinship framework of agricultural production, the Moroccan state was fighting against the disintegration of collective and kin-based forms of production in order to foster political stability in the countryside and to keep its political base.

Monarchy as Arbitrator

Another strategy of the king in the aftermath of independence was to play the role of arbitrator among the various sectors of Moroccan society. His goal was to make sure that no group took the upper hand. As long as intergroup rivalry continued, the king remained a necessary symbol and agent of political stability. The image of a political stalemate has often been used to describe Morocco in the aftermath of independence.[43] The stalemate resulted from the fact that a balance had to be maintained among the various clientele groups and patronage networks. If any one segment of the ruling groups seemed to be gaining in power, other segments would join together in order to face the threat and minimize the chances of that segment becoming more powerful than any other.

Political groups or factions also could not be allowed to disappear entirely. They were maintained in case they had to be reactivated. Kept in existence through the active support of the monarchy, factions could be used as counterbalance to one another, if need be. The role of arbitrator played by the king was facilitated by the fact that, when a Moroccan army and police were created immediately after independence, they were placed directly under the control of the monarchy. With the monopoly over the armed forces in his hands, the king was able to maintain a balance among sectors of Moroccan society as well as among political factions.

Shifts and alliances in party politics illustrate the position of the monarchy as arbitrator in a web of political forces. The Istiqlal, the dominant nationalist party, split into two parties in 1959, three years after independence. A segment broke away and formed the Union Nationale des Forces Populaires (UNFP, National Union of Popular Forces), a party with a more radical leftist bent than the Istiqlal. Although the king was far from sympathetic to leftist ideology, he nevertheless looked with favor on the weakening of the Istiqlal brought about by the split. Waterbury notes, "From early on, the palace realized that it would be to its advantage to promote the division of the Istiqlal by encouraging disputes among its leaders and by luring away its potential clientele."[44] Even though there were ideological differences between the Istiqlal (as it was after the split) and the newly created UNFP, most people did not choose sides on ideological grounds. It was rather out of loyalty for their patrons that people aligned themselves with one party or another. As frequently was the case in Moroccan politics in the aftermath of independence, patronage networks and alliances played a critical role in shaping political alignments.

Other parties mobilized tribal areas, thus providing a counterweight to the urban political elites. Whereas the Istiqlal and the UNFP were both primarily based in urban areas, two other parties, the Parti Démocratique de l'Indépendance (PDI, Democratic Party of Independence) and the Mouvement Populaire (Popular Movement), were anchored in the countryside. The PDI had gained strength in the tribal areas of the Middle Atlas and the Rif immediately after independence. Resentful of the efforts of Istiqlal officials to infiltrate their areas, tribal leaders gladly formed an alliance with a political faction opposed to the Istiqlal. Furthermore, the monarchy was eager to support a political party with a predominately rural base, as was the case of the PDI. Not only could such a party help mobilize tribal areas, which overwhelmingly had shown loyalty to the king, it could also be a useful counterweight to the Istiqlal.

The party of the Mouvement Populaire served a similar purpose, with the difference that it was more oriented toward the defense of Berber interests, although not all Berber areas supported it. Speaking for tribal areas in general, the Mouvement Populaire demanded the protection of collective tribal lands. It also argued for the creation of school programs to teach Berber dialects as a way to preserve Berber identities in local areas.[45] Most estimates indicate that Berbers constitute approximately 40 percent of the Moroccan population and some suggest that they represent as much as two thirds of the rural population.[46] Like their Algerian counterparts, Moroccan Berbers were organized in multiple communities. A major characteristic of the Mouvement Populaire was its strong support of the monarchy. In 1963, the PDI, the Mouvement Populaire, and a few independent political figures formed a coalition named the Front for the Defense of Constitutional Institutions. This was a coalition of forces loosely united on the basis of loyalty to the king.

The Moroccan monarchy thus found its strongest support in the rural areas where tribal groups preferred to ally themselves with the king rather than fall under the control of the urban-based Istiqlal party. The postindependence period witnessed what Waterbury refers to as "a territorial inversion of the blad as-siba and the blad al-makhzan."[47] He writes about that period: "The mountains were now the source of the surest support for the monarchy while the urban centers of the Atlantic plains had become the most likely environments for dissidence."[48] Political stalemate was crucial to the maintenance of the king's power and to the continuation of his role as a supreme arbitrator among competing factions. Since it was in rural areas and particularly among tribes that the monarchy found its strongest support, it was to the monarchy's advantage to refrain from policies that might bring about change. It was safer to leave in place social, economic, and political arrangements that contributed to the survival of tribal structures in Moroccan society.

ISLAMIC FAMILY LAW PRESERVED: CHOICE OF THE MONARCHY (1950S)

The policy on family law in sovereign Morocco followed from the coalition between palace and tribe. In the same way that the monarchy pursued policies that preserved kin-based solidarities in politics, administration, and agricultural production, it also preserved Islamic family law. Since Islamic family law sanctions the extended patrilineage that is the foundation of the tribal system, this should be seen as part of an overall strategy that avoided disturbing the tribal order and at times actively sought to protect it.

While the monarchy preferred to preserve Islamic family law as found in the Shari'a, others expressed interest in making some changes, although the issue never led to confrontation. Moroccan voices in favor of change belonged mostly to the urban-based Istiqlal, which was left weakened by the coalition between monarchy and tribe during the nationalist struggle and the period of independence. The voices for change remained unheard, as the monarchy chose to preserve Islamic family law in accordance with its political interests. When Morocco equipped itself with a unified family law after independence, the monarchy enforced its choice, which was to codify Islamic family law in a national body of legislation.

Voices for Change (Early to Mid-1950s)

The issue of family law had been a political battle cry during the nationalist period, especially following the manipulation of the issue by the French colonial state. As discussed in the previous chapter, the Berber decree of 1930 issued by the French had provoked a major crisis. Officially granting legitimacy to customary law and tribal councils in Berber areas, the decree had been widely perceived by Moroccans as a colonial strategy to divide and rule. The reactions to it had shown that intellectual and political figures in Morocco had an acute awareness of the necessity to unify family law. The diversity of codes of personal status was a constant reminder for the nationalist movement, the sultan, and all concerned Moroccans that the country was far from unified.[49] From the 1930s to the 1950s, customary codes constituted a topic of frequent discussion, as intellectuals and public figures spoke in favor of a uniform family law valid throughout the country. Most agreed that the application of Islamic family law to everyone was the answer, leaving open, however, the question as to how much Maliki law should be modified, if at all.

As elsewhere in the Maghrib, nationalists in favor of change in family law were heard in Morocco during the anticolonial struggle. As elsewhere, nationalists envisioned family law reform within the general framework of broad social reforms required to bring about social change in the country. As elsewhere too, discussions focused on the kind of family structure that the law would sanction. At issue was whether the law would continue to sanction extended agnatic lineages with privileges granted to extended kin and with a fragile conjugal bond (easily breakable by repudiation and made nonexclusive by polygamy), or whether the law would, on the contrary, introduce the model of a predominantly conjugal unit.

The reformist trend found a forceful exponent in Allal al-Fasi, the founder and leader of the Istiqlal. Like many other members of the Istiqlal leadership, he belonged to the urban elite that lost power in favor of the monarchy in the course of the nationalist struggle. In a book entitled *al-Naqd al-dhati* (Self-criticism), published in 1952, al-Fasi outlined a comprehensive set of social, economic, and legal reforms.[50] While they might appear tame in the contemporary context, al-Fasi's views were audacious in the context of Morocco at the time, when discussions so far had centered on legal unification rather than reform. The reformist views expressed by al-Fasi were endorsed in part by the Istiqlal party. In 1955, for example, a convention of the Istiqlal included a committee on the rights of women and children. The committee passed a resolution stating that it was "necessary to proclaim equality between the sexes," and that this equality should be "implemented in political and civil rights."[51]

The book itself, however, represented al-Fasi's individual position. His suggestions were predicated on the belief that one could be at the same time faithful to the principles of Islam and responsive to the exigencies of the twentieth century. Al-Fasi paid special attention to the kinship structure in Moroccan society and argued in favor of making changes in the legal statutes governing it. He underscored the coexistence of extended kin groupings and nuclear families in Moroccan society. He wrote: "The family, especially in some Berber areas, is sometimes so extended as to encompass a large number of men and women, boys and girls, and to become a tribal faction; whereas in cities, the family is more restricted, it is of the kind that is usually found in modern nations."[52] He saw the coexistence of these two kinds of kinship units as a source of social disharmony and potential conflicts in Morocco.

Al-Fasi suggested several concrete measures designed to foster a new conception of the family in Morocco.[53] In contrast to the deemphasis of the conjugal bond in Islamic law, al-Fasi argued that marriage ought to be based on mutual affection between the spouses and their commitment to form a new family together. To make this possible, he called for the abolition of the legal right of matrimonial constraint given by Islamic law to a woman's father or guardian over the choice of a spouse for the woman under his guardianship. Al-Fasi also urged that a minimum legal age be set for marriage and that child marriages be outlawed. As to polygamy, he thought that it should simply be abolished, as he believed that polygamy was so entrenched in Moroccan customs that a mere modification of existing rules would not work. Taking a more conservative tack on the issue of repudiation, al-Fasi recommended only that it be made compulsory for a man to compensate his repudiated wife financially, thus strengthening the admonition made in Maliki law.

Aware of the realities of kinship in Moroccan society, the leader of the nationalist party was concerned about the difficulties that they would present, were Morocco to become an independent nation-state. He recommended reforms that had two basic objectives: to reinforce the conjugal family and to eliminate local customary codes. For al-Fasi, the first step required in making reforms was not to improve the status of women, because such improvement, he thought, could not be done apart from a concomitant change in kinship organization. What Morocco needed first and foremost, he contended, was a new conception of the kinship unit, of who constituted it, and of the roles within it. He also believed that only new laws could help bring about the desired changes in the kinship structure.

After independence was achieved in 1956, the matter of family law became pressing. In the Maghrib in general, when political turmoil increased, concern for family law increased concomitantly. Following this pattern, as political events intensified in the 1950s in Morocco, so did discussions of family law. Two newspapers, *l'Istiqlal*, the publication of the party of the same name, and *Démocratie*, that of the Democratic Party for Independence, published several articles on the condition of women, stating the need to make judicial reforms to improve it.[54] The articles criticized the institutions of the veil, child marriage, and repudiation. *Démocratie* took an even more forceful line that did *l'Istiqlal*. The movement in support of liberal reforms produced a conservative reaction. Religious scholars and other defenders of Islam argued that Islam had already liberated women and that Islamic family law, as the cynosure of religious values, could not be changed. Political and public figures in Morocco thus were divided, as some wanted reforms whereas others reasserted the immutability of Islamic law.

Codification of Islamic Family Law (1950s)

The Moroccan monarchy brought the issue of family law to a close by making a decisive move. In response to the diverse opinions, the king took a conservative stand in choosing to do no more than unify the law of the country by codifying Islamic law. In March 1956, the king started by appointing an advisory commission to examine the feasibility of abolishing codes of customary law, which were widely perceived as having no place in a unified nation. Although heavily criticized for granting legitimacy to Berber customary law and councils, the Berber decree of 1930 had never been abrogated. Other customary codes were also still in effect. In August 1956, the Ministry of Justice, acting on a recommendation of the commission, declared the Berber decree of 1930 null and void. All local areas in Morocco were to be placed under Islamic jurisdiction, qaids, and regional courts of appeal. With the abolition of customary codes, the first step had been taken toward equipping Morocco with a unified, nation-wide family law.[55] The extent to which the family law of independent Morocco would remain faithful to the original texts of the Shari'a still had to be addressed, however.

In August 1957, the king declared the necessity to formulate clearly the regulations of Islamic law on matters of the family and inheritance. He appointed another special commission to undertake the task of codification. At the opening meeting of the commission, the king stated: "What is missing from our glorious heritage is finally to appear in its true light, free from sterile commentaries and abhorrent customs . . . there is need for a structured text with clearly organized articles."[56] The crown prince and the Minister of Justice reiterated the mandate of the commission: to clarify the legal regulations of Moroccan family law by organizing them in a structured text and to ground them in Islamic principles.

The commission was composed of two of the king's ministers, al-Fasi, five high officials of Islamic courts, one of the king's legal advisors, and a member of the consultative assembly. The Minister of Justice was in charge of proposing to the commission a draft reform that would serve as the basis for discussion. Al-Fasi served as rapporteur and, in that capacity, was invited to make remarks on the draft. The ultimate responsibility for the work of the commission lay with the Minister of Justice, who would submit reports to the king. No text became final and integrated into the new Moroccan family code without having received the king's approval. In this role, the king maintained his position as arbiter among potentially contending forces. He also retained ultimate authority over the content of the legal text. The composition of the commission, the procedures for approval of its work, and the nature of its mandate indicated from the start the likely conservatism of its resolutions.

The Moroccan Code of Personal Status, called the *Mudawwana*, first appeared in parts, as a series of decrees between November 1957 and March 1958.[57] It was later supplemented by legal acts and decisions of the Moroccan Supreme Court and Ministry of Justice. The set of legal regulations put in effect in Morocco was essentially what the king had indicated in his opening speech, a codification of Islamic law. It retained the prescriptions of Maliki law that had historically predominated in the Maghrib. The substance of the Mudawwana promulgated in the late 1950s was quite similar to Islamic family law as described in chapter 2. In this codification, the reforms envisioned earlier by members of the urban-based Istiqlal were absent. Instead, the kinship model of tribal collectivities was institutionalized in the family law of the newly independent Moroccan state and women's legal status remained unchanged. The following analysis centers on the content of the law as it appeared in the decrees of the late 1950s, the period when Morocco equipped itself with a national family law, following independence in 1956.[58]

Marriage. The first article of the Mudawwana defined marriage as a pact between a man and a woman, with the purpose of creating a family, under the husband's guidance. The role differences between husband and wife thus were made clear at the outset. The Mudawwana reaffirmed the expression of the spouses' consent in the presence of two witnesses and the payment of a bride price as the only two conditions necessary to make a marriage valid. As in Maliki law, however, the woman did not express her verbal consent to marriage directly and her presence at the marriage contract was not required. Instead, consent to the marriage had to be expressed by her matrimonial guardian, who should be a man. Moroccan law thereby retained the symbolism of Maliki law, in that it too defined marriage as a matter between the male representatives of two families.

The text specified that the matrimonial guardian had no constraining power over the woman, that is, he had no legal right to force her into marriage, except in case of bad conduct on the part of the woman. Left undefined in the text of the law, bad conduct should be understood in this context as sexual transgression such as loss of virginity. In this case, the matter had to be brought to the attention of a judge who would then decide whether the woman should be given in marriage against her will. The clause restricting the guardian's right of constraining power was the only change from Maliki law.[59] This restrictive clause could not, however, have its full effect as long as a woman had to be represented by a guardian during the marriage contract and did not even have to attend the signing of her own marriage contract.

A minimum age was required for marriage, eighteen for a man and fifteen for a woman, although an age exemption could be requested from a judge who was empowered to decide whether the case warranted it.[60] The minimum age for marriage, albeit low, nevertheless was a departure from Maliki law, which stipulated that marriages could be consummated once puberty had been reached. Moroccan law also set an age for legal majority, twenty-one for both males and females. Legal majority did not, however, free a woman from the requirement that a matrimonial guardian should contract the marriage in her name. The Moroccan code promulgated in the late 1950s also stipulated that the marriage of a Moroccan Muslim woman with a non-Muslim was "forbidden" and had no validity before the law.[61]

Rights and Responsibilities of Each Spouse. In this area too, the Mudawwana reiterated the prescriptions of Maliki law. It stated the obligation of the husband to support his wife, to authorize her to visit her relatives, and to leave her free to manage her own assets. Note that the woman's right to visit her own relatives was not taken for granted, but mentioned explicitly as an activity for which the husband had to give his authorization. As for the wife, she was expected, among other things, to keep her virtue, obey her husband, take good care of the household, and "honor" her husband's father, mother, and other close relatives.[62] The wife owed deference to the husband's relatives, whereas she had to have her husband's permission to see hers. This constituted one more instance of the conception of the family presented in the Mudawwana, a conception that retained the predominance of the agnatic line prevalent in Maliki law.

Civil Records and Registration of Marriage. In family law in general, the civil registration of marriage is a critical issue, because it represents a condition sine qua non for the application of other laws regulating family matters. When the law makes marriage a private act, as Maliki law does, administrative and judicial authorities are denied the possibility of enforcing other aspects of family law. The Mudawwana initially contained a clause that set conditions tantamount to registration. The clause was rescinded, however, in a subsequent law that made registration voluntary. The code first required a document called "an act of marriage," which had to be signed by two witnesses and had to show the identity of the spouses and that of the woman's matrimonial guardian.

This document was to be handed to the office of civil registry. Furthermore, in order to assure compliance with the law on the minimum age for marriage, the spouses were to deliver in person a birth certificate to the office of civil registry. Since the marriage contract was not attended by any civil or religious authority, it could very well happen that the person about to get married and the owner of the birth certificate would in reality be two different individuals. Hence, the requirement of the spouses to appear in person so that authorities could confirm the authenticity of the certificate. The woman was expected to unveil her face and be seen by the official.

Two sources of difficulty arose in the implementation of these provisions. First, the limited resources of the administrative apparatus in general, and the inadequacy of civil records in particular, hindered the preparation and recording of the act of marriage. Second, the social norms of proper behavior for women proved an insurmountable obstacle. Families did not want their daughters to be seen by a stranger or to travel the often long distance to the nearest administrative office. In March 1962, a decision of the Supreme Court suppressed the requirement of both marriage and birth certificates. It declared that judges and the courts were to accept all proofs of marriage, including verbal statements. The ruling went further. It voided the requirement that a birth certificate be deposited with the office of civil registry to validate a marriage contract. The requirement that a woman come in person to the local office of civil registry was also removed. In the absence of the woman, the verbal testimony of two relatives of hers was declared sufficient to establish her identity. The two relatives could be chosen by the woman's family and not necessarily by herself.[63]

Under these conditions—no birth certificate, no proof of marriage other than the declaration of two relatives, and no marriage certificate—the possibility of false declarations was considerably increased. In retaining the matrimonial guardian and in preventing the bride from expressing directly her consent to marriage, Moroccan family law made changes in practice unlikely. The possibility of child and compulsory marriages remained quite strong. Noting the lack of preventive measures against the marriage of minors in the family law promulgated after independence in Morocco, Borrmans writes that "the marriage of minors has not yet disappeared from Morocco and for good reasons."[64]

Divorce and Repudiation. The Mudawwana, like Maliki law, gave a man the privilege to divorce his wife simply by uttering the repudiation formula, and without any court intervention, thus leaving repudiation as a private matter. The only difference from before was that now repudiation had be observed by two witnesses who had to record it in writing after they heard the husband utter the repudiation formula. The written document became the property of the woman who could then use it as proof that she had been repudiated. Note that this was not a legal document established by judicial authorities, but simply a statement by two witnesses that the repudiation had in fact taken place. The new code also required the husband to give his repudiated wife a compensation commensurate with his means. The procedures for divorce remained very similar to what they were in Maliki law.[65] In the Moroccan code of newly independent Morocco, the prerogative of the husband to terminate the marriage at will remained unchanged, thus making the termination of marriage as easy as under Maliki law.

Polygamy. Polygamy remained legally permissible. Faithful to the Shari'a on this point as well, the Mudawwana reiterated, almost word for word, the same subjective restriction: "If one fears injustice among the spouses, then polygamy is not allowed."[66] A few minimal changes were made, as the Mudawwana gave the woman a right of option at the time of marriage. A bride could ask her husband to commit himself not to take a second wife and have this agreement recorded in the marriage contract. If the husband broke the agreement and took a second wife nevertheless, the first wife could bring the matter to a judge and ask him to evaluate the prejudice caused to her. The code was silent, however, as to what the judge should do in this case. The text did *not* state that the husband should be prevented from taking a second wife and the husband presumably could still opt to do so. Nor was it clear what accommodation should be made for the first wife, whose only choices were either to stay in a polygamous marriage or to ask for divorce.

The code also stipulated that the wives other than the first should be informed that their husband was already married. Since the Mudawwana allowed marriages to be contracted in the absence of official authorities, however, its prescriptions on polygamy should be seen as recommendations rather than legal requirements. The Mudawwana in effect kept polygamy as an option for men. It only opened up the possibility of legal recourse for women who took the precaution of including a restrictive clause in their marriage contract and who were willing to bring the matter to a judge's attention.

Filiation. There were no changes in filiation, as the Mudawwana reasserted the importance of paternal filiation. It defined legal filiation as that "by which a child becomes part of the nasab of his father."[67] The term *nasab* refers to the agnatic lineage, the line of male ancestors on the paternal side. The inclusion of this definition of filiation in the code highlights the extent to which Moroccan family law emphasized the patrilineage in its conception of the family. Commenting on the Moroccan code, J. Lapanne-Joinville remarked: "[The Moroccan family], in the legal sense of the term, is constituted by agnatic relatives . . . and among these, men enjoy a privileged position."[68]

Inheritance. On inheritance too, the Mudawwana remained faithful to Maliki law. It kept the same rigid rules, the same conditions on wills, the same principles for the identification of heirs, the same specification of shares, and the same inequality between shares of men and women. The Mudawwana required a will to be ascertained by two notaries and signed by its author in order for it to be valid. Revealing the difficulty of the Moroccan administration in controlling the registration of civil matters, however, the same article of the code relaxed the conditions for the validity of a will. If, for acceptable reasons, the will could not be established before two notaries, but only in the presence of witnesses, it was still valid. It could also be expressed verbally and did not necessarily have to exist in writing.

Maintaining the inequality between men and women, the code stated that "the share received by a man [was] twice as large as that received by a woman."[69] Like the Shari'a, the Mudawwana defined strictly the various categories of heirs and granted special inheritance privileges to male relatives in the paternal line.[70] It is noteworthy that al-Fasi, the rapporteur of the preparatory commission and leader of the Istiqlal, had suggested including uterine relatives among the individuals called to inherit under certain circumstances. His suggestion was not retained in the text of the Mudawwana, however. Such a measure would have been contrary to the dominant philosophy of maintaining the primacy of the agnatic line in all matters, especially in inheritance. Regulations on inheritance represent the most immutable part of Islamic family law. Given the general concern of Moroccan legislators for faithfulness to the Shari'a and for the protection of the extended patrilineal kin group, inheritance laws were the least likely to be modified.

· · ·

In summary, the Moroccan code kept the basic principles of Maliki law. It brought some slight changes on a number of specific points, such as the conditions for polygamy, the minimum age for marriage, and the right of paternal constraining power. Overall, however, the Mudawwana was little more than a codification of Islamic law of the Maliki school that prevailed in Morocco. Not only did the Mudawwana closely follow Maliki law, it actually identified the doctrine of Malik as the authoritative source to turn to in case of ambiguity or uncertainty. If the solution to a legal question did not appear in the text of the Mudawwana, one was advised to consult the writings of Malik to find an appropriate answer, writings that originated in the eighth century.[71] As A. Colomer notes, the codification of family law embedded in the Mudawwana represented a "triumph of the conceptions of Malik."[72] The family law of newly independent Morocco thus should be read as the triumph of a conception of the family as an extended patrilineage held together by ties of solidarity among agnates. It also should be read as the continuation of the legal subordination of women to men. This was the conception of kinship that predominated especially in rural areas, where the monarchy had found valuable allies and strong political support at the eve and in the aftermath of independence.

Legal victory was achieved not through any direct action on the part of the tribes, but as the choice of a strong monarchy that preferred to maintain the status quo in family law. The family law of newly independent Morocco was a signal to notables in rural areas that the monarchy chose a law that conformed to the vision of the world held by the population of those areas. It also showed the determination of the monarchy to safeguard kin-based social solidarities. In actively preserving a family law that sanctioned patrilineages, the monarchy avoided disturbing the tribal order of Moroccan society and nurtured its alliance with that order.

8 Elite Divisions and the Law in Gridlock
Algeria

In Algeria, the nationalist struggle culminated with the formation of a national state characterized by extensive factionalism. Engaged in an eight-year guerrilla war and lacking channels of internal communication, the nationalist movement experienced serious division. Cleavages developed mainly on the basis of regional differences and different war experiences during the decentralized guerrilla war of national liberation. Cleavages refer here to sharp divisions or splits among political groups with different social bases of power and with a tendency to engage intermittently in open conflict. Kept in check during the anticolonial struggle, the factionalism within the nationalist leadership erupted into violent conflicts after the achievement of national sovereignty in 1962.

Kin-based forms of association, which had provided Algerians with a refuge from colonial domination, remained politically significant as networks for mobilization during the nationalist war. After independence, kin-based forms of association served as a basis of support for some of the factions vying for power in the new national state. With respect to Algeria in this period, I use the term "kin-based forms of association" to indicate groupings more loosely structured than tribes. Multiple factions had ties to social groups within which they could mobilize kin-based solidarities to acquire more political leverage in the national state. Several segments of the leadership had vested interests in preserving these solidarities or at least in avoiding policies that might disrupt them.

Family law was held hostage to the political tensions generated by factionalism. The adoption of a family law in effect became one of the thorniest policy issues in the new state. The issue raised fundamental questions about the kind of society that newly independent Algeria would become. Like Morocco, Algeria adopted a highly conservative family law, but it did so through a different process. First, it took Algeria twenty-two years of hesitation and oscillation before it finally adopted its Family Code in 1984, whereas Morocco and Tunisia each adopted theirs a few months after independence. Second, shifting political alliances and factional conflicts that occurred after independence in Algeria continued to have a major influence on developments in family law, or on the lack thereof, since the result was a gridlock and a series of aborted plans for more than two decades. No faction was confident or powerful enough to institutionalize its vision of family law in a new code.

Third, by the time Algeria equipped itself with a family law, the wave of Islamic fundamentalism of the early 1980s created a political climate different from that of the 1950s when Morocco and Tunisia promulgated their family law. Fourth, in contrast to Morocco and Tunisia, conflicts directly centered on family law took place in Algeria when, in 1981, women actively opposed a government plan to codify the law in conservative terms. Women's resistance succeeded in stalling the plan for a while. But it failed to prevent the final adoption of a conservative family law, as embodied in the Algerian Family Code of 1984. The Algerian Family Code, like the Moroccan *Mudawwana* enacted in the mid-1950s, sanctioned a model of the family as an extended patrilineage in which male kin have privileges and men have power over women.

This chapter discusses the forces that led to such an outcome. It traces the role of kin-based forms of association in politics from the anticolonial war to the emergence of the new state and shows how they shaped elite factionalism. The chapter then examines the development of conflicts and alliances that, after keeping the law in prolonged gridlock, led to the adoption of a conservative family code. The influence of the rising forces of Islamic fundamentalism in the 1980s is considered.

PARTIAL RELIANCE ON KIN-BASED GROUPS (1950s–60s)

As in Morocco, the relationship of kin-based solidarities to the state at the time of independence in Algeria was in part the outcome of the politics of the nationalist struggle. French colonial rule had broken most large tribal confederations in Algeria. It had failed to destroy smaller kin-based forms of association, however, such as tribal factions, kin groupings, and extended patrilineages. The leadership of the nationalist coalition, the Front of National Liberation (called FLN, its French acronym), had an ambivalent relationship to kin-based solidarities. During the war, the nationalist leadership sometimes encouraged these forms of associations, which offered valuable organizational networks for the anticolonial struggle in local areas. At other times, it was forced to compromise with them, even though it might have been easier to proceed without them. Kin-based forms of association, anchored as they were in local areas, made coordination across regions difficult. At independence, the newly formed national state had little choice but to accommodate these forms of association in the polity of sovereign Algeria. It used an ambivalent carrot-and-stick strategy toward them, combining tolerance, special favors, and direct attacks.

Local Solidarities in the Anticolonial War

The Algerian war of national liberation was, with the Vietnam War, one of the most violent struggles of decolonization in the twentieth century. Lasting from 1954 to 1962, the war killed between 1 million and 1.5 million Algerians out of a population of 9 million.[1] It displaced entire villages and left 2 million Algerians confined to war camps. It required the prolonged intervention of the French army, one of the most powerful and modern armies engaged in a colonial war. Charles Gallagher comments that ten years after the end of colonial rule, Algeria still appeared in a state of shock from the devastation of the war.[2] The magnitude of the war affected the colonial power as well, as the Algerian war brought down the French Fourth Republic and ushered in the Fifth Republic, spearheaded by Charles de Gaulle, who forced France to confront the reality of the Algerian crisis.

The French held on to Algeria to the bitter end because Algeria represented higher stakes for France than did any of its other colonies. The French slogan according to which "Algeria was France" carried the meaning that separation was unthinkable and that Algeria should be considered an extension of the French national territory.[3] Algeria was a colony of settlement with about 1 million French people on its soil. The discovery of oil in the Sahara desert and the expected usefulness of the desert expanse for the nascent nuclear experiments further strengthened French determination to maintain its presence in Algeria. Fearing the coming of defeat in Indochina (defeat came in 1954) and facing multiple nationalist struggles at once in its colonies in the 1950s, France concentrated on retaining Algeria. As it negotiated the end of colonial rule in Tunisia and Morocco in the mid-1950s, France moved to strengthen its armed forces in Algeria in preparation for a long fight.

To understand the process of national liberation and state formation in Algeria, it is necessary to keep in mind that the process took place in a dispossessed, uprooted, disconcerted society that was fighting to regain a sense of itself in the face of sustained bloody repression. After the military might of the French army crushed active armed resistance by the 1880s, Algerians turned to passive resistance and continued to use it until the emergence of organized nationalism. With the patrilineage constituting a prime frame of reference in most of the countryside, popular resistance often expressed itself within the framework of kin-based associations, which provided a meaningful ground for mutual trust in the anticolonial fight.[4]

The geographically scattered and overwhelmingly rural population opposed the colonial administration by taking refuge in what Daho Djerbal refers to as the "counter-system of integration," represented by kinship, lineage, tribal, and village ties.[5] Algeria was a country with a heavily rural population at the beginning of the war of liberation. Estimates of the rural population at the time vary from 77 to 88 percent of the total.[6] The paradox of colonial domination in Algeria was that it often had the effect of strengthening kin-based solidarities in local areas, even though the French had made it a policy to destroy the tribes.[7] Dispossessed of their lands, language, and culture, Algerians reinforced kinship and community ties whenever possible, as a shield against the intrusion of the colonial state. For example, "occult-*jamaas*" operated alongside the colonial state. These were tribal assemblies that regulated the affairs of a community behind the backs of French administrators, often agreeing on ways to circumvent French directives.[8]

The reinforcement of kin-based forms of association in many local areas had two salient implications. The forms of association survived through the nationalist period, and they proved useful to the nationalist cause. Lineage ties were instrumental in offering organization at the local level and supplying guerrilla fighters with the necessary support. Speaking about village leaders, who often represented entire lineages, T. Bouderbala, a FLN militant said, for example: "The village leaders were those who took charge of . . . intelligence, locating medication and other goods necessary to the units of the Army of National Liberation."[9] In rural areas, although individuals occasionally embraced the quest for national liberation on their own, communities usually joined the nationalist movement en masse. In the latter case, local ties came into play, with families, clans, tribes, and entire villages joining as a group.[10]

Although local communities could respond to the nationalist call, they could not, by themselves, generate organized nationalism. They lacked the necessary channels of communication across regions. It must be remembered that Algeria was a nation in the making when it was overtaken by colonization in 1830, a time when there was no nation-state coinciding with the current national territory of Algeria. Furthermore, the French had a monopoly over channels of communication within Algeria from the 1830s onward. They used the monopoly to prevent communication among Algerians in different regions, in an effort to stifle sentiments of national unity. For example, Algerians in rural areas had to request an authorization from local colonial authorities before they could leave their locality.

Many Algerians in the countryside found meaning in their local area or region, with its network of immediately perceptible ties. Beyond that, the notion of an Algerian national entity, which would cover unknown lands, remained nebulous. In a famous remark, Ferhat Abbas, one of the future nationalist leaders, said in 1936: "I have interrogated history; I have interrogated the living and the dead; I have visited cemeteries. No one spoke to me of the Algerian nation."[11] A sense of Algerian unity had emerged nevertheless from the experience of segregation between French and Algerians. It often was grounded in religion, in that Algerians thought of themselves as united by Islam, in opposition to the Christian colonizers, who in turn defined the colonized in religious terms as the Muslims.[12] But the sense of religious unity did not (and could not under the colonial yoke) translate into a nation.

It was the armed struggle itself that acted as the catalyst for the crystallization of national identity. Forming a coalition in the early 1950s and constituting the FLN, leaders of several previously separate nationalist groups who had so far voiced nationalist demands mostly peacefully and abroad decided to launch the armed struggle on Algerian territory. On 1 November 1954, several bombs exploded at the same time in many parts of Algeria. The FLN claimed responsibility for all the explosions, which marked the beginning of the war of national liberation. One of the leaders who launched the armed struggle explained that they had two choices: "organize first and attack later or attack first and organize later. . . . We were forced to choose the second solution, that is to fire first in order to create a favorable psychological climate for the national population to support completely the revolution."[13] They chose well. As the bombs exploded in November 1954, so did a collective cry for liberation and national solidarity. Many Algerians responded by joining the FLN and creating networks of support for it, thus forging a sense of national unity in the very act of taking up arms against the French.

The FLN proved to be a remarkable force in the anticolonial war. It effectively organized resistance by mobilizing tribal and village assemblies in Algeria and by infusing them with an actively militant ethos. Although it channeled energies into national liberation, the FLN did not replace the local assemblies with a new organizational structure; nor was it likely that it could have done so. Operating in a context of regional and local diversity and in a vast territory under colonial vigilance, FLN leaders faced enormous practical obstacles to coordinated action and centralized decision making. They had to show flexibility and to respect regional and local diversity, which they did. They paid a price for it, however, as cleavages developed within the nationalist coalition.

A Nationalist Coalition with a Heterogeneous Leadership

The flexibility and internal diversity of the FLN were its strength, for these characteristics accounted for its effectiveness in the decentralized guerrilla warfare against the powerful French army. At the same time, however, the characteristics accounted for a lack of organizational unity, as the requirements of the decentralized guerrilla warfare gave rise to separate hierarchies of command in different parts of the territory. For reasons of military strategy, the FLN divided the Algerian territory into regional centers of command, or *wilayas* (shown on Map 9). Quasi-autonomous guerrilla units appeared within nationalist forces. This resulted in the emergence of relatively isolated decision-making centers in the wilayas, each with a potential claim to legitimacy in the future sovereign state.

The characteristics of the leadership reflected the social and organizational context of the Algerian nationalist movement. Terms such as cleavages, heterogeneity, divisions, factionalism, clans, and sectarianism have been fittingly used to describe Algerian nationalism.[14] The leaders who moved to the forefront of nationalist politics between the 1920s and 1950s came from different geographic areas, had different war experiences, different bases of support, and different visions of future Algeria. Furthermore, colonial repression against emerging individual leaders, coupled with internal dissension, caused at times a vertiginous turnover in the nationalist leadership. Like other nationalist movements, the FLN placed collective commitment to national liberation over conflicting aspirations for the future state. A coalition of forces, the FLN was exactly what its name indicated: a front defined by the objective of national liberation. Shared commitment to free Algeria from colonial rule held the nationalist leadership together throughout the war. Beyond the shared commitment, the many differences that existed within the Algerian nationalist leadership constituted potential sources of dissension.

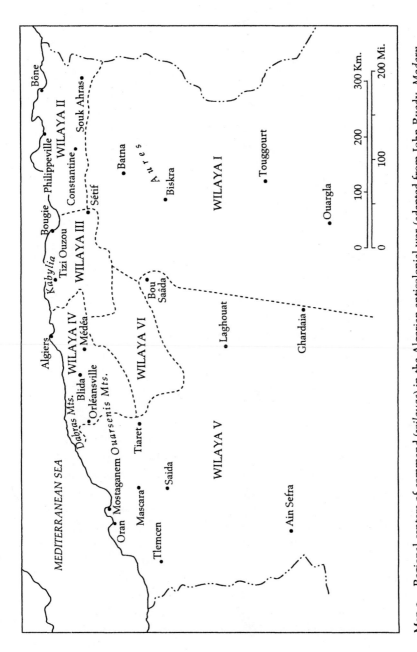

Map 9. Regional centers of command (*wilayas*) in the Algerian anticolonial war (adapted from John Ruedy, *Modern Algeria: The Origins and Development of a Nation*. Bloomington and Indianapolis: Indiana University Press, 1992, 159).

As elsewhere, the achievement of national sovereignty brought about conflicts over access to power and over policies. In contrast to Morocco, where the monarchy got the upper hand, and to Tunisia, where a victorious reformist faction finally emerged as a cohesive elite, cleavages produced a heterogeneous elite in Algeria. Some of them found their roots in the segmentation of Algerian society, and particularly in the persistence of local solidarities in politics. Others were of an ideological nature. Conflicts arose, for example, in regard to the mode of economic planning among proponents of a decentralized, "self-management" approach to economic development and those who preferred a centralized form of state capitalism. Other conflicts separated some of the Marxist nationalists and religious groups who had maintained a strong influence in Algeria. Carl Brown comments: "The Muslim reformers were of greatest importance and maintained their separate identity longest in Algeria."[15] In a similar vein, Gallagher remarks that phrases such as "a specifically Algerian socialism" expressed "a continuing undercover struggle between elements influenced by secular, Marxist principles and others who would have Algeria give primacy to Islamic values."[16]

Partly because of the decentralized guerrilla war and the ensuing divisions, the FLN never developed a centralized organizational web that would cover most of the country. As a result, the Algerian leadership found only a bare skeleton of organizational structure on which to graft the administrative authority of the national state at independence in 1962. After independence, it was the army that gradually emerged as the most powerful institution, with the strongest esprit de corps and the most effective organization. During the war, one of the nationalist forces had had the task of attacking the French army in Algeria from positions on the Tunisian and Moroccan frontiers. Called the Army of the Frontiers, it represented the largest, best organized, and best equipped single force among the Algerian fighters. After some purges and new alliances, the Army of the Frontiers later became the national army, which eventually gained the upper hand over civil political leaders, local particularisms, and regional pockets of power represented by the regional military commands of the guerrilla war.[17]

Contenders to state authority at independence wanted to gain more leverage in the newly formed political center, altogether replace the regime in place, or obtain more resources for a particular region. Challenges to state power came from heads of regional guerrilla commands (the wilayas) who felt overlooked in the distribution of power at independence. They also came from political leaders who mobilized support in local areas for the policies that they advocated in national politics. Giving rise to local and regional uprisings, the challenges showed that political leaders could activate local solidarities in their quest for power in the new state.

Mobilization of Local/Regional Solidarities in the New State

Local and regional uprisings reactivated particularistic ties after independence, although they did not necessarily aim at defending particularism. Serious uprisings erupted in the countryside in the 1960s, especially in Berber areas. In part because mountainous Berber retreats had constituted an asset in the fight against the French army, Berbers had been prominent in the guerrilla forces and had produced many well-known leaders of regional commands. After independence, some guerrilla forces and regional leaders fought the newly formed national army, while others joined forces with it. Never unified in a coordinated movement against the army or the state, Berber uprisings occurred instead in different regions at different times. Estimates on the percentage of Berbers in the Algerian population vary from more than 20 to 25 and 30 percent.[18] Regions that felt neglected by the state rose in protest to demand what they saw as their fair share of benefits from independence. Leaders who felt excluded from national politics rebelled to demand what they saw as their fair share of influence in the new polity.

Two Berber areas, the Aures and Kabylia, experienced uprisings that illustrate how political or regional guerrilla leaders mobilized kin-based solidarities after independence. Both areas had contributed substantially to the guerrilla warfare. The Aures was one of the poorest and most neglected regions of the country. Oriented toward the desert, its pastoral economy provided only minimal subsistence. People of the Aures had a long history of maintaining the cohesiveness of the kin group as a resource against extreme economic insecurity. This was because it took the labor of several members of a kin group within a single household to avoid poverty. Contrary to their expectations, small farmers of the Aures felt that they benefited little from independence and found insufficient the economic relief provided by the state. They organized rebellions. Some of the rebellions provided backing for one of the former leaders of a regional command, Colonel Zbiri, who disagreed with other members of the leadership over economic policy and wanted to gain more influence in the government. Appealing to solidarities in the Aures, his area of origin and his only base for support, Colonel Zbiri attempted a coup in 1967. The government defeated him with military force.[19]

The insurrections in the Aures took a traditional form. Jeanne Favret notes that people in the Aures were "trying to make the central government take notice of them the only way they [knew]."[20] And the only way they knew was through tribally based rebellions. They came together in protest as members of kin groupings through the reactivation of segmentary organization. As in Morocco, the meaning of the uprisings was different from that of tribal rebellions in earlier times. The goal was no longer to escape the control of the state. This time, people in the Aures rebelled to attract the attention of the state, protest its incapacity to provide the advantages expected from independence, and demand its greater intervention in the local economy. Favret states the main reason for the insurrection in the Aures as follows: "What [stirred] up rebellions [was] not so much the fear of being overrun by big-city ways as the fear of not being sufficiently overrun. The peasants [didn't] mind the state's being in charge of all economic activity; they [resented] its failure to be the driving force of the local economy."[21] As for the leader of the rebellion, Colonel Zbiri, he wanted to gain more power within the state.

Kabylia, another Berber region that experienced postindependence uprisings, offered an example of a segment of the national elite with ties to a region where kin-based solidarities had remained strong. Like the Aures, Kabylia made a major contribution to the war effort. It differed from the Aures, however, in that it had more connections to the political center. Kabyles were heavily represented in the Algerian political, administrative, business, and intellectual community. As Favret notes, members of the Kabyle elite were more likely to quote Goethe than the customary law of the area.[22] There was a long history of interchange between Kabylia and the capital city of Algiers, where close to 20 percent of the population was of Kabyle origin.[23] While Kabyle protests covered a range of issues in the aftermath of independence, some of the most violent conflicts involved the mobilization of local forces by leaders contending for power in the newly formed national state and struggling to enforce their views of policy.

The writing of the constitution precipitated conflicts that show how struggles in national politics in Algiers intersected with local uprisings in Kabylia. The conflicts occurred a year after independence, when several members of the National Assembly felt that the head of government, Ben Bella, and his close allies were making all the decisions and excluding others from composing the text of the constitution. Some members of the assembly resigned in protest.[24] Another member, Aït Ahmed, withdrew to his native Kabylia and declared dissidence to oppose the government. His protest coincided with a growing tension between leaders of previously quasi-autonomous wilayas and the Army of the Frontiers. The issue was the projected merger of all armed forces into a single organization, the newly formed national army.

Fearing a loss of influence in the projected merger, several wilaya leaders joined the Kabyle rebellion and offered logistical support to Aït Ahmed, the Kabyle leader. For example, they gave him armed protection when he held political rallies in the open in Kabylia. In addition, peasants in Kabylia, like peasants in other regions, stood ready to express their discontent at the lack of economic relief provided by the government at independence. Responding to Aït Ahmed's mobilizing effort in his homeland, many peasants joined the rebellion. While the rebellion never involved all of Kabylia, it nevertheless gained enough momentum to last two years. It was finally brought to an end by negotiations and compromise.

Insurrections that occurred in Kabylia were taken seriously by the government, precisely because they were not just rural uprisings. Through kinship and local ties, the uprisings could be manipulated by Kabyles of the intellectual, political, and economic elites. The area offered, as Favret remarks, "a plethora of traditional elements [that could] be seized upon and used as part of the strategy of different social groups in their struggle for modernization."[25] In contrast to rebellions in the Aures, which could be settled by military intervention, insurrections in Kabylia posed a real threat to the stability of the government. The danger came from the fact that discontented Kabyles in the political center were in a position to mobilize local communities in Kabylia to foster rural unrest as a way to gain power in national politics.

State Strategy: Carrot and Stick

At independence in 1962, lineages, clans, and tribal assemblies existed in a variety of relationships to the national state in formation. In some cases, kin-based forms of association remained as the major frame of reference in rural areas, where the presence of the national state was peripheral to collective life. Writing in 1967, five years after independence, Favret notes this point about many areas of Algeria. She writes that "[f]amily structures [had] hardly changed at all during the past hundred years; the same alignments persisted, and the lineage was the individual's frame of reference."[26] In other cases, kin-based solidarities coexisted in various forms of cooperation with representatives of the party, army, and central administration. In others still, they came together to protest the policies of the state. In yet others, kin-based solidarities served as fuel in elite struggles within the political center, as they offered a potential base for mobilization to segments of the elite in the internally diverse coalition that took the reins of power in the sovereign state.

One of the tasks of the newly formed national state thus was to manage the internal diversity and divisions of Algerian society, as Algeria experienced a struggle to define a new mode of articulation between the local and the central or between kin-based communities and the central organs of the national state. The heterogeneous elite that came to power in 1962 faced the challenge of building a nation and a state, that is, to give substance to a collective belief in the Algerian nation and to develop a state apparatus. The war experience had offered little preparation for the challenge. Deeply divided, the coalition in power also lacked a nationwide unified organization. Operating under the protection of the army, the leadership leaned heavily on a rural base consisting of an impoverished peasantry and a rural petty bourgeoisie made up of local notables oriented to their own areas.[27]

The coalition in power responded with ambivalence to kin-based forms of association and tendencies of local particularism. Following a carrot-and-stick strategy, state officials combined condemnation and praise, as reflected in the political discourse. Major official texts condemned the quest for autonomy on the part of local kin-based communities. The Code of the Wilayas, the official text that regulated regional institutions, rejected notions of local autonomy in making explicit that there should be no "scattering of revolutionary power."[28] The government saw a threat in what Jean Leca appropriately summarizes as a "mosaic of multiple primordial solidarities."[29] Political leaders had learned from experience that the solidarities were a potential source of division among tribes, clans, Berbers, and Arabs, as the solidarities had provoked regional conflicts within the FLN and continued to do so in the newly formed national state.

The fundamental texts of the postindependence Algerian government stated that Algeria needed a strong state to protect the society against its potential divisions. The state was repeatedly labeled as "the guarantor of unity" and "the maker of national integration," the institution best able to overcome divisions and reveal Algeria to itself.[30] The issue remained salient for a long time, as indicated in the 1976 Algerian National Charter, which stated: "The Revolution aims not only to eliminate all these relics (tribal, patriarchal and quasi-feudal structures), but also to prevent their return. Basically, it is a matter of making Algerians conscious citizens of a modern nation."[31] Criticizing the "feudal ethic," another statement called for the eradication of the "archaic, outdated and reactionary."[32]

Yet, at the same time that its texts called for their eradication, the Algerian state that emerged with national independence integrated kin-based forms of association into the political and administrative systems of the country. The state drew its legitimacy in part from rural areas, where such forms had predominated. Having taken the brunt of the anticolonial guerrilla warfare, rural areas deserved—and received—the titles of "torch bearers of the revolution" and "invulnerable fortress" of Algerian identity.[33] The leadership itself included members who drew power from their ability to mobilize supporters by activating local and regional ties. This applied not only to leaders of Berber origin, but to their Arab colleagues as well. Furthermore, the extreme shortage of trained civil servants in the aftermath of independence made it expedient for the new state to maintain kin-based forms of association as providers of law and order in local areas. The war had left newly sovereign Algeria with virtually no administrators. French administrators had departed en masse and the leaders of the new state soon expelled the majority of Algerian notables who had been co-opted by the colonial administration. A new administration had to be created and staffed, and this had to be done with scarce resources.

Where rural institutions such as tribal assemblies had persisted as functioning bodies orchestrating collective life, they were integrated into the new administrative structure, while being carefully monitored. The central government monitored tribal assemblies in an effort to have them serve as channels for the policy decisions made by the political center rather than as independent decision makers in local areas. The paucity of administrative resources made such monitoring difficult, however, with the result that representatives of the central government often had little choice but to tolerate the retention of substantial autonomy on the part of kin-based forms of association.[34]

In the years following independence, the Algerian government attempted to weaken potential rivals who found support in local and regional solidarities. For example, the government fought the regional commands that had played a critical role in the war of liberation by either eliminating the guerrilla forces or co-opting their leaders within the ranks of the army or other government institutions. In a military coup that strengthened the power of the army in 1965, Colonel Boumedienne seized the opportunity to exclude recalcitrant guerrilla fighters from positions of authority.[35] The government also sought to minimize the potential danger of Kabyle opposition. It poured vast sums of money into Kabylia and avoided moves that might be politically explosive, such as exclusion of Berbers from government positions. Arabic-speaking members of the government were careful to include Berbers within the ranks of top officials. The first government after independence, under Ben Bella, included five Berbers out of nineteen ministers, while in the next government, headed by Boumedienne and the military, important positions were also given to Berbers—in proportion to the percentage of Berbers in the population at large, about 20 percent.[36] For instance, in the Council of the Revolution, the supreme authority of the Boumedienne government, five of the twenty-six members were Berbers.[37]

To be sure, one should not necessarily equate particularism with kinship/tribal affiliation, since particularism may arise on a variety of bases other than kinship or tribe, as has been the case with ethnic nationalism, for example.[38] In the Maghrib in general in the 1950s and 1960s, however, and in the specific case of Berbers in Algeria in the nationalist struggle and the period of independence, the evidence points to the particular significance of kinship/tribal affiliations and their extension in politics, as several scholars such as Djerbal and Favret have indicated.[39] The evidence further suggests that there was no unified Berber, or even Kabyle, movement. Berbers were divided among several distinct communities that engaged in separate political actions and shared little other than the fact that their dialects had a common root.[40]

An important feature of postindependence politics in Algeria was that cleavages inherited from the anticolonial war continued while the national state was taking shape, whereas they were brought to an end in Tunisia and attenuated in Morocco in the equivalent time period. One consequence of the cleavages dividing the Algerian political elite was that contending political factions were prepared to use tribally based divisions in their contest for power in the modern state. As is evidenced by the military coup d'état of Boumedienne in 1965, only the army could keep conflicts in check. This in effect gave final power in Algeria to army officers in a context in which national unity remained threatened in the postindependence period.

Whereas the outcome of the nationalist struggle in Morocco placed power in the hands of a strengthened monarchy, which could then play the role of supreme arbitrator in Moroccan politics, the Algerian state was unable to ward off challenges. Nor did Algeria follow the Tunisian model where a relatively cohesive elite took control of party and state at independence, as the next chapter shows. There were too many divisions in Algerian nationalism, and they lasted beyond the nationalist struggle. Developments in Algeria resulted instead in the formation of a national state caught in the role of managing elite divisions and internal diversity. This could cause prolonged paralysis, as was the case with the policy on family law.

FAMILY LAW HELD HOSTAGE TO POLITICAL DIVISIONS (1950s–80s)

Family law was held hostage to politics during the anticolonial war and for two decades after independence in Algeria. A long and tortuous process of aborted reform plans and gridlock concluded with the adoption of the highly conservative Algerian Family Code of 1984. In comparing Algeria to Morocco and Tunisia, the more interesting issue concerns the process by which Algeria equipped itself with a conservative family law, rather than the content of the reforms, since the 1984 Algerian code is very similar in content to the Moroccan code of the 1950s (that has already been described in some detail). Focusing on political struggles surrounding family law, the analysis in this section covers the period from the nationalist war of the 1950s to the adoption of the Algerian Family Code in 1984.

As in the other two countries, nationalists in Algeria placed national liberation first during the anticolonial struggle. They postponed making decisions on family law until the decisions could be made in a sovereign state. The participation of women in the anticolonial guerrilla war raised hopes that women would gain legal rights after independence in 1962. The hopes went unfulfilled. Instead, divisions within the political leadership resulted in a gridlock on family law, a gridlock that lasted more than two decades, from the early 1960s to 1984. Several plans to equip Algeria with a national, unified family law aborted during that time period. In 1981 women organized grass roots resistance to one of the plans. Even though women's resistance played a role in stopping the conservative plan of 1981, it could not, in the end, prevent the enactment of a conservative family law, as embodied in the Algerian Family Code promulgated in 1984.

Family Law and Women in the Nationalist Struggle (1950s)

As in the rest of the Maghrib, both conservative and reformist trends were present in Algerian society in the nationalist period. The term "reformist" may be misleading and must be understood each time in its specific context because it was widely used in the period to apply to a range of sometimes opposite positions. From the 1920s throughout the 1950s, a group calling itself the "Reformists," yet holding conservative views, had consistently made two major demands: a return to the original sources of Islamic family law and total independence of the Islamic judicial system from any interference by the French.[41] Founded by Shaykh Ben Badis, the movement of the Reformists included religious scholars and members of the religious establishment who argued that, as the expression of Algerian authenticity, Islamic law should not only remain in effect but should also be made more faithful to its origins.

The Reformists protested moves made by the French colonial state to place the training of Islamic judges *(qadis)* under French control, which they saw as one more blow to the Islamic judicial system. That system already had received serious blows when some of the qadis' responsibilities had been transferred to French courts.[42] Calling for an end to French supervision over the training of qadis, the Reformists requested a judicial reorganization that would give Islamic courts full responsibility for the handling of all civil and penal matters. The Reformists also wanted to keep women's roles unchanged. They defended behavioral norms that they saw as part of the culture to be protected, such as the veil and the seclusion of women. They found a wide echo in Algeria, even among the educated. For example, Ali Merad describes in the following terms reactions to attempts to discuss changes in women's status at a meeting of Algerian teachers. He writes that "there were shouts and grumbles in the hall when attempts were made to raise the issue of the emancipation of women."[43] The Reformists wanted to remedy social problems that they attributed to the decline of social mores among Algerians, such as prostitution or the consumption of alcohol. They suggested that giving women a Muslim education based on the study of religious texts would help restore Algerian culture and fight the social ills that they associated with French influence.[44]

Opposing views were also expressed in Algeria from the 1920s to the 1950s as the manifestation of a trend in favor of the emancipation of women. The trend started in the 1920s primarily as the voice of a minority of French-educated young male professionals.[45] This small group was known as the Young Algerians, after the Young Turks and the Young Tunisians who argued for reforms in their respective countries in the same time period. The trend in favor of improvement in women's conditions continued to find intermittent expression through the 1950s. Although aware of the political implications of reform in a colonial situation, many argued that the status of Algerian women ought to be improved. Generally speaking, the pro-change movement did not make concrete recommendations for reform, but rather deplored the condition of women in Algerian society. For example, an observer wrote: "The veil that customs throw on the face as well as the mind of a young woman is like a gag that stifles her

. . . There are in Algeria millions of minds left uncultivated, prisoners of old customs."[46]

Denouncing compulsory and child marriages, members of the pro-change movement called for a new conception of the family in Algeria. A magazine, *République Algérienne*, launched a series of articles on the emancipation of women in the early 1950s. In the same period, a well-known woman writer, Djamila Débêche, organized conferences on the topic.[47] Committed to national liberation, supporters of change hoped that independence from French rule would bring with it greater freedom for women. They did not demand immediate reforms because they knew that the political situation was not yet appropriate. They also knew, however, that changes in the law were necessary to achieve changes in women's condition in the future.

During the war, some women played an active role in the network of resistance organized by the Front of National Liberation. The FLN expressed its gratitude for women's contribution to the war, as stated in one of its official texts: "We salute with emotion and admiration the courage of . . . our sisters who participate[d] actively, sometimes arms in hand, to the sacred struggle for the liberation of our fatherland."[48] Having interviewed women who participated in the war, Cherifa Bouatta indicates that women's roles in the war "ranged from the most spectacular to the most discreet."[49] A woman described what she did: "Sometimes, I carried weapons. Once, I gave a gun to a brother [i.e., an FLN militant] who had an action to carry out. He was wounded. I carried him through the city to our house. One of my brothers [i.e., her real brother] was still a baby at that time. When I had to carry documents through the city, I used to hide them under his push-chair."[50]

Women provided assistance to the men in combat and helped with intelligence, communication, provision of food, and care of guerrilla fighters' families.[51] Forging new roles and sometimes facing family opposition, some women went into the *maquis* (areas of guerrilla warfare). An inquiry into a catalogue of war veterans shows that among 10,949 women militants catalogued, the majority, 9,194 or 84 percent, were members of the Civil Organization of the Front of National Liberation. As such, women acted as liaison agents, collected medicines, and transported weapons. A minority of women, 1,755 or 16 percent, were involved in the armed force of the FLN, where most had responsibilities such as staffing the infirmaries, caring for the wounded, and sometimes serving as cooks.[52]

In risking their lives in the anticolonial war, women were fighting for nationalism and national liberation, not for their cause as women. They shared with the men the objective of ousting the French from Algeria. "We talked about getting the French out, that is all," commented one of the women interviewed by Bouatta.[53] In the same vein, Doria Cherifati-Merabtine notes the absence of a women's project in the nationalist struggle, despite the involvement of women in the war. She writes: "Indeed, at no time did women appear in the FLN discourse as a group who had made a claim concerning their status, on which a political position was required to be taken. In debates on the projects of society, there was no specific commitment regarding women."[54]

At the same time that it took women within its ranks, the FLN held on to images of women as guardians of Algerian culture and to conceptions of the kin group as a refuge from the destructive effects of colonial domination. When it came to family law, the FLN was cautious. Algerians experienced the family, which for most meant the patrilineage, as a refuge from colonialism. Furthermore, kin groupings provided the FLN with life-sustaining logistical support and mobilization networks. The FLN avoided any action that could alienate Algerians and tribal areas.

The FLN protested changes in family law introduced by the French colonial state. For example, its leaders disapproved of the law promulgated by the French in 1959, which, among other regulations, made the registration of marriages mandatory and set a minimum age for marriage at eighteen for a man and fifteen for a woman.[55] FLN spokesmen declared that the French had decided unilaterally to promulgate a law that attacked the essence of Islam.[56] It was an imposition of French law, they argued, in the most sacred domain—that of the family and personal status. The nationalists protested the move as one more French attempt to suppress Islamic law. In the political situation of the moment, and as long as Algeria was under colonial rule, the alternative of choice for the FLN was the retention of Islamic law in its entirety. Changes in family law were invariably perceived as the infiltration of French law into Islamic law. The FLN defined its overall position in a document outlining guidelines for its judicial committees: "We want to turn to Islamic law and take it as the basis for all prescriptions."[57] Following this principle, the document included a reference to the relevant section of the Qur'an next to each guideline, should clarification be needed.

While it offered guidelines on specific points, the FLN never spelled out a program on family law. It took position only on limited issues arising from the practical requirements of the war situation. For example, marriages took place in mountainous areas of guerrilla warfare under the control of the Front, where no Islamic or French courts were available. Committees of the Front often had to be created on the spot to take care of judicial matters, which they did on an ad hoc basis in different ways in different situations, as the conditions of the war made coordination difficult. Guerrilla war conditions, in which women sometimes were geographically separated from their families of origin, ironically led the Front to introduce modifications similar to those made by the French. For example, the Front asked its judicial committees to require that the bride attend the ceremony of her marriage contract and directly express her consent to the marriage. A rejection of the principle of the matrimonial guardian (who previously consented to marriage on behalf of the bride), this was a change from Islamic family law that had also been proposed by the French.[58]

In its *Programme de Tripoli*, published on the eve of independence and stating some of its plans for independent Algeria, the FLN expressed its intention to associate women with public life and with the development of the country. The necessity to improve women's legal conditions was also stated in the *Charte Nationale*, another central document outlining the FLN's program of action.[59] During the years of the war of independence, the position of the FLN was one of ambivalence. Desirability of reform and faithfulness to Islamic law were asserted at the same time. Leaders of the nationalist movement were well aware of the tensions surrounding family law and codes of personal status. Rather than confronting the tensions before seizing the reins of power, the FLN avoided taking a clear stand for the duration of the anticolonial struggle.

Hopes at the Time of Independence (1960s)

Hopes about reforms of family law and the expansion of women's rights were raised following independence in 1962, as a rhetoric of equality in socialist Algeria permeated a political discourse that included statements about women. The participation of women in the anticolonial guerrilla war had left many Algerians expecting changes once the war was over. The most urgent gender issue was the reform of Islamic family law and its implications for women's legal rights. Political speeches included references to women, mostly in relation to women's contribution to the anticolonial war. For example, the Minister of Justice declared in 1963: "The Algerian woman has, because of her effective contribution to the struggle for national liberation, earned her right to the city. The role of women is no longer a matter of debate."[60]

The FLN glorified the image of the *moudjahidates* (or female fighters, as the women were called who took part in the anticolonial guerrilla war).[61]

Peter Knauss, and Sophie Bessis and Souhayr Belhassen report how Djamila Bouhired, one of the famous moudjahidates, toured Arab countries
in 1963 as a folk heroine, sometimes being ranked among socialist figures
such as Mao Ze-dong and Fidel Castro.[62] A woman professor of biology at
the University of Algiers indicated the mood of the 1960s for women like
herself when she said: "In the 1960s we had the impression of living in a
secular state."[63] In 1964, then president Ben Bella made a strong statement
at a major FLN meeting. He declared: "The liberation of women is a problem the solution of which is preliminary to any kind of socialism."[64] Although political figures made statements about women, the statements
usually appeared in the context of the welfare of the country. Women's
issues, which had been subsumed to nationalism in the anticolonial war,
were now linked to socialism.

Following women's overriding commitment to nationalism and the absence of a specifically feminist discourse in the anticolonial struggle of the
1950s, there was no organized feminism in Algeria in the 1960s and 1970s.
Referring to 1962 and the aftermath of independence, Monique Gadant
remarks: "There was no feminist tradition, in the modern sense of the
term, no perception of women as women and as constituting a specific,
oppressed group."[65] Even the moudjahidates placed nation first and gender
second. They remained an informal group that included the numerous
political tendencies present in Algerian politics at the end of the anticolonial war. In the 1960s and 1970s, they did not come together in an
organization that could have taken as its agenda the defense of women's
rights. Reflecting more than her own position, Djamila Bouhired said in
an interview: "The young women of Algeria don't have time to discuss
the problems of sex right now. We are still in a struggle to make our new
country work, to rebuild the destroyed family, to preserve our identity as
a nation. In the future, perhaps we will arrive at a kind of life where men
and women relate on a more friendly basis. I hope so."[66]

Women who identified with left political tendencies shared a similar
position. For example, a small group of Algerian women (members of
immigrant families, mostly wives of male workers, a few women workers
themselves, and a few students, all associated with Algerian socialists in
Paris) met to discuss political issues. When they discussed women's issues,
they did so with reference to nation building and socialism. One of the
women explained: "Although 'marxists,' we hardly ever made the connection between Engels's thesis that we read and our present situation.
Without realizing it, we had internalized the orthodox form of thinking
about gender and the subordination of women's struggles to other strug-

gles."[67] Like the men, the women were debating the central issues of how to organize socialism in Algerian society. When they discussed women and the family, they focused on what was preoccupying the Algerian left at the time. They addressed mostly issues of the "patriarchal," "feudal" kinship structure that was prevalent in Algerian society, a structure that the left perceived as an obstacle to socialism and modern forms of social organization.[68]

Not only moudjahidates and Algerian women living in France, but most Algerian women placed nation first. Even illiterate women, who represented approximately 95 percent of the female population in 1962, were ready to make sacrifices for the Algerian nation.[69] The story of women donating their gold and silver jewelry—often a woman's dowry and only possession—to help build the Algerian nation is a poignant one. In 1963, President Ben Bella asked women to donate their gold and silver to help the National Bank of Algeria develop its reserves. Marnia Lazreg describes the response: "At televised public meetings throughout the country, women walked up to party leaders and gave them their eighteen carat gold chains (some of which were made of nineteenth-century coins), bracelets, anklets (some weighing half a pound), rings and earrings. How much gold and silver was collected is not known accurately."[70] As Algerians, men and women, took nation building and the development of the new country as the top priority at independence, issues of family law and women's rights were subordinated to other political agendas. The promises made by political leaders in the euphoria of independence went unfulfilled. Instead, family law quickly became caught in disagreements among conflicting tendencies and in struggles among forces competing for power in the new national state.

Conflicting Tendencies (1960s–84)

Although individual positions sometimes fluctuated over time depending on the political situation, it nevertheless was possible to identify a range of tendencies on family law within the FLN after independence. Segments of the post independence leadership (to which I refer in short as the progressive tendency) were interested in bringing about change in social organization, including kinship. This was particularly the case of a socialist tendency, which was powerful during the war, but lost some of its power in the factional politics of the FLN over time. At the other end of the spectrum were FLN leaders (part of what I refer to in short as the conservative tendency) supporting an association of Islamic scholars called *al-*

Qiyam (values) and committed to the preservation of Islamic law and Algerian traditions. There were many positions in between labeled secular Islam, Islamic socialism, moderate Islam, Islam with a secular bent, or socialism with an Islamic bent, with the leaders holding the positions shifting or modifying their discourse and actions at different times.

The progressive and conservative tendencies both had their roots in the FLN coalition of the war period and, as such, had a claim to legitimacy after the war. They both continued to have an impact on politics in independent Algeria. A socialist tendency had developed during the anticolonial war mostly among Algerian immigrant workers in France, where Algerians had formed the FFFLN or French Federation of the FLN. Alan Richards and John Waterbury indicate that 200,000 Algerians had found employment in the French metropolitan labor market in the mid-1950s.[71] In regular contact with socialists and communists in French trade unions, this immigrant population became the breeding ground of Algerian radicalism. Along with Algerian communists and socialists on Algerian soil, members of the FFFLN constituted the core of the Algerian left, or the progressive segment of the FLN.[72] Including many young Kabyles who belonged to the tiny minority that had received some degree of French (primary or secondary) education, the immigrant population in France had produced a number of spokesmen.[73] A major source of funds for the FLN throughout the war, the FFFLN had supported, for example, the FLN's provisional government abroad. As a provider of funds, the FFFLN had substantial political influence at the eve of independence.

For a while, the FFFLN went as far as advocating the separation of state and religion, although it quickly compromised on that issue, following pressures by Islamic scholars who attacked secularist positions in a public declaration on 22 August 1962.[74] Some of the FLN progressives called for a transformation of the family, which they perceived as a main cause of backwardness, even though they abandoned the idea of secularism. Reflecting the preoccupation of the FLN progressives with "archaic" versus "modern" institutions, the FLN fundamental texts on which the progressives had the most influence denounced "feudal" ideas and mores.[75] Some of the newspapers of the radical left promoted a new image of the family, one that devalued tradition and valued instead the couple and the nuclear family.[76] The newspapers offered a new vision of the family in future Algeria, a vision that gave place to the individual and the couple rather than extended kin groups.

Presidents and national organizations (which were all under the control of the FLN) at times reflected the preoccupations of the progressive tendency. They recognized and sometimes emphasized the desirability of promoting changes in the family structure. They spoke of ending what they saw as the harm caused by traditional kinship structures. The desirability of transforming kinship was a recurrent theme not only in the aftermath of independence, but also after the takeover by the military junta in 1965. For example, President Boumedienne, who headed the takeover of 1965, said in 1966: "We are in favor of progress. As such, we fight against the retrograde ideas that make women negotiable commodities."[77] The National Union of Algerian Women made a similar statement. Like other unions, the women's union was entirely under FLN control and its programs reflected the dominant position within the FLN at that moment. The program for action adopted by its first congress stated in 1966: "We must fight against . . . erroneous interpretations of Islam, traditional family structures. . . . [and help] put in place family structures adapted to the modern world, and a family code that conforms to our Algerian and Muslim personality as well as to the demands of the modern world."[78]

This view clashed with the conservative tendency, equally rooted in the past of the FLN and part of its outlook after independence. The Association al-Qiyam comprised mostly of *ulama*, continued to advocate for independent Algeria the position expressed by the nationalist Ben Badis in the 1930s, a position best captured in the following slogan: "Arabic is our language, Islam is our religion, Algeria is our fatherland."[79] The slogan had the advantage of differentiating Algerians from the French on the key dimensions of language, religion, and citizenship. It also served to unify otherwise separate particularistic groups and to bring them together in the nationalist struggle. The association had provided the guerrilla leadership with a useful ally during the war of national liberation, but had become too demanding for some after independence. Members of the top leadership of the FLN supported the association at times, while fighting against it at other times. For example, in 1964, the government charged the Association al-Qiyam to encourage the discussion of Islamic values. At the same time, however, its president was stripped of his post as general secretary of the university. The government banned the association in Algiers in September 1966 and then dissolved it altogether in March 1970, thus making it illegal in the entire Algerian territory.[80]

Among the many possible stands on Islam, the Association al-Qiyam on the whole emphasized Islam as tied to the concept of nation. This differed in tone from the pan-Islamic orientation prevalent in parts of the Middle East in the 1950s and 1960s, an orientation that focused instead on the concept of a transnational Islamic community enveloping individual nation-states. Members of the association insisted on the importance of recovering Algeria's specific history and culture after the loss experienced during colonization. Islam in this perspective became associated with the conservation of "specifically Algerian" forms of social organization, a theme on which the Association al-Qiyam campaigned relentlessly. The association aimed to preserve the family structure and family relationships that its members saw as part of the Algerian heritage.

The theme of preservation appeared in the political discourse of presidents and FLN-controlled national organizations. The Association al-Qiyam found enough of an echo—and enough political support from the FLN and the government—to be able to organize meetings of five thousand people in Algiers in the early 1960s.[81] One must assume that, among others, the position of the association resonated among guerrilla fighters who had played a critical role in the anticolonial war and were part of the FLN coalition. Many of the fighters were mountain and steppe people who had been deeply committed to nationalism. Richards and Waterbury describe them as pious Muslims, by no means doctrinaire socialists, suspicious of the intelligentsia, and "far less committed to a radical transformation of Algerian society."[82]

The different tendencies imbedded in the FLN sometimes clashed openly, sometimes resulted in compromises or policy fluctuations, and at other times provoked a gridlock that paralyzed policy making. The conflicts occurred overwhelmingly within the FLN and at times within the executive branch of government. When the FLN became the single party of Algeria two years after independence, in 1964, this created a situation in which political struggles took place almost exclusively within the party. Since they were under FLN control, unions and mass organizations had to conform to the orientation and fundamental texts of the FLN. In addition, one had to be a member of the FLN before one could belong to a union or mass organization. After the government that emerged from the Boumedienne military takeover in 1965 suspended the assembly indefinitely, Algeria was left without a national assembly from 1965 to 1976. In the absence of a parliament, the supreme authority in the country was the Council of the Algerian Revolution, which surrounded itself with secrecy.[83] As often is the case in situations of gridlock, there were many rumors but a paucity of accurate information about policy issues, especially about family law.

Gridlock, Aborted Plans, and Women's Resistance (1962–84)

The period from 1962 to 1984 witnessed a gridlock on the issue of family law. Gridlock refers here to a blockage caused by intersecting lines of competing political forces. The issue of family law was a pressing one in the new state. It was evident that the country could not be left without a system of law. It had to be decided at the very least whether the laws in effect under the French colonial state would remain in effect. Furthermore, the different kinds of family law that applied to different populations within Algeria were a painful reminder of particularisms. Kabyle customary law was in effect in parts of Kabylia, and Ibadite family law applied in the southern region of the Mzab. Maliki law applied to the majority of Algerians, but since it had not undergone general codification, it remained conducive to local and regional interpretations. For Algeria to achieve national unity, family law had to be unified and therefore codified. However, except for small and partial adjustments made mostly in 1962 and 1963, all attempts to codify the law aborted between 1963 and 1984.

The issue of family law became caught in the competition for power among different factions with different visions of Algerian society, different bases for power, and different roots in the heroic past of the anticolonial struggle. The structural context at the time of independence was conducive to gridlock. The factional conflicts dividing the leadership ran along several lines that intersected in different ways in a changing web of alliances. To reiterate briefly, the lines of division included among others: guerrilla forces anchored in the interior versus the army of the exterior (later made the national army), a political versus a military leadership, a Berber versus an Arab identity among the great politico-military leaders of the war, secularism versus Islam, and socialism versus liberalism. With a few exceptions, positions on family law often were shaped by politics, alliances, and conflicts. The same leader might shift positions or modify his position, depending on his allies and enemies at a particular time.

This was a period of highly volatile politics. No segment of the elite had enough control to take a firm stand and risk opposition to a family law policy, an issue that could easily serve as a battle horse for mobilization. This also was a situation in which everyone involved in politics knew or assumed that potential opponents had resources for mobilization and could use them. Although the guerrilla fighters did not organize actions centered on family law, everyone knew that they had arms left from the anticolonial war, especially before the army subdued them in the late 1960s. The guerrilla fighters also had shown the capacity to mobilize their local areas in the pursuit of political goals. Different factions had ties to local areas that had arms and could be mobilized, if need be.

Failed attempts to codify family law occurred in 1963, 1966, 1970, 1973, and 1981, as a similar scenario more or less repeated itself. Rumors on plans to codify family law, or in some cases preliminary drafts, would provoke reactions and opposition. The government would respond by shelving the project.[84] For example, in 1963, a commission was appointed to elaborate a family code, but its proposals were too conservative for some members of the government. Serious disagreements on the central issues of marriage, divorce, and polygamy made compromises unfeasible. The government withdrew the project, which never made it to the floor of the assembly. In early 1966, rumors circulated about another project of the government to reform the law. Following some of the rumors that described the project as "reactionary to the utmost," the government shelved the unpublished draft. [85] The Minister of Justice declared on 26 February 1966: "These are rumors. For now we are only at the stage of planning. There is no family code yet . . . We are trying to see how to come back to the sanest conception of Islamic law to give it a necessarily progressive character and one that conforms to our ideas about marriage and divorce."[86] Following the same course, other projects also aborted because of anticipated opposition.[87]

Unable to promulgate a family code, the Algerian government made minor adjustments to family law between 1962 and 1984. The first step was taken in December 1962 when the National Assembly declared that the body of legislation previously in effect was reconfirmed until further notice, except for those laws that called into question the sovereignty of the country.[88] It was not specified, however, which previous laws fell into this last category. The law of 1959, which had been promulgated by the French colonial state, thus remained in effect. The 1959 law had reorganized the procedure for marriage, established a minimum age for marriage, and required the registration of marriages as well as divorces.[89]

A few months later, in March 1963, a Code of Algerian Citizenship was adopted. To be Algerian, one had to be able to claim two male ascendants in the father's line born in Algeria. Only in the case of an unknown father and an Algerian mother would filiation in the mother's line be acceptable. Agnatic relations thus occupied a central place in the definition of citizenship, therefore respecting the patrilineal kinship system that had prevailed in the history of Algeria. Also emphasizing respect of the past rather than an orientation to change, the constitution stated that "the objectives of the revolution were to be faithful to the philosophical, moral and political traditions of the country."[90]

The procedure for marriage was specified in April 1963. Marriage was defined as an exchange of consent either directly by the spouses, or by the intermediary of a matrimonial guardian speaking for the woman, and always in the presence of two witnesses. It will be recalled that the 1959 law had abolished the principle of matrimonial guardian by requiring the direct consent of the woman. The 1963 decree reintroduced the principle, thus restoring previous practice. The same text also added that the marriage of an Algerian Muslim woman with a non-Muslim was null and void before Algerian law.[91]

In June 1963, a law known as the Khemisti law was passed, setting the minimum age for marriage at sixteen for a woman and eighteen for a man.[92] The Khemisti law was applicable to all Algerians. Requiring the civil registration of marriages, it stipulated that no one would be considered married unless able to provide a marriage certificate that had been registered in the civil registry at the time of marriage. The 1963 law reiterated in part what had already been done in 1959 under colonial rule. This partial step was necessary to the functioning of the newly formed Algerian bureaucracy. In the same vein, several ministerial rulings insisted on "the necessity for all the citizens of a modern state to have a clear and regularly updated *état civil*" (or be registered with the civil registry and have a set of identifications).[93]

Other partial steps occurred in 1973 and 1975. The Ordinance of 5 July 1973, abrogated all colonial legislation pertaining to marriage, divorce, and family in general, effective in 1975. The Ordinance of 26 September 1975 stipulated that the judge should resort instead to the principles of Islamic law or custom. In giving a special place to custom and various interpretations of uncodified Islamic law, the ordinance sanctioned the opposite of legal unification. The country still had no codified family law.

A codification attempt that occurred in 1981 took on a special character in that it precipitated women's resistance. This was a time when women organized themselves to block a government attempt to codify family law. In 1981, the government formed a commission again with the mandate to formulate a draft of a national family code. The commission included the Minister of Justice, a number of government figures and religious scholars. As earlier, secrecy surrounded the work of the commission. Rumors spread about the conservative tone of the draft law and a number of women managed to obtain a copy of the text. A member of the government leaked a copy of the draft to some women at the university. An Algerian woman explained what the women did, and it is worth quoting her at length:

> We had friends who were [government] ministers—they had two sessions to discuss this project. They told us that a copy of it was given to them when they entered the room, and taken back when they went out of the room . . . We had to steal this proposal. Then we duplicated twenty five copies on an old alcohol machine. . . . One of these copies reached the target . . . veteran women, women who fought in the Liberation struggle . . . They understood the situation, and they called a demonstration . . . The woman veterans also wrote to their Minister, the Minister of Veterans, saying that they hadn't fought for such a result. They also wrote to the Minister of Justice and to the President.[94]

Several women organized a protest against the draft, which was in effect as conservative as the rumors had indicated. This was a grassroots protest that involved women teachers, academics, and lawyers who belonged to a minority of professional women in independent Algeria.[95] The core group had been meeting at the university to discuss family law. The protest also involved former moudjahidates such as Djamila Bouhired, Meriem Enmihoub, and Zohra Drif Bitat. The women dared to do what had not been done before—confront the state and its single party openly and publicly by organizing highly visible street demonstrations. Women organized demonstrations mostly in Algiers, between October 1981 and January 1982.[96] The demonstrations gathered between one hundred and three hundred people, overwhelmingly women. The women also circulated a petition on which they collected ten thousand signatures and demanded primarily amendments of the family code proposed by the government. The demands included monogamy, equality in inheritance rights between men and women, and identity of divorce conditions. The police broke up the demonstrations and some of the activists were arrested. Acting outside of government-controlled organizations, the women operated with no organizational support of any kind. Constituting what Knauss appropriately calls a "minimovement," the women used informal networks of communication to organize their actions [97]

Men in the government themselves were divided over the 1981 draft law. The government press included articles and even an editorial criticizing the draft, a fact that in itself was an indication of disagreements within the FLN and the state leadership.[98] Given the level of tension raised by the draft, the then Algerian president, Chadli Benjedid, withdrew the draft bill and decided to shelve it, pending further study. Nadia Hijab reports that it was the first time a bill had been withdrawn from the assembly in independent Algeria.[99] This and the other previously aborted plans confirm the extent to which family law was a disturbing issue in Algerian politics. Two years of silence on family law followed the 1981 attempt at codification.

Conservative Outcome: The Family Code of 1984

Then, in 1984, the government suddenly proposed a revised draft law to the National Assembly, which adopted it with barely any discussion. The Family Code became law on 9 June 1984. Although the 1984 code was very similar in content to the 1981 draft, general silence followed its promulgation.[100] Lacking organizational support, the women who had constituted the core group of activists in 1981, some of whom had been arrested, did not respond immediately. The code passed essentially unopposed. About a year after the adoption of the code, reactions appeared, as small women's associations developed, expressing opposition to the code. Opposed on principle to any form of codification of family law, even if it remained faithful to the Shari'a, some fundamentalists groups also voiced criticism of the code.[101] The 1984 code nevertheless became the law of the land. Algeria had equipped itself with a national, unified, family law—one that was highly conservative.

Like the Shari'a and the Moroccan Code, with only minor differences, the Algerian Family Code of 1984 included a conception of the family as an agnatic kinship structure in which the patrilineal male line had primacy and women were subordinate to both husbands and male kin. This was the model of kinship that the Algerian state presented to the people of Algeria. The specific regulations of the 1984 Algerian Family Code resemble the Moroccan Code analyzed in chapter 7 and the Shari'a discussed in chapter 2. For example, the Algerian Family Code placed marriage within the framework of the larger kin group, instead of defining it as the choice of two individuals about to form a couple. For a marriage to be valid, a woman had to have a matrimonial guardian (father or a close agnatic relative). Only he could consent to the marriage, not the bride. The 1984 code set the minimum age of marriage at twenty-one for men and eighteen for women. As in Maliki law, polygamy remained legal, although the first wife (or second or third since four were allowed) and the new wife had to be informed of the husband's decision.[102]

The husband retained the privilege of repudiation and thus of ending the marriage at will, although repudiation now had to be registered by a judge. The legality of repudiation meant that women could find themselves divorced and thrown out of their home, sometimes with no resources. As in Maliki law, women could request a divorce in a number of specified conditions, such as in case of sexual infirmity of the husband or in case of a prolonged absence on his part. In keeping repudiation and polygamy legal, the 1984 Algerian Family Code presented a conception of the marital bond as easily breakable and nonexclusive, the same conception as in Islamic law.

The code defined filiation as exclusively patrilineal and as occurring only in marriage, which meant that the child of an unmarried woman could not have a legally recognized father. Boys would be in the custody of their mothers until the age of ten and this could be extended until the age of sixteen. Daughters would be in the custody of their mothers until the daughters married. Involving day-to-day care, custody differs from guardianship, which refers to legal responsibility for the child and will be discussed below. The 1984 Algerian Code covered succession in minute detail and accorded to it the greatest number of articles. In this respect, too, it was faithful to the prescriptions of the Shari'a on almost every point. It maintained the prerogatives of extended kin with respect of inheritance.

A few elements of the code increased the involvement of the state over kinship matters. This was the case with the mandatory registration of marriages and the registration of repudiation. Other rare elements of the code sanctioned a nuclear family system, such as the mother's right to guardianship in case of the father's death. Guardianship refers to legal prerogatives such as registering a child in school. After divorce, children might find themselves in the custody of their mothers and in the guardianship of their fathers, who thus retained legal power over children, even though mothers provided the daily care. The code stipulated that, when both parents were alive, the father was automatically the guardian. At his death, however, the mother should become the guardian. This stipulation suggested some attention paid to the nuclear family. Overall, however, the Algerian Family Code gave a privileged status to agnatic relationships within the extended patrilineal kin group and kept women in a subordinate status.

The adoption of the code in 1984 signifies that, in the end, the balance tilted toward conservatism after twenty-two years of hesitation and gridlock. The 1984 code was the outcome of the structural conditions of Algerian society, as inherited from its long-term historical trajectory and the survival of kin-based solidarities, intersecting with precipitating factors in the short term. In the late 1970s and early 1980s, the Algerian government faced several social protests at once. In that period, antigovernment Islamic fundamentalism was rising. Hugh Roberts notes that "the rise of Islamic extremism assumed alarming proportions," with an increase in violent actions in Algiers and other cities in 1981.[103] In the same period, the Algerian state faced a Berber protest, the "Berber Spring" of 1980, in which some Berbers demanded cultural rights and especially the recognition of the Berber language.[104] Furthermore, the collapse of world oil prices in the early 1980s deprived the government of one of its major sources of revenue, since the Algerian state economy was heavily dependent on oil.

The 1984 code was part of the government strategy to appeal to the base of the Islamic fundamentalist forces by meeting some of the wishes of that base. In Algeria as elsewhere in the Maghrib, a majority of the Islamic fundamentalist movement comprised members of the urban underprivileged—mostly young men and women alienated from their social environment, often of rural origin and usually unemployed.[105] Rural migration had assumed enormous proportions in Algeria in the 1960s and 1970s. The Algerian government gives a rate of urban growth of 78 percent for the period between 1956 and 1966, a period that covers part of the anticolonial war and four years after independence.[106] Richards and Waterbury indicate that between 1967 and 1978, 1.3 million Algerians left the countryside for the city.[107] This was out of a total population of close to 12 million at the beginning of the period in 1966 and a total population of 17.6 million at the end of it in 1978.[108]

Rural migrants typically had experienced the disintegration of kin groupings as a painful loss. They tended to see in a return to the past the solution to the problems of the present. Restoration of the past and reaffirmation of Islamic family law became political demands that resonated not only with segments of the FLN (still a heterogeneous coalition with conflicting views on family law), but also with the base of the Islamic fundamentalist movement and its leadership.[109] The Family Code of 1984 in part was a way for the regime in power to appease fundamentalists and to appeal to their social base.

· · ·

The origins of the gridlock from 1962 to 1984 lay mostly in internal disagreements among factions of a heterogeneous leadership formed in the social context of the decentralized anticolonial guerrilla war and each resting on different bases of power. In the wake of independence, kin-based forms of association continued to offer the most pertinent and the safest frame of reference for the majority of the population in rural areas. They also offered a potential base for mobilization by segments of the elite in the coalition that took the reins of power in the sovereign state. The paralysis of family law for two decades resulted from clashes, and ultimately irreconcilable differences, between segments of the leadership interested in transforming extended kinship and others interested in preserving it. Even those who wanted a transformation of kinship were at times ambivalent, as they feared alienating their base, which was overwhelmingly rural. The Algerian state faced internal contradictions in that it encompassed factions with conflicting agendas with respect to kinship structures and family life. It comprised some factions eager to foster the development of family structures that gave a greater place to conjugal units and other factions equally eager to remain faithful to the traditions of Algeria and thus to extended agnatic kinship. Hence the gridlock. It should come as no surprise that the factions of the FLN experienced paralysis for more than two decades.

The conservative outcome of 1984 resulted in part from the fact of a divided leadership facing a convergence of social challenges from different sectors of society in the decade preceding the adoption of the Algerian Family Code of 1984. Some of the sectors, including rural areas and rural migrants, were longing for the (partly imagined, but partly real) safety of extended kinship structures that were destabilized by migration to urban areas. For the Algerian state to enact legislation in favor of women would have required challenging extended agnatic kinship. Such a move would have risked alienating the rural areas upon which the FLN had historically relied and upon which it continued to rely in considerable measure. It also would have provided fuel to new, urban-based Islamic fundamentalist challengers who found part of their base among rural migrants. The Algerian state promulgated instead a family law likely to appeal to these groups.

In adopting the Family Code of 1984, the Algerian state catered to social and political forces with a vested interest in the preservation of the extended patrilineal kinship structure sanctioned by Islamic family law. In doing so, it sacrificed women's interests and the transformation of family law to political considerations. It also shut the door on the expansion of women's rights in the period under consideration.

9 State Autonomy from Tribe and Family Law Reform

Tunisia

The nationalist struggle in Tunisia culminated in the formation of a national state that was largely autonomous from the support of tribal areas. This was the decisive factor that distinguished Tunisia from Morocco and Algeria and permitted major reforms of family law with the resulting expansion in women's rights in the aftermath of independence. This chapter traces the balance of power between reformist and conservative forces in the Tunisian nationalist movement, their different political goals, and the course of state building reforms that the victorious liberal, reformist faction undertook after it gained power.

The chapter shows how family law reform in Tunisia was a part and a by-product of a larger project to build a modern nation-state by dismantling the foundation of kin-based solidarities. Occurring as it did in the absence of a feminist movement, the expansion of women's rights that followed from the new family law can be understood only as the outcome of a reform from above by a reformist leadership intent on encouraging social change and on marginalizing what was left of tribal communities. At the same time, it was the autonomy of the national state from kin-based tribal groups that made the transformation of family law possible.

The Tunisian struggle for independence took place in a context characterized by a tradition of national unity. Tunisia's borders had remained fairly constant for several centuries. The Berberophone population was virtually nonexistent.[1] Tunisians were overwhelmingly Arab and Muslim. Most importantly, Tunisia had fewer tribal divisions than the other two Maghribi countries. These conditions gave the country an advantage in the quest for nation building and state formation, even though they did not spare it bloodshed, caused not only by resistance to the French but also by serious cleavages that developed within the nationalist movement itself.

A conservative faction found its strongest support among the tribal areas, most of the Islamic establishment (which was concentrated in towns and cities), and some recent poor migrants to cities. A reformist, modernizing faction developed in alliance with trade unions, the professions, and most urban areas. Since the reformist faction found sustained support in the majority of urban areas, I refer to it as urban-based. In the course of the struggle, the reformist faction triumphed over the conservative one that had found a basis in the Islamic establishment and the remaining tribal areas, two constituencies that ultimately lost their political voice. This outcome resulted in policies that brought a death blow to the influence of tribal areas on politics in the newly independent state. It also left the victorious faction with no immediate rival and essentially with free rein to set national policy.

After independence, the winning reformist, urban-based faction made it a central political project to consolidate the authority of the state and develop nationwide institutions. Foremost, it moved to undermine or eradicate tribal solidarities and their political and social manifestations. To this effect, the winning faction, under the leadership of Habib Bourguiba, made reforms that attacked various traditional institutions such as the collective ownership of tribal lands, the independent power of Islamic courts, and the predominance of the extended patrilineage in matters of marriage, divorce, and inheritance. The moves accomplished two goals at once. They enforced the vision of a modern nation-state held by the victorious urban-based, reformist, nationalist faction. The moves also weakened or undermined the social bases of support of the defeated rival conservative faction.

STATE AUTONOMY FROM TRIBES (1930S–50S)

State autonomy from tribes resulted in part from the historically specific conditions of the nationalist struggle in Tunisia. In contrast to developments in Algeria and Morocco, the Tunisian nationalist party succeeded in establishing mass mobilization and tight coordination within a single organization. This was made possible by the historically greater incorporation of the hinterland into the Tunisian polity than had been the case in the other two countries. The incorporation, which had been accelerated by the bureaucratic form of colonization, gave the nationalist leadership an opportunity to coordinate among regions, something that its Maghribi counterparts had difficulty doing, given the greater tribal segmentation of Moroccan and Algerian societies.

Nationalist Party: Structure and Ideology

The Tunisian nationalist movement carried out the fight against the French through a tightly coordinated party with branches throughout the country, in cities, towns, and villages. With a democratic and centralized structure, the party served as the principal organizational instrument for national liberation from the 1930s to the 1950s.[2] Called the Neo-Destour (*Destour* means "constitution" in Arabic), the party was created in 1934, when the nationalist struggle gained momentum, following the actions of earlier nationalist associations. A broad-based party, the Neo-Destour had a membership that cut across social classes and regional groups, including intellectuals, workers from the city of Tunis, and tribesmen from the hinterland in central and southern Tunisia.[3] Charles Micaud estimates that by 1955 one out of every three male Tunisian adults belonged to the party.[4]

The inclusion of diverse social groups within its ranks, coupled with an organizational web reaching into remote villages, allowed the Neo-Destour to survive French repression and to operate in both urban and rural areas for two decades of nationalist struggle. Even though French repression forced party members to operate underground, many Tunisians felt the presence of the party in their everyday lives as it became a form of social agency. Tunisian physicians, for example, reported that local Neo-Destour leaders mobilized them to provide free medical care to party members. French reports indicate that the party had established an "Aid Service for the Indigent and Unemployed."[5] Lisa Anderson suggests that the party had become a "social club, an employment agency, a school, a sanctuary."[6]

The nationalist movement had strong urban roots and involved an alliance between the dominant labor union and the Neo-Destour party. When the Tunisian labor movement, the Union Générale des Travailleurs Tunisiens (UGTT), was established in the 1940s, the party and the union worked in collaboration.[7] Bourguiba, then a prominent nationalist leader, emphasized the mutual advantage of such collaboration for the survival of each organization. He declared in the 1950s: "The experience—I could say the proof and the counterproof—has shown that each time the solidarity between the party and the union is broken through the fault of one or the other, it is a disaster for both."[8] When the anticolonial struggle intensified in the mid-1950s, ninety thousand of the one hundred thousand members of the labor union belonged to the Neo-Destour.[9] The ties between the two organizations served to increase pressure against the colonial regime, as the owners of industries and large landholdings, who were predominantly French, became the target of combined labor and nationalist op-

position. The ties between labor and party facilitated coordination and reduced the likelihood of divisions between labor leaders and party elite.

Unique to Tunisia in the anticolonial struggles of the Maghrib was the
extent of the coordination between the political center of the nationalist
movement and guerrilla insurrections in rural areas. In contrast to Algeria
and Morocco, where semi-autonomous pockets of armed resistance developed, the control of violent actions in Tunisia rested with the political
leadership of the party for most of the nationalist period. The rural population (estimated at 65 percent of the total) was less fragmented in tribal
units than in either Algeria or Morocco and thus more amenable to coordination.[10] As elsewhere, the rural poor bore the brunt of physical violence, even though political leaders were arrested, sent to exile, and in
some cases assassinated. In the early 1950s, the party encouraged the organization of a guerrilla force. Operating in the countryside, the guerrilla
force was composed of a few thousand fighters, about three thousand according to most estimates.[11]

While its size was unimpressive, the guerrilla force showed a remarkable capacity for coordinated actions in several parts of the Tunisian territory. At the height of anticolonial violence in the early to mid-1950s, the
nationalist movement was able to synchronize armed insurrections and
harassment of colonial farms in the countryside with generalized strikes
and popular demonstrations in urban centers. This capacity for coordinated
nationalist action made the Tunisian movement a serious threat to the
French, even though the Tunisian guerrilla forces were in themselves much
less threatening than their mighty Algerian counterparts.

Nationalist movements usually must rally forces and underplay their
ideological differences in order to increase their chances of success against
the colonizer. Ideological inclusion therefore often becomes the golden rule
during the anticolonial struggle. The Neo-Destour accordingly made an
appeal to all Tunisians from the 1930s to the mid-1950s. Unambiguously
taking national sovereignty as its objective and underplaying ideologies
other than nationalism, the party leadership included liberal professionals
such as lawyers and physicians who joined forces with religious figures
and graduates of the Zaytuna (faculty of theology).[12] Following the rule
of ideological inclusion, the Neo-Destour incorporated within itself potentially conflicting tendencies, which earlier had been anchored in different
nationalist organizations.

The tendencies included among others the legacy of the club of the
"Young Tunisians," a small group of young liberal intellectuals especially
active at the turn of the century. The Young Tunisians demanded equality

with the French. Impressed with European achievements and inspired by the reformist movement of the Young Turks in Turkey, the Young Tunisians wanted to bring to Tunisia modern education and culture to replace what they saw as backwardness in their own society. Quite different in orientation, another organization, called Destour when it was founded in 1920 and later renamed Old Destour, defended an ideology of traditionalistic anticolonialism. More a pressure group than a mass movement and coming primarily from a small propertied class of Tunisians residing mostly in Tunis, the Old Destour called for the respect of Arab and Islamic culture while fighting for political rights.[13]

Facing a combination of repression and lack of resources, the Young Tunisians disbanded in the 1920s and the Old Destour dwindled over time. The Young Tunisians and the Old Destour nevertheless influenced the future course of Tunisian nationalism. The Neo-Destour, as it emerged in 1934 and later developed in the 1940s and 1950s, incorporated within itself the reformist legacy of the Young Tunisians *and* the banner of Islam raised earlier by the Old Destour. The two orientations came to clash later, when the nationalist struggle was nearing its conclusion.

Party, Islam, and Tribe: Internal Conflicts

The nationalist party maintained consensus during most of the nationalist period. Internal conflicts broke out between rival factions, however, at the eve of independence from colonial rule when power in a sovereign state appeared to be a concrete possibility. The outcome of the conflicts looked quite uncertain at the time, as it was unclear which faction would take power and what kind of state would develop in independent Tunisia. Two nationalist leaders symbolized the contending tendencies: the reformist Bourguiba and the pan-Islamist Ben Youssef, his opponent who rallied enough support to pose a serious challenge. Bourguiba and Ben Youssef disagreed on the strategy to gain sovereignty, appealed to different constituencies, offered different visions of a future Tunisia, and had different outside allies. Regardless of the ideological distance separating the two men at the start of the conflict, Bourguiba's and Ben Youssef's positions hardened as each found a different source of support in the course of the nationalist struggle. Bourguiba and Ben Youssef gradually became spokesmen for different sectors of Tunisian society.

In general terms, Ben Youssef appealed to those nationalist forces— tribal groups, uprooted rural migrants to cities, and the religious establishment—that perceived national sovereignty as an opportunity to restore a (partly real and partly imagined) Tunisian past, which they felt had been scoffed at by the colonial regime. In particular, Ben Youssef found support among the remaining tribes in the central and southern parts of the country (Map 10), where most Neo-Destour guerrilla groups fought in his name. Support for Ben Youssef was heightened as the result of a drought in the early 1950s. The drought made economic conditions precarious, especially in the arid regions where some form of tribal organization had persisted. The hard-pressed population in tribal regions saw the return to a nostalgic past as the safest shield against a threatening economic situation. In speaking the discourse of tradition, Ben Youssef gained the allegiance of guerrilla forces in tribal areas, which provided him with a rural power base. This rural base combined with a smaller base mostly in the city of Tunis among uprooted rural migrants. In addition, the Zaytuna, the religious university, had endorsed the nationalist party and the majority of its graduates backed Ben Youssef, himself a graduate of the Zaytuna.[14]

Ben Youssef insisted on three themes in his speeches: pan-Arabism, pan-Islamism, and Maghribi unity. Favoring solidarity with other Arab and Islamic countries, he claimed pan-Arabism and pan-Islamism as political anchors for the nationalist struggle and for the future Tunisian nation. Advocating Maghribi unity, he argued for the total liberation of the Maghrib as a whole. He therefore urged Tunisians to continue the fight against the French until Algeria and Morocco achieved independence from French colonial rule. Outside of Tunisia, he received encouragement from the Algerian nationalist movement and Egyptian authorities, who gave him access to radio broadcasting from Cairo. His outside allies also allegedly provided him with arms.[15]

By contrast, Bourguiba had the support of the urban labor union, the professional elites trained at the Collège Sadiqi, and the population of most of the coastal towns. Bourguiba had relatively little following in the areas where tribal organization persisted. Created before colonization, kept in place by the French as a source of educated Tunisians for the administrative apparatus, and training primarily civil servants and members of the professions, the Collège Sadiqi, located in the city of Tunis, became a cradle of nationalism. Sadiqi graduates developed an esprit de corps within an active nationalist network that backed Bourguiba.[16] Interested in social welfare and generally progressive policies, the labor union formed ties with Bourguiba's faction rather than Ben Youssef's. In terms of overall tactics, Bourguiba favored a step-by-step approach to independence and argued for negotiations, instead of the sustained armed violence advocated by Ben

Map 10. Tribal territories in central and southern Tunisia (adapted from Lisa Anderson, *The State and Social Transformation in Tunisia and Libya, 1830–1980*. Princeton: Princeton University Press, 1986, 5)

Youssef. While repeatedly asserting his allegiance to Islam, Bourguiba called for a specifically Tunisian nation and a modern state with multiple international ties. He had little sympathy for the notion of a future Tunisia free from French rule but subsumed to a pan-Arab supranation.

Whereas Ben Youssef defended pan-Islamism and pan-Arabism, Bourguiba placed nation building and the development of a distinctive Tunisian nation-state above other considerations. As early as 1932, a statement in the newspaper published by Bourguiba read: "The Tunisia we want to free [from colonial rule] will be a Tunisia for neither Muslims, nor Jews, nor Christians. It will be the Tunisia of all who will want to take it as their mother country without distinction of religion or race."[17] In a similar vein and more than thirty years later, in 1964, Bourguiba reiterated: "Whether one originates from Tunis, the South or the Sahel [coastal region], one can only react as a Tunisian, that is with a strong sense of belonging to the one and same family: the Tunisian nation."[18]

The conflict between the two nationalist factions came to a head in 1955, following disagreements on strategy. Ben Youssef was in favor of expanding armed attacks against the French, while Bourguiba preferred to enter into negotiations with them. In October 1955, Ben Youssef made a passionate speech in the highly symbolic setting of the Zaytuna mosque. Calling for the birth of a new Tunisia as an integral part of a broader Arab and Islamic supranation, Ben Youssef exhorted Tunisians to sustain the armed struggle in unity with Algeria and Morocco until the end of French rule in the entire Maghrib. Ben Youssef's discourse found an echo, since a third of the Neo-Destour cells declared themselves in his favor and recognized him as their leader, while the rest declared themselves for Bourguiba.[19] There were reports that Ben Youssef was trying to steer party militants into a rival structure.[20] Pro-Ben Youssef guerrilla fighters now attacked not only French settlers but also Neo-Destour cells known to support Bourguiba. Whole tribes favoring Ben Youssef enlisted in a guerrilla force and some joined Algerian forces fighting the French at the border. Tunisia was profoundly divided between two camps that were opposed in a bloody confrontation.[21]

Bourguiba responded to the situation by calling for an extraordinary congress of the Neo-Destour in November 1955 in Sfax, a coastal city where Ben Youssef had little support. It was the backing of the labor union that tilted the balance in favor of Bourguiba. Seriously underrepresented in the 1955 congress, the Ben Youssef forces did not have much of a fighting chance. By contrast, the Tunisian labor union, the UGTT, gave Bourguiba full tactical and political support during the congress. Drawing also on his support among professionals, Bourguiba succeeded in having Ben Youssef's faction expelled from the party by the congress, which reelected Bourguiba as party president.

French colonial officials, most of whom at that point accepted the end of colonial rule in Tunisia as inevitable, also gave help to Bourguiba. In their perspective, a sovereign Tunisia would remain important to France for strategic reasons of international security in the Mediterranean Basin. The French government preferred to face an independent Tunisia under Bourguiba than under Ben Youssef, who could be expected to remain allied with pan-Arabic Egypt and Algeria, where the French were facing an anticolonial war. In line with this policy, French troops quashed Ben Youssef's guerrilla forces in the south in a full-scale military operation.

Tunisian independence was proclaimed on 20 March 1956. The achievement of national sovereignty brought down the Tunisian monarchy headed by the bey, who had been kept in place by the French protectorate throughout the nationalist struggle, but with his prestige sapped. In the eyes of most Tunisians, the bey "seemed to perform only one function, namely to justify the exercise of power by the French."[22] Lacking any support among Tunisians, the monarchy was abolished without turmoil. Bourguiba, the leader of the winning reformist faction of the nationalist movement, became prime minister in 1956 and head of state in 1957.

The aftermath of independence witnessed the purge of Youssefist sympathizers. Using methods ranging from repression to co-optation, Bourguiba's regime moved to silence the party members and the constituencies that had supported Ben Youssef's faction. Although Ben Youssef fled to exile in January 1956, trouble continued with bloodshed through 1957. Sophie Bessis and Souhayr Belhassen suggest that the conflict within the nationalist movement caused a thousand deaths in Tunisia, more than twice the number caused by the struggle against France.[23] The Youssefist threat continued for a while despite the repression, since a Youssefist plot against Bourguiba's government was discovered among members of the army as late as six years after independence, in 1962. The purge continued in the 1960s.

Legacy of the Youssefist Crisis: The Defeat of Tribal Power

The elimination of the Ben Youssef faction from the nationalist party had several important consequences for the formation of the independent Tunisian state. First, Bourguiba's faction remained essentially unchallenged in its position of power for several years. This gave it leeway to shape

Tunisian institutions in accordance with its program to build a modern state in the aftermath of independence. Although disagreements surfaced later within Bourguiba's government regarding economic policy, they did not jeopardize the basic commitment to create a modern state. After the purge of the Ben Youssef faction, the victorious reformist, urban-based, political leadership emerged from the turmoil of the nationalist struggle as a cohesive elite committed to the national project of consolidating a strong sovereign state. This was an elite that saw the state as the primary agent of social transformation. The Neo-Destour of the independence period in effect reasserted the earlier Young Tunisian conception of the state as shaping society.

Second, the remaining tribes in Tunisia and the religious establishment no longer had a voice in politics after independence. This was the price they paid for having backed Ben Youssef and having played the losing card in the nationalist conflict. Furthermore, the crisis had shown the danger of religious and pan-Arab ideologies for the stability of the Tunisian regime that came to power after independence. The crisis had made clear that such ideologies could enflame part of the population, especially tribal areas and the religious establishment. Determined to thwart potential challengers and ready to implement its vision of the new nation-state, the Tunisian political leadership banished the pan-Arab and pan-Islamic discourse from politics, a discourse that evoked the specter of the Youssefist threat.

Third, the crisis left a fear of political chaos and an obsession with national unity. The leadership had measured the cost of division. As a result, leaders of newly independent Tunisia made the unifying project the paramount objective and defined national unity as the goal transcending all others. Commenting on the emphasis on national unity in the mass media and in political speeches in Tunisia after independence, Jean Lacouture appropriately refers to an "endless ceremony of collective identification."[24] After the bloodshed of the anticolonial battle, most Tunisians were looking forward to enjoying a period of peace, now that their country was finally free of the colonial yoke. In a general mood of national reconciliation and postcolonial enthusiasm, most people were willing to give Bourguiba's government a chance to build the new nation-state.

A word of caution should be introduced at this point about the nature of Tunisian politics in the decade following the achievement of national sovereignty. Neither national reconciliation nor the building of a nation-state means democracy. They therefore should not be confused with the development of a democratic polity. The objective of the postindependence leadership was to unify the party on the broadest base possible, to secure a virtual monopoly for it, and to make it an instrument of social transformation.[25] Single-party rule characterized Tunisian politics in the decade following independence, resulting in political authoritarianism ranging from mild to rigid, depending on the circumstances. With limited powers, the National Assembly often discussed proposals made by members of the government rather than by elected deputies. When the assembly was not in session, laws were made by presidential decree and later ratified by the assembly which, in any case, was overwhelmingly composed of members of the winning faction.[26] The executive branch of the government and the party usually had more impact on policy than did the assembly. This combined with single-party rule to make the new Tunisian state centralized, at the same time that it made it fall short of what we would expect from a democratic system.

Building the National State: A Program of Reforms

Once in power, the new leadership moved quickly to consolidate state institutions in the aftermath of independence. It sought to weaken, or preferably to eradicate, tribal solidarities and their manifestations. In its effort to undermine the social forces that had provided its rival faction with a political base, the new government wished to pull out of Tunisian society "the roots on which Youssefism had prospered."[27] Bourguiba's speeches of the period referred critically to "archaic" structures, "retrograde" mentalities, and social categories "hostile to change" that allowed Ben Youssef "to awaken the old core of anarchy and chaos."[28] Reflecting the intent of his government concerning the autonomy of tribal areas, Bourguiba declared in a speech in 1957: "I disagree with those who defend the old traditional principle according to which some freedoms predate the state and take precedence over it. . . . These freedoms must be banished if they jeopardize the collectivity and risk to cause the state to unravel."[29] Accordingly, the newly formed Tunisian state, with the government and the party working hand in hand, launched aggressive reforms designed to unify institutions and deprive local kin-based solidarities of the limited political leverage that they had retained.

The targets attacked by the reforms included the collective tribal ownership of land, the autonomy of local areas, the inheritance rights of agnates within the lineage, the independent power of Islamic courts, religious property rights, and the privileges of extended kin in family matters. Occurring all within a few years, the measures implemented the elite's vision of a future Tunisia as a modern nation-state in which the foundation of kin-based tribal solidarities would be dismantled. The measures also cemented the defeat of the Ben Youssef faction and consolidated the power of the national elite under Bourguiba's leadership.

In one of the farthest-reaching reforms, the political leadership revamped and unified local administration throughout the Tunisian territory. This was nothing short of a transformation of the national space. The newly formed government developed party and state institutions to replace solidarities based on kinship and tribal ties. The process had already started with the development of the party structure during the nationalist struggle. It intensified after independence. Referring to the expansion of the administrative network in the four years following independence, Elbaki Hermassi notes that the number of government officials almost tripled in five years, as it went from thirty thousand to eighty-six thousand between 1955 and 1960.[30] Where tribal, clan, and lineage structures had weakened or disintegrated, the Neo-Destour branch implanted its own organizational web of local and regional branches. Where the structures were still strong, the party tried to weaken them. Whenever possible, the Neo-Destour organized its branches along geographic lines, deliberately ignoring the loyalties and rivalries of kin groupings. In areas that had remained tribal, the strategy was to set up branches that cut across tribal lines.[31]

Yet, forced to adapt to local social organization, the party sometimes had to work around the tribes. For example, tribal rivalries flared up when a site had to be chosen for the construction of a new administrative center or a market because each tribal community wanted it in its territory. Neo-Destour officials made compromises such as deciding to build the center or market halfway between the two tribal territories. This forced the two tribal groups to come together despite their resistance. In southern villages, a cradle of Youssefist support, the resistance of tribes to working together in a single structure was particularly acute. For example, Clement Henry Moore indicates that near the southern town of Gafsa the Neo-Destour was divided into five local branches along tribal lines, even though the initial plan was to have one branch. Only in 1958, two years after independence, were Neo-Destour local officials able to unite the branches into a single unit accommodating the various tribal groups.[32]

Seeking to put an end to turmoil in the hinterland, the party leadership actively tried to stop the hostilities that had opposed tribes to one another in the conflict between nationalist factions in the anticolonial struggle. During the Youssefist crisis in the mid-1950s, adjacent tribes had sometimes fought on opposing sides, one for Ben Youssef's and the other for Bourguiba's. After independence, Bourguiba had to make a personal appeal to some of the victorious tribes that had supported him and implore them to refrain from decimating the defeated Youssefist tribes. In some areas, the governor and regional party representatives had to employ their diplomatic skills to maintain a balance between tribal camps and prevent more bloodshed.[33]

As party and administration officials took every occasion to erode what was left of tribal politics, they defined the local branch of the party as the local organ of national integration.[34] The overall mandate of the branch was to bring local groups into the organizational framework of party and state administration. Its role was to mobilize support for the projects of the central government, to present local grievances to higher authorities, to facilitate local administration, and to organize collective life in local areas on the basis of unified national policies. Regional committees provided the link between local branches and the central organs of the party, thus serving as channels of communication between center and periphery. The ability of the nationalist leadership to consolidate the state and party apparatus was due in part to the availability of a pool of trained administrators. Such availability in turn resulted from a long tradition of education in the country, particularly from the existence of the Collège Sadiqi, which continued to provide officials for the party and state bureaucracies.[35]

The dismantling of collective tribal lands constituted another major initiative against what remained of tribal solidarity. The law of 28 September 1957, followed by other state actions later on, established the distribution of tribal lands to individual owners with compensation to members of the tribe. Charles Micaud indicates that the policy affected about 7 million acres.[36] This was in contrast to what happened in Morocco where the monarchy pursued a land policy that strengthened kin-based social relations of production. The dismantling of tribal lands had started during colonization in Tunisia, but after independence it proceeded at a speed that Micaud describes as ten times greater than during the French Protectorate. Involving topographical surveys of the Tunisian territory, it represented a major undertaking aimed at unifying the system of property rights in land by abolishing collective tribal ownership—and with it the social foundation of the remaining tribal organization in Tunisia. In a 1961 speech about land policy, Bourguiba referred to his government's view of the relationship between tribe and state in the following terms: "In this republic of four million people, how can we leave family units, which are states in miniature ruled by autonomous chieftains, to fend for themselves? The state, which sees beyond the individual, must intervene for the sake of national solidarity."[37]

The government also moved quickly to make two other unifying reforms of major importance. Both reforms consolidated the power of the national state by developing nationwide institutions and regulations, at the same time that they weakened the religious establishment. In one of the measures, the government abolished the *habus*, or landed property given as religious donation. Habus properties had served as a financial base for the religious establishment and the landed traditional elite, which often had connections to the religious establishment. Scholars agree in estimating that between one-fourth and one-fifth of agricultural land was held in some form of habus at independence in 1956, about 4 million acres.[38] A 1956 decree and a 1957 law transferred all habus property to the public domain or private owners, thus bringing an end to the habus system in Tunisia.[39]

In the other measure, the government unified the justice system of the country by integrating all courts into a single national system. Two 1956 decrees abolished all religious courts and therefore did away with the courts that applied different schools of Islamic law (as had been the case so far with the existence of Maliki and Hanafi courts).[40] One of the decrees abolished Rabbinic courts that applied Jewish law, thus leaving a unified Tunisian, rather than religious, system of courts for all.[41] This was in effect a redefinition of justice, since citizenship came to replace religion as the central principle of the judicial system.

In summary, the strategy of the political leadership after independence was to consolidate the authority of the national state by developing nationwide institutions. The extension of the party and government institutions to all areas of the country marked what Lisa Anderson aptly refers to as "the final extinction of tribal politics" in Tunisia.[42] This was made possible by the relative homogeneity of Tunisian society and the absence of widespread tribal segmentation as existed in Algeria and Morocco. The pattern of nation building was one of national mobilization by a party and a state closely allied to each other. This occurred in a structural context in which local kin-based solidarities had been progressively weakened over the long run.

After independence, the state intervened in a way that was tantamount to a recasting of social and power relations in Tunisian society. By establishing new administrative structures, undermining the cohesion of agnatic lineages, limiting the independence of religious institutions, and eliminating collective ownership of tribal land, the political leadership of the newly formed state was launching a far-reaching program of state building. It was encouraging the unfolding of a form of social organization in which the influence of the religious establishment would be undermined and that of kin-based tribal groups eradicated. The family law reform that followed independence in Tunisia must be considered within this overall strategy of state building.

THE TRANSFORMATION OF FAMILY LAW (1930s–50s)

The policy on family law in sovereign Tunisia followed from the kind of state that took shape toward the end of the nationalist period and at the time of independence. In the same way that the state engaged in other reforms meant to build institutions and unify the country, such as the reforms of administration, land ownership, and judicial system discussed above, the state promulgated a sweeping family law reform. It promulgated the family law reform in August 1956, a few months after the achievement of national independence. It was in the same year that it reformed the judicial system and a year later, in 1957, that it eliminated the collective ownership of tribal land. In the same way as other reforms weakened what was left of tribal solidarities, so did family law reform. This stands in sharp contrast to the codification of family law in the Mudawwana of 1957–58 in Morocco and the 1984 Family Code of Algeria, where the model of the extended patrilineage was explicitly institutionalized and recognized in the new state. Tunisia in comparison equipped itself with a family law that sanctioned essentially a nuclear model of the family and expanded women's rights.

In Tunisia, as elsewhere in the Maghrib, voices in favor of change in family law started to be heard in an earlier period, in this case in the 1930s. The voices raised the question of women's condition in the context of a general critique of society and a general call for social reform. As in other countries, the reformists were part of the general current called *Nahda* or Renaissance sweeping the Islamic Middle East starting in the 1930s. Reformist voices were quickly silenced by other Tunisians. Treating Islamic family law as a sign of distinctiveness from the French colonizer, most Tunisian nationalists of the earlier period agreed that reforms should be postponed until they could be made in a sovereign state. Before I examine the family law reforms that followed independence in the 1950s, I briefly present the debate on family law during the nationalist period in the 1930s. The contrast between the two periods shows the extent to which different political contexts shaped the position of the political leadership on family law, even when the same individual leaders were involved.

A Reformist Silenced during the Nationalist Struggle (1930s)

The dominant problem that concerned Tunisians with respect to family law during the nationalist struggle from the 1930s to the 1950s was whether Islamic law should be modified or left unchanged. Since Tunisia already had virtually no customary codes of law in the colonial period, it was spared the sensitive political issues created in Algeria and Morocco by the existence of such codes.[43] Although the issue of family law and women's rights had first surfaced in Tunisia in the 1920s, it did not receive much attention until the early 1930s, when it gave rise to heated debates.

In 1930, a book appeared under the title of (in translation) *Our Women in Law and Society*.[44] The author of the book, Tahar al-Haddad, called for substantial reforms in laws governing the family and personal status. He was vehemently criticized for his views and hostile reactions were of such a magnitude that they cost him his career and reputation. Arguing that Tunisian women were constantly debased, al-Haddad stated that the purpose of his book was to argue for social reform. He was part of the broad reformist movement that developed in that period. Intellectuals throughout the Middle East saw social reform as necessary to make their respective countries able to resist encroachment by Europe. Al-Haddad called for changes in women's status and improvements in women's education as a way of making women better citizens, better wives, and better mothers. The point was not primarily to emancipate women for their own sake, but to make them better able to contribute to the stability of families and better able to educate future generations of Tunisians.

Within this general framework, al-Haddad was forceful in expressing his views. He deplored the evils stemming from unchecked paternal power in families, such as child and compulsory marriages in particular. An opponent of the veil and the seclusion of women, he highlighted their negative consequences. He argued that the veil and seclusion paralyzed the intellectual, psychological, and even physical development of women, that they fostered mutual ignorance between men and women by keeping them in separate worlds, and that they made conjugal relationships difficult, when they did not doom them to failure altogether. Among other changes, he advocated the dropping of the veil as one way of overcoming the barrier between the female and male worlds.

Presenting an image of marriage different from that contained in Islamic law, al-Haddad saw spouses as life companions. He rejected polygamy which, he contended, tears apart families by dividing them among several units, organized around each wife and her children. He condemned unilateral repudiation, the privilege that Islamic family law gives to the husband to terminate the marriage at will and in private. He urged instead the creation of divorce courts, as he considered a procedure in court, or some form of public procedure, the only appropriate way to terminate a marriage. In favor of promoting the education of women, he suggested that women be given opportunities for employment and that, in particular, positions in the public sector be progressively made available to them. Stating that "it is its women who make a nation," al-Haddad concluded with two pressing calls.[45] He urged all Tunisians to reflect on the issue and its significance for the future. He also called for reforms not only because he thought that they were desirable, but because he believed that an evolution toward greater freedom for women was ineluctable. The only realistic approach, he therefore argued, was not to fight the evolution, but to channel it in a judicious and rational manner.

Al-Haddad's book met with a storm of indignation. The Zaytuna, the center of religious education and scholarship in Tunisia, condemned it immediately as an outrageous attack against Islam. A commission was created at the Zaytuna with the task of evaluating the book. Its report was unequivocal: the book was blasphemous and it contained enticements to transgress Islamic law, and it should therefore be banned.[46] Complying with the Zaytuna's recommendation, the prime minister placed a ban on the book. Al-Haddad was the object of numerous attacks, which went beyond verbal abuse. He had been a notary and professor at the Zaytuna. Soon after the book was banned, the prime minister notified al-Haddad that he was dismissed from his position. From then on, al-Haddad was treated as a traitor and excluded from public life. He finished his days in isolation. Several other books appeared, disparaging al-Haddad and reasserting the immutable value of Islamic family law. Some bore evocative titles such as (in translation) *Mourning the Women of al-Haddad*.[47] Conservatives who refused even to contemplate the possibility of change found in al-Haddad an easy target against which to express their views. Their reactions to his book showed how bitter and effective opposition to change could be.

Al-Haddad's position in favor of change was shared by some, however. A monthly women's magazine, called *Leila* and started in 1936, discussed women's legal status. It was in that magazine that a Tunisian lawyer, Tahar Sfar, who later became one of the leaders of the nationalist movement, described the Maghribi family as "organized on the model of a small constitutional monarchy."[48] The family had to change, he argued, for Tunisia to become a modern nation. In January 1929, a woman, Habiba al-Mansari, came unveiled to a meeting in a literary club where she urged women to drop the veil. Appearing unveiled at a meeting in itself was enough to scandalize many and al-Mansari was criticized for her action. On a smaller scale than in the Algerian war, Tunisian women participated in the anti-colonial struggle, although they fought for national liberation rather than for women's causes. For example, women at times demonstrated in the streets of Tunis and were arrested along with men. Women who belonged to the Neo-Destour wrote a letter protesting the treatment of nationalist women and men in French prisons.[49]

Although a few public figures expressed their interest in seeing a change in family law, most leaders of the nationalist movement from the 1930s to the 1950s, like their Moroccan and Algerian counterparts, considered that nothing should be done until the end of colonization. For example, Habib Bourguiba, the future president of the Tunisian Republic, consistently adopted a cautious attitude prior to independence. For him, Tunisia was living a crucial period during which the French were seeking to depersonalize Tunisia. At this particular time, Bourguiba argued, Tunisians ought to hold on firmly to every component of their identity, including family law and the veil.[50]

Voicing the collective position of the leadership, Bourguiba declared in 1929: "Is it in our interest to hasten the disappearance of our ways of life and customs. . . . that constitute our identity? Given the special circumstances in which we live, my answer is categorical: No."[51] He gave his reasons: "Tunisians must safeguard their traditions, which are the sign of their distinctiveness, and therefore the last defense of a national identity in danger."[52] This was the position of the young leader who, two and a half decades later, would call the veil "a miserable rag" and under whose regime the legal status of women would be transformed. As long as the country was under colonial domination, the nationalist leadership defined the safeguard of cultural distinctiveness as a top priority.

Family Law Reform (1956)

The position of the victorious nationalist leadership quickly changed after independence. On 13 August 1956, less than five months after the proclamation of independence, a new Tunisian Code of Personal Status (CPS) was promulgated. The code profoundly changed family law and the legal status of women. The rapidity with which the new leadership under Bourguiba moved on the reform of family law after independence was not a surprise to most Tunisians involved in politics. In the 1950s, during the few years preceding independence, what became later known as the liberal, reformist wing of the nationalist party started making its position on the status of women publicly known. Its press discussed topics such as marriage, greater freedom for women, female employment, and mandatory education for girls.[53] Some people knew that a code of personal status was in preparation. It was evident that some within the leadership of the nationalist party were determined to launch a program of reforms in family law upon gaining national sovereignty.[54] This was one of the expressions of the different visions of society held by Bourguiba's victorious faction and Ben Youssef's defeated faction. As soon as it took the reins of power, Bourguiba's faction implemented its vision by promulgating the CPS.

The CPS altered regulations on marriage, divorce, alimony, custody, adoption, filiation, and to a lesser extent inheritance, leaving few, if any, aspects of family life untouched. The code dropped the vision of the family as an extended kinship group built on strong ties crisscrossing a community of male relatives. It replaced it with the vision of a conjugal unit in which ties between spouses and between parents and children occupy a prominent place. While it decreased the prerogatives of extended kin in family matters, the CPS also gave women greater rights by increasing the range of options available to them in their private lives. The code abolished polygamy, eliminated the husband's right to repudiate his wife, allowed women to file for divorce, and increased women's custody rights.

A reform from above, the CPS was initiated by the leaders of the urban, reformist, winning faction at the time of independence in the absence of a feminist grassroots mass movement. The CPS was *not* a response from the state to pressures from a women's mass protest movement. Aware of this, President Bourguiba, one the key initiators of the code, said in an interview: "Indeed, there was no feminist movement demanding the promulgation of a Code of Personal Status or the abolition of polygamy."[55] The next head of the Tunisian state, President Ben Ali, confirmed this assessment decades later, in 1992, in stating that the emancipation of Tunisian women had not been a response to feminist considerations.[56] Scholars agree with politicians on this point. Even though individual women had participated in the struggle for national liberation, some by clandestinely transporting arms, no women's mass protest movement had developed in Tunisia in the 1950s.[57]

The initiators of the family law reform embedded in the CPS described

it primarily as an instrument of change. They defined it as a way of bringing about a transformation of kinship, which they saw as a necessary condition for broader social, political, and economic changes. The initiators
saw the reform as a step toward altering kinship organization and fostering
new behavior patterns. For example, Habib Bourguiba relentlessly referred
to the theme of restructuring social relationships in his speeches on the
CPS. He said: "This change [in the law] represented in our minds a choice
in favor of progress . . . the end of a barbaric age and the beginning of an
era of social equilibrium and civilization. . . . [we must] fight anachronistic
traditions and backward mentalities."[58]

I had a rare opportunity to interview Ahmed Mestiri, who served as
Minister of Justice in the 1956 government, and to ask him directly about
the CPS. In his capacity as Minister of Justice in the first independent
government, Ahmed Mestiri played a central role in the design of the CPS.
He expressed his assessment and that of many others in stating that "the
law was in advance of the society."[59] In the same vein, political speeches
on the CPS included numerous statements such as "accelerating the march
towards progress," "we cannot wait centuries," "these revolutionary measures," "induce the people to take a first step," and "the law [may] precede
the ability of citizens to apply it."[60]

Initiators of the CPS stated that their primary objective was to encourage the development of a modern nation-state. When I asked him what
was prominent in his mind in designing the code, Ahmed Mestiri replied
that his primary interest was to help create a new society and equip it with
a uniquely Tunisian legislation. He added that he and his collaborators
wanted to eradicate practices that they considered "feudal," such as child
or compulsory marriages, polygamy, and divorce by repudiation. In forging the new Tunisian nation, it was important, he said, to orient the country toward the "modern" world.[61] In the same vein, close collaborators of
Habib Bourguiba did not recall his speaking specifically about women at
the time of the 1956 reform. Instead, they remembered his treating the
issue of women's emancipation as part of, and as a condition for, the general emancipation of Tunisian society from the effect of colonialism and
archaic forms of social organization.[62]

The lawmakers in effect intended to design a law that would alter kinship relations by also emancipating men from kin control, not only
women. For example, Bourguiba expressed his opposition to families forcing young men to marry a woman that family members would choose for
reasons of their own interest. He said in a speech to the nation:

It is inadmissible, I am sorry to say, that parents constrain their son to marry a young woman chosen for their own convenience. We have in this respect strange practices. There are the young women who have been "promised" to a young man for a long time, there are the female cousins, the female relatives with various degrees of kinship closeness, a whole series of young women to marry off. . . . Let's leave the decision to those that the marriage concerns first: the husband and wife to be."[63]

The lawmakers also hoped that the new legislation would militate against endogamy within the kin grouping. For example, Bourguiba campaigned against marriages within the same villages, which were often the equivalent of a large kin grouping. He said:

I heard that, in some villages, people find it distasteful to conclude marriage alliances between villages. This would be the case, for example, between Kalaa Kebira and Kalaa Seghira, Raf-Raf, Msaken. People in these villages, convinced of their own superiority, would see it as condescending to marry someone from a neighboring village. . . . In Monastir, one does not give his daughter in marriage to the daughter of a man from Boudher or Kenius. . . . I urge fathers and mothers to avoid as much as possible marriages among people of the same blood. . . . These marriages, which are made with the greedy objective of preserving the patrimony of the kin group from strangers, produce in the long run children who are deformed and retarded. It is necessary to revive the line by marrying outsiders.[64]

When the CPS was promulgated in 1956, the Ministry of Justice accompanied it with a communiqué that stated the Islamic character of the new laws. The communiqué indicated that "religious judges and scholars had participated in [its] preparation," that the CPS had met with their approval, and that it was based on Islamic sources.[65] Members of the 1956 government presented the code as the outcome of a new phase in Islamic thinking, similar to earlier phases of interpretation (*ijtihad*) that have marked the evolution of Islamic legal thought throughout its history. They distinguished it from the reforms made under Kamal Ataturk in Turkey, where Islamic law was abandoned altogether and replaced by the Turkish Civil Code of 1926, which was almost identical to the civil code of Switzerland.

In Tunisia, the policy makers emphasized the continuing faithfulness of the law to the Islamic heritage. They described the CPS as a step necessary to free Islamic law from past misunderstandings and restore the true spirit of Islam. For example, Ahmed Mestiri, the then Minister of Justice, wrote: "The procedure of the Tunisian lawmakers has been fundamentally different from that of Kamal Ataturk. Except for the fact that they are both resolutely reformist, they differ on the key point, that is the source and content of the law."[66] He went on, stating that the Tunisian lawmakers found inspiration in the *Shari'a* and used the principle of ijtihad. He indicated that they chose to open the doors of interpretation in order to rejuvenate the Islamic tradition. He expressed his and his collaborators' belief that a renovated Islam could serve as a basis for a modern state. The extent to which the CPS is Islamic or secular in effect has led to debate since its promulgation.

The important point is the fact that the CPS was innovative with respect to the interpretations of the Shari'a that had developed historically in the Maghrib, at the same time as it retained some elements of the Shari'a. The CPS can be interpreted either way, as an Islamic body of legislation inspired by secular norms, or a secular body of legislation inspired by Islam. Scholars alternatively have emphasized the Islamic or secular character of the CPS. Focusing on innovation within the Islamic tradition, scholars such as Abdesselem and Charfi state: "The Code of Personal Status of 1956 introduced a certain number of major innovations, inspired by the spirit of Moslem law, into the field of family law."[67] Emphasizing secular norms, Olivier Carré writes: "The Tunisian code has the features of a secular civil code inspired by religion."[68] While the Islamic influence cannot be denied, it must be placed in perspective. Although the Tunisian Constitution states that Tunisia is a Muslim country, it does not say that the law has to be Islamic law, nor does the CPS suggest going back to the Shari'a to find the solution to questions not addressed in the CPS.

The CPS was promulgated as a decree by the bey of Tunisia before the abolition of the monarchy, without being debated in a national assembly. The text of the CPS actually opens with the statement, "We, Mohamed Lamine Pacha Bey, Possessor of the Kingdom of Tunisia, have issued the following decree."[69] The text then includes the seal of the then prime minister, Habib Bourguiba. When the CPS was promulgated on 13 August 1956, the country had been independent from French rule for five months, since 20 March 1956. Ben Youssef, the leader of the defeated conservative faction, also had fled the country into exile only months earlier, in January 1956. Tunisia was still a monarchy since the abolition of the monarchy and the proclamation of the Tunisian Republic did not occur until 25 July 1957.[70] The winning reformist faction whose power was uncontested at independence was able to convince the bey to sign the CPS. Having lost all power, the bey complied, and the CPS was promulgated.

The CPS met with only minor opposition. This is to be explained in large part by the outcome of the nationalist struggle. After the defenders of tradition had been silenced with the defeat of the Ben Youssef faction, the elite in power was able to set national policy without encountering much resistance in the period of independence. The leadership made the reform of family law embodied in the CPS in the same wave as it made the other reforms, those concerning local administration, tribal land ownership, and judicial system. Ben Youssef reacted to the series of reforms by making appeals from Cairo where he had taken refuge after his defeat. He exhorted the Tunisian populace to rise in protest against Bourguiba, to whom he referred as "the one who prohibited what God has authorized and authorized what God has prohibited."[71] His appeals were in vain and the Tunisian populace failed to rise in protest.

The main center of opposition to the CPS was the most conservative segment of the religious establishment. At first, the Zaytuna, the center of religious learning, which had been adamant in its condemnation of al-Haddad twenty years earlier in the 1930s, meekly accepted the reforms, expressing neither enthusiastic endorsement nor outright opposition.[72] The Zaytuna had experienced some important changes in the 1940s. Programs had been modernized and the teaching of foreign languages and cultures had been introduced. Although, as a whole, the Zaytuna remained conservative on social and religious issues, it increasingly included individuals who were more open to new ideas. A few members of the Zaytuna even had allied themselves with the winning liberal faction led by Bourguiba at the time of independence. It was not long before the Zaytuna voiced opposition to the CPS, however. In a public statement published on 17 September 1956, the rector of the Zaytuna announced that the text of the CPS was not the same as the one that he had accepted.[73] He expressed his disagreement on several of its articles. At approximately the same time, four judges of the High Islamic Tribunal asked for early retirement and five others resigned.[74] Disagreement with the new code was also expressed in some newspapers, but overall, opposition to the reforms was minimal and most of the press reacted enthusiastically.[75]

The religious establishment, the guardian of orthodoxy and the principal defender of Islamic law, did not have enough influence or political weight to resist government decisions with any chance of success. What was left of tribal areas and the religious establishment both had lost their political voice with the defeat of the Ben Youssef faction at the end of the nationalist struggle. The reformist, urban-based elite that dominated the government at the close of the nationalist struggle had the power to enforce its vision of society and to make important changes in the legal system of the country.

The CPS is called the *Majalla* in Arabic, and I use both terms interchangeably.[76] Several additions, clarifications, and amendments in the same vein have been made at different times since 1956, and the text has been regularly updated to include them. Focusing on the reforms of family law made when the sovereign national state was taking shape, the analysis here considers the CPS as it was promulgated in 1956 and some of the early amendments.

Procedure for Marriage. "Marriage is formed only by the consent of the two spouses," stated the Majalla, which required the bride to be present at the marriage contract and directly express her consent to the union.[77] The principle of matrimonial guardian was abolished. The law thus no longer sanctioned compulsory marriages, as it took away the father's or guardian's legal prerogative to give a woman in marriage even against her will. Moreover, the CPS indicated that marriage could be concluded only before two notaries or an officer of the civil registry. Marriage also had be registered with civil authorities. A certificate delivered by the civil registry, or by two notaries after they performed the marriage, became the only valid proof of marriage. A medical certificate attesting to the good health of the spouses-to-be was made mandatory. The law no longer defined marriage as a private matter, since marriage now had to be performed and recorded by civil authorities. Marriages performed in any other way had no validity before the law.

Rights and Responsibilities of Each Spouse.[78] In contrast to the Moroccan Code, which spelled out extensively the rights and responsibilities of each spouse, the CPS was concise on the issue. It maintained a conservative tone in stating that the wife owed obedience to her husband. As to the husband, he was expected to treat his wife with kindness and provide for her and their children. A new element introduced in the Majalla concerned the financial responsibility of the woman to her husband and children. Whereas in Islamic law a woman's property remained her own without becoming part of the household assets, the Majalla required the wife to contribute to the expenses of the household, if she had the means to do so. By making the wife provide for the household when appropriate, the

Majalla placed the division of responsibilities between the spouses on a new plane.

Minimum Age for Marriage.[79] The age of legal majority was set at twenty for both men and women.[80] The minimum age for marriage had been set at fifteen for a woman and eighteen for a man in the initial text of the Majalla. Statistics on marriage revealed, however, that in 1960 and 1961, 48.5 percent of the women who got married were between the ages of fifteen and nineteen, whereas only 3.8 percent of the men were between the ages of eighteen and nineteen.[81] Believing that Tunisians, and particularly women, were still marrying too young, the lawmakers issued a new law in 1964, changing the minimum age for marriage to seventeen for a woman and twenty for a man. In introducing the new law during a press conference, the Minister of Justice urged all Tunisians to get married later than the minimum age allowed, explaining that it was only for respect of social habits that the minimum age had not been set higher. According to Maurice Borrmans, the concerns of the Tunisian lawmakers in raising the minimum age for marriage were to reduce parental intervention in decisions on marriages, indirectly to limit the birth rate, and to foster greater stability in marriages, on the assumption that marriages contracted in a more mature age would be more likely to last.[82]

Divorce. The CPS changed regulations on divorce in fundamental ways. It abolished repudiation.[83] The term "repudiation" appeared nowhere in the text of the code, which referred to the dissolution of marriage consistently as "divorce." A divorce could now take place only in court. The wife and husband were equally entitled to file for divorce, and they could do so by mutual consent. One of them could also file alone, in which case the judge would determine whether compensation should be given by one spouse to the other and what the amount ought to be. Compensation was no longer defined as payment from the husband to the wife for the harm he had caused her in dissolving the marriage. Women were now equally liable to pay a compensation to their husband, if the judge estimated that it was the husband who had been wronged. An attempt at reconciliation, to be performed by the court, became mandatory. The Majalla stated in this respect: "The court cannot pronounce the divorce until it has carefully looked into the causes of the conflict opposing the spouses and failed in its attempt to reconcile them."[84]

In addition, a law promulgated in 1968 placed men and women on the same footing in regard to adultery.[85] In the law previously in effect, only

adultery committed by the wife was defined as an offense. The husband
could commit adultery, without this being legitimate grounds for the
woman to obtain a divorce.[86] In the CPS, men lost that privilege. Adultery
committed by either women or men was considered an offense, to be punished by a fine or imprisonment.

The changes introduced go counter to the conception of divorce, and
therefore of marriage, characteristic of Maliki law. The Majalla gave men
and women equal rights and responsibilities in regard to divorce. The dissolution of marriage was no longer left to the unilateral decision of the
husband, against which the woman had no recourse whatsoever. The procedure for divorce was no longer a private act resulting from the husband's
simply saying "I divorce thee" three times. It became a judicial procedure,
requiring the intervention of civil authorities. Not only was divorce made
a public matter, it also was not as easily and quickly performed as it had
been. The emphasis on efforts at reconciliation showed a preoccupation on
the part of the Tunisian lawmakers to make decisions on divorce less im-
pulsive and to intervene in an attempt to avoid the divorce. The general
significance of the reforms on divorce was to make a marriage less easily
breakable. The concern for fostering greater stability in conjugal units,
particularly apparent in the regulations on divorce, ran through the new
Tunisian code.

Care of Children, Custody, and Adoption. The Majalla made the father
and mother both responsible for the care of a child, as long as they lived
together. If the father was no longer able to provide for the child, either
in case of death or for any other reason, the next person called upon to
assume responsibility was the mother, who now came before any other
relatives in the order of responsibility.[87] In case of divorce, the CPS initially
stipulated that the son would remain with the mother until the age of
seven, and the daughter until the age of nine, at which point the father
could request the custody of his children. The transfer from mother to
father was not to occur automatically, however. The judge was urged by
the law to consider the best interest of the child before anything else.

A new law brought an end to the right of the father to request his
children at a given age, stating that there would be no limit on the duration
of custody granted to the mother.[88] The judge was to decide to whom to
grant custody, without taking into account degrees or types of kin relations, and by considering exclusively the interest of the child. Rather than
basing custody on the nature of the kinship tie between the child and a
hierarchy of relatives, the Majalla made the well-being of the child the

determining factor. By the same token, it abolished the automatic transfer of children to the father or the paternal kin group.

Whereas Islamic law did not recognize adoption, the Majalla made it valid.[89] It allowed an adopted child to have the same rights and obligations as a natural child, to become a full member of the family, to take the name of the adopting parent, and to inherit. As long as they had reached the age of majority, men and women could both adopt a child. In this respect too, women and men were given equal rights and responsibilities. Furthermore, the person adopting a child, either man or woman, did not have to be married. The new laws on adoption represented a true "revolution in mentalities and mores."[90] They undermined the emphasis on actual blood ties and the definition of filiation only through the father's line.

Civil Status and Patronymic Name.[91] A law promulgated in August 1959 specified the responsibilities of Tunisian citizens in regard to civil status. In addition to making mandatory the declaration of birth, death, marriage, and divorce, the law of 1959 made clear the procedures to follow for each declaration. Another law stipulated that every Tunisian citizen had to have a patronymic name. In 1959, every head of household, man or women, had to choose a patronymic name, if he or she did not already have one. One could no longer be called son of X who was son of Y, as had been customary until then for the majority of Tunisians. The reform was necessary for the proper functioning of the civil registry records and other administrative procedures. It also had an important symbolic meaning. Each individual now had his or her name and life events registered in records kept by the state. Equally important symbolically, one's public identity was no longer expressed exclusively by reference to the patrilineage.

Polygamy.[92] The Majalla outlawed polygamy altogether. It stated unequivocally that "polygamy [was] forbidden."[93] An attempt at marrying again, while one was still married, was now punished with imprisonment of a year and a fine of approximately five hundred dollars, which represented the equivalent of a year's income for many Tunisians when the CPS was promulgated in 1956. The law stated that polygamy was forbidden and punished, but it did not declare a second marriage null and void. Presumably, someone could choose to incur the penalties and still marry more than one wife.

To clarify this uncertainty, a new law appeared in 1964, declaring the second marriage of a man already married null and void. Moreover, if a man and woman resumed conjugal life after their polygamous marriage had been declared null and void, they would both be subject to imprisonment and a fine, the man for having broken the law on polygamy and the woman as his accomplice. In all matters of polygamy, the judge was urged to apply the maximum sentence. Tunisian lawmakers left little doubt as to their determination to use all legal resources available to suppress polygamy once and for all.

Inheritance.[94] The initial statement on inheritance contained in the CPS was faithful to Maliki law. It maintained the same two basic categories of heirs, those who receive a well-defined part of the assets because of the nature of their kin relation to the deceased and those who are called to inherit on the basis of agnatism.[95] The rule according to which the share of a man is twice as large as that of a woman was also preserved. In the light of the other regulations of the CPS, which gave more rights to women and favored the conjugal family over the extended patrilineal kinship system, the stipulations on inheritance were surprising. They did not seem in concord with the spirit of the Majalla as a whole. Reforms affecting inheritance appeared in the regulations on wills and in separate laws and decrees, promulgated after the Majalla itself. Although, at first sight, the changes in regard to inheritance were not as striking as in other areas of family law, they nevertheless were significant for kinship relations.

For example, the Decree of 1956 and the Law of 1957, which abolished the habus institution, also had implications for family relationships and for women.[96] By donating a piece of land as habus to a religious or charitable institution, one could escape the strict inheritance rules of the Shari'a.[97] The habus were sometimes used to deprive women of their inheritance rights. They often served as a useful device for kinship units to keep their holding intact by excluding female heirs in favor of male relatives in the male line. In making the constitution of a habus illegal, the new legislation removed the availability of such a device.

The CPS regulated the procedure for wills, which could no longer be made orally. A will now had to appear in writing and be dated and signed by its author in order to be valid. As previously, a will could not apply to more than one third of a person's assets, the other two thirds going to specified heirs. But an important change was introduced in regard to wills and the children of a predeceased daughter. Suppose that a man's daughter had died and left a child. Previously, the child of his predeceased daughter could not be the beneficiary of a man's will, whereas children of a predeceased son could be. This was concordant with the rule of agnatism prevalent in Islamic family law and with the inheritance privileges granted to relatives in the male line. In contrast, the new laws allowed a man to make the child of his predeceased daughter the beneficiary of his will, thus transmitting one third of his assets to the female line. In a society in which the male line had been overwhelmingly favored in inheritance, this constituted a substantial change.

The same philosophy, striking a similar blow to agnatic privileges, appeared in two other regulations introduced in 1959.[98] The first gave the spouse greater access to inheritance. The second favored daughters and granddaughters over some agnatic relatives. According to the Maliki school of law, in case there were no agnatic heirs, the remainder of the heritage after the specified heirs (the quota sharers) received their quota, went to the state or to some communal or public fund. In Hanafi law, one of the other Islamic schools of law, this issue was handled differently. Called "return," a Hanafi rule in effect returned the remainder of the inheritance to some of the heirs. If there were no agnatic heirs, the remainder was distributed among the first category of heirs, those who were identified in the Shari'a and whose share was specified. The spouse was excluded from this kind of inheritance, however. All the other heirs would receive part of the remainder in proportion with their initial part, only the spouse would not.

Abandoning Maliki principles, Tunisian law adopted the system of "return" of the Hanafi school. In addition, it changed the rule concerning the spouse, making him or her a recipient of the return in the same way as all the other quota sharers. The implication of this legal reform was far reaching. Under the same circumstances, namely in the absence of agnatic relatives, Maliki law gave the spouse only half of the patrimony, while the other half went to a public or communal fund. In contrast, under the new law, the spouse received the totality of the patrimony, the first half as her quota share and the second half on the basis of the "return" principle. The patrimony in its entirety thus would now go to the spouse. And the rule held true whether the surviving spouse was male or female. This was another indication of the tendency of the Tunisian lawmakers to extend the inheritance rights of members of the conjugal family.

The second reform of inheritance rules went even further in shifting the direction of property transmission and in lessening the inheritance rights of extended kin. It allowed women to take precedence over or, to use the legal term, to exclude some agnatic heirs altogether. The Law of June 1959 stated: "The daughter and the granddaughter in the male line benefit from 'return' even in the presence of agnatic relatives in the category of brothers, paternal uncles and their descendants."[99] Suppose that a man died leaving a daughter and a brother or a paternal uncle. Under the new law, the daughter now received the whole patrimony, thereby excluding from inheritance the brother or the paternal uncle of the deceased. Under Maliki law, the daughter would have received only half of the patrimony and the other half would have gone to the brother or paternal uncles who would have inherited as agnates. In the same kinship configuration, a woman now received twice as much as she previously did. At the death of the daughter, the property that she had received to the detriment of her uncle or granduncle would then pass to her children, thus escaping the agnatic kin group altogether.

The Tunisian reforms as a whole have been interpreted as favoring women.[100] Like other laws in the CPS, the laws on inheritance certainly expanded women's rights. Inheritance laws also did something else, which was to sanction the nuclear family. For what was noteworthy about the new laws was not only that women excluded some men, but it was the particular category of male relatives that women excluded versus those that they did not. A careful reading of the law of 1959, for example, shows that daughters and granddaughters now excluded collateral male relatives of the deceased, namely brothers, paternal uncles, and their children. But they did not exclude the son, grandson, or father of the deceased. There are two kinds of male relatives in the paternal line: descendants such as son and grandson and collateral kin such as brothers and uncles. In Maliki law, they were all called to inherit as agnates. Under the new law, sons and grandsons of the deceased retained their inheritance rights whereas his brothers and uncles were excluded by daughters.

The key to understanding the reforms of inheritance laws is that they favored descendants of both sexes over collateral relatives. They did not directly favor women as such. In the transmission of property, a child, whether male *or* female, now had priority over other kin, even if the other kin were males. The male relatives that were excluded, brothers, uncles, and cousins, constituted the center of the circle within which relations of solidarity and reciprocal obligations were historically emphasized in the Maghribi kin group. One of the Tunisian reforms favored the spouse and the other favored descendants over other kin. Taken together, the reforms represented a strengthening of the conjugal unit and its progeny, to the detriment of the extended agnatic group.

In summary, the CPS made drastic innovations, even though it retained some aspects of Islamic family law, such as the rule according to which a woman inherits half as much as a man in the same kinship configuration.

As a whole, the CPS departed from Islamic law in its general conception of the family and in its specific regulations. Among the innovations, it abolished polygamy, repudiation, and the father's or guardian's right of matrimonial constraint. It required the bride to express her voluntary consent for the marriage to be valid. It gave men and women equal rights and responsibilities in regard to divorce. It made divorce less easy than it had been and required that it take place in court. It made the wife responsible for contributing to the expenses of the household and for support of her children. It gave custody to the mother if this was in the child's best interest. It reorganized civil status by making the registration of marriages and divorces mandatory. It made adoption legally valid. It required a patronymic name for all citizens. It abolished the institution of the habus. It modified the rules on inheritance so as to favor the spouse and female descendants over several agnatic relatives and, like the Moroccan and Algerian codes but with a fundamentally different content, it provided clearly formulated legal documents that facilitated the work of the judicial and administrative systems.

The promulgation of the CPS was followed by extensive efforts on the part of the government to explain the reforms to the Tunisian population and to enforce their application. Assigned a social responsibility, judges were called upon as social educators whose mission was not only to apply the new laws, but also to make the mutations required in family life more understandable to Tunisian citizens.[101] The code was presented to Tunisians as the expression of national goals and aspirations. Conferences and seminars were organized to provide explanations and clarifications of the code. August 13, the anniversary of the promulgation of the CPS, was made Women's Day. The party of the Neo-Destour and all national organizations were urged to share in the effort required to help make the social transition that the new laws entailed. The CPS became a matter of national pride. It also became a national project to which all parts of the government were asked to contribute and in which all Tunisians were invited to participate.

•　　•　　•

The Tunisian political leadership that took the reins of power enjoyed a period of internal consensus from 1956 to the early 1960s. The consensus was crucial in shaping state institutions and state policies. The faction that emerged victorious from the nationalist factional conflicts of the mid-1950s constituted a cohesive and pragmatic political elite united behind strategy and ideology during the critical period following independence. In that period, the leadership made administrative and legal reforms that had one feature in common. The reforms converged toward creating or reinforcing nationwide institutions at the expense of local forms of association, especially those based on tribal allegiances. The reforms implemented the vision of the victorious leadership, the reformist, urban-based elite allied with Bourguiba. This was a vision in which tribal kin groupings were marginalized. It involved in particular a kinship transformation from extended patrilineages to nuclear-family structures. The general program of state-building reforms also further weakened the social base of the defeated faction that had relied heavily on tribal areas and the Islamic establishment.

The newly formed national state was able to make a radical family law reform because a modernizing faction faced no political challenger at the critical moment when it took the reins of power in 1956. Defeated in factional conflicts at the eve of independence from French rule, the potential opposition, which could have spoken for a conservative interpretation of Islamic law and blocked the reforms, had lost all political leverage at that particular time. Made possible by the relative autonomy of the national state from kin groupings, family law reform was part and by-product of the broader national policy to create a new nation-state in which tribal allegiances would no longer serve as a basis for political action. Once victorious and unchallenged, the elite in power in Tunisia treated family law reform as part of the transformation of society deemed necessary for the development of a modern state.

Conclusion
State Building, Family Law, and Women's Rights

The purpose of this book has been to explain differences in state policies on family law and women's rights in the three Maghribi countries. A reform of the version of Islamic law that historically came to prevail throughout the region was a prerequisite for expanding women's rights. The central question posed in the book, why the state engaged in—or refrained from—reform, has been compelling in the light of cultural similarities shared by Tunisia, Algeria, and Morocco with respect to religion, gender relations, and kinship structure. It has been made even more intriguing by the presence of a reformist ideology that favored changing the law within the nationalist movement in each of the countries.

The study has argued that the particular fate of family law was shaped by the process of state formation in each country, especially the degree of autonomy of the state from—versus reliance upon—kin-based solidarities. Family law served as an instrument for the maintenance of the social and political status quo in Morocco. It was held hostage to political divisions and then subject to political expediency in Algeria. It was treated as a force for change in Tunisia. In all three Maghribi countries, family law policy came "from above" as a strategic choice by the elites in power. Postindependence family law was formulated by the political leadership, which chose to maintain Islamic law, oscillated between alternatives or actively promulgated reforms.

The closer the ties of the victorious nationalist leadership with kin groupings, the smaller were the prospects for family law reform at independence. Allied with coalitions anchored in tribal areas, Morocco promptly took a conservative stand, restricting its action almost entirely to a codification of Islamic law in a concise text (1957–58). Using a carrot-and-stick strategy toward kin-based solidarities, the postindependence Al-

233

gerian government shied away from either a conservative codification of family law or substantive reforms from independence in 1962 until 1984, as several plans for a national legislation aborted. The Algerian Family Code finally enacted in 1984 maintained the thrust of Islamic law on most matters. A disappointment for many who expected a legislation more favorable to women's rights from socialist Algeria, the Algerian Code dashed the hopes generated during the struggle of national liberation. Autonomous from tribes and opposed to their perpetuation, the Tunisian leadership fundamentally reformed its family law and thereby expanded women's rights. There is near consensus among analysts of the Maghrib in describing the 1956 Tunisian Code of Personal Status and its amendments as revolutionary and a daring break from the past.

HISTORY, STRATEGY, AND POLICY

To understand the politics and policies of the newly independent Maghribi states, it is necessary to include long-term historical trajectories in the analysis. Attention must be paid to the fact that tribal kin groupings historically have acted as corporate structures in the economic and political spheres. Until recent times, the "republics of cousins," as Germaine Tillion cleverly calls the Maghribi kin groupings, engaged in intermittent conflict, latent or overt, with central authority.[1] Throughout much of their history, the states of Maghribi societies had to contend with politics involving kin-based solidarities.

In all three countries, long-term historical trajectories set the stage on which the political strategies of the national leadership and family law policies would later unfold. But they set a different stage in each country, as different developments in the precolonial and colonial periods affected the political leverage retained by kin groupings. Such developments created different conditions that influenced the ways in which people could be mobilized in the nationalist struggle, especially the extent to which kin or tribal ties provided a basis for collective political action. Different historical developments also shaped the degree of autonomy from tribal kin groupings achieved by the elites in power and their incentives to further undermine kin-based solidarities.

In Morocco, the French strategy of indirect administration and divide and rule left tribal organization little affected by colonization. At independence, the Moroccan monarchy co-opted coalitions based on tribal kin groupings. It relied on these coalitions not because its power was rooted in the allegiance of any one group, but because the existence of kin-based solidarities allowed for the playing-off of factions as a way to prevent any single force from emerging as a significant political rival.

In Algeria, the effect of colonization was to destroy some of the tribes and to leave others in place while the country as a whole experienced devastation. Divided by ideological and tribally rooted cleavages, the Algerian leadership included segments that mobilized the republics of cousins as a way of gaining political leverage in the politics of the national state. Showing ambivalence toward kin-based associations, the Algerian state combined tolerance with an attempt to control these associations.

The Tunisian state, in contrast to the Moroccan and Algerian cases, inherited a strong state bureaucracy from the precolonial and colonial periods. A mostly urban-based political elite developed in relative autonomy from tribal kin groupings. It then engaged in a broad range of policies meant to eradicate what was left of tribal solidarities in politics. The Tunisian state, and the urban-based reformist faction that led it, in effect used all means available to marginalize tribal groups in the aftermath of independence.

When a nation-state had to be built on the structure left by the colonial regime, law constituted a major tool at the disposal of the political leadership as it implemented its vision of the future country. Law represents a summation of objectives for the social system. One of the functions of the law is to structure social relations and to imprint on social dynamics a certain direction. The type of family law enacted in each country was a direct expression of the model of kinship favored by the elites in power in the newly formed national state. It carried a specific message regarding the preferred course of development for the kinship structure as envisaged by those elites.

The Tunisian Code of Personal Status (CPS) promulgated in 1956 by the mostly urban, reformist leadership presented a new ideal or norm, that of the conjugal unit. The code gave greater individual rights and responsibilities to women in the family and by extension in the larger society. It decreased considerably the legal control of male kin over women in marriage. It also weakened the legal privileges of the extended patrilineal kin group in matters of inheritance while strengthening those of the conjugal unit. Although the law did not preclude the practice of endogamy or kin-controlled exogamy, it no longer sanctioned it. Whereas Islamic family law previously in effect in Tunisia portrayed the conjugal unit as easily breakable, the CPS emphasized the durability and importance of marriage. The message of the reforms left little ambiguity. The CPS legitimated the conjugal family and shifted the lines of solidarity from the extended agnatic group to the conjugal unit.

This was in keeping with the nation-building strategy of the victorious and cohesive Tunisian leadership that sought to expand the state apparatus and re-orient political loyalties from kin-based local solidarities to the nation-state. Accordingly, family law reform in Tunisia redefined the rights and responsibilities of individuals by presenting a concept of kinship that not only departed from the model associated with kin groupings, but steered individuals away from the extended kin group. The new Tunisian laws thus challenged the extended patrilineage and therefore its extension, the tribal kin grouping.

In Morocco, in contrast, the family law supported by the monarchy and enacted in the Code of Personal Status, *Mudawwana*, of 1957–58 favored a strongly agnatic kinship structure. Its message was that the extended patrilineage that served as the building block of kin groupings remained the locus of critical ties for reciprocal obligations and support. The model of the family embodied in the postindependence Moroccan Code of Personal Status remained the same as in Maliki law. The Mudawwana kept women in a subordinate legal status. In leaving the legal control of marriages in the hands of the patrilineage, the law continued to sanction endogamy and kin-controlled exogamy. The marital bond was still easily breakable through repudiation. Inheritance rules, taken unchanged from Maliki law, maintained the inheritance privileges of agnates in the extended patrilineage to the detriment of daughters and wives.

By opting for a legal system in favor of agnatism, Moroccan lawmakers, under the direct supervision of the monarchy, maintained the model typical of the Maghribi kinship structure as defined by the preservation of property for the agnatic kinship network, the primacy of internal cohesiveness, and the significance of kin-based solidarities. Moroccan law thereby retained the model of kinship that had been central to the collective identity of tribal kin groupings. The preservation of Maliki family law in Morocco in the 1950s avoided disrupting kin-based solidarities in those tribal areas where the monarchy found its staunchest allies in the aftermath of independence. And, because it kept in place tribal segmentation, such preservation could only serve to facilitate the monarchy's strategy of acting as orchestrator among regions and factions.

Like the Moroccan Mudawwana, the conservative Algerian Family Code finally adopted in 1984 remained faithful to Maliki law from which it differed only on minor points. On most issues such as divorce, polygamy, and inheritance, Maliki regulations continued to apply. Like the Moroccan Mudawwana, the 1984 Algerian Code defined the conjugal unit as fragile and continued to sanction kin-based solidarities. The Algerian Code thus embodied a model of the kinship structure as an extended patrilineage in which male kin have privileges and men have power over women.

The political paralysis over family law in Algeria from 1962 to 1984 resulted in part from the divisions of the leadership among multiple factions. Only some segments of the Algerian national leadership voiced support for family law reform, as they wished to foster the development of a conjugal family. Opposed to such reform, other segments chose to leave the extended patrilineage in place. Family law thus was held hostage to the political tensions generated by factionalism and the ensuing climate of distrust and uncertainty. The impasse in the law and the aborted plans resulted from a confrontation between two different blueprints for Algerian society with two different visions of the family.

The code finally enacted in 1984 was of the kind that would satisfy those social groups that saw the extended patrilineage as the appropriate family form for Algerian society. It found an echo among the republics of cousins in the countryside at the same time as it preserved their kin-based social organization. It also was likely to appeal to rural migrants in urban areas, who longed for the restoration of extended patrilineages. In promulgating the code, the Algerian government of the mid-1980s sought to preserve its base of support in rural and urban areas and to diminish the appeal of Islamic fundamentalism, which by then represented an increasingly serious rival. With the conservative Family Code, the Algerian government of the mid-1980s in effect sacrificed family law reform to political expediency.

It is notable that the only Maghribi country to experience family law reform in the years following independence, Tunisia, had no grassroots feminist movement in that period. Furthermore, the only country to experience grassroots women's activism before the promulgation of its family code, Algeria, did not reform its family law. It should also be noted that neither conservative family legislation (Morocco and Algeria) nor liberal reform (Tunisia) can be explained by the ideology on family law during the nationalist period. In all three countries, regardless of organizational structure, pattern of mobilization, or tactics, nationalists usually agreed on the necessity to retain Islamic family law as the cornerstone of Maghribi identity in the face of French domination. Although some individual leaders made concrete proposals for changes in the law, most nationalists agreed that reforms should be postponed until they could be made in a sovereign country. Besides, the three nationalist movements held a fairly similar range of positions on Islamic family law during the nationalist period, as all three countries had a reformist and conservative trend.

In retrospect, it is clear how family law policy followed from different political strategies of the elites in power in the newly formed national state. Such strategies made family law reform and the concomitant threat to kin-based solidarities possible in Tunisia, improbable in Algeria, and unlikely in Morocco. In Tunisia, it was in the best interest of the state leadership to break kin-based solidarities, and it was possible for it to do so because tribal groups had already lost much of their leverage as politically relevant actors. In Algeria, it was also in the best interest of some segments of the factionalized leadership to foster a rearrangement of kinship by weakening agnatic kin groupings. This was not the case, however, for other segments of the leadership for whom it made political sense to oppose policies that could alienate or weaken their base in tribal areas. In Morocco, it was in the interest of the monarchy to refrain from forcing major changes in kinship as its power derived to a considerable extent from its ability to maintain a balance among tribally rooted communities. Furthermore, its political challengers found their greatest support in the nontribal sectors of society.

The reasons for the different family policies of the three sovereign states in the aftermath of independence thus lie neither in the ideology of the nationalists nor in pressures from below, but instead in struggles for state power and in state-building strategies. What made the most important difference was neither the history of family law itself nor the history of opinions about the law, but the history of politics.

SOME THEORETICAL IMPLICATIONS

The framework developed to analyze differences among the three countries has called attention to long-term historical trajectories, strategies of the political leadership at critical historical moments, and policy outcomes. In theoretical terms, the book has argued that the process of state formation, especially the integration of tribal kin groupings into the nation-state, as mediated by the political conflicts and alliances of the political leadership of the newly formed national state, shaped the development of family law policy. Like the states of other newly independent nations in the wave of decolonization of the mid-twentieth century, those of the Maghrib faced the tasks of developing a nation-state in the context of the historically specific social structure left by colonization. Structural conditions inherited from the precolonial and colonial period delineated the range of options and strategies available to the leadership as it made alliances in seeking power. They also shaped the advantages—or costs—involved in autonomy from kin-based communities and in family law reform.

I have indicated that social segmentation versus state bureaucratization in the aftermath of independence resulted mostly from the way in which the following three dimensions combined in the particular history of each country: 1) the strength of tribal groups prior to colonization, 2) the form of colonial rule, and 3) the characteristics and strategies of the national state that emerged from the nationalist struggle. The notion of structural conditions aims to identify potential allies for the groups in power and to elucidate the basis on which such groups made alliances. In considering state-building strategies, I have addressed the question whether, from the standpoint of their own interests, the powerholders found it advantageous to engage in reforms of family law given the matrix of political conflicts and alliances in which they were involved.

Although structural conditions inherited from the colonial and precolonial periods defined a range of possible alliances for the nationalist leadership in the Maghrib, they did not determine the outcomes of the nationalist struggles. Nor were the outcomes accidental. Precolonial and colonial histories analyzed in part 2 of the book generated the potential for state autonomy from tribes and for the kind of nationwide centralization that was the hallmark of modern states in the mid-twentieth century. It is more useful to think of structural conditions as delimiting a range of possible variations than as determining outcomes. Within the structurally delineated range, historically specific occurrences then contributed to the outcome, as shown in part 3. While several alliances and divisions were possible, the range of options available to each nationalist movement was far from identical. The three movements operated in very different social contexts, offering different potential roles to tribes as allies in the anticolonial struggle and as social bases for power in the new state.

The book has treated the issue of family law and women's rights as an inherent part of the larger struggles to build a modern state in the Maghrib. In reforming family law, a state redefines rights and obligations for men and women in the family, the community, and, by extension, the society at large. Neither neutral nor benevolent, states are inherently institutions of control. They are not disinterested actors. Unless forced to do otherwise, a state elite selects among alternative family law policies those that either conform with its interests or at least do not jeopardize them. At times, the interests of a state elite and those of women overlap, as in the period of independence in Tunisia. At other times they diverge, as in

Morocco and Algeria. National states in newly sovereign countries do not necessarily strive toward the weakening of kin-based local solidarities and the redefinition of the relationship between individuals and social groups. There is more than one strategy for holding power, as is evinced by the three paths followed in the Maghrib.

Whether the structural framework developed in this book sheds light on cases other than those considered can be assessed only by further comparative research. The framework addresses cases where pressure from women's grassroots movements is either absent or ineffective, as in the Maghrib in the period under consideration. Can the argument simply be transposed unmodified to cases beyond Tunisia, Algeria, and Morocco in the aftermath of independence? The answer is no. The specific structural and historical arguments developed for the three countries cannot mechanically be extended to other societies. A structural and historical analysis by definition requires that systematic attention be paid to the particular social structure and history of the society considered, thus placing built-in limits on generalizing.

The theoretical framework has delineated a conceptualization and pointed to questions that should prove useful in the analysis of state policies on women's rights in other cases, however. It applies best to kin-based social structures where ties within lineages, clans, or tribes serve as a major basis for political mobilization and collective action.[2] Key issues to consider in the structural and comparative-historical analysis of state policies on women's rights proposed in this book include: the legacy of historical trajectories and structural forces on the polity; the state-building strategies as shaped by state autonomy from—versus reliance on—kin-based formations; the political strength of the coalitions that find support among kin groupings; the extent to which women serve as a resource for kin groups; and the social-structural issues involved in the state policy under investigation, such as the potential strengthening versus weakening of kin-based solidarities.

The framework applies especially to historical periods when kin-based societies emerge from colonization. This is a time when a central state expands its control over territory and consolidates its power in the context of a kin-based social structure left by colonial rule. For colonization may have the effect of strengthening tribal organization. If there is a process that tends to reactivate kin-based political solidarities, it is the achievement of independence itself. This is a moment when access to power is at stake. Contenders to state power mobilize their followers, sometimes on the basis of particularistic ties. Groups that feel left out demand the attention of the state by reawakening local allegiances.

After the newly formed state develops authority and administrative control over the national territory, issues of state power tend to change. So do the contenders for power and the potential partners in alliances and conflicts. State formation in kin-based societies may or may not resolve old contradictions involving the relationship between states and tribes at the same time as it is likely to generate new bases for conflict. Once the state is in place, kin-based solidarities may present themselves differently, pose new challenges, or become irrelevant to state policies. The important point is that the development of a national state in a postcolonial society is a critical historical moment that brings the relationship between state and kin-based solidarities to center stage in politics and thus in the formulation of policies.

In broad terms, the book has sought to make the relationship between state and tribe and its political consequences for family law a central problem of comparative history. It suggests expanding the analysis of policies on women's rights by considering the long-term historical development of states in kin-based, non-Western societies. A task in comparative history is to contextualize the analysis of states and their policies. It is also to decipher the structural conditions that shape state policies on women's rights in a wide range of societies. Sensitivity to variations among countries outside the West has the potential to open the door to a deeper understanding of the forces behind state politics and policies.

At the most general level, a central point of this book has been to show how state formation and struggles over state power play a key role in the development of state policies on women's rights. The focus has been on historically derived conflicts and alliances between the state elite and social groups that have the highest stakes in women's subordination. In the absence of women's agency, states handle women's rights in a variety of ways, depending on their own sources of support, their projects for the future society, and the nature of other contenders to power within each historical context. Policies on family law and women's rights thus become pawns in broader conflicts and alliances. They become the outcome and sometimes a tool of struggles among social and political groups fighting over state power.

Glossary

The glossary follows the guidelines indicated in the "Note on Foreign Words and Transliteration." When two words appear, the first shows the form I have used in the book, and the second the transliteration with diacritics if there is a difference between the two.

agnate	male relative in the paternal line
amm, ʿamm	paternal uncle
asabiyya, ʿaṣabiyya	solidarity, *esprit de clan*, tribal cohesion
Aures	a predominantly Berber region in Algeria
ayla, ʿāʾila	used in this book to mean extended patrilineage, also to refer to family or kin group in a general sense
ibn (also often *ben* in the Maghrib)	son
beni, banū	sons, members of a tribe recognizing a common ancestor
beni amm, banū ʿamm	literally the sons of the father's brother; circle of cousins, tribal faction, entire tribal group
bey	monarch, ruler (in Tunisia), nominally under Ottoman suzerainty
beylical	under the bey, that belongs to the bey
bilad al-makhzan (also *bled* or *blad makhzen*), *bilād al-makhzan*	land of government, territory under the control of central authority
bilad es-siba (also *bled siba*), *bilād al-sība*	land of dissidence, tribal areas outside the control of central authority

bint (also often *bent* in the Maghrib)	daughter
CPS	the Tunisian Code of Personal Status
dahir, ẓahīr	decree issued by the monarch
destour, al-dustūr	constitution
FBD	father's brother's daughter
FLN	Algerian Front of National Liberation referred to by its French acronym; FLN stands for Front de Liberation Nationale
FFFLN	French Federation of the FLN
habus, ḥubus	pious endowment
Hadith, Ḥadīth	narrative relating the deeds and pronouncements of the Prophet Muhammad and his companions
hadiya, hadīya	tribute (taxation)
Hanafi, Ḥanafī	one of the schools of legal interpretation in Islam, historically the law of a minority in the Maghrib
Hanbali, Ḥanbalī	one of the schools of legal interpretation in Islam
hanut, ḥanūt	room, shop
ijma, ijmā'	community consensus
ijtihad, ijtihād	interpretation, the exertion of independent reasoning in legal and theological matters
ird, 'irḍ	collective reputation of a kin group, honor, prestige in the community
jabr	legal prerogative of a man to constrain a woman under his guardianship to take the husband of his choice
jamaa (also *djemmaa* in the Maghrib), *jamā'a*	tribal council, local assembly
Kabylia	a predominantly Berber region in Algeria
khal	maternal uncle
latif, laṭīf	invocation to God, special form of prayer usually in time of distress
Majalla	the Tunisian Code of Personal Status
makhzan (also *makhzen*)	storehouse, treasury, and, by extension, government

Maliki, Mālikī	one of the schools of legal interpretation in Islam; the school that has historically predominated in the Maghrib
maquis	area of guerilla warfare
moudjahidates (plural of *moudjahida*), *mujāhidāt*	female fighters, women who took part in the anticolonial guerilla war in Algeria
Mudawwana	the Moroccan Code of Personal Status
nasab	agnatic lineage, line of male ancestors on the paternal side, filiation
qadi (also *cadi*), *qāḍi*	religious judge
qaid (also *caid*), *qāʾid*	administrator of a rural district or a region, governor of a province
qiyas, qiyās	reasoning by analogy
résident général	supreme representative of France during colonization
Rif, Rīf	a region in northern Morocco
Shafii, Shāfiʿī	one of the schools of legal interpretation in Islam
Shariʿa, Sharīʿa	the holy law of Islam
sharif, sharīf	descendant of the Prophet
shaykh (also shaikh)	chief, leader, head of a tribe, administrative authority in local areas
Shii, Shīʿī	minority branch of Islam, divided from the Sunni majority by issues of theology and doctrine; the Shiʿis have a more formally organized religious establishment
siba, sība	dissidence
Sunna	deeds and pronoucements of the Prophet Muhammad as recorded in compendia called *Hadiths*
Sunni, Sunnī	majority branch of Islam
sura, sūra	a chapter in the Qurʾan
transhumant	semi-nomadic; applies to tribes that typically made two moves a year, one to the mountains in the spring and the other to the lower valleys in the fall
transhumance	periodic nomadic moves
ulama (pl.of *ʿalim*), *ʿulamāʾ*	religious scholars
watan, waṭan	nation

waqf	pious endowment
wazir, wazīr	court official, government minister
wilaya, wilāya	district, region, military zone in the Algerian anticolonial war
Zaytuna, Zaytūna	faculty of theology and center of religious scholarship (Tunisia)

Notes

All translations are the author's unless otherwise indicated.

INTRODUCTION

1. International Women's Rights Action Watch (IWRAW), the Committee on the Elimination of Discrimination against Women (CEDAW), 1995 Country Reports, prepared by Sharon Ladin (Minneapolis: Humphrey Institute of Public Affairs, University of Minnesota, 1995).

2. Maghrib means "west" in Arabic. The region to which the term refers is the western tip of the Arab-Islamic world. I have chosen not to include Libya in the analysis because Libya was colonized by Italy, whereas the other three countries were all under French rule. In this study, the terms "Middle East" and "Middle East and the Maghrib" are used interchangeably to denote the region between Morocco and Iran.

3. I borrow the expression from Robert Descloitres and Laid Debzi, "Système de parenté et structures familiales en Algérie," *Annuaire de l'Afrique du Nord* (Paris: Editions du Centre National de la Recherche Scientifique, 1963): 23–59.

4. Asma Khadar, president of the Jordanian Women's Union, quoted in the *Association for Middle East Women's Studies Newsletter* 10, no. 4 (Jan. 1996): 2.

5. Charles Tilly, ed., *The Formation of National States in Western Europe* (Princeton: Princeton University Press, 1975); Lisa Anderson, *The State and Social Transformation in Tunisia and Libya, 1830–1980* (Princeton: Princeton University Press, 1986); Immanuel M. Wallerstein, *The Modern World-System. 1. Capitalist Agriculture and the Origins of the European World-Economy in the Sixteenth Century* (New York: Academic Press, 1974); and Perry Anderson, *Lineages of the Absolutist State* (London: New Left Books, 1974).

6. Theda Skocpol, *States and Social Revolutions: A Comparative Analysis*

of France, Russia, and China (Cambridge: Cambridge University Press, 1979); Peter B. Evans, Dietrich Rueschemeyer, and Theda Skocpol, eds., *Bringing the State Back In* (Cambridge: Cambridge University Press, 1985); Theda Skocpol, *Protecting Soldiers and Mothers: The Political Origins of Social Policy in the United States* (Cambridge: Belknap Press of Harvard University Press, 1992); Fred L. Block, *Revising State Theory: Essays in Politics and Postindustrialism* (Philadelphia: Temple University Press, 1987); and Ann S. Orloff, *The Politics of Pensions: A Comparative Analysis of Britain, Canada, and the United States, 1880–1940* (Madison: University of Wisconsin Press, 1993).

7. My initial formulation of the relationship between state and kin-based solidarities as shaping family law policy in the Maghrib appeared in Mounira M. Charrad, "State and Gender in the Maghrib," *Middle East Report* (Mar.– Apr. 1990), reprinted in *Gendering Political Cultures in the Middle East*, Suad Joseph and Susan Slyomovics, eds. (Philadelphia: University of Pennsylvania Press, 2001), and "State, Civil Society and Gender: Examples from the Maghrib," Conference on "Retreating States and Expanding Societies," Social Science Research Council and American Council of Learned Societies, Aix-en-Provence, France, 25–27 March 1988. Abbreviated versions of the theoretical framework developed in this book appear in Mounira M. Charrad, "Policy Shifts: State, Islam and Gender in Tunisia, 1930s–1990s," *Social Politics* 4, no. 2 (summer 1997): 284–319, and "Formation de l'état et statut personnel au Maghreb: Esquisse d'une analyse comparative et théorique," in *Femmes, culture et société au Maghreb*, ed. Rahma Bourqia, Mounira M. Charrad, and Nancy Gallagher, vol. 2 (Casablanca: Afrique Orient, 1996), 15–32.

8. See, for example, Louise A. Tilly and Patricia Gurin, eds., *Women, Politics, and Change* (New York: Russell Sage Foundation, 1990); Ann Bookman and Sandra Morgen, eds., *Women and the Politics of Empowerment* (Philadelphia: Temple University Press, 1988); Joyce Gelb and Marian L. Palley, *Women and Public Policies*, rev. ed. (Princeton: Princeton University Press, 1987); and Sylvia B. Bashevkin, *Women on the Defensive: Living through Conservative Times* (Chicago: University of Chicago Press, 1998).

9. A theoretical elaboration may be found in the works of Suad Joseph, "Gender and Citizenship in Middle Eastern States," *Middle East Report* 26, no. 198 (Jan.–Mar. 1996): 4–10; "Problematizing Gender and Relational Rights: Experiences from Lebanon," *Social Politics* 1, no. 3 (fall 1994): 271–85; "Elite Strategies for State Building: Women, Family, Religion and the State in Iraq and Lebanon," in *Women, Islam and the State*, ed. Deniz Kandiyoti (Philadelphia: Temple University Press, 1991); and the introduction to *Citizenship and Gender in the Middle East*, ed. Suad Joseph (Syracuse: Syracuse University Press, 2000). Many other important studies are included in Michelle R. Kimball and Barbara R. von Schlegell, *Muslim Women throughout the World: A Bibliography* (Boulder: Lynne Rienner, 1997).

10. Jacques Berque, *Structures sociales du Haut-Atlas* (Paris: Presses Universitaires de France, 1955); Ernest Gellner, *Saints of the Atlas* (Chicago: Chicago University Press, 1961), and *Muslim Society* (Cambridge: Cambridge

University Press, 1981); Clifford Geertz, Hildred Geertz, and Lawrence Rosen, *Meaning and Order in Moroccan Society* (Cambridge: Cambridge University Press, 1979); Julia A. Clancy-Smith, *Rebel and Saint: Muslim Notables, Populist Protest, Colonial Encounters (Algeria and Tunisia, 1800–1904)* (Berkeley and Los Angeles: University of California Press, 1994).

11. Elbaki Hermassi, *Leadership and National Development in North Africa: A Comparative Study* (Berkeley and Los Angeles: University of California Press, 1972), 11. On the concept of tribe in the context of the Maghrib and the Middle East, see also Dale F. Eickelman, "What Is a Tribe?" in *The Middle East and Central Asia: An Anthropological Approach*, 3d ed. (Upper Saddle River, N.J.: Prentice Hall, 1998), 123–46.

12. As did Barrington Moore Jr. in his classic study, *Social Origins of Dictatorship and Democracy: Lord and Peasant in the Making of the Modern World* (Boston: Beacon, 1966). My analysis also is informed by Lipset's approach to comparative politics, *The First New Nation: The United States in Historical and Comparative Perspective* (New York: Basic Books, 1963). See also Skocpol, *States and Social Revolutions;* Anderson, *Lineages;* Wallerstein, *Modern World-System;* and John Markoff, *The Abolition of Feudalism: Peasants, Lords and Legislators in the French Revolution* (University Park: Pennsylvania State University Press, 1996).

13. John Stuart Mill, *A System of Logic, Ratiocinative and Inductive*, 8th ed. (London: Longmans, 1970); Neil J. Smelser, *Comparative Methods in the Social Sciences* (Englewood Cliffs, N.J.: Prentice-Hall, 1976), 69, 104, 201–2, 205; Theda Skocpol, "Emerging Agendas and Recurrent Strategies in Historical Sociology," in *Vision and Method in Historical Sociology*, ed. Theda Skocpol (Cambridge: Cambridge University Press, 1984), 356–91; Philip Abrams, *Historical Sociology* (Ithaca, N.Y.: Cornell University Press, 1982), 156–57.

14. H. H. Gerth and C. W. Mills, eds., "Methods of Social Science," introduction to part III, section 3 of *From Max Weber: Essays in Sociology* (New York: Oxford University Press, 1970), 59–61; and Max Weber, *The Methodology of the Social Sciences*, trans. (from German) and ed. Edward A. Shils and Henry A. Finch (New York: Free Press, 1949), 183–84. See also Smelser's discussion of Weber in *Comparative Methods*, chap. 5; and, on Weber's comparative sociology and his approach to theory and history, Randall Collins, *Weberian Sociological Theory* (Cambridge: Cambridge University Press, 1986).

CHAPTER 1. STATE FORMATION IN KIN-BASED SOCIETIES

1. An example is in the title of Clifford Geertz, ed., *Old Societies and New States: The Quest for Modernity in Asia and Africa* (New York: Free Press, 1963).

2. Tunisia and Morocco were French "protectorates," whereas Algeria was declared a French "province." Tunisians and Moroccans participated nominally

in government, although actual power was in the hands of the French. On the different forms of colonial rule in the Maghrib, see chapter 6, "Colonial Rule."

3. On the development of the state in the Maghrib and other parts of the Middle East, see Roger Owen, *State, Power, and Politics in the Making of the Modern Middle East* (London: Routledge, 1992), 8–133; Nazih N. Ayubi, *Over-Stating the Arab State: Politics and Society in the Middle East* (London: Tauris, 1995), 38–134; Lisa Anderson, *The State and Social Transformation in Tunisia and Libya, 1830–1980* (Princeton: Princeton University Press, 1986), and "The State in the Middle East and North Africa," *Comparative Politics* 20 (Oct. 1987): 1–18; Ghassan Salamé, ed., *The Foundations of the Arab State* (London: Croom Helm, 1987); and Sami Zubaida, *Islam, the People and the State: Essays on Political Ideas and Movements in the Middle East* (London: Routledge, 1989).

4. Clifford Geertz, "The Integrative Revolution: Primordial Sentiments and Civil Politics in the New States," in *Old Societies*, ed. Geertz, 106.

5. Max Weber, *The Theory of Social and Economic Organization*, trans. A. M. Henderson and T. Parsons (from German) (New York: Free Press, 1964), 154.

6. Charles Tilly sees state formation in Western Europe as involving "territorial consolidation, centralization, differentiation of the instruments of government from other sorts of organization, and monopolization (plus concentration) of the means of coercion." Charles Tilly, "Reflections on the History of European State-Making," in *The Formation of National States in Western Europe*, ed. Charles Tilly (Princeton: Princeton University Press, 1975), 27. The formulation in this book is close to that used by Tilly. A key difference is that I consider states that had to contend with lineages, tribes, and kin-based coalitions, which Tilly does not examine. Nevertheless, the development of a modern state involves similar processes in both cases.

7. Reinhard Bendix, *Kings or People: Power and the Mandate to Rule* (Berkeley and Los Angeles: University of California Press, 1978) appropriately warns that the variations are numerous, with national movements transcending the geographic territories of states, and dissident minorities contesting the legitimacy of nation-states. He nevertheless makes a useful distinction between the concepts of state and nation. He writes: "Nation refers to at least two phenomena: 1) an historically developed community with a distinctive culture and language in common; 2) the juxtaposition of the central government and a citizenry which consists of individuals who are equal under the law, a principle of government introduced by the French Revolution" (605). As to the emergence of the modern state, he defines it as "the gradual concentration of administrative functions in the hands of the central government" (605). On Bendix's treatment of nation building, see also his *Nation-Building and Citizenship: Studies of Our Changing Social Order* (New York: John Wiley, 1964). On nation and nationalism, see E. J. Hobsbawm, *Nations and Nationalism since 1780: Programme, Myth, and Reality* (Cambridge: Cambridge University Press, 1990); and Benedict Anderson, *Imagined Communities: Re-*

flections on the Origin and Spread of Nationalism, rev. ed. (London: Verso, 1991).

8. Geertz, "Integrative Revolution," 109.

9. Reinhard Bendix, "Tradition and Modernity Reconsidered," *Comparative Studies in Society and History* 9, no. 3 (Apr. 1967): 326.

10. Jack Goody, *The Development of the Family and Marriage in Europe* (Cambridge: Cambridge University Press, 1983).

11. Tilly, "Reflections," 35.

12. This formulation has benefited from discussions I had with Seymour Martin Lipset, Theda Skocpol, and Ann Swidler.

13. This is exemplified by the case of Libya. See Anderson, *State and Social Transformation*.

14. Nikki R. Keddie, "Is There a Middle East?" *International Journal of Middle East Studies* 4, no. 3 (July 1973): 270. On tribes in countries of the Middle East outside the Maghrib, see Dawn Chatty, *Mobile Pastoralists: Development Planning and Social Change in Oman* (New York: Columbia University Press, 1996); Mehran Kamrava, *The Political History of Modern Iran: From Tribalism to Theocracy* (Westport, Conn.: Praeger, 1992); Linda L. Layne, *Home and Homeland: The Dialogics of Tribal and National Identities in Jordan* (Princeton: Princeton University Press, 1994); Schirin H. Fathi, *Jordan — An Invented Nation? Tribe-State Dynamics and the Formation of National Identity* (Hamburg: Deutsches Orient-Institut, 1994); Andrew Shryock, *Nationalism and the Genealogical Imagination: Oral History and Textual Authority in Tribal Jordan* (Berkeley and Los Angeles: University of California Press, 1997); Philip S. Khoury and Joseph Kostiner, *Tribes and State Formation in the Middle East* (Berkeley and Los Angeles: University of California Press, 1990) (the individual case studies include Iran, Saudi Arabia, Yemen, and Libya); Paul Dresch, *Tribes, Government and History in Yemen* (Oxford: Clarendon Press, 1989); and Martha Mundy, *Domestic Government: Kinship, Community and Polity in North Yemen* (London: Tauris, 1995).

15. Elbaki Hermassi, *Leadership and National Development in North Africa: A Comparative Study* (Berkeley and Los Angeles: University of California Press, 1972), 36. For an example of tribal life in the twentieth century, see Dale F. Eickelman, "What Is a Tribe?" in *The Middle East and Central Asia: An Anthropological Approach* (Upper Saddle River, N.J.: Prentice Hall, 1998), 123–46.

16. On tribal organization in the history of the Maghrib, see the following overviews: Daniel Nordman, *Profils du Maghreb: Frontières, figures et territoires (XVIIIe–XXe siècles)* (Rabat: Université Mohamed V, Publications de la Faculté des Lettres et des Sciences Humaines, 1996), 23–126; Rahma Bourqia and Nicholas Hopkins, eds., *Le Maghreb: Approches des mécanismes d'articulation* (Casablanca: Al Kalam, 1991), 118–222; and Ernest Gellner and Charles Micaud, eds., *Arabs and Berbers: From Tribe to Nation in North Africa* (Lexington, Mass.: D. C. Heath, 1972). Historical and anthropological studies on each Maghribi country are cited in relevant chapters.

17. There were variations on this dimension among the three Maghribi countries, as discussed in part 2.

18. Keddie, "Is There a Middle East," 271.

19. In the French translation from Arabic, the phrase goes as follows: "Cela (la charrue) n'entrera pas dans la demeure d'une famille sans que Dieu y fasse entrer (aussi) l'avilissement," *El Bokhari, L'authentique tradition musulmane, choix de H'adiths*, G. H. Bousquet, trans. from Arabic, 1964. Quoted in Germaine Tillion, *Le harem et les cousins* (Paris: Seuil, 1966), 190–91, trans. Q. Hoare and published in English as *The Republic of Cousins: Women's Oppression in Mediterranean Society* (London: Al Saqi Books, 1983).

20. Ibn Khaldun, *An Arab Philosophy of History: Selections from the Prolegomena of Ibn Khaldun of Tunis (1332–1406)*, trans. and arranged by Charles Issawi (Princeton: Darwin Press, 1987). On Ibn Khaldun's socio-political model, see also Ernest Gellner, "Cohesion and Identity: The Maghreb from Ibn Khaldun to Emile Durkheim," chap. 2 in *Muslim Society* (Cambridge: Cambridge University Press, 1981), and "Problems Facing the Ibn Khaldun Model of Traditional Muslim Society," in *Leadership and Development in Arab Society*, ed. Fuad I. Khuri (Beirut: American University of Beirut, 1981), 14–29. On Ibn Khaldun's views on economic issues, see Dieter Weiss, "Ibn Khaldun on Economic Transformations," *International Journal of Middle East Studies* 27, no. 1 (Feb. 1995): 29–37.

21. David Hart proposed the translation, as cited by John Waterbury, *The Commander of the Faithful: The Moroccan Political Elite—A Study in Segmented Politics* (New York: Columbia University Press, 1970), 17, in a note as a personal communication made to him by David Hart, 16 Sep. 1966.

22. Tillion, *Le harem et les cousins*.

23. Jeanne Favret, "Traditionalism through Ultra-Modernism," in *Arabs and Berbers*, ed. Gellner and Micaud, 308.

24. Clifford Geertz, *Islam Observed: Religious Developments in Morocco and Indonesia* (Chicago: University of Chicago Press, 1971), 9.

25. Ernest Gellner, "Patterns of Rural Rebellion in Morocco during the Early Years of Independence," in *Arabs and Berbers*, ed. Gellner and Micaud, 367.

26. Classic formulations include William J. Goode, *World Revolution and Family Patterns* (New York: Free Press, 1963); and Tamara K. Hareven, *Family Time and Industrial Time: The Relationship between Family and Work in a New England Industrial Community* (Cambridge: Cambridge University Press, 1982).

27. Judith Stacey, *Patriarchy and Socialist Revolution in China* (Berkeley and Los Angeles: University of California Press, 1983). See also Arland Thorton and Thomas E. Fricke, "Social Change and the Family: Comparative Perspectives from the West, China and South Asia," in *Demography as an Interdiscipline*, ed. J. Mayone Stycos (New Brunswick, N.J.: Transaction Publishers, 1989), 128–61. On the persistence of extended kinship systems in the United States longer than previously suggested, see Betty G. Farrell, *Elite*

Families: Class and Power in Nineteenth-Century Boston (Albany: State University of New York Press, 1993).

28. I. William Zartman, "A Review Article: The Elites of the Maghreb," *International Journal of Middle East Studies* 6, no. 4 (Oct. 1975): 501; and Waterbury, *The Commander of the Faithful,* chaps. 4 and 7. See also Jean-Francois Clément, "Maroc: Les atouts et les défis de la monarchie," in *Maghreb: Les années de transition,* ed. Bassma Kodmani-Darwish with May Chartouni-Dubarry (Paris: Masson, 1990), 63, 68–69.

29. Favret, "Traditionalism," 308.

30. I discuss this in part 3.

31. Immanuel M. Wallerstein, *The Modern World-System 1. Capitalist Agriculture and the Origins of the European World-Economy in the Sixteenth Century* (New York: Academic Press, 1974).

CHAPTER 2. ISLAM AND FAMILY LAW

1. Philippe Ariès, *Centuries of Childhood: A Social History of Family Life,* trans. R. Baldick (from French) (New York: Vintage Books, 1962); Jack Goody, *The Development of the Family and Marriage in Europe* (Cambridge: Cambridge University Press, 1983); Peter Laslett, *The World We Have Lost: Further Explored,* 3d ed. (New York: Scribner, 1984); Michael Anderson, *Approaches to the History of the Western Family, 1500–1914* (London: Macmillan, 1980); Mary Ann Glendon, *The Transformation of Family Law: State, Law and Family in the United States and Western Europe* (Chicago: University of Chicago Press, 1989), 35–147; and Martha Albertson Sineman, *The Neutered Mother, the Sexual Family, and Other Twentieth Century Tragedies* (New York: Routledge, 1995).

2. The actual application of the law varied with the particular community and its interpretation of the legal principles. The analysis presented here considers common elements of the law rather than variations in community or individual practice.

3. The discourse on normative images of gender in Islam has produced conservative and liberal positions throughout history and in different parts of the Islamic world, as discussed, for example, in the following: Barbara Freyer Stowasser, *Women in the Qur'an, Traditions, and Interpretation* (New York: Oxford University Press, 1994); Leila Ahmed, *Women and Gender in Islam: Historical Roots of a Modern Debate* (New Haven: Yale University Press, 1992); Barbara Daly Metcalf, *Perfecting Women: Maulana Ashraf 'Ali Thanawi's Bihishti Zewar, A Partial Translation with Commentary* (Berkeley and Los Angeles: University of California Press, 1990); Fatima Mernissi, *The Veil and the Male Elite: A Feminist Interpretation of Women's Rights in Islam,* trans. M. J. Lakeland (from French) (Reading, Mass.: Addison-Wesley, 1991); Mervat Hatem, "Egyptian Discourses on Gender and Political Liberalization: Do Secularist and Islamic Views Really Differ?" *Middle East Journal* 48, no. 4 (1994): 661–76; and "Secularist and Islamist Discourses on Modernity in

Egypt and the Evolution of the Postcolonial Nation-State," in *Islam, Gender, and Social Change*, ed. Yvonne Y. Haddad and John L. Esposito (New York: Oxford University Press, 1998); Deniz Kandiyoti, "Islam and Patriarchy: A Comparative Perspective," in *Women in Middle Eastern History: Shifting Boundaries in Sex and Gender*, ed. Nikki R. Keddie and Beth Baron (New Haven: Yale University Press, 1991). Mounira M. Charrad, "Policy Shifts: State, Islam and Gender in Tunisia, 1930s–1990s," *Social Politics* 4, no. 2 (summer 1997): 284–319, and "Cultural Diversity within Islam: Veils and Laws in Tunisia," in *Women in Muslim Societies: Diversity within Unity*, ed. Herbert L. Bodman and Nayereh Tohidi (Boulder, Col.: Lynne Rienner, 1998), 63–79.

4. On the sources and development of Islamic law, see especially Wael B. Hallaq, *A History of Islamic Legal Theories: An Introduction to Sunnī Usūl al-Fiqh* (Cambridge: Cambridge University Press, 1997); and John L. Esposito, *Women in Muslim Family Law* (Syracuse: Syracuse University Press, 1982), chaps. 1 and 4. For classic studies, see J. N. D. Anderson, *Islamic Law in the Modern World* (New York: New York University Press, 1959); and Joseph Schacht, *An Introduction to Islamic Law* (Oxford: Clarendon Press, 1964).

5. Issues of theology have divided the Islamic world into a Sunni majority and a minority to which the Shiis belong, as in Iran for example. The Sunni tradition heavily predominates in the Islamic world with approximately 90 percent of Muslims subscribing to it. In contrast to the Shii minority, which has a highly structured religious establishment, the Sunni majority has no organized clergy. The Maghrib overwhelmingly belongs to the Sunni tradition (with only pockets of other sects).

6. Abdelwahab Bouhdiba, "L'Islam maghrébin: Essai d'une typologie," *Revue Tunisienne de Sciences Sociales* no. 4 (Dec. 1965): 5.

7. Clifford Geertz, *Islam Observed: Religious Developments in Morocco and Indonesia* (Chicago: University of Chicago Press, 1971). On the diversity of legal interpretations in the Islamic world from early Islam to the contemporary period, see Mohammad Khalid Masud, Brinkley Messick, and David S. Powers, eds., *Islamic Legal Interpretation: Muftis and Their Fatwas* (Cambridge: Harvard University Press, 1996). On the importance of taking into account the historical manifestations of Islam in different settings, see Mohammed Arkoun, *Rethinking Islam: Common Questions, Uncommon Answers*, trans. R. D. Lee (from French) (Boulder, Col.: Westview, 1994).

8. Ann Swidler, "Culture in Action," *American Sociological Review* 51, no. 2 (1986).

9. The four schools of law in Sunni Islam are the Maliki, the Hanafi, the Shafii, and the Hanbali. On similarities and differences among these schools, see J. N. D. Anderson, *Law Reform in the Muslim World* (London: Athlone, 1976), chaps. 1 and 2; Erwin I. Rosenthal, *Islam in the Modern National State* (Cambridge: Cambridge University Press, 1965). On historical developments in Islamic law, see Noel J. Coulson, *A History of Islamic Law* (Edinburgh: Edinburgh University Press, 1964); and James P. Piscatori, *Islam in a World of Nation-States* (Cambridge: Cambridge University Press, 1986).

10. E. F. Gautier, quoted in Bouhdiba, "Islam maghrébin," 5.

11. Given the existence of several legal schools, it is important to use sources specifically dealing with the legal tradition of the Maghrib. In analyzing Islamic family law as it existed in the Maghrib until the end of colonization in the mid-twentieth century, I rely in particular on Maurice Borrmans's classic study, *Statut personnel et famille au Maghreb: de 1940 à nos jours* (Paris: Mouton, 1977). This 708-page book, covering family law in the Maghrib from the 1940s to the 1960s is a thorough, descriptive treatment of the subject. On the Maliki school as understood in the history of the Maghrib before the end of colonization, see also Ibn Abi Zayd al-Qayrawani, *La Risâla, ou Epître sur les éléments du dogme et de la loi de l'Islam selon le rite mâlikite*, Arabic text with French translation by L. Bercher, 3d ed. (Algiers: Carbonal, 1949); and Khalil Ibn Ishaq, *Abrégé de la loi musulmane selon le rite de l'imâm Mâlik*, vol. 2, *Le statut personnel*, trans. G. H. Bousquet (Paris: A. Maisonneuve, 1958–62); see also Y. Linant de Bellefonds, *Traité de droit musulman comparé*, 3 vols. (Paris: Mouton, 1965–73). On family law in the Hanafi school, see John A. Williams, ed., *The Word of Islam* (Austin: University of Texas Press, 1994), 87–92.

12. See, for example, Stowasser, *Women in the Qur'an*; Ahmed, *Women and Gender in Islam*; Fatima Mernissi, *Beyond the Veil: Male-Female Dynamics in a Modern Muslim Society*, rev. ed. (Bloomington: Indiana University Press, 1987); Fatna A. Sabbah, *Woman in the Muslim Unconscious*, trans. M. J. Lakeland (from French) (New York: Pergamon, 1984); John L. Esposito, "Women's Rights in Islam," *Islamic Studies* 14, no. 2 (summer 1975): 99–114, and *Women in Muslim Family Law*; and Mohammad Fadel, "Two Women, One Man: Knowledge, Power, and Gender in Medieval Sunni Legal Thought," *International Journal of Middle East Studies* 29, no. 2 (May 1997): 185–204.

13. Anderson, *Law Reform*, 102; Borrmans, *Statut personnel*, 16.

14. Borrmans, *Statut personnel*, 16; Anderson, *Law Reform*, 103.

15. This does not imply that all families control marriage alliances by arranging child marriages, but only that Islamic law makes it possible for them to do so. In his classic article, Goode shows how child marriage constitutes one of the mechanisms by which families control marriage alliances: William J. Goode, "The Theoretical Importance of Love," in *The Family, Its Structures and Functions*, ed. Rose Laub Coser, 2d ed. (New York: St. Martin's, 1974).

16. Borrmans, *Statut personnel*, 16–17. In only one case does the law allow a woman to escape her father's or guardian's legal control over whom she will marry. If she has already been married once and divorced, then she is legally allowed to choose her next husband. But even so, she cannot give her own verbal consent at her second marriage contract and still must be represented by a guardian. Why different rules apply to a woman's first and second marriage is an intriguing question. One interpretation is that a family prefers to see a divorced woman remarry rather than remain unmarried, hence the more flexible rules in the particular case of remarriage after divorce.

17. The minority Hanafi school in the Maghrib is somewhat more lenient

toward women and gives slightly less control over the choice of marriage partners to the male members of the kin group. If a woman has not yet reached puberty, her father or legal guardian has the right to give her in marriage to a man of his choice, just as in the Maliki school. After puberty, however—and this is where the difference resides—a woman is granted the right of choice, although it is recommended that she leave the choice to her father or guardian. Still, in the Hanafi rite, if the woman has been given in marriage before puberty, and if the choice was made by a guardian other than her father or grandfather, she has a right of option on reaching puberty and may reject her guardian's decision. If the decision was made by her father or grandfather, however, the decision is then irrevocable (Borrmans, *Statut personnel*, 16, 17, 20.) In principle, as long as the woman has not reached puberty and the marriage has not yet been consummated, and only the marriage contract has been made, the woman has therefore the possibility of negating its effects.

18. Borrmans, *Statut personnel*, 17.

19. Barbara F. Stowasser, "Women and Citizenship in the Qur'an," in *Women, the Family, and Divorce Laws in Islamic History*, ed. Amira El Azhary Sonbol (Syracuse: Syracuse University Press, 1996), 29–33; and Esposito, *Women in Muslim Family Law*, chap. 2.

20. Borrmans, *Statut personnel*, 32.

21. Y. Linant de Bellefonds, "La répudiation dans l'Islam d'aujourd'hui," *Revue Internationale de Droit Comparé*, no. 3 (1962); Dalenda Largueche, "Confined, Battered and Repudiated Women in Tunis since the Eighteenth Century," in *Women, the Family*, ed. Sonbol, 274–78; and Mounira M. Charrad, "Repudiation versus Divorce: Responses to State Policy in Tunisia," in *Women, the Family and Policy: A Global Perspective*, ed. Esther N. Chow and Catherine W. Berheide (Albany: State University of New York Press, 1994), 54–55.

22. Borrmans, *Statut personnel*, 24.

23. Lawrence Rosen, "I Divorce Thee," *Transactions* 7, no. 8 (June 1970): 35.

24. Borrmans, *Statut personnel*, 27.

25. The *Koran* [Qur'an], trans. N. J. Dawood (London: Penguin, 1990), sura 4: verse 3.

26. For example, Marnia Lazreg, *The Eloquence of Silence: Algerian Women in Question* (New York: Routledge, 1994), 186–87; Stowasser, *Women in the Qur'an*, 121; Mernissi, *Beyond the Veil*, part I; Goode, *World Revolution*, "Polygyny," 101–4.

27. Other cultures have developed other heir-producing devices such as adoption and concubinage or a combination thereof.

28. Goode, *World Revolution*, 90.

29. Dominique Tabutin, "La polygamie en Algérie," *Population* 29, no. 2 (Apr. 1974): 312–26. On polygamy rates over time in Algeria, see also Noureddine Saadi, *La femme et la loi en Algérie* (Casablanca: Le Fennec, 1991), 77 n. 20. Lazreg, *Eloquence of Silence*, 187, comments that only a very small

minority of Algerian men have practiced polygamy. Statistics on the Arab world show that in 1955 polygamy was practiced by 2 percent of married Muslim men: Halim Barakat, *The Arab World: Society, Culture and State* (Berkeley and Los Angeles: University of California Press, 1993), 112.

30. A. M. Baron, "Mariage et divorce à Casablanca," *Hesperis* 40, nos. 3–4 (1953): 419–40. In a similar vein and referring to Baron, Ziba Mir-Hosseini, *Marriage on Trial: A Study of Islamic Family Law — Iran and Morocco Compared* (London: Tauris, 1993), 127, comments on "the rarity of polygyny." See also Jack Goody, "Polygyny, Economy and the Role of Women," in *The Character of Kinship*, ed. Jack Goody (Cambridge: Cambridge University Press, 1973), 176.

31. Mernissi, *Beyond the Veil*, 115.

32. Borrmans, *Statut personnel*, 22. This contrasts with restrictions on women's ownership in the history of the West.

33. At independence, the Tunisian government required all citizens who did not have a patronymic name to choose one for purposes of identification on official papers such as on the national identity card.

34. *Ibn* (also often *ben* in the Maghrib) means "son of."

35. *Bint* (also often *bent* in the Maghrib) means "daughter of."

36. Borrmans, *Statut personnel*, 32.

37. Noel J. Coulson, *Succession in the Muslim Family* (Cambridge: Cambridge University Press, 1971); see also Louis Milliot, *Introduction à l'étude du droit musulman* (Paris: Recueil Sirey, 1953); and Anderson, *Law Reform*. On the formation of inheritance law, see David S. Powers, *Studies in Qur'an and Hadīth: The Formation of the Islamic Law of Inheritance* (Berkeley and Los Angeles: University of California Press, 1986).

38. *Koran* [Qur'an], sura 4: verses 11, 12.

39. Only one Islamic sect, that of the Shiis, has different laws of inheritance. In particular, they do not recognize the right of agnates. For a discussion of succession in the law of the Shiis, see Coulson, *Succession in the Muslim Family*, chap. 8.

40. Borrmans, *Statut personnel*, 33; see also Anderson, *Law Reform*.

41. Only full or consanguine brothers (brothers by both parents or by the father but not the mother) are considered heirs as agnates. Uterine brothers (by the mother but not the father), inherit as quota sharers.

42. Borrmans, *Statut personnel*, 34.

43. This is true in all cases except for the uterine brother and sister, who inherit the same share.

44. On the habus system and its complexities, see Sophie Ferchiou, ed., *Hasab wa nasab: Parenté, alliance et patrimoine en Tunisie* (Paris: Editions du Centre National de la Recherche Scientifique, 1992); and Randi Deguilhem, ed., *Le waqf dans l'espace islamique: Outil de pouvoir socio-politique* (Damascus: Institut Français d'Etudes Arabes de Damas, 1995).

45. Sophie Ferchiou, "Catégorie des sexes et circulation des biens habous," in *Hasab wa nasab*, ed. Ferchiou, 251–70. On habus and women, see also

Sophie Ferchiou, "Le rôle des femmes dans la transmission du patrimoine familial," in *Femmes du Maghreb au présent: La dot, le travail, l'identité,* ed. Monique Gadant and Michèle Kasriel (Paris: Editions du Centre National de la Recherche Scientifique, 1990).

46. Lucette Valensi, *Tunisian Peasants in the Eighteenth and Nineteenth Centuries,* trans. B. Archer (from French) (Cambridge: Cambridge University Press, 1985), 70.

47. David S. Powers, "The Maliki Family Endowment: Legal Norms and Social Practices," *International Journal of Middle East Studies* 25, no. 3 (Aug. 1993): 386.

48. Germaine Tillion, *Le harem et les cousins* (Paris: Seuil, 1966), 177.

49. Milliot, "Introduction," 588; and Vanessa Maher, *Women and Property in Morocco: Their Changing Relation to the Process of Social Stratification in the Middle Atlas* (London: Cambridge University Press, 1974). On control of property and gender in many parts of the world, see Rae L. Blumberg, *Engendering Wealth and Well-Being: Empowerment for Global Change* (Boulder, Col.: Westview, 1995).

50. Berbers constitute between 20 and 25 percent of the population in Algeria and approximately 40 percent in Morocco, according to most estimates. See, for example, Yves Lacoste, "Peuplements et organisation sociale," in *L'Etat du Maghreb,* ed. Camille Lacoste et Yves Lacoste (Tunis: Cérès Productions, 1991), 229–34; and Michael Brett and Elizabeth Fentress, *The Berbers* (Oxford: Blackwell, 1996), 3.

51. Jacques Berque, *French North Africa: The Maghrib between Two World Wars,* trans. J. Stewart (from French)(New York: Praeger, 1967), 217.

52. Some information is included in the following: Makilam, *La magie des femmes kabyles et l'unité de la société traditionnelle* (Paris: Harmattan, 1996), 216–88; Fadhma A. M. Amrouche, *My Life Story: The Autobiography of a Berber Woman,* trans. D. S. Blair (from French) (New Brunswick, N.J.: Rutgers University Press, 1989); Pierre Bourdieu, *Sociologie de l'Algérie,* rev. ed. (Paris: Presses Universitaires de France, 1961); David C. Gordon, *Women of Algeria; An Essay on Change,* Harvard Middle Eastern Monographs, no. 19 (Cambridge: Harvard University Press, 1968); Jacques Berque, *Structures sociales du Haut-Atlas* (Paris: Presses Universitaires de France, 1955); and G. H. Bousquet, *Les Berbères: Histoire et institutions* (Paris: Presses Universitaires de France, 1957). On tribal law in the Arab world outside of the Maghrib, see Frank H. Stewart, "Tribal Law in the Arab World: A Review of the Literature," *International Journal of Middle East Studies* 19, no. 4 (Nov. 1987). For a study that traces the history of the Berbers from Antiquity to the present, see Michael Brett and Elizabeth Fentress, *The Berbers* (Oxford: Blackwell, 1996). The special issue, *Berbères: Une identité en construction,* of the *Revue de l'Occident Musulman et de la Méditerranée* (Aix-en-Provence), no. 44 (1987), is devoted to the Maghrib and includes detailed bibliographies on Berber culture. A special issue of the *International Journal of the Sociology of Language,* no. 123 (1997), devoted to Berber sociolinguistics and edited

by Moha Ennaji, includes several articles on the place of Berber culture in the Maghrib.

53. On Kabyle code and customs, see Bourdieu, "Les Kabyles," chap. 1 of *Sociologie de l'Algérie;* Makilam, *La magie des femmes kabyles;* and Gordon, *Women of Algeria.*

54. Gordon, *Women of Algeria,* 16.

55. Borrmans, *Statut personnel,* 38; see also Bourdieu, *Sociologie de l'Algérie,* chap. 1.

56. Bousquet, *Les Berbères,* 110.

57. Examples include the women in the Aures and among the Touaregs, ibid.; see also Gordon, *Women of Algeria,* 16–17.

58. On women in the Aures, see Mathéa Gaudry, *La femme chaouia de l'Aurès; étude de sociologie berbère* (Paris: Librarie Orientaliste Paul Geuthner, 1929); and Bourdieu, *Sociologie de l'Algérie,* chap. 2, "Les Chaouia."

59. Information on several codes of customary law can be found in studies of Moroccan tribal areas, especially in two journals, *Archives Berbères* and *Hesperis.* See also Berque, *Structures sociales du Haut-Atlas.*

60. Robert Descloitres and Laid Debzi, "Système de parenté et structures familiales en Algérie," *Annuaire de l'Afrique du Nord* (Paris: Editions du Centre Nationale de la Recherche Scientifique, 1963): 35.

CHAPTER 3. WOMEN ALLY WITH THE DEVIL

1. Jacques Berque, "Clôture du séminaire," *Revue Tunisienne de Sciences Sociales,* no. 11 (special issue on mutations of the family in the Maghrib) (Oct. 1967): 127.

2. René Maunier, *Mélanges de sociologie nord-africaine* (Paris: F. Alcan, 1930), 46.

3. Lois Beck and Nikki R. Keddie, eds., introduction to *Women in the Muslim World* (Cambridge: Harvard University Press, 1978), 3.

4. Robert Descloitres and Laid Debzi, "Système de parenté et structures familiales en Algérie," *Annuaire de l'Afrique du Nord* (Paris: Editions du Centre National de la Recherche Scientifique, 1963): 23–59. Even in Tunisia where kin-based solidarities have been the most weakened, lineages retain meaning in some regions. Kilani shows how the history of the lineage has remained central to collective identity in the oasis of El Ksar in southern Tunisia: Mondher Kilani, *La construction de la mémoire: Le lignage et la sainteté dans l'oasis d'El Ksar* (Geneva: Editions Labor et Fidès, 1992), chaps. 1, 2, 3, and 8.

5. Carroll McC. Pastner, "Access to Property and the Status of Women in Islam," in *Women in Contemporary Muslim Societies,* ed. Jane I. Smith (Cranbury, N.J.: Associated University Presses, 1980), 175.

6. Suad Joseph, "Gender and the Family in the Arab World," *Middle East Report* (1994), reprinted in *Arab Women: Between Defiance and Restraint,* ed. Suha Sabbagh (New York: Olive Branch Press, 1996), 194–202.

7. Keddie and Beck, "Introduction," *Women in the Muslim World.*

8. Descloitres and Debzi, "Système de parenté."

9. Halim Barakat, *The Arab World: Society, Culture and State* (Berkeley and Los Angeles: University of California Press, 1993), 97–118.

10. Lilia Ben Salem, "Structures familiales et changement social en Tunisie," *Revue Tunisienne de Sciences Sociales* 27, no. 100 (1990): 165–79; Carmel Camilleri, *Jeunesse, famille et développement: Essai sur le changement socioculturel dans un pays du tiers-monde (Tunisie)* (Paris: Editions du Centre National de la Recherche Scientifique, 1973), chap. 16. See also Sophie Ferchiou, *Les femmes dans l'agriculture tunisienne* (Aix-en-Provence: Edisud, 1985).

11. Maurice Borrmans, *Statut personnel et famille au Maghreb: de 1940 à nos jours* (Paris: Mouton, 1977), 3.

12. Historical change and variations among countries are discussed in parts II and III.

13. The historical present used for stylistic reasons in this chapter is thus that of the 1920s–1970s. I made the following assumption concerning change in the kinship structure: If features usually referred to as "traditional" were reported in studies done in the 1970s and 1980s, I considered that there were good reasons to assume that the features applied to the earlier period as well. Since there was a relative dearth of research until the early 1970s, this assumption opened up a broader range of anthropological and sociological studies as sources useful for this chapter.

14. On the Touaregs, for example, see Hélène Claudot-Hawad, "Femmes touarègues et pouvoir politique," in *Femmes et pouvoir*, ed. Monique Gadant, special issue of *Peuples Méditerranéens*, nos. 48–49 (July-Dec. 1989): 69–79. See also Michael Brett and Elizabeth Fentress, *The Berbers* (Oxford: Blackwell, 1996), 209–13, 221–22.

15. There is a long history of scholarship on the issue of agnatic descent in the Maghrib. Scholars from a variety of disciplines have considered how different communities have adapted the basic principle. See the special issue on the Proceedings of a Conference on Population in North Africa, "Actes du colloque de démographie maghrébine," *Revue Tunisienne de Sciences Sociales*, nos. 17–18 (June-Sep. 1969); Vanessa Maher, *Women and Property in Morocco: Their Changing Relation to the Process of Social Stratification in the Middle Atlas* (London: Cambridge University Press, 1974), and "Divorce and Property in the Middle Atlas of Morocco," *Man* 9, no. 1 (1974): 103–22; Claudine Chaulet, "Les fonctions de la famille patriarcale dans le 'secteur traditionnel' et leurs modifications possibles dans le cadre de la révolution agraire," *Revue Algérienne des Sciences Juridiques, Economiques et Politiques* 11, no. 3 (Sep. 1974): 119–26; Jean Cuisenier, *Economie et parenté: Leurs affinités de structure dans le domaine turc et dans le domaine arabe* (Paris: Mouton, 1975); Hildred Geertz, "The Meaning of Family Ties," in *Meaning and Order in Moroccan Society: Three Essays in Cultural Analysis*, Clifford Geertz, Hildred Geertz, and Lawrence Rosen (Cambridge: Cambridge University Press, 1979); Francoise Corrèze, *Femmes des Mechtas: Témoignage sur l'Est algérien* (Paris: Editeurs Français Réunis, 1976); Descloitres and Debzi, "Système de

parenté"; Geneviève Bédoucha, "Le cercle des proches: La consanguinité et ses détours (Tunisie, Yémen)," in *Epouser au plus proche: Inceste, prohibitions et stratégies matrimoniales autour de la Méditerranée,* ed. Pierre Bonte (Paris: Editions de l'Ecole des Hautes Etudes en Sciences Sociales, 1994), 189–219; Raymond Jamous, *Honneur et baraka: Les structures sociales traditionnelles dans le Rif* (Cambridge: Cambridge University Press, 1981), 44–61; Mokhtar el Harras, "Evaluation critique de quelques études récentes sur la famille rurale au Maroc," in *Portraits de femmes,* Mohamed Alahyane et al. (Casablanca: Le Fennec, 1987); Faouzi Adel, "Formation du lien conjugal et nouveaux modèles familiaux en Algérie," in *Femmes, culture et société au Maghreb,* ed. Rahma Bourqia, Mounira M. Charrad and Nancy Gallagher (Casablanca: Afrique Orient, 1996), 139–45.

16. Maher, "Relationships among Women," in *Women and Property in Morocco,* chap. 8.

17. Descloitres and Debzi, "Système de parenté," 49.

18. Germaine Tillion, *Le harem et les cousins* (Paris: Seuil, 1966), chaps. 1 and 4.

19. This does not apply to marriages between paternal cousins. If the woman marries her father's brother's son, her own son de facto remains in the patrilineage.

20. Divorce in Islamic law is discussed in chapter 2.

21. L. Massignon, quoted in Berque, "Clôture du séminaire," 127.

22. Descloitres and Debzi, "Système de parenté," 42.

23. Fatna A. Sabbah, *Woman in the Muslim Unconscious,* trans. M. J. Lakeland (from French) (New York: Pergamon, 1984); and Mounira M. Charrad, review of Sabbah's book, *Bulletin of the Middle East Studies Association* 20, no. 2 (Dec. 1986): 191–92. On the acceptance of sexuality in the Islamic tradition, see Abdelwahab Bouhdiba, *Sexuality in Islam,* trans. A. Sheridan (from French) (London: Routledge and Kegan Paul, 1985). On Arab-Islamic writing on the woman's body, see Fedwa Malti-Douglas, *Woman's Body, Woman's Word: Gender and Discourse in Arabo-Islamic Writing* (Princeton: Princeton University Press, 1991).

24. Quoted in Fatima Mernissi, *Beyond the Veil: Male-Female Dynamics in Modern Muslim Society,* rev. ed. (Bloomington: Indiana University Press, 1987), 42.

25. Ibid.

26. Robert Fernea and James M. Malarkey, "Anthropology of the Middle East and North Africa: A Critical Assessment," *Annual Review of Anthropology* 4 (1975): 188.

27. On the time period that is the focus of this chapter—the twentieth century until the 1970s—see Cuisenier, "Le domaine arabe ou l'économie et la parenté en système de lignages à segmentation réglée," livre 2 in *Economie et parenté,* and "Endogamie et exogamie dans le mariage arabe," *L'Homme* 4 (1962): 71–89; Pierre Bourdieu, "Case Study: Parallel-cousin Marriage," chap. 1, sec. 2 in *Outline of a Theory of Practice,* trans. R. Nice (from French)

(Cambridge: Cambridge University Press, 1977); Fernea and Malarkey, "Anthropology of the Middle East and North Africa" (includes an extensive bibliography, a considerable proportion of which is on FBD marriage); H. Geertz, "The Meaning of Family Ties"; Fredrik Barth, "Descent and Marriage Reconsidered," in *The Character of Kinship*, ed. Jack Goody (Cambridge: Cambridge University Press, 1973) 3–19; William J. Goode, *World Revolution and Family Patterns* (New York: Free Press, 1970), 88–101; Camilleri, *Jeunesse, famille et développement*; Cecil H. Brown and Saad Sowayan, "Descent and Alliance in an Endogamous Society: A Structural Analysis of Arab Kinship," *Social Science Information* 16, no. 5 (1977): 581–99; Anne-Marie Baron, "Mariages et divorces à Casablanca," *Hesperis* 40 (1953): 419–40; Millicent R. Ayoub, "Parallel Cousin Marriage and Endogamy: A Study in Sociometry," *Southwestern Journal of Anthropology* 15 (1959): 266–75; M. Bchir, A. Bouraoui, M. Rouissi, and A. Zghal, "L'Influence sur le taux de fécondité du statut et du rôle de la femme dans la société tunisienne," *Revue Tunisienne de Sciences Sociales*, nos. 32–35 (1973): 103–59; Tillion, *Le harem et les cousins*, 131–34; Jamil M. Hilal, "Father's Brother's Daughter Marriage in Arab Communities: A Problem for Sociological Explanation," *Middle East Forum* 46, no. 4 (1970); Adel, "Formation du lien conjugal"; and Abdelhamid Bouraoui, "Mariages préférentiels? Evolution et répartition des mariages consanguins en Tunisie (1970–1982)," *Cahiers du C.E.R.E.S.*, Série Psychologique, no. 6 (Tunis: Centre d'Etudes et de Recherches Economiques et Sociales, 1988).

For recent discussions covering a range of time periods including the present, see Pierre Bonte, "Manière de dire ou manière de faire: Peut-on parler d'un mariage 'arabe'?" in *Epouser au plus proche*, 371–98; Lilia Ben Salem, "Introduction à l'analyse de la parenté et de l'alliance dans les sociétés arabo-musulmanes," in *Hasab wa nasab: Parenté, alliance et patrimoine en Tunisie*, ed. Sophie Ferchiou (Paris: Editions du Centre National de la Recherche Scientifique, 1992), 79–104; Judith E. Tucker, "The Arab Family in History: 'Otherness' and the Study of the Family," in *Arab Women: Old Boundaries, New Frontiers*, ed. Judith E. Tucker (Bloomington: Indiana University Press, 1993), 201, 204.

28. Primogeniture makes the eldest child (usually the eldest son) and ultimogeniture the youngest child the only heir of the family estate.

29. Nayra Atiya, *Khul-Khaal: Five Egyptian Women Tell Their Stories* (Syracuse: Syracuse University Press, 1982), 29.

30. Ibid., 5.

31. H. Geertz, "The Meaning of Family Ties," 373.

32. Ibid.

33. Descloitres and Debzi, "Système de parenté," 43.

34. The bride price in Islamic law is discussed in chapter 2.

35. Pastner, "Access to Property," 161.

36. Raphael Patai, *Society, Culture and Change in the Middle East*, 3d. ed. (Philadelphia: University of Pennsylvania Press, 1971), 141.

37. Goode, *World Revolution*, 93–95.

38. Barth, "Descent and Marriage," 11. The figure of 10 percent is quoted in M. R. Ayoub, "Parallel Cousin Marriage and Endogamy: A Study in Sociometry," *Southwestern Journal of Anthropology* 15, no. 3 (autumn 1959); and F. Khuri, "Parallel Cousin Marriage Reconsidered: A Middle Eastern Practice that Nullifies the Effects of Marriage on the Intensity of Family Relationships," *Man* 5, no. 4 (Dec. 1970). The figure of 20 percent appears in Raphael Patai, "The Structure of Endogamous Unilineal Descent Groups," *Southwestern Journal of Anthropology* 21, no. 4 (winter 1965); and that of 30 percent in Fredrik Barth, "Father's Brother's Daughter Marriage in Kurdistan," *Southwestern Journal of Anthropology* 10, no. 2 (summer 1954). On rates of endogamy among different social groups within a country, see Martha Mundy, *Domestic Government: Kinship, Community and Polity in North Yemen* (London: Tauris, 1995), 179–95, 291–95.

39. Bonte, "Manière de dire," 375, table 1.

40. Ben Salem, "Introduction à l'analyse de la parenté," 87.

41. Susan S. Davis, *Patience and Power: Women's Lives in a Moroccan Village* (Cambridge, Mass.: Schenkman, 1983), 27.

42. H. Geertz, "The Meaning of Family Ties," 325.

43. Dale F. Eickelman, *Moroccan Islam: Tradition and Society in a Pilgrimage Center* (Austin: University of Texas Press, 1976), 202–5.

44. Kilani, *Construction,* 166–70.

45. Barth, "Descent and Marriage," 11; for a similar estimate, see also Pastner, "Access to Property," 159. Camilleri's report is based on data collected after independence in Tunisia, between 1958 and 1960, *Jeunesse, famille et développement,* 140–42. On Tunisia, see also Ferchiou, *Les femmes dans l'agriculture tunisienne.*

46. Cuisenier, "Endogamie et exogamie." Baron obtains the figure of 30 percent by considering marriages and divorces recorded in the city of Casablanca in 1951, "Mariages et divorces à Casablanca"; Vanessa Maher, "Women and Social Change in Morocco," in *Women in the Muslim World,* Beck and Keddie, eds., 113; H. Geertz, "The Meaning of Family Ties," 325; and Bonte, "Manière de dire," 376–78.

47. Bonte, "Manière de dire," 375.

48. With a focus different from that of this book, ethnographic studies have shown how women accept or escape social and cultural norms in everyday life experiences in the Maghrib. Most studies concern the 1980s and 1990s, and not the 1920s to 1970s as does this chapter. On the contemporary period see, for example, the articles on the Maghrib in *Everyday Life in the Muslim Middle East,* ed. Donna Lee Bowen and Evelyn A. Early (Bloomington: Indiana University Press, 1993); the sources on the Maghrib in the bibliography by Herbert L. Bodman, *Women in the Muslim World* (Providence, R.I.: Association for Middle East Women's Studies, 1990); and in Michelle R. Kimball and Barbara R. von Schlegell, *Muslim Women throughout the World: A Bibliography* (Boulder, Col.: Lynne Rienner, 1997). See also Bourquia, Charrad, and Gallagher, eds., *Femmes, culture et société au Maghreb.*

49. See the discussion on Islamic family law in chapter 2.

50. The term "ird" is used in the Maghrib.

51. Lois Beck, "The Religious Lives of Muslim Women," in *Women in Contemporary Muslim Societies*, ed. Smith, 39 ff.

52. Descloitres and Debzi, "Système de parenté," 41.

53. On the history and types of veil, see Fatima Mernissi, *The Veil and the Male Elite: A Feminist Interpretation of Women's Rights in Islam*, trans. M. J. Lakeland (from French) (Reading, Mass.: Addison-Wesley, 1991), 85–101, 180–88; Leila Hessini, "Wearing the Hijab in Contemporary Morocco: Choice and Identity," in *Reconstructing Gender in the Middle East*, ed. Fatma M. Göçek and Shiva Balaghi (New York: Columbia University Press, 1994), 40–56; Hinde Taarji, *Les voilées de l'Islam* (Paris: Editions Balland, 1990); and Mounira M. Charrad, "Cultural Diversity within Islam: Veils and Laws in Tunisia," in *Women in Muslim Societies: Diversity within Unity*, ed. Herbert L. Bodman and Nayereh Tohidi (Boulder, Col.: Lynne Rienner, 1998), 64–79.

54. See the discussion of female sexuality in "Women as Division," above in this chapter.

55. Tillion, *Le harem et les cousins*, 24–29, 194–97.

56. Ibid., 190; and Joëlle Bahloul, *The Architecture of Memory: A Jewish-Muslim Household in Colonial Algeria, 1937–1962* (Cambridge: Cambridge University Press, 1996), 30.

57. Hanut also means "shop." The same word is used to refer to a grocery store, or generally a space where commercial activities are carried on, and the room reserved for male visitors. This reflects the public character of the room called hanut in a house.

58. Jean-Paul Charnay, "De la grande maison au couple moderne: Interférences entre droit, psychologie et économie dans l'évolution de la famille maghrébine," *Revue Algérienne des Sciences Juridiques, Economiques et Politiques* 11, no. 3 (Sep. 1974): 73–74. See also Dale F. Eickelman, *The Middle East and Central Asia: An Anthropological Approach*, 3d ed. (Upper Saddle River, N.J.: Prentice Hall, 1998), 101–2. Many streets in the old parts of Maghribi cities such as Tunis, Algiers, Marrakech, or Fez are about three yards wide and wind around in a tight web.

59. Rooftops are flat in the Maghrib. A stairway located inside the house leads to the roof, where women can thus go without stepping outside the house. Since streets are narrow, rooftops are close enough together for conversations to be easily carried on from one rooftop to another. See Elizabeth W. Fernea, *A Street in Marrakech* (Garden City, N.Y.: Anchor Books, 1976), 97–111. On women's gatherings, see also Monia Hejaiej, *Behind Closed Doors: Women's Oral Narratives in Tunis* (New Brunswick, N.J.: Rutgers University Press, 1996).

60. Descloitres and Debzi, "Système de parenté," 48.

CHAPTER 4. MEN WORK WITH ANGELS

1. Abdelkader Zghal, "L'Edification nationale au Maghreb," *Revue Tunisienne de Sciences Sociales*, no. 27 (Dec. 1971): 20; see also Lisa Anderson, *The State and Social Transformation in Tunisia and Libya, 1830–1980* (Princeton: Princeton University Press, 1986), chap. 1; Neil MacMaster, *Colonial Migrants and Racism: Algerians in France, 1900–62* (New York: Macmillan and St. Martin's, 1997), 24–25; David Prochaska, *Making Algeria French: Colonialism in Bône, 1870–1920* (Cambridge: Cambridge University Press, 1990), 54–57; Abdelkader Zghal, "La participation de la paysannerie maghrébine à la construction nationale," *Revue Tunisienne de Sciences Sociales*, no. 22 (July 1970); Jacques Berque, *Structures sociales du Haut-Atlas* (Paris: Presses Universitaires de France, 1955).

2. This was the case more clearly in Algeria and Morocco than in Tunisia, as is shown when differences among countries are examined in part 2 and part 3.

3. Geneviève Bédoucha, "Le cercle des proches: La consanguinité et ses détours (Tunisie, Yémen)," in *Epouser au plus proche: Inceste, prohibitions et stratégies matrimoniales autour de la Méditerranée*, ed. Pierre Bonte (Paris: Editions de l'Ecole des Hautes Etudes en Sciences Sociales, 1994), 189–219.

4. The proverb is discussed in chapter 3.

5. See, for example, Dale F. Eickelman, "What Is a Tribe," in *The Middle East and Central Asia: An Anthropological Approach*, 3d ed. (Upper Saddle River, N.J.: Prentice Hall, 1998), 125–35; Fredrik Barth, "Descent and Marriage Reconsidered," in *The Character of Kinship*, ed. Jack Goody (Cambridge: Cambridge University Press, 1973), 3–19; Paul Dresch, "Segmentation: Its Roots in Arabia and Its Flowering Elsewhere," *Cultural Anthropology* 3, part I (1988): 50–67; and Meyer Fortes, *The Dynamics of Clanship among the Tallensi: Being the First Part of an Analysis of the Social Structure of a Trans-Volta Tribe* (London: Oxford University Press, 1945). On the relation between kinship and politics in comparative perspective, see Charles Lindholm, "Kinship Structure and Political Authority: The Middle East and Central Asia," *Comparative Studies in Society and History* 28, no. 2 (Apr. 1986): 334–55. See also Jeffery M. Paige, "Kinship and Politics in Stateless Societies," and Guy E. Swanson, "Descent and Polity: The Meaning of Paige's Findings," both in *American Journal of Sociology* 80, no. 2 (Sep. 1977). The Maghrib, which has had a form of state for the last several centuries, differs from stateless societies as considered by Paige. His analysis offers insights that are nevertheless useful for the understanding of kin-group solidarity and politics in a general way.

6. Fortes, *Dynamics of Clanship*, 14–29, 191–230.

7. Barth, "Descent and Marriage," 18.

8. See, for example, the debate between Henry Munson Jr. and Ernest Gellner: Henry Munson Jr., "Rethinking Gellner's Segmentary Analysis of Morocco's Ait 'Atta," *Man* 28, no. 2 (June 1993): 267–80; Ernest Gellner's

response, "Segmentation: Reality or Myth?" *Journal of the Royal Anthropological Institute* 1, no. 4 (Dec. 1995): 821–29; and Munson's reply, 829–32 in the same issue.

9. For classic formulations of some of the issues, see Jacques Berque, "Qu'est-ce qu'une 'tribu' nord-africaine?" in *Eventail de l'histoire vivante: Mélanges à Lucien Fèbvre*, vol. 1 (Paris: A. Colin, 1953), 261–71; and Pierre Bourdieu, *Outline of a Theory of Practice*, trans. R. Nice (from French) (Cambridge: Cambridge University Press, 1977), 33–43. On the history of the debate, see Dale F. Eickelman, "New Directions in Interpreting North African Society," in *Connaissances du Maghreb: Sciences sociales et colonisation*, Centre de Recherches et d'Etudes sur les Societies Méditerranéennes (Paris: Editions du Centre National de la Recherche Scientifique, 1984), 279–89; and Eickelman, *The Middle East*, 123–46. See also Wilfrid J. Rollman, "Some Reflections on Recent Trends in the Study of Modern North African History," in *The Maghrib in Question: Essays in History and Historiography*, ed. Michel Le Gall and Kenneth Perkins (Austin: University of Texas Press, 1997), 73–74. The lines between theoretical positions are sometimes blurred. Segmentation theory has been associated with British anthropology, especially with the work of Ernest Gellner, for example, *Saints of the Atlas* (Chicago: Chicago University Press, 1969) and *Muslim Society* (Cambridge: Cambridge University Press, 1981). The emphasis on fluidity in cultural meanings is associated with American anthropology, particularly with the work of Clifford Geertz, for example, Clifford Geertz, Hildred Geertz, and Lawrence Rosen, *Meaning and Order in Moroccan Society* (Cambridge: Cambridge University Press, 1979); and Clifford Geertz, "In Search of North Africa," *The New York Review of Books*, 22 April 1971. Lawrence Rosen includes a discussion relevant to the issue in *The Anthropology of Justice: Law as Culture in Islamic Society* (Cambridge: Cambridge University Press, 1989). For Maghribi scholarship on issues involved in the debate, see for example Abdallah Hammoudi, "Segmentarity, Social Stratification, Political Power and Sainthood: Reflections on Gellner's Theses," *Economy and Society* 9 (1980): 279–303; Abdallah Laroui, *Les origines sociales et culturelles du nationalisme marocain, 1830–1912* (Paris: Maspéro, 1977); Lilia Ben Salem, "Intérêt des analyses en termes de segmentarité pour l'étude des sociétés du Maghreb," *Revue de l'Occident Musulman et de la Méditerranée*, no. 33 (1982): 113–35, and "Questions méthodologiques posées par l'étude des formes du pouvoir: Articulation du politique et du culturel, du national et du local," in *Le Maghreb: Approches des mécanismes d'articulation*, ed. Rahma Bourqia and Nicholas Hopkins (Casablanca: Al Kalam, 1991), 197–98.

10. Germaine Tillion, *Le harem et les cousins* (Paris: Seuil, 1966). The concept of asabiyya is central to the work of Ibn Khaldun (1332–1406). David Hart proposed the translation of asabiyya as "unifying structural cohesion," as cited by John Waterbury, *The Commander of the Faithful: The Moroccan Political Elite—A Study in Segmented Politics* (New York: Columbia University Press, 1970), 17, in a note as a personal communication made to him by

David Hart, 16 Sep. 1966. On asabiyya, see also Halim Barakat, *The Arab World: Society, Culture and State* (Berkeley and Los Angeles: University of California Press, 1993), 53.

11. Bédoucha, "Le cercle des proches." Mondher Kilani, *La construction de la mémoire: Le lignage et la sainteté dans l'oasis d'El Ksar* (Geneva: Editions Labor et Fidès, 1992), shows how social organization in an oasis in the region of Gafsa in south central Tunisia is based on lineages whose members share a myth of common origin (thought to have occurred four to five centuries ago).

12. Wendy Griswold, "The Writing on the Mud Wall: Nigerian Novels and the Imaginary Village," *American Sociological Review* 57, no. 6 (Dec. 1992): 709–24; and Benedict Anderson, *Imagined Communities: Reflections on the Origin and Spread of Nationalism*, rev. ed. (London: Verso, 1991).

13. David M. Hart, "The Tribe in Modern Morocco: Two Case Studies," in *Arabs and Berbers: From Tribe to Nation in North Africa*, ed. Ernest Gellner and Charles Micaud (Lexington, Mass.: D. C. Heath, 1972), 25.

14. Hart, "The Tribe in Modern Morocco," 39. See also David M. Hart, *Dadda 'Atta and His Forty Grandsons: The Socio-Political Organization of the Ait 'Atta of Southern Morocco* (Cambridge, Eng.: Middle East and North African Studies Press, 1981); "Segmentary Systems and the Role of 'Five Fifths' in Tribal Morocco," in *Islam in Tribal Societies: From the Atlas to the Hindus*, ed. Akbar S. Ahmed and David M. Hart (London: Routledge and Kegan Paul, 1984), 66–105; and *The Aith Waryaghar of the Moroccan Rif: An Ethnography and History* (Tucson: University of Arizona Press, 1976); and Bernhard Venema, *Les Khroumirs: Changements politiques et religieux dans la période 1850–1987* (Amsterdam: VU University Press, 1990), 49–64. For a discussion of tribal ethnography and the work of David M. Hart, see E. G. H. Joffé and C. R. Pennell, eds., *Tribe and State: Essays in Honour of David Montgomery Hart* (Wisbech, Cambridgeshire, Eng.: Middle East and North African Press, 1991).

15. Lucette Valensi, *Tunisian Peasants in the Eighteenth and Nineteenth Centuries*, trans. B. Archer (from French) (Cambridge: Cambridge University Press, 1985), 25.

16. Hart, "The Tribe," 39.

17. Bryan C. Clarke, *Berber Village: The Story of the Oxford University Expedition to the High Atlas Mountains of Morocco* (London: Longmans, 1959), 75–76.

18. Claudine Chaulet, "Les fonctions de la famille patriarchale dans le 'secteur traditionnel' et leurs modifications possibles dans le cadre de la révolution agraire," *Revue Algérienne des Sciences Juridiques, Economiques et Politiques* 11, no. 3 (Sep. 1974): 119–26.

19. Robert Descloitres and Laid Debzi, "Système de parenté et structures familiales en Algérie," *Annuaire de l'Afrique du Nord* (Paris: Editions du Centre National de la Recherche Scientifique, 1963): 23–59.

20. Barth, "Descent and Marriage," 17.

21. Chaulet, "Les fonctions de la famille patriarchale," 121.

22. Robert Fernea and James M. Malarkey, "Anthropology of the Middle East and North Africa: A Critical Assessment," *Annual Review of Anthropology*, vol. 4 (1975): 191. Sophie Ferchiou shows how the rural area of Sidi Bou Zid in central western Tunisia went from collective property before the 1950s to a blurring of the lines between the private and the collective in subsequent years: *Les femmes dans l'agriculture tunisienne* (Aix-en-Provence: Edisud, 1985), 17–19.

23. Hart, "The Tribe," 31.

24. Descloitres and Debzi, "Système de parenté," 32.

25. Abdelhamid Henia, "Mécanisme d'articulation des communautés oasiennes du Jerid avec le pouvoir central de Tunis au cours du XVIIIe et de la première moitié du XIXe siècles," in *Le Maghreb*, ed. Bourqia and Hopkins; Raymond Jamous, *Honneur et baraka: Les structures sociales traditionnelles dans le Rif* (Cambridge: Cambridge University Press, 1981), 161–74; Ben Salem, "Intérêt des analyses en termes de segmentarité"; Ernest Gellner, "Tribalism and the State in the Middle East," in *Tribes and State Formation in the Middle East*, ed. Philip S. Khoury and Joseph Kostiner (Berkeley and Los Angeles: University of California Press, 1990); Hart, "The Tribe"; and Edward E. Evans-Pritchard, *The Sanusi of Cyrenaica* (Oxford: Clarendon, 1949).

26. On the changing allocation of water rights in different historical periods respectively in a Moroccan and a Tunisian community, see Abdallah Hammoudi, "Substance and Relation: Water Rights and Water Distribution in the Dra Valley"; and Habib Attia, "Water Sharing Rights in the Jerid Oases of Tunisia," both in *Property, Social Structure, and Law in the Modern Middle East*, ed. Ann Elizabeth Mayer (Albany: State University of New York Press, 1985), 27–57, 85–106.

27. Evans-Pritchard, *The Sanusi of Cyrenaica*, 59–60. A shaykh in this context is a tribal chief. On authority in tribal groups, see also Charles Lindholm, "Quandaries of Command in Egalitarian Societies: Examples from Swat and Morocco," in *Comparing Muslim Societies: Knowledge and the State in a World Civilization*, ed. Juan R. I. Cole (Ann Arbor: The University of Michigan Press, 1992), 63–77.

28. William J. Goode, *World Revolution and Family Patterns* (New York: Free Press, 1970), 138. On norms and sanctions, see also Hart, "The Tribe."

29. Berque, *Structures sociales du Haut-Atlas;* Bédoucha, "Le cercle des proches."

30. Barth, "Descent and Marriage," 13.

31. E. Braunlich, quoted in Goode, *World Revolution*, 138.

32. L. Carl Brown, "Islam's Role in North Africa," in *Man, State and Society in the Contemporary Maghreb*, ed. I. William Zartman (New York: Praeger, 1973), 32. Although it unified tribes in the precolonial and colonial history of the Maghrib, Islam has nevertheless given rise to conflicting interpretations and to divisions, as has been evident especially in the late 1980s and 1990s. See, for example, François Burgat and William Dowell, *The Islamic Movement in North Africa* (Austin: Center for Middle Eastern Studies, University of

Texas, 1993); John Ruedy, ed., *Islamism and Secularism in North Africa* (New York: St. Martin's, 1994); and John P. Entelis, ed., *Islam, Democracy, and the State in North Africa* (Bloomington: Indiana University Press, 1997). The focus in this book is on Islam as a unifying factor from the precolonial to the colonial and independence periods.

33. Jean Dejeux, "Meeting of Two Worlds in the Maghrib," in *Man, State and Society*, ed. Zartman, 22.

34. Ernest Gellner, "Introduction," *Arabs and Berbers*, ed. Gellner and Micaud, 11.

35. Ibid.

36. Marvin W. Mikesell, "The Role of Tribal Markets in Morocco," in *Man, State and Society*, ed. Zartman, 416; Peter von Sivers, "Rural Uprisings as Political Movements in Colonial Algeria, 1851–1914," in *Islam, Politics, and Social Movements*, ed. Edmund Burke III and Ira M. Lapidus (Berkeley and Los Angeles: University of California Press, 1988).

37. Habib Attia, "L'Evolution des structures sociales et économiques dans les Hautes Steppes," *Revue Tunisienne de Sciences Sociales*, no. 6 (June 1966): 11. Making a similar point, Donald C. Holsinger, "Islam and State Expansion in Algeria: Nineteenth-Century Saharan Frontiers," in *Islamism and Secularism*, ed. Ruedy, 13, comments on the involvement of the Saharan community of the Mzab in southern Algeria in a mutually beneficial exchange of goods and services with its neighbors.

38. Julia A. Clancy-Smith, *Rebel and Saint: Muslim Notables, Populist Protest, Colonial Encounters (Algeria and Tunisia, 1800–1904)* (Berkeley and Los Angeles: University of California Press, 1994), 63.

39. Hermassi, *Leadership*, 26.

40. Berque, *Structures sociales du Haut Atlas*.

41. Mikesell, "The Role of Tribal Markets," 416.

42. Ibid., 422.

43. Pierre Boyer, *L'Evolution de l'Algérie médiane (Ancien département d'Alger) de 1830 à 1956* (Paris: Adrien-Maisonneuve, 1960), 48–53.

44. Gellner, "Introduction," *Arabs and Berbers*, ed. Gellner and Micaud, 18.

45. Abdellah Ben Mlih, *Structures politiques du Maroc colonial* (Paris: Harmattan, 1990), 108–14, 122–23.

46. Clifford Geertz, "The Integrative Revolution: Primordial Sentiments and Civil Politics in the New States," in *Old Societies and New States: The Quest for Modernity in Asia and Africa*, ed. Clifford Geertz (New York: Free Press, 1963), 146. See also the interesting story of how the life trajectory of a Moroccan Berber intersected with the changing political circumstances of his tribe, the Ait Ndhir: Edmund Burke III, "Mohand N'Hamoucha: Middle Atlas Berber," in *Struggle and Survival in the Modern Middle East*, ed. Edmund Burke III (Berkeley and Los Angeles: University of California Press, 1993), 100–113; and the long-term history of that same tribe in Amal Rassam Vinogradov, *The Ait Ndhir of Morocco: A Study of the Social Transformation of*

a Berber Tribe, Anthropological Papers no. 15 (Ann Arbor: The University of Michigan, 1974), 15–33.

47. For a discussion of systems of alliances, see Hart, "The Tribe"; David J. Seddon, "Local Politics and State Intervention: Northeast Morocco from 1870 to 1970"; and Gellner, "Political and Religious Organization of the Berbers of the Central High Atlas," in *Arabs and Berbers,* ed. Gellner and Micaud; see also Waterbury, "The Social Context of Moroccan Politics," chap. 3 in Waterbury, *The Commander of the Faithful,* 61–80; Vinogradov, "Sociopolitical Organization," chap. 4 in Vinogradov, *The Ait Ndhir;* Hermassi, "The State, Medieval and Patrimonial," chap. 1 in Hermassi, *Leadership;* and Zghal, "L'Edification nationale."

48. Zghal, "L'Edification nationale," 18; and Clancy-Smith, *Rebel and Saint,* 85–86.

49. Hermassi, *Leadership,* 88 ff.

50. For example, Emile F. Gautier, *Le passé de l'Afrique du Nord: Les siècles obscurs* (Paris: Payot, 1937).

51. Berbers have become more vocal in asserting a common Berber cultural heritage separate from the dominant Arab culture in recent years. It must be noted, however, that this is a recent phenomenon that should not be read into the past when divisions among Berbers prevailed. Proportions of Berbers in the overall population are given in chapter 2, section on Customary Law.

52. Hermassi, *Leadership,* 36.

53. Gellner, "Introduction," *Arabs and Berbers,* ed. Gellner and Micaud, 13.

CHAPTER 5. THE PRECOLONIAL POLITY

1. This was not the only factor, but without it, one had little chance of success in building a power base.

2. Julia A. Clancy-Smith, *Rebel and Saint: Muslim Notables, Populist Protest, Colonial Encounters (Algeria and Tunisia, 1800–1904)* (Berkeley and Los Angeles: University of California Press, 1994), 7.

3. Abdelkader Zghal, "L'Edification nationale au Maghreb," in *Revue Tunisienne de Sciences Sociales,* no. 27 (Dec. 1971): 25; Elbaki Hermassi, *Leadership and National Development in North Africa: A Comparative Study* (Berkeley and Los Angeles: University of California Press, 1972), 51.

4. Lucette Valensi, *Tunisian Peasants in the Eighteenth and Nineteenth Centuries,* trans. B. Archer (from French) (Cambridge: Cambridge University Press, 1985). On political organization in the region of Khroumirie in northwest Tunisia, see Bernhard Venema, *Les Khroumirs: Changements politiques et religieux dans la période 1850–1987* (Amsterdam: VU University Press, 1990), 49.

5. Henri de Montety, "Old Families and New Elites in Tunisia," in *Man, State and Society in the Contemporary Maghrib,* ed. I. William Zartman (New York: Praeger, 1973), 171–72.

6. Nazih N. Ayubi, *Over-Stating the Arab State: Politics and Society in the Middle East* (London: Tauris, 1995), 119.

7. Jean Lacouture, *The Demigods: Charismatic Leadership in the Third World* (New York: Knopf, 1970), 138.

8. L. Carl Brown, "Towards a Comparative History of Modernization in the Arab World: Tunisia and Egypt," in *Identité culturelle et conscience nationale, Cahiers du C.E.R.E.S.*, Série Sociologique, no. 2 (Tunis: Centre d'Etudes et de Recherches Economiques et Sociales, June 1975), 76.

9. Ibid., 172.

10. On precolonial Tunisia, see Valensi, *Tunisian Peasants;* Lisa Anderson, *The State and Social Transformation in Tunisia and Libya, 1830–1980* (Princeton: Princeton University Press, 1986), 59–133; Clancy-Smith, *Rebel and Saint*, 11–32, 125–67, 201–3; Abdelhamid Henia, "Mécanisme d'articulation des communautés oasiennes du Jerid au cours du XVIIIe et de la première moitié du XIXe siècles," in *Le Maghreb: Approches des mécanismes d'articulation*, ed. Rahma Bourqia and Nicholas Hopkins (Casablanca: Al Kalam, 1991), 153–72; L. Carl Brown, *The Tunisia of Ahmad Bey, 1837–1855* (Princeton: Princeton University Press, 1974). For a broad overview of Tunisian history before colonization, see Mohamed Hédi Cherif, "Tunis de la fin du XVIIème siècle à 1956: Introduction historique," in *Hasab wa nasab: Parenté, alliance et patrimoine en Tunisie*, ed. Sophie Ferchiou (Paris: Editions du Centre National de la Recherche Scientifique, 1992), 27–40. On the establishment of Ottoman domination in Tunisia, see André Raymond, "The Ottoman Legacy in Arab Political Boundaries," in *Imperial Legacy: The Ottoman Imprint on the Balkans and the Middle East*, ed. L. Carl Brown (New York: Columbia University Press, 1996), 123–27. See also Asma Larif-Béatrix, *Edification étatique et environnement culturel: Le personnel politico-administratif dans la Tunisie contemporaine* (Paris: Publisud, 1988), 61–89; F. Robert Hunter, "Recent Tunisian Historical Writing on State and Society in Modern Tunisia," *Middle East Studies Association Bulletin* 20, no. 1 (July 1986): 23–28; Hermassi, *Leadership*, part I; and Noureddine Sraieb, "Elite et société: L'Invention de la Tunisie: De l'état-dynastie à la nation moderne," in *Tunisie au présent: Une modernité au-dessus de tout soupçon?* Michel Camau et al. (Paris: Editions du Centre National de la Recherche Scientifique, 1987).

11. Augustin Bernard, *L'Evolution du nomadisme en Algérie* (Algiers: A. Jourdan, 1906), 293–94.

12. Valensi, *Tunisian Peasants*, 50. See also Venema, *Khroumirs*, 50.

13. Habib Attia, "Evolution des structures sociales et économiques dans les Hautes Steppes," *Revue Tunisienne de Sciences Sociales*, no. 6 (June 1966).

14. See table in ibid., 13.

15. Ibid., 10.

16. Jamil M. Abun-Nasr, *A History of the Maghrib*, 2d ed. (Cambridge: Cambridge University Press, 1975), 267; and Abdelkader Zghal, "Participation de la paysannerie maghrébine à la construction nationale," *Revue Tunisienne de Sciences Sociales*, no. 22 (July 1970): 145. For an extensive discussion of

the rebellion of 1864, see *Rabii al Orbane, printemps des Arabes: Aux origines de l'insurrection populaire de 1864*, ed. Taoufik Bachrouch (Tunis: Editions Bayt al-Hikma, Fondation Nationale pour la Traduction, l'Etablissement des Textes, et les Etudes, 1992); and Bice Slama, *L'Insurrection de 1864 en Tunisie* (Tunis: Maison Tunisienne de l'Edition, 1967). See also Anderson, *State and Social Transformation*, 69–70, 84–86. On the devastating effect of the 1864 crisis and its aftermath for the Tunisian population, see Nancy E. Gallagher, *Medicine and Power in Tunisia, 1780–1900* (Cambridge: Cambridge University Press, 1983), 65–68.

17. Abun-Nasr, *History*, 267.

18. Zghal, "Participation," 146.

19. Ibid., 147.

20. John Waterbury, "Peasants Defy Categorization (as well as Landlords and the State)," in *Peasants and Politics in the Modern Middle East*, ed. Farhad Kazemi and John Waterbury (Miami: Florida International University Press, 1991), 6.

21. Valensi, *Tunisian Peasants*, 240.

22. Hermassi, *Leadership*, 51.

23. Ibid., 52.

24. On differences in state centralization within the Maghrib in the pre-colonial period, see Michel le Gall, "The Historical Context," in *Polity and Society in Contemporary North Africa*, ed. I. William Zartman and William M. Habeeb (Boulder, Col.: Westview, 1993), 6–12. On state centralization in Tunisia, see Anderson, *State and Social Transformation*, 59–113. On center-periphery relations in southern Tunisia, see Clancy-Smith, *Rebel and Saint*, 131–34; and Henia, "Mécanisme d'articulation au Jerid."

25. De Montety, "Old Families," 171.

26. Hermassi, *Leadership*, 25.

27. Ibid.; de Montety, "Old Families," 171.

28. Henia, "Mécanisme d'articulation au Jerid," 153–72; Attia, "Evolution," 11.

29. Quoted in Attia, "Evolution," 2.

30. Kenneth J. Perkins, "The Masses Look Ardently to Istanbul: Tunisia, Islam and the Ottoman Empire, 1837–1931," in *Islamism and Secularism in North Africa*, ed. John Ruedy (New York: St. Martin's, 1994), 23–28.

31. Clancy-Smith, *Rebel and Saint*, 157.

32. Brown, *The Tunisia of Ahmad Bey* and "Towards a Comparative History."

33. Brown, *The Tunisia of Ahmad Bey*.

34. Abun-Nasr, *History*, 261.

35. L. Carl Brown, "Tunisia: Education, 'Cultural Unity' and the Future," in *Man, State and Society*, ed. Zartman, 367. Each class of Sadiki graduates formed a network that often lasted a lifetime.

36. For pivotal research on the *ulama* and the religious establishment in Tunisian history, see the work of Arnold H. Green. On reforms, see his *The*

Tunisian Ulama, 1873–1915: Social Structure and Response to Ideological Currents (Leiden: Brill, 1978), 113–15, and "Political Attitudes and Activities of the Ulama in the Liberal Age: Tunisia as an Exceptional Case," *International Journal of Middle East Studies* 7, no. 2 (Apr. 1976): 227. See also Arnold H. Green, "A Comparative Historical Analysis of the Ulama and the State in Egypt and Tunisia," *Revue de l'Occident Musulman et de la Méditerranée* 29 (1980): 28–34; Mahmoud Abdel Moula, *L'Université Zaytounienne et la société tunisienne,* Thèse de 3ème cycle en Sociologie (Tunis: published with the assistance of the Centre National de la Recherche Scientifique, Paris, 1971); and Perkins, "The Masses Look Ardently," 28–34.

37. Islamic schools taught primarily the Qur'an, but also elementary reading and writing.

38. Cherif, "Tunis," 36.

39. On Algeria in the precolonial period and in the early phase of the French conquest, see John Ruedy, *Modern Algeria: The Origins and Development of a Nation* (Bloomington: Indiana University Press, 1992), 16–57; David Prochaska, *Making Algeria French: Colonialism in Bône, 1870–1920* (Cambridge: Cambridge University Press, 1990), 31–61; Clancy-Smith, *Rebel and Saint,* 11–124; Donald C. Holsinger, "Islam and State Expansion in Algeria: Nineteenth Century Sahara Frontiers," in *Islamism,* ed. Ruedy, 3–21; Neil MacMaster, *Colonial Migrants and Racism: Algerians in France, 1900–62* (New York: St. Martin's, 1997), 22–26; Jean Claude Vatin, *L'Algérie politique: Histoire et société* (Paris: Fondation Nationale des Sciences Politiques, 1974), chap. 2; Charles-André Julien, *Histoire de l'Algérie contemporaine,* vol. 1, *La conquête et les débuts de la colonisation (1927–1871)* (Paris: Presses Universitaires de France, 1964), 1–163; Lucette Valensi, *On the Eve of Colonialism: North Africa before the French Conquest,* trans. K. J. Perkins (from French) (New York: Africana, 1977); Hermassi, *Leadership,* part I; and Rachid Tlemcani, *State and Revolution in Algeria* (Boulder, Col.: Westview, 1986), chaps. 2 and 3.

40. Ruedy, *Modern Algeria,* 48–50.

41. Carette, *Recherches sur l'origine et les migrations des principales tribus de l'Afrique septentrionale* (Paris: 1853), 341, cited in Hermassi, *Leadership,* 36.

42. Louis Rinn, "Le royaume d'Alger sous le dernier dey," *Revue Africaine,* (1897): 121–52, 331–50; (1898): 5–21, 113–39, 289–309; (1899): 105–41, 297–320 (reprinted in a special volume, Paris: Editions Jourdan, 1900), cited in Hermassi, *Leadership,* 46.

43. Hermassi, *Leadership,* 47.

44. André Nouschi, *Enquête sur le niveau de vie des populations rurales constantinoises, de la conquête jusqu'en 1919* (Paris: Presses Universitaires de France, 1961), 99. See also Prochaska, *Making Algeria French,* 58.

45. Ruedy, *Modern Algeria,* 57–66; Julien, *Histoire,* 137–209; Clancy-Smith, *Rebel and Saint,* 71–72, 76; and Abun-Nasr, *History,* 240–47.

46. Ruedy, *Modern Algeria,* 64. On the pledge of allegiance to Abd al-Qadir

by anti-French tribes on 27 November 1832, in Gheris in eastern Algeria, see Khalifa Chater, "A Rereading of Islamic Texts in the Maghrib in the Nineteenth and Early Twentieth Centuries: Secular Themes or Religious Reformism?" in *Islamism*, ed. Ruedy (New York: St. Martin's, 1994), 41.

47. Abun-Nasr, *History*, 243–44.

48. Ibid., 246–47.

49. Julien, *Histoire*, 204–9; Ruedy, *Modern Algeria*, 65.

50. Alexis de Tocqueville, "Ecrits et discours politiques," *Oeuvres Complètes*, vol. 3 (Paris: Gallimard, 1962), 223–24.

51. Clancy-Smith, *Rebel and Saint* and "Saints, Mahdis, and Arms: Religion and Resistance in Nineteenth-Century North Africa," in *Islam, Politics and Social Movements*, ed. Edmund Burke III and Ira M. Lapidus (Berkeley and Los Angeles: University of California Press, 1988), 60–80. On insurrections in Algeria in the nineteenth century, see also the studies discussed by Kenneth Perkins, "Recent Historiography of the Colonial Period in North Africa: The 'Copernican Revolution' and Beyond," in *The Maghrib in Question*, ed. Michel Le Gall and Kenneth Perkins (Austin: The University of Texas Press, 1997), 126.

52. Abun-Nasr, *History*, 252.

53. Julien, *Histoire*, 475–500; Ruedy, *Modern Algeria*, 77–79.

54. Zghal, "Participation," 156.

55. Although scholars have debated the proper meaning of *makhzan* and *siba* in the history of Morocco, most agree on the usefulness of the concepts especially for the precolonial period. For a discussion on the historiography of Morocco, see Mohamed El Mansour, "Moroccan Historiography since Independence," in *The Maghrib in Question*, ed. Le Gall and Perkins, 114–18. On precolonial Morocco, see Abdellah Ben Mlih, *Structures politiques du Maroc colonial* (Paris: Harmattan, 1990), 85–126; Daniel Nordman, *Profils du Maghreb: Frontières, figures et territoires (XVIIIe-XXe siècles)* (Rabat: Faculté des Lettres et Sciences Humaines, Université Mohamed V, 1996), 101–26; Janet L. Abu-Lughod, *Rabat: Urban Apartheid in Morocco* (Princeton: Princeton University Press, 1980), 75–130; Abdallah Laroui, *Les origines sociales et culturelles du nationalisme marocain (1830–1912)* (Paris: Maspéro, 1977); Ernest Gellner, "The Struggle for Morocco's Past," in *Man, State and Society*, ed. Zartman, 37–49; Clifford Geertz, *Islam Observed* (Chicago: University of Chicago Press, 1971); Edmund Burke III, *Prelude to Protectorate in Morocco: Precolonial Protest and Resistance, 1860–1912* (Chicago: University of Chicago Press, 1976); David J. Seddon, "Local Politics and State Intervention: Northeast Morocco from 1870 to 1970"; and Ernest Gellner, "Patterns of Rural Rebellion in Morocco during the Years of Independence," both in *Arabs and Berbers: From Tribe to Nation in North Africa*, ed. Ernest Gellner and Charles Micaud (Lexington, Mass.: D. C. Heath, 1972); Clifford Geertz, "The Integrative Revolution: Primordial Sentiments and Civil Politics in the New States," in *Old Societies and New States: The Quest for Modernity in Asia and Africa*, ed. Clifford Geertz (New York: Free Press, 1963); and Hermassi, *Leadership*,

chaps. 1 and 2. A stereotyped view of the concepts of makhzan and siba appears in the writings of Robert Montagne, *Révolution au Maroc* (Paris: Editions France-Empire, 1953); and *Les Berbères et le makhzen dans le sud du Maroc* (Paris: F. Alcan, 1930).

56. With the title of "sultan," members of the Alawi dynasty had ruled Morocco since the mid-1600s and claimed descent from the Prophet Muhammad. In the nineteenth century, however, this was a weak dynasty and a weak form of monarchy. See Le Gall, "Historical Context," 8; Yves Lacoste, "De l'antiquité à la colonization, une histoire mouvementée," in *L'Etat du Maghreb*, ed. Camille Lacoste and Yves Lacoste (Tunis: Cérès Productions, 1991), 46. For a genealogy of the Alawi dynasty, see M. E. Combs-Schilling, *Sacred Performances: Islam, Sexuality, and Sacrifice* (New York: Columbia University Press, 1989), 312–13; and Ben Mlih, *Structures*, 344.

57. On the gradual penetration of Morocco by European powers in the mid-nineteenth century, see Mohammed Kenbib, "Quelques mutations de l'état et de la société au Maroc au XIXème siècle," in *L'Etat marocain dans la durée (1850–1985)*, ed. Abdelali Doumou (Rabat and Paris: Publisud, 1987), 19–34; and Ben Mlih, *Structures*, 63–72. On the perception of French society by a Moroccan scholar in the mid-1840s, see *Disorienting Encounters: Travels of a Moroccan Scholar in France in 1845–1846*, ed. Susan Gilson Miller (Berkeley and Los Angeles: University of California Press, 1992).

58. John Waterbury, *The Commander of the Faithful: The Moroccan Political Elite—A Study in Segmented Politics* (New York: Columbia University Press, 1970), 20. On the expression of allegiance to the sultan in zones of submissiveness, see Rahma Bourqia, "L'Etat et la gestion du symbolique au Maroc précolonial," in *Le Maghreb*, ed. Bourqia and Hopkins, 137–51.

59. Gellner, "The Struggle for Morocco's Past," 44; and Yves Lacoste, "Peuplements et organisation sociale," in *L'Etat du Maghreb*, ed. Lacoste and Lacoste, 32–33.

60. Geertz, *Islam Observed*, 78; Abu-Lughod, *Rabat*, 125–30; Ben Mlih, *Structures*, 104–26.

61. Geertz, "Integrative Revolution," 146.

62. Hermassi, *Leadership*, 35; Michael Brett and Elizabeth Fentress, *The Berbers* (Oxford: Blackwell, 1996), 3. Earlier sources gave estimates that varied from 35 percent, as in Nevill Barbour, ed., *A Survey of North West Africa (the Maghrib)* (London: Oxford University Press, 1959), 79, to 60 percent, as in D. Rustow, "The Politics of the Near East," in *The Politics of the Developing Areas*, ed. G. Almond and J. Coleman (Princeton: Princeton University Press, 1960), 369–453.

63. Ernest Gellner, "Patterns of Rural Rebellion," 364. For an example of changing relations between a Berber tribe (the Ait Ndhir) and the makhzan, see Edmund Burke III, "Mohand N'Hamoucha: Middle Atlas Berber," in *Struggle and Survival in the Modern Middle East*, ed. Edmund Burke III (Berkeley and Los Angeles: University of California Press, 1993), 100–113. On rural rebellions and tribal ethnography, see George Joffé and C. R. Pennell,

eds., *Tribe and State: Essays in Honour of David Montgomery Hart* (Wisbech, Cambridgeshire, Eng.: Middle Eastern and North African Studies Press, 1991).

64. Abun-Nasr, *History*, 284.

65. Waterbury, *Commander*, 15.

66. Ibid., 17–18.

67. Ibid., 20. On Moulay Hassan's expeditions to tribal areas, see also Nordman, *Profils*, 101–26.

68. Abun-Nasr, *History*, 285; Waterbury, *Commander*, 21–24; Abu-Lughod, *Rabat*, 127–30; and Ben Mlih, *Structures*, 104–14.

69. Waterbury, *Commander*, 29.

70. Abun-Nasr, *History*, 301–2.

71. Waterbury, *Commander*, 25.

72. Ibid., 30.

73. Seddon, "Local Politics," 118.

74. Hermassi, *Leadership*, 42; Brett and Fentress, *Berbers*, 187–88.

75. Waterbury, *Commander*, 25.

76. Ibid., 29; and Abun-Nasr, *History*, 285–99.

77. Seddon, "Local Politics," 128–29.

78. Abun-Nasr, *History*, 293–96.

79. Ibid., 297.

80. Ibid.

81. Especially the Shrarda and Beni Mtir tribes.

82. Kenbib, "Quelques mutations," 33; and William A. Hoisington Jr., *Lyautey and the French Conquest of Morocco* (New York: St. Martin's, 1995), 21–39. The text of the treaty of 30 March 1912, establishing the French Protectorate, appears in Ben Mlih, *Structures*, 353–54.

83. Gellner, "Struggle for Morocco's Past," 45.

84. Seddon, "Local Politics," 120.

85. Ibid., 124.

86. See "Customary Law" in chapter 2. On variations among Kabyle tribes, see Patricia M. E. Lorcin, *Imperial Identities: Stereotyping, Prejudice and Race in Colonial Algeria* (London: Tauris, 1995), 72.

87. Green, "Political Attitudes," 229.

88. Ibid., 227.

89. See "Customary Law" in chapter 2.

CHAPTER 6. COLONIAL RULE

1. John Entelis, *Comparative Politics of North Africa: Algeria, Morocco, and Tunisia* (Syracuse: Syracuse University Press, 1980), 17.

2. Lisa Anderson, *The State and Social Transformation in Tunisia and Libya, 1830–1980* (Princeton: Princeton University Press, 1986), 141–57.

3. Elbaki Hermassi, *Leadership and National Development in North Africa: A Comparative Study* (Berkeley and Los Angeles: University of California Press, 1972), 67. On reforms made by the French colonial state with respect

to central administration, local administration, judicial system, and land ownership, see also Asma Larif-Béatrix, *Edification étatique et environnement culturel: Le personnel politico-administratif dans la Tunisie contemporaine* (Paris: Publisud, 1988), 93–122.

4. Nazih N. Ayubi, *Over-Stating the Arab State: Politics and Society in the Middle East* (London: Tauris, 1995), 119.

5. Larif-Béatrix, *Edification*, 99.

6. Jamil M. Abun-Nasr, *A History of the Maghrib*, 2d ed. (Cambridge: Cambridge University Press, 1975), 280; and Magali Morsy, "Des régimes coloniaux differents selon les pays," *L'Etat du Maghreb*, ed. Camille Lacoste and Yves Lacoste (Tunis: Cérès Productions, 1991), 56. On the establishment of French authority over Tunisian qaids in the region of Khroumirie in northwest Tunisia, see Bernhard Venema, *Les Khroumirs: Changements politiques et religieux dans la période 1850–1987* (Amsterdam: VU University Press, 1990), 71.

7. Abun-Nasr, *History*, 351.

8. Habib Attia, "L'Evolution des structures sociales et économiques dans les Hautes Steppes," *Revue Tunisienne de Sciences Sociales*, no. 6 (June 1966), 7–12.

9. Venema, *Khroumirs*, 69–70.

10. Anderson, *State and Social Transformation*, 150.

11. Ibid.

12. M. Dellagi, "Les débuts du syndicalisme tunisien et la C.G.T.T. de M'hamed Ali," ms. cited in Abdelkader Zghal, "Conscience ouvrière et identité culturelle dans une société coloniale: Le cas de la Tunisie," *Identité Culturelle et Conscience Nationale en Tunisie, Cahiers du C.E.R.E.S.*, Série Sociologique, no. 2 (Tunis: Centre d'Etudes et de Recherches Economiques et Sociales, June 1975), 128. On the trade-union movement in Tunisia in the 1920s, see also Eqbal Ahmad and Stuart Schaar, "M'hamed Ali: Tunisian Labor Organizer," in *Struggle and Survival in the Modern Middle East*, ed. Edmund Burke III (Berkeley and Los Angeles: University of California Press, 1993), 191–204.

13. State-Councillor Pascal, quoted in Hermassi, *Leadership*, 79.

14. Abun-Nasr, *History*, 344; and Venema, *Khroumirs*, 65–67, 81–96. In an example from the Sahel on the eastern coast of Tunisia, Kenneth Brown ("Muhammad Ameur: A Tunisian Comrade," in *Struggle and Survival*, ed. Burke, 255–56), indicates that the economy of the village of Ksibet was dominated by saltworks owned by the French company Cotusal established in 1903.

15. Jean Lacouture, *The Demigods: Charismatic Leadership in the Third World* (New York: Knopf, 1970), 136.

16. Comte de Raousset-Boulbon, *De la colonisation et des institutions civiles en Algérie* (Paris, 1847), 24–25, quoted in Peter von Sivers, "Insurrection and Accommodation: Indigenous Leadership in Eastern Algeria, 1840–1900," *International Journal of Middle East Studies* 6, no. 3 (July 1975): 259. On perceptions of the Maghrib in writings of the colonial period, see Centre de Recherches et d'Etudes sur les Sociétés Méditerranéennes, *Connaissances du*

Maghreb: Sciences sociales et colonisation (Paris: Editions du Centre National de la Recherche Scientifique, 1984).

17. John Ruedy, *Modern Algeria: The Origins and Development of a Nation* (Bloomington: Indiana University Press, 1992), 66–68; Jean-Claude Vatin, *L' Algérie politique: Histoire et société* (Paris: Presses de la Fondation Nationale des Sciences Politiques, 1974), chap. 3.

18. Hermassi, *Leadership*, 59.

19. Julia A. Clancy-Smith, *Rebel and Saint: Muslim Notables, Populist Protest, Colonial Encounters (Algeria and Tunisia, 1800–1904)* (Berkeley and Los Angeles: University of California Press, 1994), 95–96.

20. David Prochaska, *Making Algeria French: Colonialism in Bône, 1870–1920* (Cambridge: Cambridge University Press, 1990), 72.

21. Hermassi, *Leadership*, chap. 3; Vatin, *Algérie politique*, chap. 3. On the use of military force by French authorities to subdue the Saharan community of the Mzab in the 1850s, for example, see Donald C. Holsinger, "Islam and State Expansion in Algeria: Nineteenth-Century Saharan Frontiers," in *Islamism and Secularism in North Africa*, ed. Ruedy (New York: St. Martin's, 1994), 14–20.

22. A discussion of conflicts between Algerian tribes and the French during the military conquest of Algeria appears in the preceding chapter.

23. Abun-Nasr, *History*, 249; Ruedy, *Modern Algeria*, 68–72; Prochaska, *Making Algeria French*, 68–76, 81–85; Neil MacMaster, *Colonial Migrants and Racism: Algerians in France, 1900–62* (New York: St. Martin's, 1997), 25–33.

24. René Maunier, *The Sociology of Colonies*, vol. 2, *The Progress of Law*, trans. E. O. Lorimer (from French) (London: Routledge and Kegan Paul, 1949), 481, quoted in Hermassi, *Leadership*, 65.

25. See Henri Brenot, *Le douar, cellule administrative de l'Algérie du Nord* (Algiers: V. Heintz, 1938), 113–14, cited in von Sivers, "Insurrection," 260.

26. Colette Establet, *Etre caïd dans l'Algérie coloniale* (Paris: Editions du Centre National de la Recherche Scientifique, 1991), 21–141; and von Sivers, "Insurrection" (where the transliteration form *banu* is used instead of *beni*).

27. Von Sivers, "Insurrection," 266–67.

28. Peter von Sivers, "Rural Uprisings as Political Movements in Colonial Algeria, 1851–1914," in *Islam, Politics and Social Movements*, ed. Edmund Burke III and Ira M. Lapidus (Berkeley and Los Angeles: University of California Press, 1988), 39–59.

29. Von Sivers, "Insurrection," 269.

30. Ibid., 272.

31. Establet, *Etre caïd*, 191–254.

32. Von Sivers, "Insurrection," 262.

33. This contrasts with Tunisia, where tribal organization had already been weakened.

34. John Waterbury, *The Commander of the Faithful: The Moroccan Political Elite—A Study in Segmented Politics* (New York: Columbia University

Press, 1970), 4. On French colonial rule in Morocco, see also William A. Hoisington Jr., *Lyautey and the French Conquest of Morocco* (New York: St. Martin's, 1995); Abdellah Ben Mlih, *Structures politiques du Maroc colonial* (Paris: Harmattan, 1990), 127–339; Daniel Nordman, *Profils du Maghreb: Frontières, figures et territoires (XVIIIe–XXe siècles)* (Rabat: Faculté des Lettres et Sciences Humaines, Université Mohamed V, 1996), 56–71; Robin Bidwell, *Morocco under Colonial Rule: French Administration of Tribal Areas, 1912–1956* (London: Frank Cass, 1973); Ernest Gellner, "Patterns of Rural Rebellion in Morocco during the Early Years of Independence," in *Arabs and Berbers: From Tribe to Nation in North Africa,* ed. Ernest Gellner and Charles Micaud (Lexington, Mass.: D. C. Heath, 1972), 365–68; Kenneth Brown, "The Impact of the Dahir Berbère in Salé," in *Arabs and Berbers,* ed. Gellner and Micaud, 201–6; Edmund Burke III, "The Image of the Moroccan State in French Ethnological Literature: A New Look at the Origin of Lyautey's Berber Policy," ed. in *Arabs and Berbers,* Gellner and Micaud, 175–99.

35. Abdeslam Baita, "La 'retraditionalisation' des structures étatiques dans le Maroc colonial," in *L'Etat marocain dans la durée (1850–1985),* ed. Abdelali Doumou (Rabat and Paris: Edino and Publisud, 1987), 35–64.

36. Abun-Nasr, *History,* 364. The life story told by David Seddon, "Muhammad El Merid: The Man Who Became Qaid," in *Struggle and Survival,* ed. Burke, 211–23, illustrates the complex situation generated by the coexistence of French and Spanish jurisdictions in northeastern Morocco and its implications for local notables and politics.

37. Abun-Nasr, *History,* 365; Hoisington, *Lyautey,* 185–204.

38. Abun-Nasr, *History,* 365.

39. Général Guillaume, quoted in Waterbury, *Commander,* 37.

40. Ibid.

41. Bidwell, *Morocco under Colonial Rule.* On Lyautey's style with its inconsistencies, see Hoisington Jr., *Lyautey;* and Nordman, *Profils,* 56–65.

42. Ben Mlih, *Structures,* 292–97; Baita, "La 'retraditionalisation,' " 44–48; Waterbury, *Commander,* 36; and Hoisington Jr., *Lyautey,* 93–108, 163–84.

43. Abun-Nasr, *History,* 357.

44. Gellner, "Patterns of Rural Rebellion," in *Arabs and Berbers,* ed. Gellner and Micaud, 367.

45. Ibid.

46. Waterbury, *Commander,* 34.

47. Ibid.

48. Ernest Gellner, "Political and Religious Organization of the Berbers of the Central High Atlas," in *Arabs and Berbers,* ed. Gellner and Micaud, 59; and Waterbury, *Commander,* 4.

49. R. Gaudefroy-Démombynes, doctoral thesis on French education in Morocco (1928), 72, cited in Kenneth Brown, "Impact of the Dahir Berbère," 206 n. 1.

50. Berber speakers constitute approximately 40 percent of the Moroccan

population and are divided among three distinct major dialects. See Michael
Brett and Elizabeth Fentress, *The Berbers* (Oxford: Blackwell, 1996), 3.

51. Burke III, "The Image of the Moroccan State," 188.

52. Ibid., 191.

53. On differences between codes of customary law and the Shariʿa, see
"Customary Law" in chapter 2.

54. Allan Christelow, *Muslim Law Courts and the French Colonial State
in Algeria* (Princeton: Princeton University Press, 1985). See also Mounira M.
Charrad, review of Christelow's book in *Middle East Journal* 41, no. 2 (spring
1987): 281–82.

55. Maurice Borrmans, *Statut personnel et famille au Maghreb: de 1940
à nos jours* (Paris: Mouton, 1977), 103–7. Borrmans includes detailed information on major laws and ordinances from the colonial period. On French
policy in Kabylia and sustained efforts to foster a separate Kabyle identity, see
Patricia M. E. Lorcin, *Imperial Identities: Stereotyping, Prejudice and Race in
Colonial Algeria* (London: Tauris, 1995).

56. Jules Roussier, *Le mariage et sa dissolution dans le statut civil local
algérien* (Algiers: n.p., 1960), 120 n. 93, cited in Borrmans, *Statut personnel*,
438.

57. Decree of 1 January 1883 and Decree of 29 December 1890, cited in
Borrmans, *Statut personnel*, 105. On number of courts, see ibid., 438.

58. Decree of 1950, cited in ibid., 438.

59. Roussier, *Le mariage*, 120 n. 93, quoted in ibid.

60. Ibid., 106–13. On the history of family law in Algeria, see Ghaouti
Benmelha, *Eléments du droit algérien de la famille* (Paris: Publisud, 1985).

61. Marcel Morand quoted in Borrmans, *Statut personnel*, 108.

62. Islamic sources are discussed in chapter 2.

63. Ordinances of 7 March 1944 and 23 November 1944; and Law of 20
September 1947, in Borrmans, *Statut personnel*, 428–31.

64. Ordinance of 23 November 1944, in ibid., 429–30.

65. Laws of 23 March 1882 and 2 April 1930, in ibid., 467, and note 2 on
same page.

66. Law No. 57 777 of July 1957, discussed in ibid., 467.

67. Decree of 1 August 1902, discussed in ibid., 439.

68. Ordinance of 4 February 1959 on marriage and additional Decree of 17
September 1959, in ibid., 481.

69. Individual members of tribal areas could have recourse to Islamic courts
and judges for issues of family law. The acceptance of Islamic law was left to
individual choice; it was not made a matter of general policy.

70. Brown, "Impact of the *Dahir*," 205.

71. Roger Le Tourneau, *Evolution politique de l'Afrique du Nord musulmane, 1920–1961* (Paris: A. Colin, 1962), 182.

72. Brown, "Impact of the *Dahir*," 206.

73. Charles-André Julien, *L'Afrique du Nord en marche: Nationalismes
musulmans et souveraineté française* (Paris: Julliard, 1952), 145–53; Le Tour-

neau, *Evolution politique*, 180–95; Henry Munson Jr., *Religion and Power in Morocco* (New Haven: Yale University Press, 1993), 103; Dale F. Eickelman, *Knowledge and Power in Morocco: The Education of a Twentieth Century Notable* (Princeton: Princeton University Press, 1985), 102–3, 135–36; and Brown, "Impact of the *Dahir*." The text of the dahir appeared in *Bulletin Officiel du Maroc* (May 1930): 652.

74. Article 6 of the dahir of 1930, *Bulletin Officiel*: 652.
75. Le Tourneau, *Evolution politique*, 183.
76. Brown, "The Impact of the *Dahir*."
77. Ibid., 213; Eickelman, *Knowledge and Power*, 135–36.
78. Borrmans, *Statut personnel*, 159.
79. Brown, "The Impact of the *Dahir*," 159.
80. Gellner, "Patterns of Rural Rebellion," 366.
81. Clifford Geertz, *Islam Observed: Religious Development in Morocco and Indonesia* (Chicago: University of Chicago Press, 1971), 80.
82. Dahir of 8 April 1934, discussed in Borrmans, *Statut personnel*, 161.
83. Hermassi, *Leadership*, 66. See also Pierre Bourdieu, rev. ed., *Sociologie de l'Algérie* (Paris: Presses Universitaires de France, 1961).

CHAPTER 7. PALACE, TRIBE, AND PRESERVATION OF ISLAMIC LAW

1. On the historiography of Morocco in the nationalist and postindependence period, see Mohamed El Mansour, "Moroccan Historiography since Independence," in *The Maghrib in Question: Essays in History and Historiography*, ed. Michel Le Gall and Kenneth Perkins (Austin: The University of Texas Press, 1997), 112–19. On the social and political landscape, see Abdallah Hammoudi, *Master and Disciple: The Cultural Foundations of Moroccan Authoritarianism* (Chicago: Chicago University Press, 1997), 11–43, 120–33; Jean-François Clément, "Maroc: Les atouts et les défis de la monarchie," in *Maghreb: Les années de transition*, ed. Bassma Kodmani-Darwish with May Chartouni-Dubarry (Paris: Masson, 1990), 68–69; Rémy Leveau, *Le fellah marocain: Défenseur du trône* (Paris: Presses de la Fondation Nationale des Sciences Politiques, 1976); Abdelali Doumou, "Etat et légitimation dans le Maroc post-colonial," in *L'Etat marocain dans la durée (1850–1985)*, ed. Abdelali Doumou (Rabat and Paris: Edino and Publisud, 1987); Marvin W. Mikesell, "The Role of Tribal Markets in Morocco," in *Man, State and Society in the Contemporary Maghrib*, ed. I. William Zartman (New York: Praeger, 1973); Ernest Gellner, *Saints of the Atlas* (Chicago: Chicago University Press, 1969); David Seddon, *Moroccan Peasants: A Century of Change in the Eastern Rif, 1870–1970* (Folkstone, Kent, Eng.: Dawson, 1981), and "Aspects of Kinship and Family Structure among the Ulad Stut of Zaio Rural Commune, Nador Province, Morocco," in *Mediterranean Family Structures*, ed. J. G. Peristiany (Cambridge: Cambridge University Press, 1976), 173–94; Dale F. Eickelman, *Moroccan Islam: Tradition and Society in a Pilgrimage Center* (Aus-

tin: The University of Texas Press, 1976); David M. Hart, *Dadda 'Atta and His Forty Grandsons: The Socio-Political Organisation of the Ait 'Atta of Southern Morocco* (Cambridge, Eng.: Middle Eastern and North African Studies Press, 1981); I. William Zartman, *Morocco: Problems of New Power* (New York: Atherton, 1964).

2. Jamil M. Abun-Nasr, *A History of the Maghrib*, 2d ed. (Cambridge: Cambridge University Press, 1975), 374. On Moroccan nationalism, see Abdallah Laroui, *Les origines sociales et culturelles du nationalisme marocain, 1830–1912* (Paris: Maspéro, 1977); Benjamin Stora, "Tunisie, Algérie, Maroc: Aux origines des mouvements indépendantistes," in *L'Etat du Maghreb*, ed. Camille Lacoste and Yves Lacoste (Tunis: Cérès Productions, 1991); and Hammoudi, *Master and Disciple*, 16, 129–31.

3. On al-Fasi's views, see Henry Munson Jr., *Religion and Power in Morocco* (New Haven: Yale University Press, 1993), 78–79; and Mohamed El Mansour, "Salafis and Modernists in the Moroccan Nationalist Movement," in *Islamism and Secularism in North Africa*, ed. John Ruedy (New York: St. Martin's, 1994), 65–68.

4. Stora, "Tunisie, Algérie, Maroc," 63.

5. Ibid.; Elbaki Hermassi, *Leadership and National Development in North Africa: A Comparative Study* (Berkeley and Los Angeles: University of California Press, 1972), 108.

6. Quoted in Hermassi, *Leadership*, 108.

7. Quoted in Abun-Nasr, *History*, 376.

8. Ibid., 375.

9. Ibid.

10. M. E. Combs-Schilling, *Sacred Performances: Islam, Sexuality, and Sacrifice* (New York: Columbia University Press, 1989), 9–12, 175–87.

11. Ibid., 10.

12. On the role of the Moroccan monarchy, see Susan E. Waltz, *Human Rights and Reform: Changing the Face of North African Politics* (Berkeley and Los Angeles: University of California Press, 1995), 107–9; Nazih N. Ayubi, *Over-Stating the Arab State: Politics and Society in the Middle East* (London: Tauris, 1995), 120–22; Munson, *Religion and Power*, 125–34; Mark A. Tessler, "Morocco: Institutional Pluralism and Monarchical Dominance," in *Political Elites in Arab North Africa*, I. William Zartman et al. (New York: Longman, 1982); Mark A. Tessler and John P. Entelis, "Kingdom of Morocco," in *The Government and Politics of the Middle East and North Africa*, ed. David E. Long and Bernard Reich (Boulder, Col.: Westview, 1980), 382–406; Stora, "Tunisie, Algérie, Maroc"; John Waterbury, *The Commander of the Faithful: The Moroccan Political Elite—A Study of Segmented Politics* (New York: Columbia University Press, 1970), 53–58; and Hermassi, *Leadership*, 100–112. On the resilience of the Moroccan and other Middle Eastern monarchies, see Lisa Anderson, "Absolutism and the Resilience of Monarchy in the Middle East," *Political Science Quarterly*, no. 1 (1991): 1–15.

13. Quoted in Clifford Geertz, "The Integrative Revolution: Primordial

Sentiments and Civil Politics in the New States," in *Old Societies and New States: The Quest for Modernity in Asia and Africa*, ed. Clifford Geertz (New York: Free Press, 1963), 148.

14. Ibid.

15. Philippe Fargues, "Un siècle de transition démographique en Afrique méditerranéenne, 1885–1985," in *Population* 41, no. 2 (1986): 207. Under colonization, from 1912 to 1956, the zones under French and Spanish occupation never had a census at the same time (Fargues, 204).

16. Leveau, *Fellah marocain*, 36.

17. Douglas E. Ashford, *Political Change in Morocco* (Princeton: Princeton University Press, 1961), 185. On urban/rural population, see also *United Nations Demographic Yearbook, 1960* (New York: United Nations Publication, 1961), 373; and I. William Zartman and William M. Habeeb, eds., *Polity and Society in Contemporary North Africa* (Boulder, Col.: Westview, 1993), 257.

18. Geertz, "Integrative Revolution," 148.

19. David Seddon, "Local Politics and State Intervention: Northeast Morocco from 1870 to 1970," in *Arabs and Berbers: From Tribe to Nation in North Africa*, ed. Ernest Gellner and Charles Micaud (Lexington, Mass.: D. C. Heath, 1972).

20. Quoted in Ashford, *Political Change in Morocco*, 214.

21. See chapter 5.

22. Zartman, *Morocco*, 10.

23. Geertz, "Integrative Revolution," 149.

24. Seddon, "Local Politics," 134.

25. Ibid.; Geertz, "Integrative Revolution," 149–50.

26. Ernest Gellner, "Patterns of Rural Rebellion in Morocco during the Early Years of Independence," in *Arabs and Berbers*, ed. Gellner and Micaud, 373.

27. Ibid.

28. Ibid.

29. Leveau, *Fellah marocain*.

30. Clément, "Maroc," 64, 70.

31. Hammoudi, *Master and Disciple*, 36; see also 30–31 and 36–43.

32. Doumou, "Etat et légitimation," 72–81. See also Dale F. Eickelman, *Knowledge and Power: The Education of a Twentieth Century Notable* (Princeton: Princeton University Press, 1985), 156–57.

33. King Hassan II was trained in law in France (Tessler and Entelis, "Kingdom of Morocco," 386).

34. Leveau, *Fellah marocain*, 26–27.

35. Ibid., 26.

36. Ibid., 84.

37. Clément, "Maroc," 68–70.

38. Leveau, *Fellah marocain*, 23.

39. Ibid.

40. Waterbury, *Commander*, 83.

41. Article 22 of the Decree of 29 September 1972, quoted in Doumou, "Etat et légitimation," 75–76.

42. Doumou, "Etat et légitimation," 75–79.

43. For example, Waterbury, *Commander*, 61.

44. Ibid., 170. On the power of the king and his role as arbitrator, see also Clement Henry Moore, "Political Parties," in *Polity and Society*, ed. Zartman and Habeeb, 44; Clément, "Maroc," 85; Hammoudi, *Master and Disciple*, 12–24; and Waltz, *Human Rights*, 117–21.

45. Waterbury, *Commander*, 244.

46. Halim Barakat, *The Arab World: Society, Culture and State* (Berkeley and Los Angeles: University of California Press, 1993), 40, gives the figure of 40 percent. So do John P. Entelis, *Comparative Politics of North Africa: Algeria, Morocco, and Tunisia* (Syracuse: Syracuse University Press, 1980), 3, and Hermassi, *Leadership*, 35. Yves Lacoste, "Peuplements et organisation sociale," in *L'Etat du Maghreb*, ed. Lacoste and Lacoste, 29, uses the figure of 33 percent.

47. Waterbury, *Commander*, 315.

48. Ibid.

49. Kenneth Brown, "The Impact of the *Dahir Berbère* in Salé," in *Arabs and Berbers*, ed. Gellner and Micaud, 215.

50. Allal al-Fasi, *al-Naqd al-dhati* (Self-criticism) (Cairo: al-Matba'at al-'Alamiyya, 1952). Chapters on family and kinship are reproduced in Maurice Borrmans, *Documents sur la famille au Maghreb de 1940 à nos jours*, special issues of *Oriente Moderno* 59, nos. 1–5 (1979): 125–59.

51. Resolution of the *Istiqlal*, *Revue de Presse (Maghreb, Proche-Orient, Moyen-Orient)*, no. 4 (Apr. 1956).

52. Al-Fasi, *al-Naqd al-dhati*, in Borrmans, *Documents*, 128.

53. Al-Fasi, ibid., passim.

54. For example, *l'Istiqlal*, 16 March 1957, and *Démocratie*, 4 and 25 February 1957.

55. This applied to the Muslim population in Morocco, whether Arab or Berber. The Jewish population was under a different family legislation.

56. Mohammed V, king of Morocco, quoted in Borrmans, *Statut personnel*, 194–95.

57. The Mudawwana (books 1, 2, and 3, and a commentary) appears in book form in Mohamed Chafi, *Code du statut personnel annoté* (Marrakech: Walili, 1996). The text of the Mudawwana was initiaily published in parts in the *Bulletin Officiel du Maroc*, books 1 and 2 (23 May 1958); book 3 (25 July 1958); book 4 (7 November 1958); book 5 (20 February 1959). The complete text also appears in A. Colomer, "Le code du statut personnel marocain (texte et commentaire)," *Revue Algérienne, Tunisienne et Marocaine de Législation et de Jurisprudence* 79 (1961): 201. Borrmans, *Statut personnel*, 197–232, includes sections of the Mudawwana.

58. Limited amendments were made to the Mudawwana in 1993, and appear in Chafi, *Code*. For a discussion of the Mudawwana by a legal scholar, see

also Abderrazak Moulay Rchid, "La Mudawwana en question," in *Femmes, culture et société au Maghreb*, vol. 2, ed. Rahma Bourqia, Mounira M. Charrad, and Nancy Gallagher (Casablanca: Afrique Orient, 1996), 53–66; and Abderrazak Moulay Rchid, *La femme et la loi au Maroc* (Casablanca: Le Fennec, 1991), 51–96. For an anthropological study based on fieldwork among litigants in family courts in Morocco and conducted in 1988–89 (thus three decades after the promulgation of the Mudawwana), see Ziba Mir-Hosseini, *Marriage on Trial: A Study of Islamic Family Law—Iran and Morocco Compared* (London: Tauris, 1993).

59. On marriage, Mudawwana, articles 1–31.

60. Ibid., article 8.

61. Ibid., article 29.

62. Ibid., article 35.

63. On registration, Mudawwana, articles 5, 41, 42; and Decision of the Moroccan Supreme Court, 19 March 1962, *Al-Qada wa-l-Qanun*, cited in Borrmans, *Statut personnel*, 249. On unregistered marriages in Morocco still in the 1980s, see Mir-Hosseini, *Marriage on Trial*, 171–74.

64. Borrmans, *Statut personnel*, 250.

65. On repudiation and other forms of divorce, Mudawwana, articles 44–65.

66. Ibid., article 30, first section. On the subjective restriction placed on polygamy by Islamic law, see chapter 2 of this book. On the regulations on polygamy in the Mudawwana, see articles 30 and 31.

67. Mudawwana, article 83.

68. J. Lapanne-Joinville, "Le code marocain de statut personnel," *Revue Juridique et Politique de l'Union Française* (1959): 79, quoted in Borrmans, *Statut personnel*, 217. The same emphasis on agnatic ties and the patrilineage appears in Moroccan citizenship law: see Mounira M. Charrad, "Becoming a Citizen: Lineage versus Individual in Morocco and Tunisia," in *Citizenship and Gender in the Middle East*, ed. Suad Joseph (Syracuse: Syracuse University Press, 2000).

69. Mudawwana, article 215.

70. On wills and inheritance, see ibid., articles 173–297.

71. Ibid., articles 82, 172, 216, and 267.

72. Colomer, "Code du statut personnel marocain," 200.

CHAPTER 8. ELITE DIVISIONS AND THE LAW IN GRIDLOCK

1. The estimate of the deaths caused by the war varies depending on the source. Benjamin Stora indicates that Algerian sources present the figure of 1.5 million, whereas French sources present the figure of 500,000: Benjamin Stora, "La guerre d'indépendance algérienne," in *L'Etat du Maghreb*, ed. Camille Lacoste and Yves Lacoste (Tunis: Cérès Productions, 1991), 64. Elbaki Hermassi suggests a figure of 1 million: *Leadership and National Development in*

North Africa: A Comparative Study (Berkeley and Los Angeles: University of California Press, 1972), 131. On the death-toll debate, see John Ruedy, *Modern Algeria: The Origins and Development of a Nation* (Bloomington: Indiana University Press, 1992), 190.

2. Charles F. Gallagher, "A Note on the Maghrib," in *Man, State and Society in the Contemporary Maghrib,* ed. I. William Zartman (New York: Praeger, 1973), 9. For sources on the Algerian war of independence, including memoirs and personal accounts, see Kenneth Perkins, "Recent Historiography of the Colonial Period in North Africa: The 'Copernican Revolution' and Beyond," in *The Maghrib in Question: Essays in History and Historiography,* ed. Michel Le Gall and Kenneth Perkins (Austin: The University of Texas Press, 1997), 127. On the development of the war and its stages between 1954 and 1962, see Ruedy, *Modern Algeria,* 156–90.

3. Algeria was declared a French province even earlier (1830) than other territories that are now an integral part of France. The province of Savoy, for example, did not become French until 1860. On settler colonialism and its culture in Algeria, see David Prochaska, *Making Algeria French: Colonialism in Bône, 1870–1920* (Cambridge: Cambridge University Press, 1990), 206–29.

4. Daho Djerbal, "Aux origines de l'état-nation ou comment comprendre les relations de légitimité et d'autorité politiques dans l'Algérie des années 1940–1950," in *Le Maghreb: Approches des mécanismes d'articulation,* ed. Rahma Bourqia and Nicholas Hopkins (Rabat: Al Kalam, 1991), 201–22; and Jeanne Favret, "Traditionalism through Ultra-Modernism," in *Arabs and Berbers: From Tribe to Nation in North Africa,* ed. Ernest Gellner and Charles Micaud (Lexington, Mass.: D. C. Heath, 1972).

5. Djerbal, "Aux origines," 202.

6. The *United Nations Demographic Yearbook, 1960* (New York: United Nations Publications, 1961), 373, gives a figure of 22.9 percent for the urban population. Favret, "Traditionalism," 318, indicates that the urban population made up only 12 percent of the total.

7. See chapter 6.

8. Djerbal, "Aux origines," 205–15.

9. Quoted in ibid., 213.

10. Jean Claude Vatin, *L'Algérie politique: Histoire et société* (Paris: Fondation Nationale des Sciences Politiques, 1974), 280.

11. Quoted in Hermassi, *Leadership,* 133.

12. Marnia Lazreg, *The Eloquence of Silence: Algerian Women in Question* (New York: Routledge, 1994), 51–52; and Lisa Anderson, "Obligation and Accountability: Islamic Politics in North Africa," *Daedalus* 120, no. 3 (summer 1991): 99–100.

13. Quoted in Hermassi, *Leadership,* 134.

14. On divisions within the Algerian political leadership, see Vatin, *L'Algérie politique;* Jean Leca, "Etat et société en Algérie," in *Maghreb: Les années de transition,* ed. Bassma Kodmani-Darwish with May Chartouni-Dubarry (Paris: Masson, 1990), 17–32; Halim Barakat, *The Arab World: So-*

ciety, Culture and State (Berkeley and Los Angeles: University of California Press, 1993), 168–69; Susan E. Waltz, *Human Rights and Reform: Changing the Face of North African Politics* (Berkeley and Los Angeles: University of California Press, 1995), 84–87; Jean Leca and Jean Claude Vatin, *L'Algérie politique, institutions et régime* (Paris: Presses de la Fondation Nationale des Sciences Politiques, 1975); Bruno Etienne, "Le socialisme algérien," in *Introduction à l'Afrique du Nord contemporaine,* Centre de Recherches et d'Etudes sur les Societies Méditerranéennes (Paris: Editions du Centre National de la Recherche Scientifique, 1975); Mohammed Harbi, *Aux origines du Front de Libération Nationale: La scission du P.P.A.-M.T.L.D.* (Paris: C. Bourgeois, 1975); William Quandt, *Revolution and Political Leadership: Algeria 1954– 1968* (Cambridge: M.I.T. Press, 1969); Rachid Tlemcani, *State and Revolution in Algeria* (Boulder, Col.: Westview, 1986); John P. Entelis, *Algeria: The Revolution Institutionalized* (Boulder, Col.: Westview, 1986), 57–59; and Ruedy, *Modern Algeria,* 190–94.

15. L. Carl Brown, "Islam's Role in North Africa," in *Man, State and Society,* ed. Zartman, 33.

16. Gallagher, "A Note on the Maghrib," 11.

17. In 1962, at the time of independence, three separate bodies contended for power: a provisional government in exile, regional guerrilla command centers on the Algerian territory itself, and the Army of the Frontiers.

18. Michael Brett and Elizabeth Fentress, *The Berbers* (Oxford: Blackwell, 1996), 3, and Yves Lacoste, "Peuplements et organisation sociale," in *L'Etat du Maghreb,* ed. Lacoste and Lacoste, 29, give the figure of 20 percent; John P. Entelis, *Comparative Politics of North Africa: Algeria, Morocco, and Tunisia* (Syracuse: Syracuse University Press, 1980), 3, indicates 25 percent; Hermassi, *Leadership,* 35, gives 30 percent.

19. Favret, "Traditionalism." Colonel Zbiri argued for a decentralized, self-management approach to the economy and against a centralized system.

20. Ibid., 315.

21. Ibid.

22. Ibid., 308.

23. Ibid., 319.

24. Hermassi, *Leadership,* 150–53; Leca and Vatin, *Algérie politique,* 400–412.

25. Favret, "Traditionalism," 323.

26. Ibid., 313.

27. There was not much of an Algerian urban financial or industrial bourgeoisie in any case, since finance and the little industry that existed were in the hands of the French. See Charles-Robert Ageron, "Les classes moyennes dans l'Algérie coloniale: Origine, formation et évaluation quantitative," in *Les classes moyennes au Maghreb,* Centre de Recherches et d'Etudes sur les Sociétés Méditerranéennes (Paris: Centre National de la Recherche Scientifique, 1980); and Leca, "Etat et société en Algérie," 35. On the impoverished peasantry, see Ruedy, *Modern Algeria,* 189–90.

28. Pierre Robert Baduel, "Etat, pouvoir et territoire," in *L'Etat du Maghreb*, ed. Lacoste and Lacoste, 347.

29. Leca, "Etat et société en Algérie," 18.

30. Jean Leca, "Villes et systèmes politiques: L'Image de la ville dans le discours officiel algérien," in *Système urbain et développement au Maghreb*, ed. Amel Rassam and Abdelkader Zghal (Tunis: Cérès Productions, 1980), 290–317.

31. Quoted in Leca, "Villes et systèmes politiques," 295.

32. Ibid.

33. Ibid., 293–94.

34. Fanny Colonna, "Paysans et encadreurs: A propos des transferts de savoirs et de modèles entre villes et campagnes en Algérie," in *Système urbain*, ed. Rassam and Zghal, 318–40.

35. The military coup occurred with barely a ripple. At the same time a film about the Algerian war, *Battle of Algiers*, was being shot, with tanks and guns deployed in the streets of Algiers. It took a while for people to realize that a coup was taking place in addition to a film being shot.

36. William B. Quandt, "The Berbers in the Algerian Political Elite," in *Arabs and Berbers*, ed. Gellner and Micaud, 295, 298.

37. Ibid., 298.

38. Witness, for example, instances of ethnic nationalism in former Yugoslavia and the former Soviet Union. These instances are not, for the most part, linked to a kin-based social organization.

39. Djerbal, "Aux origines de l'état-nation"; Favret, "Traditionalism."

40. Quandt, "The Berbers"; also *Berbères: Une identité en construction*, special issue of *Revue de l'Occident Musulman et de la Méditerranée*, no. 44 (1987). The four most important and distinct Berber communities in Algeria are the Kabyles, the Shawiyas (in the region of Aures), the Mzabites and the Touaregs. More remote geographically than the others, the Mzabites and the Touaregs had relatively little say in national politics in the aftermath of independence, whereas the Kabyles and the Shawiyas were very much involved.

41. Maurice Borrmans, *Statut personnel et famille au Maghreb: de 1940 à nos jours* (Paris: Mouton, 1977), 447–53; Ruedy, *Modern Algeria*, 134–36; Entelis, *Algeria*, 42–43. On positions on gender and family law among the nationalists from the 1920s to 1962, see Monique Gadant, *Le nationalisme algérien et les femmes* (Paris: Harmattan, 1995), 121–36.

42. Allan Christelow, *Muslim Law Courts and the French Colonial State* (Princeton: Princeton University Press, 1985).

43. Ali Merad, *Le réformisme musulman en Algérie de 1925 à 1940: Essai d'histoire religieuse et sociale* (Paris: Mouton, 1967), cited in Doria Cherifati-Merabtine, "Algeria at a Crossroads: National Liberation, Islamization and Women," in *Gender and National Identity: Women and Politics in Muslim Societies*, ed. Valentine M. Moghadam (London: Zed Books, 1994), 45.

44. Lazreg, *The Eloquence of Silence*, 80–88; and "Gender and Politics in

Algeria: Unraveling the Religious Paradigm," *Signs: Journal of Women in Culture and Society* 15, no. 41 (1990).

45. Lazreg, "Gender and Politics"; and Prochaska, *Making Algeria French*, 234–38.

46. Houria Hizb, "La situation sociale de la musulmane algérienne," *Rhythmes du Monde* (Paris), no. 4 (1947): 42.

47. Borrmans, *Statut personnel*, 457. On pro-change trend, see the same, 115–17, 454–58.

48. Statement of the National Liberation Front at the Congress of Soumman, 20 August 1956, quoted in ibid., 498–99.

49. Cherifa Bouatta, "Feminine Militancy: Moudjahidates during and after the Algerian War," in *Gender and National Identity*, ed. Moghadam, 20.

50. Quoted in Bouatta, "Feminine Militancy," 27.

51. See the account given by the Moroccan journalist Zakya Daoud, *Féminisme et politique au Maghreb: Sept décennies de lutte* (Casablanca: Eddif, 1996), 138–40; and David C. Gordon, *Women of Algeria; An Essay on Change*, Middle Eastern Monograph 19 (Cambridge: Harvard University Press, 1968), 53–56.

52. Cited in Cherifati-Merabtine, "Algeria at a Crossroads," 47.

53. Bouatta, "Feminine Militancy," 29.

54. Cherifati-Merabtine, "Algeria at a Crossroads."

55. See chapter 6.

56. *Al-Moujahid* (Algiers), no. 45 (6 July 1959), in Borrmans, *Statut personnel*, 494.

57. Document of the National Liberation Front outlining guidelines for its judicial committees, reproduced in Borrmans, *Statut personnel*, 499–500, note 106.

58. See chapter 6.

59. Front de Libération Nationale, *Charte nationale* (République Algérienne Démocratique et Populaire: Editions Populaire de l'Armée, 1976), 72. The *Programme of Tripoli* appears in *Annuaire de l'Afrique du Nord* (Paris: Editions du Centre National de la Recherche Scientifique, 1962), 683–704. The *Charte nationale*, called *Charte d'Alger* (*Charter of Algiers*), was first published in 1964, two years after independence, but was written before 1962. It represented one of the most important statements of the objectives of the FLN for independent Algeria.

60. Quoted in Peter R. Knauss, "Algerian Women since Independence," in *State and Society in Algeria*, ed. John P. Entelis and Phillip C. Naylor (Boulder, Col.: Westview, 1992), 155. On popular discourse on women's roles in the aftermath of independence, see Gadant, *Nationalisme*, 86–94.

61. Fatima-Zohra Sai, "Les femmes algériennes: Citoyennes, moudjahidates, soeurs," in *Femmes, culture et société au Maghreb*, ed. Rahma Bourqia, Mounira M. Charrad, and Nancy Gallagher, vol. 2 (Casablanca: Afrique Orient, 1996), 86–87, 91–94.

62. Sophie Bessis and Souhayr Belhassen are two journalists who report extensively on the Maghribi press and provide a wealth of interviews in *Femmes du Maghreb: L'enjeu* (Tunis: Cérès Productions, 1992), 67; see also Knauss, "Algerian Women," 156.

63. Bessis and Belhassen, *Femmes du Maghreb,* 69.

64. Declaration of President Ben Bella in 1964, quoted in Borrmans, *Statut personnel,* 539.

65. Monique Gadant, "Les communistes algériens et l'émancipation des femmes," *Femmes et pouvoir,* special issue of *Peuples Méditerranéens,* nos. 48–49 (July–Dec. 1989): 201. On the absence of a feminist tradition in this period, see also Chérifa Bouatta, "Evolution of the Women's Movement in Contemporary Algeria: Organization, Objectives and Prospects," *Working Papers* (United Nations University/Wider), no. 124 (1997): 1–3.

66. The interview took place in 1971. It is quoted in Knauss, "Algerian Women," 159.

67. Kamila Sefta, "Le 'collectif femmes' du Parti de la Révolution Socialiste à Paris, 1972–74. Les raisons d'une crise," in *Femmes et pouvoir,* 196.

68. Sefta, "Collectif femmes," 196.

69. Gadant, "Communistes algériens," 206.

70. As Lazreg points out, this was a time when the gold standard served as a measure for national currencies (*Eloquence of Silence,* 145–46).

71. Alan Richards and John Waterbury, *A Political Economy of the Middle East: State, Class, and Economic Development* (Boulder, Col.: Westview, 1990), 424.

72. Mohammed Tozy, "Islam and the State," in *Polity and Society in Contemporary North Africa,* ed. I. William Zartman and William M. Habeeb (Boulder, Col.: Westview, 1993), 104.

73. For the reasons discussed in chapter 6, the French implanted more schools in Kabylia than elsewhere. The figures given by Richards and Waterbury show how little Algerians benefitted from French education. In the mid-1950s, Algeria included approximately 1 million Europeans, mostly French, and 9 million Muslim Algerians. French children in Algeria "enjoyed universal primary education, made up 90 percent of the secondary school population and 98 percent of all those from Algeria who went to France for higher education" (Richards and Waterbury, *A Political Economy,* 423). In contrast, there were only seventy living Muslim Algerians who had a university education in 1954, after 124 years of colonial rule.

74. Tozy, "Islam and the State," 104; and Etienne, "Socialisme algerien," 365.

75. Two major texts were the *Programme of Tripoli,* 683–704, and the *Charte nationale.*

76. Gadant, "Les communistes algériens," 208–9.

77. Quoted in Borrmans, *Statut personnel,* 540.

78. Ibid., 540–41.

79. Abdelbaki Hermassi, "The Political and the Religious in the Modern

History of the Maghrib," in *Islamism and Secularism in North Africa*, ed. John Ruedy (New York: St. Martin's, 1994), 90.

80. Francois Burgat and William Dowell, *The Islamic Movement in North Africa* (Austin: Center for Middle Eastern Studies, The University of Texas at Austin, 1993), 248–50; Tozy, "Islam and the State," 104, 108; John Ruedy, "Continuities and Discontinuities in the Algerian Confrontation with Europe," in *Islamism and Secularism*, ed. John Ruedy, 80; Leca and Vatin, *Algérie Politique*, 308–12; Jean-Claude Vatin, "Puissance d'état et résistances islamiques en Algérie, XIX–XX siècles. Approche mécanique" in *Islam et politique au Maghreb*, Centre de Recherches et d'Etudes sur les Sociétés Méditerranéennes (Paris: Editions du Centre National de la Recherche Scientifique, 1981), 263–65.

81. Leca and Vatin, *l'Algérie politique*, 308; Vatin, "Puissance d'état," 261.

82. Richards and Waterbury, *A Political Economy*, 310.

83. Etienne, "Le socialisme algérien," 363; Leca, "Etat et société en Algérie," 23; Knauss, "Algerian Women," 157; Entelis, *Comparative Politics*, 85–101; Hugh Roberts, "The Politics of Algerian Socialism," in *North Africa: Contemporary Politics and Economic Development*, ed. Richard Lawless and Allan Findlay (London: Croom Helm, 1984), 6.

84. Nouredine Saadi, *La femme et la loi en Algérie* (Casablanca: Le Fennec, 1991), 44–47; and Borrmans, *Statut personnel*, 521–35.

85. Saadi, *La femme et la loi*, 45.

86. *Revolution et travail*, 3 March 1966, quoted in ibid.

87. Before 1965, rumors circulated that a reform plan was in the works and the government withdrew the projects without presenting them to the assembly. From 1965 to 1976 (when the assembly was suspended), rumors would circulate that a governmental commission was working on a project, followed by the government's denial of them.

88. Law of 31 December 1962, articles 1 and 2, in *Annuaire de l'Afrique du Nord* (1962): 741.

89. Discussed in chapter 6.

90. Preamble to the Algerian Constitution, quoted in Borrmans, *Statut personnel*, 515. The complete text of the constitution appears in *Annuaire de l'Afrique du Nord* (1963): 852–59.

91. Decree of 23 April 1963, cited in Borrmans, *Statut personnel*, 520. Ghaouti Benmelha, *Eléments du droit algérien de la famille* (Paris: Publisud, 1985), provides details on family law in independent Algeria before the promulgation of the 1984 Family Code.

92. Law of 31 December 1962; articles 1 and 2 in *Annuaire de l'Afrique du Nord* (1963): 852–59.

93. For example, Ruling no. 17, 11 February 1963, quoted in Borrmans, *Statut personnel*, 520.

94. Interview in the March 1985 edition of the American newspaper, *Off Our Backs*, quoted in Nadia Hijab, *Womanpower: The Arab Debate on Women at Work* (Cambridge: Cambridge University Press, 1988), 27–28.

95. Lazreg (*Eloquence of Silence*, 158) reports that, according to official statistics published in 1986, women represented 6 percent of the labor force and that 86 percent of those were in clerical white collar jobs. Saadi (*La femme et la loi*, 92) reports that a survey by the Algerian National Office of Statistics indicates that in 1989 women represented 4.7 percent of the paid labor force.

96. A classic source on women's resistance to the 1981 draft law is the article that Louis wrote following a trip to Algeria in that period: Marie-Victoire Louis, "Les Algériennes, la lutte," *Les Temps Modernes*, nos. 432–33 (July–Aug. 1982): 152–93. For other sources on the events, some of which use Louis, see Knauss, "Algerian Women"; Lazreg, *Eloquence of Silence*, 153–55; Hijab, *Womanpower*, 27; Bouatta, "Evolution," 4–5; Willy Jansen, *Women without Men: Gender and Marginality in an Algerian Town* (Leiden: Brill, 1987), 232–38; and Boutheina Cheriet, "Islamism and Feminism: Algeria's 'Rites of Passage' to Democracy," in *State and Society*, ed. Entelis and Naylor, 192–94. On Algerian women's activism in a global context, see Valentine M. Moghadam "Organizing Women: The New Women's Movement in Algeria," in *Women and Politics in the Middle East*, ed. Mary Jane Deeb and Mary Ann Tetreault (forthcoming).

97. Knauss, "Algerian Women," 164.

98. Hijab, *Womanpower*, 28.

99. Ibid.; on the withdrawal of the draft, see also Louis, "Les Algériennes."

100. Louis, "Les Algériennes" includes the text of the 1981 draft law. See also Hélène Vandevelde, "Le code algérien de la famille," *Maghreb-Machrek* 107 (Jan.–Mar. 1985): 30–58; and Peter R. Knauss, *The Persistence of Patriarchy: Class, Gender and Ideology in Twentieth Century Algeria* (New York: Praeger, 1987).

101. Saadi (*La femme et la loi*, 48) reports that some members of the Islamic fundamentalist movement were opposed to the very principle of codification of the law and proposed a return to an uncodified Islamic law, as in the Shari'a and as had been the case historically in Algeria.

102. Law no. 84-11 of 9 June 1984, constitutes the Algerian Family Code of 1984. The text appeared in the *Journal Officiel de la République Algérienne Démocratique et Populaire*, no. 24 (12 June 1984). For a detailed analysis of the content of the code, see Saadi, *La femme et la loi*; Leila Hamdan, "Les difficultés de codification du droit de la famille algérien," *Revue Internationale de Droit Comparé* 37, no.4 (1985): 1001–15; Maurice Borrmans, "Le nouveau code algérien de la famille dans l'ensemble des codes musulmans de statut personnel, principalement dans les pays arabes," *Revue Internationale de Droit Comparé* 38, no. 1 (1986): 133–39; and Ramdane Babadji and Mohamed N. Mahieddin, "Le Fiqh islamique, source non exclusive de droit de la famille en Algérie," *Revue Internationale de Droit Comparé* 39, no.1 (1987): 163–73. For an approach to the enactment of the 1984 Family Code different from the one presented in this book, see the interesting analysis of the process of enactment as a legitimation crisis for the official ideology of "specific socialism," in Cheriet, "Islamism and Feminism."

103. Roberts, "Politics of Algerian Socialism," in *North Africa*, ed. Lawless and Findlay, 39.

104. The government faced intermittent unrest in Kabylia, where Kabyles demanded recognition of their language and culture. The most serious incident occurred in the spring of 1980 in the city of Tizi Ouzou. See Ronald Koven, "Algerian Government Challenged by Unrest in Berber Homeland," *Washington Post*, 23 April 1980; Ruedy, *Modern Algeria*, 240; and Lisa Anderson, "North Africa: Changes and Challenges," *Dissent* 43, no. 3 (summer 1996): 115. On arabization and Berbers, see Ruedy, *Modern Algeria*, 239–44; and Brett and Fentress, *Berbers*, 271–82. On language as a basis for Berber identity and protest, see Salem Chaker, "L'Affirmation identitaire berbère à partir de 1900–constantes et mutations (Kabylie)," in *Berbères: Une identité en construction*, special issue of *Revue de l'Occident Musulman et de la Méditerranée*, no. 44 (1987). On the aggressive state policy of deberberization and, for example, the requirement that all newborn babies be given Arabic rather than Berber-sounding names, see Salem Mezhoud, "Glasnost the Algerian Way: The Role of Berber Nationalists in Political Reform," in *North Africa: Nation, State, and Region*, ed. George Joffé (London: Routledge, 1993).

105. Mark Tessler, "Alienation of Urban Youth," in *Polity and Society*, ed. Zartman and Habeeb, 97–98; Martin Stone, *The Agony of Algeria* (New York: Columbia University Press, 1997), 154–55; Ruedy, *Modern Algeria*, 241. On the leadership of the movement, see Severine Labat, "Islamism and Islamists: The Emergence of New Types of Politico-Religious Militants," in *Islamism and Secularism*, ed. Ruedy, 103–21.

106. Secrétariat Social d'Alger, *Information rapide, de l'explosion à la révolution? Etude socio-démographique de l'Algérie*, 6th series, nos. 7–8 (Oct. 1968): 46, quoted in Borrmans, *Statut personnel*, 542.

107. Richards and Waterbury, *Political Economy*, 267.

108. The figure of 12 million (actual number 11,905,500) in 1966 appears in *Information rapide*, Secrétariat Social d'Alger, cited in Borrmans, *Statut personnel*, 542. The figure of 17.6 million in 1978 appears in *World Development Report, 1980* (Washington, D.C.: World Bank, 1980), 110.

109. Burgat and Dowell, *Islamic Movement*, 257–58.

CHAPTER 9. STATE AUTONOMY FROM TRIBE
AND FAMILY LAW REFORM

1. Estimates vary between 1 and 3 percent. See Michael Brett and Elizabeth Fentress, *The Berbers* (Oxford: Blackwell, 1996), 3; Yves Lacoste, "Peuplements et organisation sociale," in *L'Etat du Maghreb*, ed. Camille Lacoste and Yves Lacoste (Tunis: Cérès Productions, 1991), 29; John P. Entelis, *Comparative Politics of North Africa: Algeria, Morocco, and Tunisia* (Syracuse: Syracuse University Press, 1980), 3; and John P. Entelis and Mark A. Tessler, "Republic of Tunisia," in *The Government and Politics of the Middle East and*

North Africa, ed. David E. Long and Bernard Reich (Boulder, Col.: Westview, 1980), 446.

2. On Tunisian nationalism and the Neo-Destour, see Lisa Anderson, *The State and Social Transformation in Tunisia and Libya, 1830–1980* (Princeton: Princeton University Press, 1986), 158–77; Kenneth Brown, "Muhammad Ameur: A Tunisian Comrade," in *Struggle and Survival in the Modern Middle East,* ed. Edmund Burke III (Berkeley and Los Angeles: University of California Press, 1993), 251–67; Susan E. Waltz, *Human Rights and Reform: Changing the Face of North African Politics* (Berkeley and Los Angeles: University of California Press, 1995), 54–58; Clement Henry Moore, *Tunisia since Independence: The Dynamics of One-Party Government* (Berkeley and Los Angeles: University of California Press, 1965); Charles A. Micaud with L. Carl Brown and Clement Henry Moore, *Tunisia: The Politics of Modernization* (New York: Praeger, 1964), 22–110, Lars Rudebeck, *Party and People: A Study of Political Change in Tunisia* (Stockholm: Almqvist and Wiksell, 1967), 25–66; and Nadia M. Abu-Zahra, "Inequality of Descent and Egalitarianism of the New National Organizations in a Tunisian Village," in *Rural Politics and Social Change in the Middle East,* ed. Richard Antoun and Iliya Harik (Bloomington: Indiana University Press, 1972), 267–86.

3. Anderson, *State and Social Transformation,* 174–77; Micaud, *Tunisia,* 79–86; Jamil Abun-Nasr, *A History of the Maghrib,* 2d ed. (Cambridge: Cambridge University Press, 1975), 348; and Benjamin Stora, "Tunisie, Algérie, Maroc: Aux origines des mouvements indépendantistes," in *L'Etat du Maghreb,* ed. Lacoste and Lacoste, 60–61. On involvement of communities in southern Tunisia, see Mondher Kilani, *La construction de la mémoire: Le lignage et la sainteté dans l'oasis d'El Ksar* (Geneva: Labor and Fidès, 1992), 265–74.

4. Micaud, *Tunisia,* 83. On membership, see also Roger Owen, *State, Power, and Politics in the Making of the Modern Middle East* (London: Routledge, 1992), 256.

5. Cited in Anderson, *State and Social Transformation,* 174.

6. Ibid., 173.

7. Abun-Nasr, *History,* 345.

8. Habib Bourguiba, *La Tunisie et la France* (Paris: Julliard, 1954), 386.

9. Elbaki Hermassi, *Leadership and National Development in North Africa: A Comparative Study* (Berkeley and Los Angeles: University of California Press, 1972), 155. On the alliance between party and labor in the nationalist struggle, see also Stora, "Tunisie, Algérie, Maroc," 60 ff.; Nazih N. Ayubi, *Over-Stating the Arab State: Politics and Society in the Middle East* (London: Tauris, 1995), 211–12; and Micaud, *Tunisia,* 79–88. On the early period of the labor movement (1920s), see Eqbal Ahmad and Stuart Schaar, "M'hamed Ali: Tunisian Labor Organizer," in *Struggle and Survival,* ed. Burke, 191–204.

10. United Nations, *Demographic Yearbook, 1960* (New York: United Nations Publications, 1961), 374, gives a total population of 3,783,000 and an urban population of 1,347,500 or 35 percent in 1956. The figure on urban

population appears inflated for the period and relative to the Maghrib as a whole. This is due to the fact that the Tunisian census of 1956 defined as "urban" a locality of one thousand inhabitants or more, whereas a census taken a few years later in Morocco defined as "urban" a locality of two thousand inhabitants or more, United Nations, *Demographic Yearbook, 1960*, 391.

11. Micaud, *Tunisia*, 85.

12. Anderson, *State and Social Transformation*, 174–75.

13. Ibid., 166.

14. Mohsen Toumi, *Tunisie, pouvoirs et luttes* (Paris: Sycomore, 1978), 205–24; Moore, *Tunisia*, 89–92.

15. Asma Larif-Béatrix, *Edification étatique et environnement culturel: Le personnel politico-administratif dans la Tunisie contemporaine* (Paris: Publisud, 1988), 139–45; Hermassi, *Leadership*, 155–56; Moore, *Tunisia*, 61–70; Sophie Bessis and Souhayr Belhassen, *Bourguiba*, vol. 1 (Paris: Groupe Jeune Afrique, 1988), 147–76.

16. Hermassi, *Leadership*, 121–22.

17. Quoted in Larif-Béatrix, *Edification étatique*, 138.

18. Quoted in Entelis, *Comparative Politics*, 151.

19. Bessis and Belhassen, *Bourguiba*, vol. 1, 159.

20. Micaud, *Tunisia*, 90.

21. Larif-Béatrix, *Edification étatique*, 139–45; Moore, *Tunisia*, 61–70; Bessis and Belhassen, *Bourguiba*, vol. 1, 147–76.

22. Abun-Nasr, *History*, 354.

23. Bessis and Belhassen, *Bourguiba*, vol. 1, 171.

24. Jean Lacouture, *The Demigods: Charismatic Leadership in the Third World* (New York: Knopf, 1970), 191.

25. Entelis and Tessler, "Republic of Tunisia."

26. Micaud, *Tunisia*, 120; Anderson, *State and Social Transformation*, chap. 11.

27. Bessis and Belhassen, *Bourguiba*, vol. 2, 10.

28. Quoted in ibid.

29. Quoted in ibid., 11–12.

30. Elbaki Hermassi, "Elite et société en Tunisie: Intégration et mobilisation," in *Social Stratification and Development in the Mediterranean Basin*, ed. Mubeccel B. Kiray (The Hague: Mouton, 1973), 182.

31. Moore, *Tunisia*, 132–40; Micaud, *Tunisia*, 121–28.

32. Moore, *Tunisia*, 135.

33. Ibid.; and Micaud, *Tunisia*, 121–28.

34. There are two separate questions with respect to efforts to erode what was left of tribal politics. One concerns the actions of the political leadership to implant state and party in local areas and replace kin-based solidarities. The other question involves the response of the populace. My focus is on the actions of the political leadership. In her field research in rural Tunisia (near le Kef and in the central region where kin-based solidarities used to prevail), Larson considers the extent to which individuals now feel that they belong to

a national entity. Despite a variety of specific responses, the population in the rural areas that Larson studied identified with the Tunisian nation. See Barbara K. Larson, "L'Etat bureaucratique et l'articulation locale-nationale," in *Le Maghreb: Approches des mécanismes d'articulation,* ed. Rahma Bourqia and Nicholas Hopkins (Casablanca: Al Kalam, 1991), 173–86; and Larson, "Local-National Integration in Tunisia," *Middle Eastern Studies* 20, no. 1 (Jan. 1984): 17–26.

35. "Tunisia," in chapter 5.

36. Micaud, *Tunisia,* 163. On land reform policies and communities with tribal roots in the lower Medjerda Valley in Tunisia, see Mira F. Zussman, *Development and Disenchantment in Rural Tunisia: The Bourguiba Years* (Boulder, Col.: Westview, 1992).

37. Quoted in Micaud, *Tunisia,* 166. On the history of collective lands in Tunisia and the government policies that affected them after independence, see Hafedh Ben Salah, *Les terres collectives en Tunisie* (Tunis: Centre d'Etudes, de Recherches et de Publications de la Faculté de Droit et des Sciences Politiques et Economiques de Tunis, 1977).

38. Anderson, *State and Social Transformation,* 235; Micaud, *Tunisia,* 159.

39. On reforms and liquidation of habus, see Anderson, *State and Social Transformation,* 234–35; Micaud, *Tunisia,* 159–67; Moore, *Tunisia,* 50–54; and Entelis and Tessler, "Republic of Tunisia," 447.

40. This action implemented the plan that the early reformers of precolonial Tunisia had contemplated almost a century earlier, but could not implement (discussed in chapter 5). On the Maliki and Hanafi schools of Islamic family law, see chapter 2.

41. Decrees of 25 September 1956 and 25 October 1956, discussed in Maurice Borrmans, *Statut personnel et famille au Maghreb: de 1940 à nos jours* (Paris: Mouton, 1977), 293.

42. Anderson, *State and Social Transformation,* 231.

43. Tunisia had two schools of Islamic law, Maliki and Hanafi, with the majority of religious judges applying Maliki law, as discussed in chapters 2 and 6.

44. Tahar al-Haddad [al-Haddad, al-Tahir], *Imra'atuna fi al-shari'a wa al-mujtama'a* (Our women in law and society) (Tunis: al-Matba'at al-Fanniyya, 1930). On al-Haddad's position, intellectual trends of the late 1920s and early 1930s, and controversies over al-Haddad's book, see Aziza Medimegh Darghouth, *Droits et vécu de la femme en Tunisie* (Lyon: Hermès, 1992), 45–47; Christiane Lamourette, "Polémique autour du statut de la femme musulmane en Tunisie en 1930," *Bulletin d'Etudes Orientales* 30 (1978): 11–31; Souad Chater, *La femme tunisienne: Citoyenne ou sujet* (Tunis: Maison Tunisienne de l'Edition, 1978), 68–76; Norma Salem, "Islam and the Status of Women in Tunisia," in *Muslim Women,* ed. Freda Hussain (London: Croom Helm, 1984).

45. Al-Haddad, *Imra'atuna,* 113.

46. Borrmans, *Statut personnel,* 139–40.

47. Mohamed al-Salih Ben Mrad [Ibn Murad, Muhammad al-Salih], *al-*

Hidad 'ala imra'at al-Haddad (Mourning the women of al-Haddad) (Tunis: al-Matba'at al-Tunisiyya, 1931).

48. Tahar Sfar in *Leila*, no. 2 (1936): 2, quoted in Borrmans, *Statut personnel*, 151.

49. *Tunis-Socialiste* (5 Jan. 1939) announced the arrest of the twelve women. The letter of protest is included with unsorted archival materials concerning the 1930s in the Archives of the Centre de Documentation Nationale, Tunis.

50. On Habib Bourguiba's position prior to independence, see *l'Action* (Tunis), 22 October 1956, 13, and 29 October 1956, 17, Archives of the Centre de Documentation Nationale, Tunis.

51. Habib Bourguiba, "Le voile," *l'Etendard Tunisien*, 11 January 1929, 1, Archives of the Centre de Documentation Nationale, Tunis.

52. Ibid.

53. Numerous articles on these topics appeared in the newspaper *l'Action* (Tunis), 22 October 1956, 13, and 29 October 1959, 17.

54. Borrmans, *Statut personnel*, 288.

55. Interview of President Habib Bourguiba, "Notre code de statut personnel est un sujet de fierté pour la femme tunisienne" (Our code of personal status is a source of pride for the Tunisian woman)," *Revue Fémina* (Tunis), 20 March 1973, Archives of the Centre de Documentation Nationale, Tunis.

56. President Zine el Abidine Ben Ali, speech of 13 August (Woman's Day in Tunisia) 1992, *La Presse* (Tunis), 14 August 1992, 4.

57. Ilhem Marzouki, founder of the Club for the Study of Women's Condition in Tunisia (Club Tahar Haddad), and the journalist Zakya Daoud agree on locating the emergence of a feminist protest movement in Tunisia in the early 1980s. See Zakya Daoud, *Féminisme et politique au Maghreb: Sept décennies de lutte* (Casablanca: Eddif, 1996), 77–99; and Ilhem Marzouki, *Le mouvement des femmes en Tunisie au XXème siècle: Féminisme et politique* (Tunis: Cérès Productions, 1993), 227–75, 291–301. See also Sophie Ferchiou, "Féminisme d'état en Tunisie: Ideologie dominante et résistance féminine," in *Femmes, culture et société au Maghreb*, vol. 2, ed. Rahma Bourqia, Mounira M. Charrad, and Nancy Gallagher (Casablanca: Afrique Orient, 1996).

58. Habib Bourguiba, speech of 13 August 1965, *Discours*, tome 14, 1965 (Tunis: Publications du Secrétariat à l'Information, 1978), 158.

59. Ahmed Mestiri, Minister of Justice in 1956, interview granted to the author.

60. Habib Bourguiba, speech of 13 August 1965, *Discours*, tome 14, 1965 (Tunis: Publications du Secrétariat à l'Information, 1978), 158; and speech of 13 August 1960, *Discours*, tome 8, 1960–61 (Tunis: Publications du Secrétariat d'Etat à l'Information, 1976).

61. "Feudal" and "modern" are the terms actually used by the interviewee. "Feudal" should be taken as a metaphor, not literally. Tunisian history does not include feudalism of the kind that existed in Western Europe.

62. Sophie Bessis and Souhayr Belhassen, *Bourguiba*, vol. 2 (Tunis: Groupe Jeune Afrique, 1989), 13.

63. Habib Bourguiba, speech of 13 August 1965, in *Discours*, tome 14, 1965 (Tunis: Publications du Secrétariat à l'Information, 1978), 166–67.

64. Ibid., 169–70.

65. *L'Action Tunisienne*, 3 September 1956, Archives of the Centre de Documentation Nationale, Tunis.

66. Ahmed Mestiri, letter to *Révolution Africaine*, 17 February 1966, Archives of the Centre de Documentation Nationale, Tunis.

67. Mustapha Abdesselem and Mohamed Charfi, "Tunisia," in *National Reports*, vol. 1 of *International Encyclopedia of Comparative Law*, under the auspices of the International Association of Legal Science, ed. Victor Knapp (The Hague: Mouton, 1973), T-38.

68. Olivier Carré, *L'Islam laïque ou le retour à la grande tradition* (Paris: A. Colin, 1993), 111.

69. The *Code du statut personnel* was promulgated as the Decree of 13 August 1956 and was officially published in the *Journal Officiel*. The text has since appeared as a readily available booklet entitled *Code du statut personnel* and published in Arabic and French by the Imprimerie Officielle de la République Tunisienne, Tunis. It is regularly updated and reprinted. I rely in this chapter on the *Code du statut personnel* as presented and annotated by M. T. es-Snoussi, 5th ed. (Tunis: Imprimerie Al-Asria, 1965) because that edition is close to the initial code of 1956. On amendments and other laws of the 1950s and 1960s, I use in part Borrmans's thorough, seven-hundred-page study, *Statut personnel*, which provides extensive and detailed chronological information on legislation.

70. For a chronology of events, see Sophie Bessis, "Tunisie 1943–1990," in *L'Etat du Maghreb*, ed. Lacoste and Lacoste, 74.

71. Quoted in Bessis and Belhassen, *Bourguiba*, vol. 2, 15.

72. Borrmans, *Statut personnel*, 291.

73. *L'Action*, no. 67 (17 Sep. 1956).

74. Borrmans, *Statut personnel*, 292.

75. Ibid.

76. Code du Statut Personnel. For commentaries on the code by legal scholars, see Alya Chérif Chamari, *La femme et la loi en Tunisie* (Casablanca: Le Fennec, 1991), 35–78; and Naziha Ayyat Lakihal, *La femme tunisienne et sa place dans le droit positif* (Tunis: Editions Dar al-Amal, 1978). See also Samya El Mechat, "Femmes et pouvoir en Tunisie," *Les temps modernes*, no. 436 (Nov. 1982): 975–1010.

77. Code du Statut Personnel, article 3.

78. Ibid., article 23.

79. Ibid., article 5; and Law of 20 February 1964, quoted in Borrmans, *Statut personnel*, 290.

80. République Tunisienne, *Code de la nationalité tunisienne* (Code of Tunisian Citizenship) (Tunis: Imprimerie Officielle, 1983), article 4.

81. Borrmans, *Statut personnel*, 335.

82. Ibid., 337.

83. Code du Statut Personnel, book 2, articles 29–33. On divorce law, see Mounira M. Charrad, "Repudiation versus Divorce: Responses to State Policy in Tunisia," in *Women, the Family, and Policy: A Global Perspective*, ed. Esther N. Chow and Catherine W. Berheide (Albany: State University of New York Press, 1994), 51–69.

84. Code du Statut Personnel, article 32.

85. Law of 8 March 1968, discussed in Borrmans, *Statut personnel*, 343–45.

86. See "Divorce and Repudiation" in chapter 2.

87. Code du Statut Personnel, article 47.

88. Law of 3 June 1966, in Borrmans, *Statut personnel*, 343–45.

89. Laws of 8 March 1958 and 19 June 1959, ibid., 351–53.

90. Ibid., 353.

91. Laws of 1 August 1957; 4 July 1958; 26 May 1959; and 10 March 1962, ibid., 348–50.

92. Code du Statut Personnel, article 18; and Law-Decree of 20 February 1964, in Borrmans, *Statut personnel*, 339–42.

93. Code du Statut Personnel, article 18.

94. Ibid., book 9, articles 89–152.

95. See the discussion of inheritance rules in Islamic law in chapter 2.

96. Law of 31 May 1956 and Decree of 18 July 1957, in Borrmans, *Statut personnel*, 346–47.

97. The habus institution is discussed in chapter 2.

98. Law of 19 June 1959, in Borrmans, *Statut personnel*, 333–35. The same principle—weakening the agnatic patrilineage—appears also in the Tunisian legislation on citizenship. See Mounira M. Charrad, "Becoming a Citizen: Lineage versus Individual in Morocco and Tunisia," in *Citizenship and Gender in the Middle East*, ed. Suad Joseph (Syracuse: Syracuse University Press, 2000).

99. Quoted in Borrmans, *Statut personnel*, 334.

100. This has been the case since the 1960s and among observers writing from a variety of perspectives. See Arlie Hochschild, "Le travail des femmes dans une Tunisie en voie de développement," *Revue Tunisienne de Sciences Sociales*, no. 9 (Mar. 1967); Cynthia Grenier, "Tunisia: Out from behind the Veil," *Ms.* (Aug. 1974); J. N. D. Anderson, *Law Reform in the Muslim World* (London: Athlone, 1976); Naziha Ayyat Lakihal, "Le divorce et la femme tunisienne," *El Mar'a* (publication of the National Union of Tunisian Women), no. 12 (Mar. 1976); "Tunisia," *New York Times*, 15 August 1977; Robert J. Lapham, "Population Policies in the Middle East and North Africa," *Middle East Studies Association Bulletin* 11, no. 2 (May 1977); Mark A. Tessler, "Women's Emancipation in Tunisia," in *Women in the Muslim World*, ed. Lois Beck and Nikki R. Keddie (Cambridge: Harvard University Press, 1978), 145; Nancy Adams Shilling, "The Social and Political Roles of Arab Women:

A Study of Conflict," in *Women in Contemporary Muslim Societies*, ed. Jane I. Smith (Cranbury, N.J.: Associated University Press, 1980); Souad Chater, *Les émancipées du harem: Regard sur la femme tunisienne* (Tunis: Edition La Presse, 1992), 7–10; Ann E. Mayer, "Rhetorical Strategies and Official Policies on Women's Rights: The Merits and Drawbacks of the New World Hypocrisy," in *Faith and Freedom: Women's Human Rights in the Muslim World*, ed. Mahnaz Afkhami (Syracuse: Syracuse University Press, 1995), 114; and Nadia Hijab, "Islam, Social Change and the Reality of Arab Women's Lives," in *Islam, Gender, and Social Change*, ed. Yvonne Y. Haddad and John L. Esposito (New York: Oxford University Press, 1998), 46–47.

101. Speech by President Habib Bourguiba, 25 July 1965, cited in Borrmans, *Statut personnel*, 379.

CONCLUSION

1. Germaine Tillion, *Le harem et les cousins* (Paris: Seuil, 1966), 182.

2. The particular kinship ties that matter for politics vary, and the terms of the relationship between kinship and politics must be specified for each context and each historical period. Examples of kin-based societies include China in the mid-twentieth century, parts of Central Asia, and parts of the Middle East.

Selected Bibliography

This selected bibliography identifies national codes of law, newspapers, and books that I have consulted in the course of my research. The literature in political science, history, sociology, anthropology, and law relevant to the themes of this study is rich and extensive. I am indebted not only to scholars whose books are listed below, but also to the authors of the many articles and book chapters that I have used. Limitations of space preclude their inclusion here. These appear in the backnotes to each chapter and their authors are listed in the author index.

The bibliography is organized alphabetically under five major headings:
National Codes of Law and Other Statutes
Tunisia, Algeria, Morocco, Maghrib as a whole
Middle East, Muslim World, Islam
Theory, General
Newspapers and Magazines

NATIONAL CODES OF LAW AND OTHER STATUTES

Algeria. *Charte nationale.* République Algérienne Démocratique et Populaire: Editions Populaires de l'Armée, 1976. First published in 1964 as the *Charte d'Alger* (Charter of Algiers).

Algeria. *Constitution,* in *Annuaire de l'Afrique du Nord.* Paris: Editions du Centre National de la Recherche Scientifique (1963): 852–59.

Algeria. Law no. 84–11 of 9 June 1984 constitutes the Algerian Family Code of 1984. The text appeared in the *Journal Officiel de la République Algérienne Démocratique et Populaire* 23, no. 24 (12 June 1984).

Algeria. *Programme de Tripoli,* in *Annuaire de l'Afrique du Nord.* Paris: Editions du Centre National de la Recherche Scientifique, 1962.

Morocco. *Code du statut personnel* (Code of Personal Status, or *Mudawwana*), *Bulletin Officiel du Maroc.* Books 1 and 2, 23 May 1958; Book 3, 25 July 1958; Book 4, 7 November 1958; Book 5, 20 February 1959. Updated and reprinted in Mohamed Chafi, *Code du statut personnel annoté.* Marrakech: Imprimerie Walili, 1996.

Morocco. *Constitution.* Rabat: Ministry of Communication and Al-Anbaa Press, 1996.

Morocco. *Dahir berbère* (Berber Decree) of 1930. *Bulletin Officiel du Maroc.* May 1930.

Tunisia. *Code de la nationalité tunisienne* (Code of Tunisian Citizenship). Tunis: Imprimerie Officielle de la République Tunisienne, 1983. Updated and reprinted since its inception on 26 January 1956.

Tunisia. *Code du statut personnel* (Code of Personal Status, or *Majalla*), promulgated on 13 August 1956. Presented and annotated by M. T. es-Snoussi. 5th ed. Tunis: Imprimerie Al-Asria, 1965. Updated and periodically reprinted since by the Imprimerie Officielle de la République Tunisienne, Tunis.

Tunisia. *Constitution de la République Tunisienne.* Tunis: Imprimerie Officielle de la République Tunisienne, 1998. First promulgated 1 June 1959.

TUNISIA, ALGERIA, MOROCCO, MAGHRIB
AS A WHOLE

Abu-Lughod, Janet L. *Rabat: Urban Apartheid in Morocco.* Princeton: Princeton University Press, 1980.

Abun-Nasr, Jamil M. *A History of the Maghrib.* 2d ed. Cambridge: Cambridge University Press, 1975.

Amrouche, Fadhma A. M. *My Life Story: The Autobiography of a Berber Woman.* Translated from French by Dorothy S. Blair. New Brunswick, N.J.: Rutgers University Press, 1989.

Anderson, Lisa. *The State and Social Transformation in Tunisia and Libya, 1830–1980.* Princeton: Princeton University Press, 1986.

Ashford, Douglas E. *Political Change in Morocco.* Princeton: Princeton University Press, 1961.

Bachrouch, Taoufik, ed. *Rabii al Orbane, Printemps des Arabes: Aux origines de l'insurrection populaire de 1864.* Tunis: Editions Bayt al-Hikma, Fondation Nationale pour la Traduction, l'Etablissement des Textes, et les Etudes, 1992.

Baddou, Tajeddine. *La population du Maroc.* Rabat: I.N.S.E.A., 1976.

Bahloul, Joëlle. *The Architecture of Memory: A Jewish-Muslim Household in Colonial Algeria, 1937–1962.* Cambridge: Cambridge University Press, 1996.

Baker, Alison. *Voices of Resistance: Oral Histories of Moroccan Women.* Albany: State University of New York Press, 1998.

Barakat, Halim, ed. *Contemporary North Africa: Issues of Development and Integration.* Washington, D.C.: Center for Contemporary Arab Studies, 1985.

Barbour, Nevill, ed. *A Survey of North West Africa (the Maghrib)*. London: Oxford University Press, 1959.

Benmelha, Ghaouti. *Elements du droit algérien de la famille*. Paris: Publisud, 1985.

Ben Mlih, Abdellah. *Structures politiques du Maroc colonial*. Paris: Harmattan, 1990.

Ben Mrad, Mohamed al-Salih [Ibn Murad, Muhammad al-Salih]. *al-Hidad 'ala imra'at al-Haddad* (Mourning the women of al-Haddad). Tunis: al-Matba'at al-Tunisiyya, 1931.

Ben Salah, Hafedh. *Les terres collectives en Tunisie*. Tunis: Centre d'Etudes, de Recherches et de Publications de la Faculté de Droit et des Sciences Politiques et Economiques de Tunis, 1977.

Bernard, Augustin. *L'Evolution du nomadisme en Algérie*. Algiers: A. Jourdan, 1906.

Berque, Jacques. *French North Africa: The Maghrib between Two World Wars*. Translated from French by Jean Stewart. New York: Praeger, 1967.

———. *Structures sociales du Haut-Atlas*. Paris: Presses Universitaires de France, 1955.

Bessis, Sophie, and Souhayr Belhassen. *Femmes du Maghreb: L'enjeu*. Tunis: Cérès Productions, 1992.

———. *Bourguiba*. 2 vols. Paris: Groupe Jeune Afrique, 1988, 1989.

Bidwell, Robin. *Morocco under Colonial Rule: French Administration of Tribal Areas, 1912–1956*. London: Frank Cass, 1973.

Borrmans, Maurice. *Documents sur la famille au Maghreb de 1940 à nos jours*. Special issues of *Oriente Moderno* 59, nos. 1–5 (1979): 125–59.

———. *Statut personnel et famille au Maghreb: de 1940 à nos jours*. Paris: Mouton, 1977.

Bourdieu, Pierre. *Sociologie de l'Algérie*. Rev. ed. Paris: Presses Universitaires de France, 1961. Published in English as *The Algerians*. Translated from French by Alan C. M. Ross. Boston: Beacon Press, 1962.

Bourguiba, Habib. *Discours*, tome 59, 1965. Tunis: Publications du Secrétariat à l'Information, 1978.

———. *La Tunisie et la France: Vingt-cinq ans de lutte pour une coopération libre*. Paris: Julliard, 1954.

Bourqia, Rahma, Mounira M. Charrad, and Nancy Gallagher, eds. *Femmes, culture et société au Maghreb*. 2 vols. Casablanca: Afrique Orient, 1996.

Bourqia, Rahma, and Nicholas Hopkins, eds. *Le Maghreb: Approches des mécanismes d'articulation*. Casablanca: Al Kalam, 1991.

Bousquet, G. H. *Les Berbères: Histoire et institutions*. Paris: Presses Universitaires de France, 1957.

Boyer, Pierre. *L'Evolution de l'Algérie médiane (Ancien département d'Alger) de 1830 à 1956*. Paris: Adrien-Maisonneuve, 1960.

Brenot, Henri. *Le douar, cellule administrative de l'Algérie du Nord*. Algiers: V. Heintz, 1938.

Brett, Michael, and Elizabeth Fentress. *The Berbers.* Oxford: Blackwell, 1996.

Brown, L. Carl. *The Tunisia of Ahmad Bey, 1837–1855.* Princeton: Princeton University Press, 1974.

Burgat, François, and William Dowell. *The Islamic Movement in North Africa.* Austin: Center for Middle Eastern Studies, The University of Texas, 1993.

Burke, Edmund, III. *Prelude to Protectorate in Morocco: Precolonial Protest and Resistance, 1860–1912.* Chicago: University of Chicago Press, 1976.

Camau, Michel. *Pouvoir et institutions au Maghreb.* Tunis: Cérès Productions, 1978.

Camau, Michel et al. *Tunisie au présent: Une modernité au-dessus de tout soupçon?* Paris: Editions du Centre National de la Recherche Scientifique, 1987.

Camilleri, Carmel. *Jeunesse, famille et développement: Essai sur le change-ment socio-culturel dans un pays du tiers-monde (Tunisie).* Paris: Editions du Centre National de la Recherche Scientifique, 1973.

Centre de Recherches et d'Etudes sur les Sociétés Méditerranéennes. *Con-naissances du Maghreb: Sciences sociales et colonisation.* Paris: Editions du Centre National de la Recherche Scientifique, 1984.

———. *Introduction à l'Afrique du Nord contemporaine.* Paris: Editions du Centre National de la Recherche Scientifique, 1975.

Chater, Souad. *La femme tunisienne: Citoyenne ou sujet.* Tunis: Maison Tu-nisienne de l'Edition, 1978.

———. *Les émancipées du harem: Regard sur la femme tunisienne.* Tunis: La Presse, 1992.

Chérif Chamari, Alya. *La femme et la loi en Tunisie.* Casablanca: Le Fennec, 1991.

Christelow, Allan. *Muslim Law Courts and the French Colonial State in Al-geria.* Princeton: Princeton University Press, 1985.

Clancy-Smith, Julia A. *Rebel and Saint: Muslim Notables, Populist Protest, Colonial Encounters (Algeria and Tunisia, 1800–1904).* Berkeley and Los Angeles: University of California Press, 1994.

Clarke, Bryan C. *Berber Village: The Story of the Oxford University Expe-dition to the High Atlas Mountains of Morocco.* London: Longmans, 1959.

Combs-Schilling, M. E. *Sacred Performances: Islam, Sexuality, and Sacrifice.* New York: Columbia University Press, 1989.

Corrèze, Françoise. *Femmes des mechtas, Témoignage sur l'Est algérien.* Paris: Editeurs Français Réunis, 1976.

Daoud, Zakya. *Féminisme et politique au Maghreb: Sept décennies de lutte.* Casablanca: Eddif, 1996.

Darghouth Medimegh, Aziza. *Droits et vécu de la femme en Tunisie.* Lyon: Hermès, 1992.

Davis, Susan S. *Patience and Power: Women's Lives in a Moroccan Village.* Cambridge, Mass.: Schenkman, 1983.

Demeerseman, André. *La famille tunisienne et les temps nouveaux; essai de psychologie sociale.* Tunis: Maison Tunisienne de l'Edition, 1967.

Duvignaud, Jean. *Change at Shebika; Report from a North African Village.* Translated from French by Frances Frenaye. New York: Pantheon, 1970.

Eickelman, Dale F. *Knowledge and Power in Morocco: The Education of a Twentieth-Century Notable.* Princeton: Princeton University Press, 1985.

———. *Moroccan Islam: Tradition and Society in a Pilgrimage Center.* Austin: The University of Texas Press, 1976.

Ennaji, Moha, ed. *Berber Sociolinguistics,* special issue of the *International Journal of the Sociology of Language,* no. 123 (1997).

Entelis, John P. *Algeria: The Revolution Institutionalized.* Boulder, Col.: Westview, 1986.

———. *Comparative Politics of North Africa: Algeria, Morocco, and Tunisia.* Syracuse: Syracuse University Press, 1980.

———, ed. *Islam, Democracy, and the State in North Africa.* Bloomington: Indiana University Press, 1997.

Entelis, P. John, and Phillip C. Naylor, eds. *State and Society in Algeria.* Boulder, Col.: Westview, 1992.

Establet, Colette. *Etre caïd dans l'Algérie coloniale.* Paris: Editions du Centre National de la Recherche Scientifique, 1991.

Fanon, Frantz. *The Wretched of the Earth.* Translated from French by Constance Farrington. New York: Grove, 1968.

al-Fasi, 'Allal. *al-Naqd al-dhati* (Self-criticism). Cairo: al-Matba'at al-'Alamiyya, 1952.

Ferchiou, Sophie. *Les femmes dans l'agriculture tunisienne.* Aix-en-Provence: Edisud, 1985.

———, ed. *Hasab wa nasab: Parenté, alliance et patrimoine en Tunisie.* Paris: Editions du Centre National de la Recherche Scientifique, 1992.

Fernea, Elizabeth W. *A Street in Marrakech.* Garden City, N.Y.: Anchor Books, 1976.

Gadant, Monique. *Le nationalisme algérien et les femmes.* Paris: Harmattan, 1995.

Gadant, Monique, and Michele Kasriel, eds. *Femmes du Maghreb au présent: La dot, le travail, l'identité.* Paris: Editions du Centre National de la Recherche Scientifique, 1990.

Gallagher, Nancy E. *Medicine and Power in Tunisia, 1780–1900.* Cambridge: Cambridge University Press, 1983.

Gaudry, Mathéa. *La femme chaouia de l'Aurès; étude de sociologie berbère.* Paris: Librarie Orientaliste Paul Geuthner, 1929.

Gautier, Emile F. *Le passé de l'Afrique du Nord: Les siècles obscurs.* Paris: Payot, 1937.

Geertz, Clifford. *Islam Observed: Religious Developments in Morocco and Indonesia.* Chicago: University of Chicago Press, 1971.

Geertz, Clifford, Hildred Geertz, and Lawrence Rosen. *Meaning and Order in Moroccan Society: Three Essays in Cultural Analysis.* Cambridge: Cambridge University Press, 1979.

Gellner, Ernest. *Saints of the Atlas.* Chicago: University of Chicago Press, 1969.

Gellner, Ernest, and Charles Micaud, eds. *Arabs and Berbers: From Tribe to Nation in North Africa.* Lexington, Mass.: D. C. Heath, 1972.

Gellner, Ernest, Jean-Claude Vatin, et al. *Islam et politique au Maghreb.* Paris: Editions du Centre National de la Recherche Scientifique, 1981.

Gordon, David C. *Women of Algeria; An Essay on Change.* Middle Eastern Monograph 19. Cambridge: Harvard University Press, 1968.

Green, Arnold H. *The Tunisian Ulama 1873–1915: Social Structure and Response to Ideological Currents.* Leiden: Brill, 1978.

al-Haddad, Tahar [al-Haddad, al-Tahir]. *Imra'atuna fi al-shari'a wa al-mujtama'a* (Our women in law and society). Tunis: al-Matba'at al-Fanniyya, 1930.

Hammoudi, Abdellah. *Master and Disciple: The Cultural Foundations of Moroccan Authoritarianism.* Chicago: Chicago University Press, 1997.

Hammoudi, Abdellah, and Stuart Schaar, eds. *Algeria's Impasse.* Monograph Series, no. 8. Princeton: Center of International Studies, Princeton University, 1995.

Harbi, Mohammed. *Aux origines du Front de Libération Nationale: La scission du P.P.A.-M.T.L.D.* Paris: C. Bourgeois, 1975.

Hart, David M. *Dadda 'Atta and His Forty Grandsons: The Socio-Political Organisation of the Ait 'Atta of Southern Morocco.* Cambridge, Eng.: Middle East and North African Studies Press, 1981.

———. *The Aith Waryaghar of the Moroccan Rif: An Ethnography and History.* Tucson: University of Arizona Press, 1976.

Hejaiej, Monia. *Behind Closed Doors: Women's Oral Narratives in Tunis.* New Brunswick, N.J.: Rutgers University Press, 1996.

Hermassi, Elbaki. *Leadership and National Development in North Africa: A Comparative Study.* Berkeley and Los Angeles: University of California Press, 1972.

Hoisington, William A., Jr. *Lyautey and the French Conquest of Morocco.* New York: St. Martin's, 1995.

Ibn Khaldun. *The Muqaddimah: An Introduction to History.* Translated from Arabic by Franz Rosenthal. 2d ed. 3 vols. Princeton: Princeton University Press, 1967. A briefer selection appears in *An Arab Philosophy of History: Selections from the Prolegomena of Ibn Khaldun of Tunis (1332–1406).* Translated and arranged by Charles Issawi. Princeton: Darwin Press, 1987.

Ishaq, Khalil Ibn. *Abrégé de la loi musulmane selon le rite de l'imâm Mâlik.* Vol. 2, *Le statut personnel.* Translated by G. H. Bousquet. Paris: A. Maisonneuve, 1958–62.

Jamous, Raymond. *Honneur et baraka: Les structures sociales traditionnelles dans le Rif.* Cambridge: Cambridge University Press, 1981.

Jansen, Willy. *Women without Men: Gender and Marginality in an Algerian Town.* Leiden: Brill, 1987.

Joffé, George, ed. *North Africa: Nation, State, and Region*. London: Routledge, 1993.

Joffé, George, and C. R. Pennell, eds. *Tribe and State: Essays in Honour of David Montgomery Hart*. Wisbech, Cambridgeshire, Eng.: Middle East and North African Studies Press, 1991.

Julien, Charles-André. *Histoire de l'Algérie contemporaine: La conquête et les débuts de la colonisation (1827–1871)*. Paris: Presses Universitaires de France, 1964.

———. *L'Afrique du Nord en marche: Nationalismes Musulmans et souveraineté française*. Paris: Julliard, 1952.

Kilani, Mondher. *La construction de la mémoire: Le lignage et la sainteté dans l'oasis d'El Ksar*. Geneva: Editions Labor et Fidès, 1992.

Knauss, Peter R. *The Persistence of Patriarchy: Class, Gender and Ideology in Twentieth-Century Algeria*. New York: Praeger, 1987.

Kodmani-Darwish, Bassma, ed., with May Chartouni-Dubarry. *Maghreb: Les années de transition*. Paris: Masson, 1990.

Lacoste, Camille, and Yves Lacoste, eds. *L'Etat du Maghreb*. Tunis: Cérès Productions, 1991.

Lakihal Ayyat, Naziha. *La femme tunisienne et sa place dans le droit positif*. Tunis: Editions Dar al-Amal, 1978.

Larif-Béatrix, Asma. *Edification étatique et environnement culturel: Le personnel politico-administratif dans la Tunisie contemporaine*. Paris: Publisud, 1988.

Laroui, Abdallah. *Les origines sociales et culturelles du nationalisme marocain, 1830–1912*. Paris: Maspéro, 1977.

Layachi, Azzedine. *State, Society and Democracy in Morocco: The Limits of Associative Life*. Washington, D.C.: Center for Contemporary Arab Studies, Georgetown University, 1998.

Lazreg, Marnia. *The Eloquence of Silence: Algerian Women in Question*. New York: Routledge, 1994.

Leca, Jean, and Jean Claude Vatin. *L'Algérie politique, institutions et régime*. Paris: Presses de la Fondation Nationale des Sciences Politiques, 1975.

Le Gall, Michel, and Kenneth Perkins, eds. *The Maghrib in Question: Essays in History and Historiography*. Austin: The University of Texas Press, 1997.

Le Tourneau, Roger. *Evolution politique de l'Afrique du Nord musulmane, 1920–1961*. Paris: A. Colin, 1962.

Leveau, Rémy. *Le fellah marocain: Défenseur du trône*. Paris: Presses de la Fondation Nationale des Sciences Politiques, 1976.

Lorcin, Patricia M. E. *Imperial Identities: Stereotyping, Prejudice and Race in Colonial Algeria*. London: Tauris, 1995.

MacMaster, Neil. *Colonial Migrants and Racism: Algerians in France, 1900–62*. New York: St. Martin's, 1997.

Maher, Vanessa. *Women and Property in Morocco: Their Changing Relation* to the Process of Social Stratification in the Middle Atlas. London: Cambridge University Press, 1974.

Makilam. La magie des femmes kabyles et l'unité de la société traditionnelle. Paris: Harmattan, 1996.

Marzouki, Ilhem. Le mouvement des femmes en Tunisie au XXème siècle: Féminisme et politique. Tunis: Cérès Productions, 1993.

Maunier, René. Coutumes algériennes. Paris: Domant-Montchrestien, 1935.

———. Mélanges de sociologie nord-africaine. Paris: F. Alcan, 1930.

Merad, Ali. Le réformisme musulman en Algérie de 1925 à 1940: Essai d'histoire religieuse et sociale. Paris: Mouton, 1967.

Mernissi, Fatima. Beyond the Veil: Male-Female Dynamics in a Modern Muslim Society. Rev. ed. Bloomington: Indiana University Press, 1987.

Micaud, Charles A., with L. Carl Brown and Clement Henry Moore. Tunisia: The Politics of Modernization. New York: Praeger, 1964.

Miller, James A. Imlil: A Moroccan Mountain Community in Change. London: Westview, 1984.

Miller, Susan Gilson. Disorienting Encounters: Travels of a Moroccan Scholar in France in 1845–1846. Berkeley and Los Angeles: University of California Press, 1992.

Mir-Hosseini, Ziba. Marriage on Trial: A Study of Islamic Family Law—Iran and Morocco Compared. London: Tauris, 1993.

Montagne, Robert. The Berbers: Their Social and Political Organization. Originally published as La vie sociale et la vie politique des Berbères, 1931. Translated by David Seddon. London: Frank Cass, 1973.

———. Révolution au Maroc. Paris: Editions France-Empire, 1953.

———. Les Berbères et le makhzen dans le sud du Maroc. Paris: F. Alcan, 1930.

Moore, Clement Henry. Tunisia since Independence: The Dynamics of One-Party Government. Berkeley and Los Angeles: University of California Press, 1965.

Moula, Mahmoud Abdel. L'Université Zaytounienne et la societé tunisienne. Thèse de 3ème Cycle en Sociologie. Tunis: Published with the assistance of the Centre National de la Recherche Scientifique, 1971.

Moulay Rchid, Abderrazak. La femme et la loi au Maroc. Casablanca: Le Fennec, 1991.

M'rabet, Fadela. Les algériennes. Paris: Maspéro, 1967.

Munson, Henry, Jr. Religion and Power in Morocco. New Haven: Yale University Press, 1993.

Nordman, Daniel. Profils du Maghreb: Frontières, figures et territoires (XVIIIe-XXe siècles). Rabat: Faculté des Lettres et Sciences Humaines, Université Mohamed V, 1996.

Nouschi, André. Enquête sur le niveau de vie des populations rurales constantinoises, de la conquête jusqu'en 1919. Paris: Presses Universitaires de France, 1961.

Prochaska, David. *Making Algeria French: Colonialism in Bône, 1870–1920*. Cambridge: Cambridge University Press, 1990.

al-Qayrawani, Ibn Abi Zayd. *La Risâla, ou, Epître sur les éléments du dogme et de la loi de l'Islam selon le rite mâlikite*. Arabic text with French translation by Léon Bercher. 3d ed. Algiers: Carbonal, 1949.

Quandt, William B. *Revolution and Political Leadership: Algeria 1954–1968*. Cambridge: M.I.T. Press, 1969.

Raousset-Boulbon, Comte de. *De la colonisation et des institutions civiles en Algérie*. Paris, 1847.

Revue de l'Occident Musulman et de la Méditerranée, no. 44 (1987). Special issue, *Berbères: Une identité en construction*.

Revue Tunisienne de Sciences Sociales (Tunis) 1969. Special issue on the Proceedings of a Conference on Population in the Maghrib, *Actes du colloque de démographie maghrébine*, nos. 17–18, June-September.

Rosen, Lawrence. *The Anthropology of Justice: Law as Culture in Islamic Society*. Cambridge: Cambridge University Press, 1989.

Roussier, Jules. *Le mariage et sa dissolution dans le statut civil local algérien*. Algiers: n.p., 1960.

Rudebeck, Lars. *Party and People: A Study of Political Change in Tunisia*. Stockholm: Almqvist and Wiksell, 1967.

Ruedy, John. *Modern Algeria: The Origins and Development of a Nation*. Bloomington: Indiana University Press, 1992.

———, ed. *Islamism and Secularism in North Africa*. New York: St. Martin's, 1994.

Saadi, Nouredine. *La femme et la loi en Algérie*. Casablanca: Le Fennec, 1991.

Salem, Norma. *Habib Bourguiba, Islam and the Creation of Tunisia*. London: Croom Helm, 1984.

Seddon, David. *Moroccan Peasants: A Century of Change in the Eastern Rif, 1870–1970*. Folkstone, Kent, Eng.: Dawson and Sons, 1981.

Slama, Bice. *L'Insurrection de 1864 en Tunisie*. Tunis: Maison Tunisienne de l'Edition, 1967.

Stone, Martin. *The Agony of Algeria*. New York: Columbia University Press, 1997.

Tillion, Germaine. *Le harem et les cousins*. Paris: Seuil, 1966. Published in English as *The Republic of Cousins: Women's Oppression in Mediterranean Society*. Translated by Quintin Hoare. London: Al-Saqi Books, 1983.

Tlemcani, Rachid. *State and Revolution in Algeria*. Boulder, Col.: Westview, 1986.

Toumi, Mohsen. *Tunisie, pouvoirs et luttes*. Paris: Sycomore, 1978.

Valensi, Lucette. *Tunisian Peasants in the Eighteenth and Nineteenth Centuries*. Translated from French by Beth Archer. Cambridge: Cambridge University Press, 1985.

———. *On the Eve of Colonialism: North Africa before the French Conquest*. Translated from French by K. J. Perkins. New York: Africana, 1977.

Vatin, Jean Claude. *L'Algérie politique: Histoire et société.* Paris: Fondation Nationale des Sciences Politiques, 1974.

Venema, Bernhard. *Les Khroumirs: Changements politiques et religieux dans la période 1850–1987.* Amsterdam: VU University Press, 1990.

Vinogradov, Amal Rassan. *The Ait Ndhir of Morocco: A Study of the Social Transformation of a Berber Tribe.* Anthropological Papers, no. 55. Ann Arbor: University of Michigan, 1974.

Waltz, Susan E. *Human Rights and Reform: Changing the Face of North African Politics.* Berkeley and Los Angeles: University of California Press, 1995.

Waterbury, John. *The Commander of the Faithful: The Moroccan Political Elite—A Study in Segmented Politics.* New York: Columbia University Press, 1970.

Zartman, I. William. *Morocco: Problems of New Power.* New York: Atherton, 1964.

―――, ed. *Man, State and Society in the Contemporary Maghrib.* New York: Praeger, 1973.

Zartman, I. William, and William M. Habeeb, eds. *Polity and Society in Contemporary North Africa.* Boulder, Col.: Westview, 1993.

Zartman, I. William, Mark A. Tessler, John P. Entelis, Russell A. Stone, Raymond A. Hinnebusch, and Shahrough Akhavi. *Political Elites in Arab North Africa: Morocco, Algeria, Tunisia, Libya, and Egypt.* New York: Longman, 1982.

Zussman, Mira F. *Development and Disenchantment in Rural Tunisia: The Bourguiba Years.* Boulder, Col.: Westview, 1992.

MIDDLE EAST, MUSLIM WORLD, ISLAM

Afkhami, Mahnaz, ed. *Faith and Freedom: Women's Human Rights in the Muslim World.* Syracuse: Syracuse University Press, 1995.

Ahmed, Leila. *Women and Gender in Islam: Historical Roots of a Modern Debate.* New Haven: Yale University Press, 1992.

Anderson, J. N. D. *Law Reform in the Muslim World.* London: Athlone, 1976.

―――. *Islamic Law in the Modern World.* New York: New York University Press, 1959.

Antoun, Richard, and Iliya Harik, eds. *Rural Politics and Social Change in the Middle East.* Bloomington: Indiana University Press, 1972.

Arkoun, Mohammed. *Rethinking Islam: Common Questions, Uncommon Answers.* Translated from French by Robert D. Lee. Boulder, Col.: Westview, 1994.

Atiya, Nayra. *Khul-khaal: Five Egyptian Women Tell Their Stories.* Syracuse: Syracuse University Press, 1982.

Ayubi, Nazih N. *Over-Stating the Arab State: Politics and Society in the Middle East.* London: Tauris, 1995.

Badran, Margot. *Feminists, Islam and Nation: Gender and the Making of Modern Egypt.* Princeton: Princeton University Press, 1995.

Barakat, Halim. *The Arab World: Society, Culture and State.* Berkeley and Los Angeles: University of California Press, 1993.

Beck, Lois, and Nikki R. Keddie, eds. *Women in the Muslim World.* Cambridge: Harvard University Press, 1978.

Bellefonds, Y. Linant de. *Traité de droit musulman comparé.* 3 vols. Paris: Mouton, 1965–73.

Bodman, Herbert L. *Women in the Muslim World: A Bibliography of Books and Articles Primarily in the English Language.* Providence, R.I.: Assoc. for Middle East Women's Studies, 1990.

Bodman, Herbert L., and Nayereh Tohidi, eds. *Women in Muslim Societies: Diversity within Unity.* Boulder, Col.: Lynne Rienner, 1998.

Bouhdiba, Abdelwahab. *Sexuality in Islam.* Translated from French by Alan Sheridan. London: Routledge and Kegan Paul, 1985.

Bowen, Donna Lee, and Evelyn A. Early, eds. *Everyday Life in the Muslim Middle East.* Bloomington: Indiana University Press, 1993.

Brand, Laurie A. *Women, the State and Political Liberalization: Middle Eastern and North African Experiences.* New York: Columbia University Press, 1998.

Brown, L. Carl, ed. *Imperial Legacy: The Ottoman Imprint on the Balkans and the Middle East.* New York: Columbia University Press, 1996.

Burke, Edmund, III, ed. *Struggle and Survival in the Modern Middle East.* Berkeley and Los Angeles: University of California Press, 1993.

Carré, Olivier. *L'Islam laïque ou le retour à la grande tradition.* Paris: A. Colin, 1993.

Chatty, Dawn. *Mobile Pastoralists: Development Planning and Social Change in Oman.* New York: Columbia University Press, 1996.

Cole, Juan R. I., ed. *Comparing Muslim Societies: Knowledge and the State in a World Civilization.* Ann Arbor: University of Michigan Press, 1992.

Coon, Carleton S. *Caravan: The Story of the Middle East.* New York: Holt, 1951.

Coulson, Noel J. *Succession in the Muslim Family.* Cambridge: Cambridge University Press, 1971.

———. *A History of Islamic Law.* Edinburgh: Edinburgh University Press, 1964.

Cuisenier, Jean. *Economie et parenté: Leurs affinités de structure dans le domaine turc et dans le domaine arabe.* Paris: Mouton, 1975.

Deguilhem, Randi, ed. *Le Waqf dans l'espace islamique: Outil de pouvoir socio-politique.* Damascus: Institut Français d'Etudes Arabes de Damas, 1995.

Dresch, Paul. *Tribes, Government and History in Yemen.* Oxford: Clarendon, 1989.

Eickelman, Dale F. *The Middle East and Central Asia: An Anthropological Approach.* 3d ed. Upper Saddle River, N.J.: Prentice Hall, 1998.

Esposito, John L. *Women in Muslim Family Law.* Syracuse: Syracuse University Press, 1982.

Evans-Pritchard, Edward E. *The Sanusi of Cyrenaica.* Oxford: Clarendon, 1949.

Fathi, Schirin H. *Jordan—An Invented Nation? Tribe-State Dynamics and the Formation of National Identity.* Hamburg: Deutsches Orient-Institute, 1994.

Fernea, Elizabeth W., ed. *Women and the Family in the Middle East: New Voices of Change.* Austin: The University of Texas Press, 1985.

Gallagher, Nancy E. *Approaches to the History of the Middle East: Interviews with Leading Middle East Historians.* Reading, Eng.: Ithaca Press, 1994.

Gellner, Ernest. *Muslim Society.* Cambridge: Cambridge University Press, 1981.

Gibb, Hamilton A. R. *Mohammedanism: An Historical Survey.* 2d ed. London: Oxford University Press, 1961.

Göçek, Fatma Müge, and Shiva Balaghi, eds. *Reconstructing Gender in the Middle East: Tradition, Identity, and Power.* New York: Columbia University Press, 1994.

Haddad, Yvonne Y., and John L. Esposito, eds. *Islam, Gender, and Social Change.* N.Y.: Oxford University Press, 1998.

Hale, Sondra. *Gender Politics in Sudan: Islamism, Socialism, and the State.* Boulder, Col.: Westview, 1996.

Hallaq, Wael B. *A History of Islamic Legal Theories: An Introduction to Sunnī Usūl al-Fiqh.* Cambridge: Cambridge University Press, 1997.

Hijab, Nadia. *Womanpower: The Arab Debate on Women at Work.* Cambridge: Cambridge University Press, 1988.

Joseph, Suad, ed. *Citizenship and Gender in the Middle East.* Syracuse: Syracuse University Press, 2000.

Joseph, Suad, and Susan Slyomovics, eds. *Gendering Political Cultures in the Middle East.* Philadelphia: University of Pennsylvania Press, 2001.

Kamrava, Mehran. *The Political History of Modern Iran: From Tribalism to Theocracy.* Westport, Conn.: Praeger, 1992.

Kazemi, Farhad, and John Waterbury, eds. *Peasants and Politics in the Modern Middle East.* Miami: Florida International University Press, 1991.

Keddie, Nikki R., and Beth Baron, eds. *Women in Middle Eastern History: Shifting Boundaries in Sex and Gender.* New Haven: Yale University Press, 1991.

Khoury, Philip S., and Joseph Kostiner, eds. *Tribes and State Formation in the Middle East.* Berkeley and Los Angeles: University of California Press, 1990.

Kimball, Michelle R., and Barbara R. von Schlegell. *Muslim Women throughout the World: A Bibliography.* Boulder, Col.: Lynne Rienner, 1997.

Koran [Qur'an]. Translated by N. J. Dawood, with parallel Arabic text. London: Penguin, 1990.

Layish, Aharon. *Women and Islamic Law in a Non-Muslim State: A Study Based on Decisions of the Shari'a Courts in Israel.* New York: Wiley, 1975.

Layne, Linda L. *Home and Homeland: The Dialogics of Tribal and National Identities in Jordan.* Princeton: Princeton University Press, 1994.

Long, David E., and Bernard Reich, eds. *The Government and Politics of the Middle East and North Africa.* Boulder, Col.: Westview, 1980.

Malti-Douglas, Fedwa. *Woman's Body, Woman's Word: Gender and Discourse in Arabo-Islamic Writing.* Princeton: Princeton University Press, 1991.

Massell, Gregory J. *The Surrogate Proletariat: Moslem Women and Revolutionary Strategies in Soviet Central Asia, 1919–1929.* Princeton: Princeton University Press, 1974.

Masud, Mohammad Khalid, Brinkley Messick, and David S. Powers, eds. *Islamic Legal Interpretation: Muftis and Their Fatwas.* Cambridge: Harvard University Press, 1996.

Mayer, Ann E., ed. *Property, Social Structure, and Law in the Modern Middle East.* Albany: State University of New York Press, 1985.

Mernissi, Fatima. *The Veil and the Male Elite: A Feminist Interpretation of Women's Rights in Islam.* Translated from French by Mary Jo Lakeland. Reading, Mass.: Addison-Wesley, 1991.

Metcalf, Barbara Daly. *Perfecting Women: Maulana Ashraf 'Ali Thanawi's Bihishti Zewar, A Partial Translation with Commentary.* Berkeley and Los Angeles: University of California Press, 1990.

Michalak, Laurence O., and Jeswald W. Salacuse, eds. *Social Legislation in the Contemporary Middle East.* Berkeley: Institute of International Studies, University of California, 1986.

Milliot, Louis. *Introduction à l'étude du droit musulman.* Paris: Recueil Sirey, 1953.

Moghadam, Valentine M., ed. *Gender and National Identity: Women and Politics in Muslim Societies.* London: Zed Books, 1994.

Mundy, Martha. *Domestic Government: Kinship, Community and Polity in North Yemen.* London: Tauris, 1995

Owen, Roger. *State, Power, and Politics in the Making of the Modern Middle East.* London: Routledge, 1992.

Patai, Raphael. *Society, Culture, and Change in the Middle East.* 3d ed. Philadelphia: University of Pennsylvania Press, 1971.

Peteet, Julie M. *Gender in Crisis: Women and the Palestinian Resistance Movement.* New York: Columbia University Press, 1991.

Piscatori, James P. *Islam in a World of Nation-States.* Cambridge: Cambridge University Press, 1986.

Powers, David S. *Studies in Qur'an and Hadīth: The Formation of the Islamic Law of Inheritance.* Berkeley and Los Angeles: University of California Press, 1986.

Richards, Alan, and John Waterbury. *A Political Economy of the Middle East: State, Class, and Economic Development.* Boulder, Col.: Westview, 1990.

Rosenthal, Erwin I. *Islam in the Modern National State.* Cambridge: Cambridge University Press, 1965.

Sabbah, Fatna A. *Woman in the Muslim Unconscious.* Translated from French by Mary Jo Lakeland. New York: Pergamon, 1984.

Salamé, Ghassan, ed. *The Foundations of the Arab State.* London: Croom Helm, 1987.

Schacht, Joseph. *An Introduction to Islamic Law.* Oxford: Clarendon, 1964.

Shryock, Andrew. *Nationalism and the Genealogical Imagination: Oral History and Textual Authority in Tribal Jordan.* Berkeley and Los Angeles: University of California Press, 1997.

Sonbol, Amira El Azhary, ed. *Women, the Family, and Divorce Laws in Islamic History.* Syracuse: Syracuse University Press, 1996.

Starr, June. *Law as Metaphor: From Islamic Courts to the Palace of Justice.* Albany: State University of New York Press, 1992.

Stowasser, Barbara Freyer. *Women in the Qur'an, Traditions, and Interpretation.* New York: Oxford University Press, 1994.

Taarji, Hinde. *Les voilées de l'Islam.* Paris: Editions Balland, 1990.

Tucker, Judith E. *In the House of the Law: Gender and Islamic Law in Ottoman Syria and Palestine.* Berkeley and Los Angeles: University of California Press, 1998.

———, ed. *Arab Women: Old Boundaries, New Frontiers.* Bloomington: Indiana University Press, 1993.

UNESCO. *Social Science Research and Women in the Arab World.* London and Dover, N.H.: Frances Pinter, 1984.

Williams, John A., ed. *The Word of Islam.* Austin: The University of Texas Press, 1994.

Zubaida, Sami. *Islam, the People and the State: Essays on Political Ideas and Movements in the Middle East.* London: Routledge, 1989.

THEORY, GENERAL

Abrams, Philip. *Historical Sociology.* Ithaca: Cornell University Press, 1982.

Anderson, Benedict. *Imagined Communities: Reflections on the Origin and Spread of Nationalism.* Rev. ed. London: Verso, 1991.

Anderson, Michael. *Approaches to the History of the Western Family, 1500–1914.* London: Macmillan, 1980.

Anderson, Perry. *Lineages of the Absolutist State.* London: New Left Books, 1974.

Ariès, Philippe. *Centuries of Childhood: A Social History of Family Life.* Translated from French by Robert Baldick. New York: Vintage Books, 1962.

Bashevkin, Sylvia B. *Women on the Defensive: Living through Conservative Times.* Chicago: University of Chicago Press, 1998.

Bendix, Reinhard. *Kings or People: Power and the Mandate to Rule.* Berkeley and Los Angeles: University of California Press, 1978.

————. *Nation-Building and Citizenship: Studies of Our Changing Social Order.* New York: Wiley, 1964.

————, ed. *State and Society: A Reader in Comparative Political Sociology.* Berkeley and Los Angeles: University of California Press, 1973.

Block, Fred L. *Revising State Theory: Essays in Politics and Postindustrialism.* Philadelphia: Temple University Press, 1987.

Blumberg, Rae Lesser. *Engendering Wealth and Well-Being: Empowerment for Global Change.* Boulder, Col.: Westview, 1995.

Bookman, Ann, and Sandra Morgen, eds. *Women and the Politics of Empowerment.* Philadelphia: Temple University Press, 1988.

Bonte, Pierre, ed. *Epouser au plus proche: Inceste, prohibitions et stratégies matrimoniales autour de la Méditerranée.* Paris: Editions de l'Ecole des Hautes Etudes en Sciences Sociales, 1994.

Boserup, Ester. *Women's Role in Economic Development.* London: Allen and Unwin, 1970.

Bourdieu, Pierre. *Outline of a Theory of Practice.* Translated from French by Richard Nice. Cambridge: Cambridge University Press, 1977.

Collins, Randall. *Theoretical Sociology.* San Diego: Harcourt Brace Jovanovich, 1988.

————. *Weberian Sociological Theory.* Cambridge: Cambridge University Press, 1986.

Durkheim, Emile. *The Division of Labor in Society.* Translated from French by George Simpson. New York: Free Press, 1933.

Evans, Peter B., Dietrich Rueschemeyer, and Theda Skocpol, eds. *Bringing the State Back In.* Cambridge: Cambridge University Press, 1985.

Farrell, Betty G. *Elite Families: Class and Power in Nineteenth-Century Boston.* Albany: State University of New York Press, 1993.

Fortes, Meyer. *The Dynamics of Clanship among the Tallensi: Being the First Part of an Analysis of the Social Structure of a Trans-Volta Tribe.* London: Oxford University Press, 1945.

Geertz, Clifford, ed. *Old Societies and New States: The Quest for Modernity in Asia and Africa.* New York: Free Press, 1963.

Gelb, Joyce, and Marian L. Palley. *Women and Public Policies.* Rev. ed. Princeton: Princeton University Press, 1987.

Gerschenkron, Alexander. *Economic Backwardness in Historical Perspective.* Cambridge: Harvard University Press, 1966.

Gerth, H. H., and C. W. Mills, eds. *From Max Weber: Essays in Sociology.* New York: Oxford University Press, 1970.

Glendon, Mary Ann. *The Transformation of Family Law: State, Law and Family in the United States and Western Europe.* Chicago: University of Chicago Press, 1989.

Goode, William J. *World Revolution and Family Patterns.* New York: Free Press, 1970.

Goody, Jack. *The Development of the Family and Marriage in Europe.* Cambridge: Cambridge University Press, 1983.

Hareven, Tamara K. *Family Time and Industrial Time: The Relationship between the Family and Work in a New England Industrial Community.* Cambridge: Cambridge University Press, 1982.

Hobsbawm, E. J. *Nations and Nationalism since 1780: Program, Myth, Reality.* Cambridge: Cambridge University Press, 1990.

Lacouture, Jean. *The Demigods: Charismatic Leadership in the Third World.* New York: Knopf, 1970.

Laslett, Peter. *The World We Have Lost: Further Explored.* 3d ed. New York: Scribner, 1984.

Lipset, Seymour Martin. *The First New Nation: The United States in Historical and Comparative Perspective.* New York: Basic Books, 1963.

———. *Political Man: The Social Bases of Politics.* Garden City, N.Y.: Doubleday, 1960.

Markoff, John. *The Abolition of Feudalism: Peasants, Lords and Legislators in the French Revolution.* University Park: Pennsylvania State University Press, 1996.

Maunier, René. *The Sociology of Colonies.* Vol. 2, *The Progress of Law.* Translated from French by E. O. Lorimer. London: Routledge and Kegan Paul, 1949.

Mill, John Stuart. *A System of Logic, Ratiocinative and Inductive.* 8th ed. London: Longman, 1970.

Moore, Barrington, Jr. *Social Origins of Dictatorship and Democracy: Lord and Peasant in the Making of the Modern World.* Boston: Beacon Press, 1966.

Orloff, Ann S. *The Politics of Pensions: A Comparative Analysis of Britain, Canada, and the United States, 1880–1940.* Madison: University of Wisconsin Press, 1993.

Peristiany, J. G., ed. *Mediterranean Family Structures.* Cambridge: Cambridge University Press, 1976.

Sineman, Martha Albertson. *The Neutered Mother, the Sexual Family, and Other Twentieth Century Tragedies.* New York: Routledge, 1995.

Skocpol, Theda. *Protecting Soldiers and Mothers: The Political Origins of Social Policy in the United States.* Cambridge: Belknap Press of Harvard University, 1992.

———. *States and Social Revolutions: A Comparative Analysis of France, Russia, and China.* Cambridge: Cambridge University Press, 1979.

Smelser, Neil J. *Comparative Methods in the Social Sciences.* Englewood Cliffs, N.J.: Prentice-Hall, 1976.

Stacey, Judith. *Patriarchy and Socialist Revolution in China.* Berkeley and Los Angeles: University of California Press, 1983.

Tilly, Charles. *Big Structures, Large Processes, Huge Comparisons.* New York: Russell Sage Foundation, 1984.

———, ed. *The Formation of National States in Western Europe.* Princeton: Princeton University Press, 1975.

Tilly, Louise A., and Patricia Gurin, eds. *Women, Politics, and Change.* New York: Russell Sage Foundation, 1990.

Tilly, Louise A., and Joan W. Scott. *Women, Work, and Family.* New York: Holt, Rinehart and Winston, 1978.

Tomason, Richard F. *Comparative Social Research.* Vol. 9, *Historical Studies.* Greenwich, Conn.: JAI Press, 1986.

United Nations. *Demographic Yearbook, 1960.* New York: United Nations Publications, 1961.

Wallerstein, Immanuel M. *The Modern World-System 1. Capitalist Agriculture and the Origins of the European World-Economy in the Sixteenth Century.* New York: Academic Press, 1974.

Weber, Max. *Economy and Society: An Outline of Interpretive Sociology.* Edited by Guenther Roth and Claus Wittich. 3 vols. New York: Bedminster, 1968.

———. *The Theory of Social and Economic Organization.* Translated from German by A. M. Henderson and Talcott Parsons. New York: Free Press, 1964.

———. *The Methodology of the Social Sciences.* Translated and edited from German by Edward A. Shils and Henry A. Finch. New York: Free Press, 1949.

NEWSPAPERS AND MAGAZINES

l'Action (Tunisia)
Démocratie (Morocco)
l'Etendard Tunisien (Tunisia)
Istiqlal (Morocco)
Leila (Tunisia)
le Monde (France)
al-Moujahid (Algeria)
The New York Times (USA)
la Presse (Tunisia)
Revue Fémina (Tunisia)
Tunis-Socialiste (Tunisia)
Révolution Africaine (Maghreb)
Revue de Presse—Maghreb, Proche-Orient, Moyen Orient (Algeria)
The Washington Post (USA)

Author Index

Abdesselem, Mustapha, 298n67
Abrams, Philip, 249n13
Abu-Lughod, Janet L., 274n55, 275n60, 276n69
Abu-Zahra, Nadia M., 294n2
Abun-Nasr, Jamil M., 105, 129, 271nn16, 17, 272n34, 273n45, 274nn47, 52, 276nn64, 68, 70, 76, 78, 277nn6, 7, 14, 278n23, 279nn36, 37, 38, 43, 282nn2, 7, 294nn3, 7, 295n22
Adel, Faouzi, 261n15, 262n27
Ageron, Charles-Robert, 287n27
Ahmad, Eqbal, 277n12, 294n9
Ahmed, Leila, 253n3
Amrouche, Fadhma, A. M., 258n52
Anderson, Benedict, 70, 250n7, 267n12
Anderson, J. N. D., 254nn4, 9, 255nn13, 14, 257nn37, 40, 299n100
Anderson, Lisa, 21, 118, 203, 214, 247n5, 250n3, 251n13, 265n1, 271n10, 272nn16, 24, 276n2, 277n10, 282n12, 293n104, 294nn2, 3, 5, 295nn12, 26, 296nn38, 39, 42
Anderson, Michael, 253n1
Anderson, Perry, 247n5, 249n12
Antoun, Richard, 294n2

Ariès, Philippe, 253n1
Arkoun, Mohammed, 254n7
Ashford, Douglas E., 152, 283nn17, 20
Atiya, Nayra, 262n29
Attia, Habib, 78, 91, 95, 268n26, 269n37, 271n13, 272nn28, 29, 277n8
Ayoub, M. R., 262n27, 263n38
Ayubi, Nazih N., 89, 116, 272n6, 277n4

Babadji, Ramdane, 292n102
Bachrouch, Taoufik, 272n16
Baduel, Pierre Robert, 288n28
Bahloul, Joëlle, 65, 254n56
Baita, Abdeslam, 126, 279nn35, 42
Balaghi, Shiva, 264n53
Barakat, Halim, 52, 257n29, 260n9, 267n10, 284n46, 286n14
Barbour, Nevill, 275n62
Baron, Anne-Marie, 38, 61, 257n30, 262n27, 263n46
Baron, Beth, 254n3
Barth, Fredrik, 60, 61, 69, 74, 77, 262n27, 263nn38, 45, 265nn5, 7, 267n20, 268n30
Bashevkin, Sylvia B., 248n8
Bchir, M., 262n27

319

Subject Index

Abbas, Ferhat, 173
Abd al-Qadir, Amir, 100–102
Abdelkader. *See* Abd al-Qadir
Abdulkrim, 127
Addi ou Bihi, 155
adoption: allowed in postcolonial Tunisia, 219, 227, 231; and heirs, 256n27; and Islamic law, 40
adultery: avenging shame of, 62; in Tunisian law, 225–26
age: legal majority of, 137, 138, 163, 225; at marriage, 33, 49, 138, 160, 163, 186, 194, 195, 197, 225
agnatism, defined, 53. *See also* patrilineage
Ahmad Bey, 95, 97
Ahmed, Aït, 179
Alawi dynasty, 105, 109, 150, 275n56
Algeria, precolonial polity, 87–89, 98–103, 109–13; and Abd al-Qadir's movement, 100–101; customary law, 46–48, 111–12, 258n50; distribution of tribes, 99; marriage alliances and tribal politics, 110; and particularism in family law, 111–12; and taxation, 99; tribal autonomy, 80, 85, 98–99; uprisings in, 100–102

Algeria, colonial rule, 115–16, 120–25, 131–39; bureaucratization, 132, 134; compared, 85, 114–16, 125, 126, 132, 142–44, 249n2; contradictions of indirect local administration, 123–25; and customary law, 132–34; and direct local administration, 121, 123; fragmentation of tribes, 120–25, 142–44; French stakes, 115–16, 171, 249n2, 286n3, 287n27, 289n59; land appropriation, 120–22; local particularisms exacerbated, 133–34, 136; manipulation of family law, 131–39; marriage laws promulgated, 137–38; plan to codify family law in Code Morand, 134–35; tribal leaders used, 123–24; uprisings, 124
Algeria, nationalist struggle, 6–7, 24, 147, 151, 202, 204, 218, 169, 171–77, 183–87; and anticolonial guerilla war, 171–74, 285n1; and armed struggle as catalyst, 173; conservative trend, 191–92; family law, 183–87; female fighters, 185–87; casualties, 171; heterogeneous leadership, 174–76, 287n17; and independence proclaimed, xix, 169; and Islam, 173, 186;

327

Istiqlal party: and family law, 157–
62; in independent state, 154–
55; and nationalist struggle, 148–
51

jabr. See matrimonial guardian
jamaa. See tribal council
Kabyles, 46–49, 78, 83, 102, 112,
190; under colonial rule, 133,
136, 137; in independent state,
177–79, 181, 182, 193, 288n40,
293n104
Khadar, Asma, 5
Khayr al-Din, 95–97, 111
Khemisti law, 195
kin-based societies: bases for collective action, 23–26; central/local
tension in, 21–23; defined, 4;
other than the Maghrib, 240–41;
state formation in, 17–27, 234,
238–41. *See also* kin-based solidarities; patrilineage; tribes
kin-based solidarities: and agricultural production in postcolonial
Morocco, 156, 213; in anticolonial Algerian war, 85, 169, 170–74;
and central/local tension, 21–23,
80–83, 234; and circle of cousins
(Beni Amm), 72; used by colonial
state, 114–31; in different historical periods in Algeria, Morocco,
and Tunisia (*See* Algeria; Morocco; Tunisia); economic and political functions, 68–83; and gender relations, 51–67 (*See also*
women); included in independent
Moroccan state, 147, 151–56, 158;
in labor union in Tunisia, 118;
and long term political change,
compared, 24–25; and limits of
loyalties, 71–73; Maghribi history, 21–23, 70–77; marginalized
in independent Tunisian state,
201–2, 211–13, 215, 259n4,

267n11, 295n34; mobilized in independent Algerian state, 21,
151, 169, 177–79; and nationalism, 148–51, 171–74, 202, 205–8;
and power of tribes, 68–80; in
precolonial polity, 87–89, 91–94,
98–113; as refuge from colonial
domination in Algeria, 143, 169;
and state formation, 2, 4–10, 17–
27, 233–41; treated with ambivalence in independent Algerian
state, 169, 170–71, 177–82, 200.
See also kin-based societies; kinship; patrilineage; tribes
kin groupings. *See* kin-based societies; kin-based solidarities; kinship; patrilineage; tribes
kinship: in Algerian Family Code,
197–98, 200; in Bourguiba'd
views, 57–61; and Christian
Church, 141; and endogamy, 57–
61; and family law in postcolonial
states (*See* family law: compared
in independent states); in al-Fasi's
views, 160; French Federation of
FLN on, 190; in Islamic law, 5, 31–
45; men and unity in, 53–55; in
Morrocan Code of Personal
Status, 162, 166–68; organizing
principles, 51–61, 66–67; and
ownership, 73–74; political significance, 2, 4, 68–83; and responses
to political change, 24–25; and
styles of interaction, 53–55; in
Tunisian Code of Personal Status,
215, 219–21, 227–32; women as
threat, 55–56. *See also* kin-based
societies; kin-based solidarities;
patrilineage

labor unions: French, and Algerian
immigrants, 190; and Tunisian
nationalism, 118, 119, 202–4,
206, 208